THE LAW OF GOOD PEOPLE

Currently, the dominant enforcement paradigm is based on the idea that states deal with "bad people" – or those pursuing their own self-interests – with laws that exact a price for misbehavior through sanctions and punishment. At the same time, by contrast, behavioral ethics posits that "good people" are guided by cognitive processes and biases that enable them to bend the laws within the confines of their conscience. In this illuminating book, Yuval Feldman analyzes these paradigms and provides a broad theoretical and empirical comparison of traditional and nontraditional enforcement mechanisms to advance our understanding of how states can better deal with misdeeds committed by normative citizens blinded by cognitive biases regarding their own ethicality. By bridging the gap between new findings of behavioral ethics and traditional methods used to modify behavior, Feldman proposes a "law of good people" that should be read by scholars and policy makers around the world.

Yuval Feldman is the Mori Lazarof Professor of Legal Research at Bar-Ilan University. He holds a PhD in Jurisprudence and Social Policy from the University of California, Berkeley (2004). His research focuses on compliance, law and behavioral economics, and empirical legal studies. He has coauthored more than 50 papers and has won more than 20 research grants and fellowships, including one at the Edmond J. Safra Research Lab at Harvard University. Feldman is a Senior Research Fellow at the Israel Democracy Institute, where he advises various governmental bodies on the usage of behavioral sciences, in areas related to regulatory design, corruption, and enforcement. In 2016, he was elected to the Israel Young Academy.

"A fascinating, comprehensive exploration of the complexities of human motivations – and of how to get good people to do really good things. Opens up new vistas in behavioral science, and also in public policy. Highly recommended."

Cass R. Sunstein, Robert Walmsley University Professor,
Harvard University, and coauthor of Nudge

"In mid-twentieth century, Hannah Arendt was criticized for speaking about the banality of evil in describing Adolf Eichmann, and even today Stanley Milgram's experiments showing the ease of ordering people to harm others is difficult to comprehend. Since then, psychological evidence has accumulated, revealing the undeniable daily harms that emerge from the unintended actions of 'good' people. In this excellent book, Yuval Feldman brings all the best research to those interested in imagining the good society. He admirably polishes the grimy results of behavioral science experiments until they shine with solutions for political and legal reform. It is rare to see a scholar write with the broad sweep Feldman does, and even rarer to have one so effectively persuade that central concepts in the law – property, conflict of interest, discrimination – cannot remain in their present form if only we would confront the evidence already before us."

Mahzarin R. Banaji, Richard Clarke Cabot Professor of Social Ethics
and Chair, Department of Psychology, Harvard University

"More than 40 years ago, economics revolutionized legal theory by analyzing the incentive effects of laws on people who are rationally self-interested. In recent years, cognitive psychology revolutionized law and economics by showing how legal incentives affect real people who are not purely rational. In *The Law of Good People,* Yuval Feldman provides a fresh perspective on laws aimed at motivating good people, as opposed to just deterring bad people. His creativity and knowledge of law, economics, and psychology will make readers rethink the incentive effects of laws and current theories of law and economics."

Robert Cooter, Herman Selvin Professor of Law and Co-Director
of Law and Economics Program, Berkeley Law School

"Should the law target the infamous Mr. Hyde? No, says Yuval Feldman, who demonstrates why most individuals are not hard-nosed Mr. Hydes. In fact, the law should be much more concerned with Dr. Jekyll, who could turn into Mr. Hyde at all times, but who will nevertheless convince himself that he remains the good-natured Dr. Jekyll. In short, motivational plasticity, as Feldman explains, is a much bigger normative problem than merely being a 'bad person' in the first place. This book not only alerts legal academia to this idea but also carefully discusses the implications for legal analysis and design."

Christoph Engel, Director, Max Planck Institute for Research on Collective Goods

"This book is the first to introduce the large and heterogeneous body of work on behavioral ethics to the world of law and legal policy. Drawing in part on the author's own pioneering experimental work, the book moves beyond the reigning enforcement-based approach with its focus on cognition and deliberation and takes greater account of complex motivations, especially of people with a self-conception as being a good person. Feldman provides an important first installment on evaluating law and related interventions in the light of this promising new paradigm."

Henry Smith, Fessenden Professor of Law, and Director, Project
on the Foundations of Private Law, Harvard Law School

"Weaving in disparate threads of economics and psychology, Professor Feldman delivers an exciting new approach to our understanding of ethical behavior. The implications of this work will influence our understanding of how to regulate good and evil for many years to come."

Jeffrey Rachlinski, Henry Allen Mark Professor of Law, Cornell Law School

The Law of Good People

CHALLENGING STATES' ABILITY TO REGULATE
HUMAN BEHAVIOR

YUVAL FELDMAN

Bar-Ilan University

CAMBRIDGE
UNIVERSITY PRESS

University Printing House, Cambridge CB2 8BS, United Kingdom

One Liberty Plaza, 20th Floor, New York, NY 10006, USA

477 Williamstown Road, Port Melbourne, VIC 3207, Australia

314–321, 3rd Floor, Plot 3, Splendor Forum, Jasola District Centre,
New Delhi – 110025, India

79 Anson Road, #06–04/06, Singapore 079906

Cambridge University Press is part of the University of Cambridge.

It furthers the University's mission by disseminating knowledge in the pursuit of
education, learning, and research at the highest international levels of excellence.

www.cambridge.org
Information on this title: www.cambridge.org/9781107137103
DOI: 10.1017/9781316480328

First published 2018

Printed in the United Kingdom by Clays, St Ives plc.

A catalogue record for this publication is available from the British Library.

Library of Congress Cataloging-in-Publication Data
NAMES: Feldman, Yuval, 1971– author.
TITLE: The law of good people : challenging states' ability to regulate human
behavior / Yuval Feldman.
DESCRIPTION: Cambridge [UK] ; New York, NY : Cambridge University Press, [2018]
IDENTIFIERS: LCCN 2017055939 | ISBN 9781107137103
SUBJECTS: LCSH: Law – Psychological aspects. | Law and ethics. | CYAC: Behavior.
Classification: LCC K346 .F43 2018 | DDC 340/.19–dc23
LC record available at https://lccn.loc.gov/2017055939

ISBN 978-1-107-13710-3 Hardback

Contents

Preface

Plato has famously argued that "laws are made to instruct the good, and in the hope that there may be no need of them; also to control the bad, whose hardness of heart will not be hindered from crime."[1]

The premise of this book is that "good" people need laws, but with a different regulatory approach. For law to be able to operate effectively and lead to behavioral change, it needs to understand why "good" people engage in wrongdoing. Yet, even today, the law's main purpose is understood as protecting others from the actions of "bad" people. In contrast, this book argues that it is "good" people (more accurately, those who think of themselves as good people) whose behavior should occupy more of the attention of the law. While, for understandable reasons, the legal system is primarily focused on the upper tail of the distribution of misconduct, in fact most misconduct – those acts we refer to in the book as ordinary unethicality – is actually found in the middle of that curve; in many contexts, its treatment requires completely different assumptions and consequently a modified set of regulatory and enforcement tools from those used to punish serious misconduct.

This book assumes that ordinary unethicality is the most common and relevant type of behavior that legal policy makers should attempt to regulate. Acts of ordinary unethicality are part of most private law disputes in areas such as contact breach, tortious behavior, and lack of respect for people's property rights.[2] In addition, much of people's misconduct in public law, such as tax law, administrative law, and corporate law, involve ordinary unethicality.

Research into behavioral ethics, a growing field within the psychology and management literatures, has demonstrated in numerous field and lab experiments that people's unethical behavior stems from numerous cognitive and social processes that are only partially related to people's deliberative and aware reasoning;

---

[1] Taken from Jowett, B. (1871). *The dialogues of Plato* (Vol. 8). Oxford: Oxford University Press, p. 128. Interestingly, the following "Good people do not need laws to tell them to act responsibly, while bad people will find a way around the laws" is a misquoted phrase of Plato that is indeed better for the purposes of the book.

[2] Both tangible property and even more so with regard to intellectual property.

hence, people can engage in misconduct and still think of themselves as "good" people.

For the purposes of the book, we divide good people into "authentic good people," who through various implicit self-serving processes, such as blind spots or moral forgetting, understand reality in a biased way without recognizing it, and situational wrongdoers who use various justifications in the situation to behave badly without feeling immoral.[3] In contrast to the current dominant enforcement paradigm, which assumes that states are dealing with bad people who are pursuing their own self-interest and that the law needs to increase the price for misbehavior through sanctions and punishment, behavioral ethics posits that good people are guided by both automatic and deliberative processes and biases that enable them to bend the laws within the confines of their conscience. The book claims that the regulatory treatment of the good people who commit many of these misconducts is the neglected task of the law and of legal theory. A focus on those good people will enable regulators to determine in advance which types of situations are likely to encourage acts of ordinary unethicality and to develop an effective regulatory toolbox.

Although behavioral approaches have been introduced into legal theory and practice in the past two decades, they have been narrowly focused on the biases and heuristics literature, which has served as the foundation of the field of behavioral economics: that dominant field deals with cognitive biases in decision making in contexts related to probability, risk, and money. In contrast, behavioral ethics, which focuses on people's biases in making ethical decisions, has received little attention. Yet, ethical biases are not only stronger in many ways than the cognitive biases of behavioral economics but also far more relevant for the regulation of people's ethical behavior. For example, whereas behavioral economics uses the optimism bias to understand why people pursue legal disputes in courts, the behavioral ethics approach suggests that people go to court because they fail to fully understand how problematic their own behavior is, both legally and morally; various self-maintenance mechanisms prevent them from recognizing their wrongdoing. In addition, loss aversion affects not just risk perception but also the likelihood that people will behave unethically.

To regulate the involvement of "good" people in various types of noncooperative behaviors, this book provides a broad theoretical and empirical comparison of traditional and nontraditional enforcement mechanisms. It argues that many of the existing regulatory enforcement strategies are not suitable for addressing misconduct stemming from both deliberative and non-deliberative reasoning processes and biases. The insights of behavioral ethics into the cognitive and motivational factors guiding the behavior of good people require the development of innovative

[3] Obviously the majority of good people are found on a spectrum between those prototypes of good people, using both deliberative and implicit mechanisms to justify their unethically.

approaches to the normative treatment of a diverse population consisting of both good and bad people. These new approaches use an *ex ante* approach that attempts to regulate behavior in advance rather than an *ex post* approach that tries to determine responsibility, which behavioral ethics suggests is quite complex. The move to an *ex ante* design reduces the need to find the smoking guns required by evidentiary rules; hence, it gives more importance to dealing with minor misconducts that cannot justify *ex post* legal examination but in the aggregate are not less important. Good people's ignorance and unawareness of the moral meaning of their behavior provide another justification for a greater focus on detection than on punishment. This new paradigm facilitates a more nuanced understanding by regulators of the likely implicit and explicit effects on behaviors of specific situations. Finally, it suggests that differentiated approaches focusing on variation in people's level of intrinsic motivation should be supplemented by strategies that account for variation in people's level of self-awareness of the moral and legal meaning of their behavior.

The book examines the law's effectiveness in preventing people from engaging in uncooperative behaviors and wrongful conducts, such as breaching contracts, engaging in corruption and employment discrimination, and eschewing professional duties. More specifically, it compares the impact of traditional methods, including deterrence, social norms, and procedural justice, with that of behaviorally informed enforcement mechanisms, such as nudges, framing, and debiasing. The book discusses the pros and cons of these various intervention mechanisms, drawing practical conclusions for legal policy makers on how to optimize their regulatory and enforcement effects on both the deliberative and non-deliberative components of unethical behavior.

In addition, this book addresses key unresolved theoretical questions from several directions. How much can we know ex ante about good people's awareness and ability to control their unethical behaviors? How can we know that their goodness is genuine and not faked? Are considerations of morality and traditional enforcement practices, such as deterrence, effective in curbing behaviors that are only partly deliberative? Can states regulate simultaneously different types of individuals by using different intervention methods? Should the nudge approach, which avoids direct communication between the state and the people it regulates, replace all other intervention methods? Do we know what is lost in the sustainability of behavioral change and in autonomy when we abandon traditional intervention methods and replace them with interventions that don't require any deliberative reasoning by people? Is there still a benefit derived from changing people's intrinsic motivation when many of their misconducts are not done with full awareness? The book addresses these questions and examines in what way the existing research falls short of offering a coherent behavioral and normative picture of the person we are trying to regulate.

In its call for regulatory reform, the book does not focus only on theoretical discussions; instead, it draws on extensive empirical research that other researchers and I have conducted on these questions. It examines through case studies, the effect of social norms on the perception of legality in the context of intellectual property, the effect of legal incentives on people's intrinsic and extrinsic motivations in the area of environmental protection and whistle-blowing laws, the effect of legal uncertainty on the compliance and performance of people with different motivational backgrounds, and the effectiveness of deterrence and morality in enabling people to avoid subtle conflicts of interest and refrain from engaging in implicit discrimination toward different social groups.

Chapters 1 and 2 lay the groundwork for this innovative approach to the law. Chapter 1 outlines the main argument of the book, briefly describing the potential of behavioral ethics, exposing existing gaps in the behavioral analysis of law, and showing how the book proposes to fill them. Chapter 2 explains how both deliberate mechanisms, (e.g. moral disengagement) and non-deliberate mechanisms, (e.g. moral forgetting and motivated blindness) prevent people from recognizing the wrongdoing in their behavior and their own unethicality.

Chapters 3–5 address how to expand the regulatory toolbox, focusing on both formal and non-formal controls and their ability to deal with both explicit and implicit types of misconducts by both "good" and "bad" people. These chapters outline factors such as situational design, behavioral incentives, social and ethical nudges, fairness, social norms, and education. The focus on good people requires a shift in the focus of the legal regime from *ex post* liability to *ex ante* design. *Ex post* mechanisms that focus on liability and are designed to change people's *ex ante* calculations will not be effective because most "good" people are not likely to be aware of why they behaved in a certain way in the first place. We also argue for the importance of designing policies that make it difficult for people to interpret fairness in a self-serving way. There is a need to provide people with accurate information on the nature of social norms and their prevalence, because various cognitive mechanisms are likely to cause people to underestimate the true prevalence of cooperative norms. Incentives need to be sensitive to the crowding-out effect of intrinsic motivation and hence should account for people's motivational sensitivities. Ethical nudges need to be distinguished from other kinds of behavioral nudges, so that appeals to self-interest do not reduce their effectiveness.

Chapter 6, which focuses on individual differences, complicates the picture of good vs. bad people by arguing that good people should be divided into at least two types[4], based on the variation in self-deception mechanisms reviewed in Chapter 2. Good people of the first type genuinely do not understand their behavior or the relevant situation as it is, because of cognitive mechanisms, such as Bazerman's blind spot, Haidt's "emotional dog" approach to morality, or Balcetis's motivated

---

[4] This dichotomy is first developed in Chapter 4.

seeing, which rely mostly on non-deliberative processes. In that camp of morally blind people belong those who engage in implicit job discrimination or in implicit corruption in subtle conflict of interest situations. In contrast, good people of the second type know that what they are doing is impermissible, but they find various rationales that allow them to do bad things without harming their moral self-image. The related work of Bandura on moral disengagement and Shalvi's work on justified dishonesty in the dice-under-the-cup paradigm shows that this is mostly a deliberate process. In the camp of the deliberative justifiers, we can find those committing various parking violations, cutting corners, or using personal contacts to bypass a certain bureaucratic procedure.[5] In this chapter, we also analyze relevant individual differences scales, such as moral identity and social value orientation. Recognizing the limitations of identifying individual variation ex ante, the chapter concludes with a discussion of alternative ways to differentiate between different types of people based on their commitment to the law or the norms of their profession. Such approaches are more likely to be known ex ante by regulators.

The complex effects of law, the existence of various types of regulatory tools, the power of the situation, and the variation among people together create a highly complex regulatory picture. Both Chapter 7 on the pluralistic account of law and Chapter 8 on the trade-offs between the different likely effects of laws present research that guides how policy makers can balance the effects of different aspects of the law, on different people, with regard to different compliance behaviors. The concept of the pluralistic approach to law refers to the fact that the law tries to change the behavior of people with different compliance motivations and different levels of awareness, and through the use of both implicit and explicit signals; thus, there are many possible conflicting behavioral outcomes to any law that is enacted. The concept of behavioral trade-offs suggests that each type of intervention produces a different behavioral reaction, because the behavioral ethics perspective on people's approach to unethicality is far more complex than is assumed by traditional enforcement methods. It is rarely the case that any one policy will be superior in terms of every behavioral dimension. Developing an effective policy requires taking many factors into consideration, as well as the particular context of the situations in which people make decisions.

This book's approach to law enforcement is applied in Chapters 9 and 10 to corruption and employment discrimination, respectively; these two case studies demonstrate how to create an effective balance between regulatory tools that address different types of populations with different mind-sets toward the behavior to be regulated. For both corruption and employment discrimination, it is not the behavior itself, but the state of mind of the individual when doing it that is problematic – and that is very hard to prove in court. For example, when a mayor hires a contractor,

---

[5] As suggested above, many good people are on a spectrum between those two prototypes, depending on the specific situation.

that behavior is only of concern when that decision is made based at least partially on his or her self-interest. When an employer decides not to hire someone for a job, that decision is problematic if he or she based it on prejudice. These chapters examine the different set of regulatory tools to be used *ex ante* rather than *ex post* to deal with legal violations in these two fields.

Chapter 11 concludes with a discussion of some key policy-making concepts derived from the book's assumptions about wrongdoing and the good vs. bad people typology. It first examines the role of intrinsic motivation and moral education when decisions are non-deliberative. It then outlines the use of taxonomies of regulatory contexts to determine which regulatory tools to use in which contexts and for which purposes and reviews possible approaches to deal with people's unethical and illegal behavior, such as differentiated or targeted regulation and responsive or sequential regulation. It concludes with a discussion of the future of the field of behavioral ethics in the theory of legal enforcement and some of its limitations.

Acknowledgments

I wish to thank a number of people and institutions for their important assistance while writing this book. First, I would like to thank Matt Gallaway from Cambridge University Press for proposing the initial idea to write this book. Without his encouragement, this project may not have come to fruition. I would like to thank Catherine Smith and Meera Seth from the Press for managing the production of the book. I would also like to thank Mathivathini Mareesan and the Production team at Integra software services Pvt., Ltd.

This book has been published with the help of generous funding by the Bar-Ilan Faculty of Law, where I have worked for the past 13 years. The support this faculty has shown me over the years truly knows no bounds. I would like to express thanks in particular to former dean Prof. Sahar Lifstitz, as well as the entering dean Prof. Oren Perez. So as not to leave anyone out, I would like to express my thanks to the faculty as a whole. Many of the ideas for this book were formulated as a result of my countless conversations with other faculty members. The individual help I received from many of them, particularly from Tsilly Dagan and Adi Leibson, does not go unnoticed. Over the past four years, I have also been fortunate to conduct my more applied research on the implications of behavioral economics and ethics to regulation and compliance in the Israel Democracy Institute. It was there that I learned the gap between lab experiments and behaviorally based policy making by governmental institutions.

Earlier drafts of the book were presented in seminars at Berkeley, Stanford, UC Hastings, Oxford, Dublin, Turin, Munich, the Israeli Democracy Institute in Jerusalem, Tel-Aviv University, and Bar-Ilan University. I appreciate the helpful comments I have received from those attending.

In addition to my institutional colleagues, I wanted to thank Christoph Engel, Jeff Rachlinski, Shaul Shalvi, Dan Arielly, Hanoch Dagan, Tom Tyler, Max Bazerman and Ariel Porat, whose conversations with me have afforded much insight into the topics discussed in this book.

I was fortunate enough to spend a number of productive years in the Corruption Lab at Harvard University headed by Larry Lessig and the Implicit Social Cognition lab headed by Mahzarin Banaji, also at Harvard University. Most of my knowledge about behavioral ethics was attained during this time. The intellectual tools I gained while working in these labs have exerted a considerable influence on the course and direction of my research. The creation of this book evinces this influence, for which I am deeply grateful.

Some of the research in this book can also be traced to an even earlier – my doctoral studies at the University of California–Berkeley. Naturally, my advisors Bob Cooter and Rob MacCoun – whose different but equally sophisticated and coherent views on rationality and decision-making processes helped shape my current view about "good people" – require much gratitude. I would also like to thank the entire Jurisprudence and Social Policy faculty at Boalt Hall for their indirect help with the creation of this book. It took me many years to recognize the importance of studying not just the behavioral and economic approaches to law but also the sociological, philosophical, and political science views on decision making in legal contexts.

The vast majority of my research has been conducted in collaboration with scholars from numerous disciplines, such as law, psychology, sociology, political science, philosophy, economics, and game theory. Generally, credit is given to each person in the appropriate chapter.

However, since so much of my research has emerged from that collaborative work, I feel the need to thank each one of them for their specific contribution to this work as a whole:

To Doron Teichman, for a series of joint papers regarding the nuanced effect of law on behavior, the last three being in collaboration with Amos Schur and Uriel Haran.

To Henry Smith, Constantine Boassalis, and Alon Harel, for our joint work on theoretical and empirical aspects of legal ambiguity.

To Orly Lobel, for our joint work on legal instruments, behavioral trade-offs, whistle-blowing, and new regulatory tools.

To Oren Perez, for our joint work on various legal incentives and their effect on environmental behavior.

To Tom Tyler, for our joint work on the effect of law on procedural justice.

To Eliran Halali, for our joint work on competing approaches to enforcing behavior in subtle conflict of interest situations.

To Michal Feldman and Bob Cooter, for our joint work on biases in the perception of norms.

To Tammi Krichelli-Katz and Haggay Porat, for our joint work regarding employment discrimination.

To Maryam Koachaki and Francesca Gino, for our joint work regarding the expressive effects of ethical codes.

Finally, I would like to extend my gratitude to the numerous research assistants who helped in various stages of this book's preparation: Noam Loshinsky, Jasmin Goldofsky, Russel Shitrit-Leibovitch, Or Ashual, Aelet Sender, Maryam Jacobi,

Sapir Malachi, Shira Saidler, Shira Kahan, Zachi Shimon, Gal Ben Haim, Matt Firestone, Yoel Felsen, Yakira Markus, Na'ama Gutman, Guy Opatovsky. Special thanks to Sivan Ratzon for her work on the final stages of the book preparation, particularly the index. Finally, I would like to thank the team at Academic Language Experts – Avi Staiman, project manager; Gail Naron Chalew, editor; and Avi Kallenbach, proofreader – for their thorough and comprehensive edit, which helped raise the level of the final manuscript and prepare it for publication.

On a more personal note, I would like to express my deepest gratitude to my family. To my wonderful kids: Liav, Yaara, Adva, Ori, and Daniel, for constantly reminding me of what is most important in life, as well as for their participation, each one according to his or her own age, through various conversations on the topics of this book. Their genuine goodness continues to act as a wellspring of motivation and inspiration to me.

To my beloved wife, Professor Michal Feldman, who is a rare combination of a loving partner and advisor. I have gained so much support from her, both emotionally and intellectually throughout this process; her ability to perfectly synthesize these two roles is truly remarkable.

To my mother Rachel, for her endless and constant love and support, for the simple belief that whatever I do is always the best, even when it isn't. To her husband, Bernie, who has been part of our family for so many years and has always shown interest in my research.

To my brothers Ronen and Amir, for their friendship and encouragement.

To my parents-in-law, Zippi and Menachem, for their interest and support in the ongoing struggle to balance family and work.

This book is dedicated to my late father, Itzchak Feldman, who passed away at a young age. Even though I only knew him during my childhood and adolescent years, his wisdom and sharp understanding of people have always accompanied me and acted as an ongoing source of inspiration to my work.

1

Introduction

The focus of this book is on how governments may effectively use recent advances in the understanding of human behavior to guide their efforts to modify people's behavior. To date, the insights of behavioral ethics that have completely revolutionized the business and management fields have yet to be applied in legal theory and policy research, especially in the context of legal enforcement and compliance. The growing recognition that misconduct can be facilitated by structural issues and is not just the product of a few "bad apples" has important implications for the creation and fine-tuning of institutional design and enforcement mechanisms. States need to modify their regulatory roles and functions based on the understanding that discrimination does not just stem from certain employers who hate minorities, that corruption is not just about greedy individuals, or that trade secrets are not just divulged for mercenary motives.

This book argues that the good-people rationale – the idea that ordinary people could engage in all types of wrongdoing without being aware of the full meaning of their behavior – greatly complicates the regulatory challenge of states. Because of various psychological and social mechanisms that prevent people from recognizing their wrongdoing and encourage them to feel as if they are far more moral, unbiased, and law abiding than they actually are, individuals today are less likely to react, at least not explicitly, to classical legal signals, which they view as directed to other, "bad" people. Similar self-serving mechanisms affecting their perception of social norms and fairness cause people to have very inaccurate views of the normative status of their behavior. Moreover, a great deal of uncertainty surrounds the good-people rationale and, as we will show from the literature, there is clearly more than one type of good person – different people use a variety of different mechanisms to justify their unethical and illegal behavior. We do not yet know how "good" the good

---

* Parts of specific chapters are based on joint work with my coauthors. This chapter includes some text that appeared in "Behavioral Ethics Meets Behavioral Law and Economics," in *The Oxford Handbook of Behavioral Law and Economics*, ed. Eyal Zamir and Doron Teichman (2014).

people are in terms of their awareness and ability to control their conduct. Nor can we accurately quantify *ex ante* the ratio of good to bad people in society with regard to any particular behavior. Although we appreciate the need to address the misconduct of good and bad people differently, we do not know the costs of using the "wrong" intervention techniques to deal with various types of bad behavior. Bringing about the needed shifts in regulatory design first requires a shift in the behavioral analysis of law.

1.1 LIMITED COGNITION, LIMITED SELF-INTEREST, AND BEHAVIORAL ETHICS

The past 40 years have seen a dramatic increase in the influence of psychology on the field of economics in general and on the law and economics movement in particular. As a result, significant efforts have been devoted to mapping the flaws in human cognition and examining their implications for how individuals deviate from making optimal decisions.[1] For example, the literature has investigated how irrelevant factors of context, framing, or situation can cause individuals to make decisions that are contrary to their best interest. Daniel Kahneman's book, *Thinking, Fast and Slow*, popularized the concept of two systems of reasoning, which now is at the core of extensive research in behavioral law and economics.[2] Kahneman differentiates between an automatic, intuitive, and mostly unconscious process (System 1) and a controlled and deliberative process (System 2). Although many scholars – for example, Gigerenzer et al.[3] and Kruglanski[4] – have criticized this paradigm, recognition of the role of automaticity in decision making has played an important role in the emergence of behavioral law and economics.

It is essential to clarify at the outset the dramatic difference between the highly popular behavioral law and economics (BLE) and behavioral ethics (BE). BLE is concerned with people's limited ability to make "rational" decisions, whereas behavioral ethics addresses people's inability to fully recognize the ethical, moral and legal aspects of their behavior. How BE and BLE approach self-interest illustrates the main difference between them. BLE assumes that people cannot be fully trusted on their own to make decisions that enhance their self-interest because of the bounded rationality argument – that available information, cognitive ability, and

---

[1] Jolls, C., Sunstein, C. R., & Thaler, R. (1998). A behavioral approach to law and economics. *Stanford Law Review*, 50, 1471–1550. See also Korobkin, R. B., & Ulen, T. S. (2000). Law and behavioral science: Removing the rationality assumption from law and economics. *California Law Review*, 88, 1051–1144; Langevoort, D. C. (1998); Behavioral theories of judgment and decision making in legal scholarship: A literature review. Vanderbilt Law Review, 51, 1499; Jolls, C. (2007). *Behavioral law and economics* (No. w12879). National Bureau of Economic Research.

[2] Kahneman, D. (2011). *Thinking, slow and fast*. New York: Farrar, Straus and Giroux.

[3] Gigerenzer, G., Todd, P. M., & ABC Research Group. (1999). *Simple heuristics that make us smart*. New York: Oxford University Press.

[4] Kruglanski, A. W., & Gigerenzer, G. (2011). Intuitive and deliberate judgments are based on common principles. *Psychological Review*, 118(1), 97.

time constraints limit individuals' ability to make rational decisions. In contrast, BE focuses on people's inability to recognize the extent to which self-interest in its broader sense affects their behavior. BE assumes that many people's actions are based on self-interest, in that they serve the need to maintain a positive and coherent view of the self. It also accounts for the effect that self-interest has on cognitive processes (e.g., visual perception and memory), as opposed to simply looking at how self-interest affects motivation. Finally, BE is more concerned with how our self-interest affects us implicitly than with how it shapes our explicit choices. In light of these differences, the fact that BLE is so popular within the legal literature[5] while BE is almost entirely ignored[6] is quite counterintuitive.[7]

As I discuss in more detail in Chapter 2 – which focuses on the psychological foundations of behavioral ethics – good people are those who find themselves in situations in which they are not fully aware of the legal, moral, and ethical meanings of their behavior for a combination of reasons.[8] They then engage in motivated reasoning, in which their desires affect the types of information they pay attention to and how they process it.[9] Self-deception also plays an important role in their ability to accurately assess the nature of their actions and motives, causing them to believe they are acting more ethically than they actually are.[10] To use a common

---

[5]   For example, Sunstein, C. R. (1999). Behavioral law and economics: A progress report. *American Law and Economics Review*, 1(1/2), 115–157. See also Langevoort, *supra* note 1.

[6]   For some comparison of the potential of the two literatures, see Amir, O., & Lobel, O. (2008). Stumble, predict, nudge: How behavioral economics informs law and policy. *Columbia Law Review*, 108(8), 2098–2137.

[7]   I discuss this point in Chapter 1, page 6.

[8]   For example, see Mazar, N., Amir, O., & Ariely, D. (2008). The dishonesty of honest people: A theory of self-concept maintenance. *Journal of Marketing Research*, 45(6), 633–644. See also Bersoff, D. M. (1999). Why good people sometimes do bad things: Motivated reasoning and unethical behavior. *Personality and Social Psychology Bulletin*, 25(1), 28–39; Kidder, R. M. (2009). *How good people make tough choices: Resolving the dilemmas of ethical living* (Rev. ed.). New York: Harper Perennial; Pillutla, M. M. (2011). When good people do wrong: Morality, social identity, and ethical behavior, in D. De Cremer, R. van Dijk & J. K. Murnighan (Eds.), *Social psychology and organizations* (p. 353). New York: Routledge; Hollis, J. (2008). *Why good people do bad things: Understanding our darker selves*. New York: Penguin; and Banaji, M. R., & Greenwald, A. G. (2013). *Blindspot: Hidden biases of good people*. New York: Delacorte Press. Many other authors do not use the term but make the same argument in the text (see, e.g., De Cremer, D., van Dick, R., Tenbrunsel, A., Pillutla, M., & Murnighan, J. K. (2011). Understanding ethical behavior and decision making in management: A behavioural business ethics approach. *British Journal of Management*, 22(s1), S1–S4. This is also the view held by Bazerman, M. H., & Tenbrunsel, A. E. (2011). *Blind spots: Why we fail to do what's right and what to do about it*. Princeton: Princeton University Press. This line of scholarship is completely different from the type of research conducted by Zimbardo, P. G. (2007). *The Lucifer effect*. New York: Random House Trade Paperbacks. These works generally try to explain how ordinary people end up doing evil or at least engaging in gross criminal behaviors.

[9]   Kunda, Z. (1990). The case for motivated reasoning. *Psychological Bulletin*, 108(3), 480.

[10]   Chugh, D., Bazerman, M. H., & Banaji, M. R. (2005). Bounded ethicality as a psychological barrier to recognizing conflicts of interest. In D. A. Moore, D. M. Cain, G. Loewenstein, & M. H. Bazeman (Eds.), *Conflicts of interest: Challenges and solutions in business, law, medicine, and public policy* (pp. 74–95). Cambridge: Cambridge University Press.

example, a mayor will find it difficult admitting to himself that his behavior is driven by anything other than the benefit of the city he runs – even if his specific actions[11] seem to be, on the surface, motivated primarily by his own self-interest.

As discussed in more details in Chapter 2 and especially in Chapter 9 that focuses on implicit corruption, the BE literature has produced many important and counter-intuitive insights with regard to the predictors of unethical behavior. For example, people behave less ethically in groups than when alone[12] and also when they are acting on behalf of other people, rather than for themselves. Another example is that good people might ignore blatant conflicts of interest, having few qualms about accepting tickets to a sports event from a client, although they would shy away from taking a monetary bribe. Individuals who consider themselves to be "good" based on their past behavior may permit themselves to bend the rules (moral licensing) and are more likely to make unethical decisions when time constraints increase.[13] These findings described in the literature pose a substantial challenge to the ability of the state to change the behavior of the public across many domains of law.

As will be developed throughout the book, current research on behavioral ethics could explain a long line of uncooperative behaviors and wrongful conducts, such as breaching contracts due to biased interpretation of the contractual negotiation, engaging in corruption for undermining the effect of self-interest on one's reasoning, employment discrimination due to social cognition processes, and eschewing professional duties of loyalty in various corporate and administrative contexts.

These psychological mechanisms not only amplify the effect of self-interest but also tend to limit people's awareness of the role of self-interest in determining their behavior. Indeed, one of the unresolved issues is the degree to which individuals are aware of their ethical behavior,[14] and BE research has proceeded along several paths that argue different views on this topic. On the one hand, Marquardt and Hoeger showed that individuals make decisions based on implicit rather than explicit attitudes.[15] Along similar lines, when examining the automatic system, Moore and Loewenstein[16] found that the effect of self-interest is automatic, and Epley and

[11] For example, in choosing people he wants to promote, areas in the city he decides to develop, and contractors with whom he interacts. In Chapter 9, the fact that the contribution of the "best interest of the city" is an ambiguous concept is developed.

[12] Weisel, O., & Shalvi, S. (2015). The collaborative roots of corruption. *Proceedings of the National Academy of Sciences*, 112(34), 10651–10656.

[13] Shalvi, S., Eldar, O., & Bereby-Meyer, Y. (2012). Honesty requires time (and lack of justifications). *Psychological Science*, 23(10), 1264–1270.

[14] Hochman, G., Glöckner, A., Fiedler, S., & Ayal, S. (2016). "I can see it in your eyes": Biased processing and increased arousal in dishonest responses. *Journal of Behavioral Decision Making*, 29(2–3), 322–335.

[15] Marquardt, N., & Hoeger, R. (2009). The effect of implicit moral attitudes on managerial decision-making: An implicit social cognition approach. *Journal of Business Ethics*, 85(2), 157–171.

[16] Moore, D. A., & Loewenstein, G. (2004). Self-interest, automaticity, and the psychology of conflict of interest. *Social Justice Research*, 17(2), 189–202.

Caruso[17] concluded that automatic processing leads to egocentric ethical interpretations. However, within BE can be found theories such as Bandura's theory of moral disengagement that maps *post hoc* deliberative and aware self-serving justifications, creating a taxonomy of how people come to explicitly rationalize their unethical behavior.[18]

Another body of literature that stands in contrast to BE is that on limited self-interest, which emphasizes the role of fairness and morality in compliance with the law. A good example is the important line of research that derives from the prosocial account of human behavior (see, e.g., works of Stout[19] and Benkler[20] on prosocial behavior). According to this literature, rational choice models cannot account for our ability to cooperate and engage in prosocial behavior beyond what is in our self-interest.

Both BE and the prosocial behavior literature agree on the need to take a broader view of how self-interest operates relative to traditional economics, and both disagree with the notion that money is the main force motivating people. However, they do not agree on the implications of these assumptions: BE argues that a broad account of self-interest should reveal our tendency toward selfish action, whereas the prosocial literature claims the opposite. In this book, I do not suggest that we look at people's selfish choices to understand their behavior. On the contrary, I offer a more complex view of what it means for a choice to be in one's broader self-interest and how self-interest affects people's understanding of the legal and moral meaning of their behavior.

1.2 THE CONTRIBUTION OF ECONOMICS TO THE DEVELOPMENT OF THE BEHAVIORAL ANALYSIS OF LAW

The contribution of economics to law and psychology, which cannot be overstated, has brought about a shift in focus from the individual to the collective. Before the field of BLE developed, the law and psychology scholarship mostly took a forensic approach, evaluating individuals for the courts, primarily in criminal and family law contexts. Even research exposing biases at work in criminal and civil procedures, which is closely related to research in empirical legal studies (ELS),[21] was often carried out in the context of individuals involved in particular court cases (e.g., jury selection and jury decision making). This orientation has limited the applicability of the traditional law and psychology scholarship to regulatory and legislative contexts.

[17] Epley, N., & Caruso, E. M. (2004). Egocentric ethics. *Social Justice Research*, 17(2), 171–187.
[18] Bandura, A., Barbaranelli, C., Caprara, G. V., & Pastorelli, C. (1996). Mechanisms of moral disengagement in the exercise of moral agency. *Journal of Personality and Social Psychology*, 71(2), 364.
[19] Stout, L. (2010). *Cultivating conscience: How good laws make good people.* Princeton: Princeton University Press.
[20] Benkler, Y. (2011). *The penguin and the leviathan: How cooperation triumphs over self-interest.* New York: Crown Business.
[21] Rachlinski, J. J., Johnson, S. L., Wistrich, A. J., & Guthrie, C. (2009). Does unconscious racial bias affect trial judges? *Notre Dame Law Review*, 84(3), 1195.

In contrast, BLE scholarship focuses on understanding the behavior of ordinary people in everyday situations, with attention to situational context and the general effect of law on those actions. Many BLE findings have found practical application through communications with regulators, legislatures, and Behavioral Insight Teams (BIT).[22]

BLE incorporates psychological insights into law through an economic lens. At the same time, it ignores many noneconomic areas of psychology, focusing instead on theories related to judgment and decision making. The implications of the limited attention paid to the role of psychological mechanisms in people's behavior are discussed in the next chapter.

This book challenges the excessive focus on cognitive biases at the expense of ethical biases that allow immoral behavior. Whereas the economics literature stresses rationality – that is, the outcome as a utility-maximizing decision relative to preference – I argue that it is the understanding of the importance of non-deliberative decision making that truly matters for legal theory; in addition, it is precisely the nuanced effect of this process on immoral behavior that economics fails to address.

1.2.1 Demonstration through the "Self-serving Bias"

The danger of BLE's over-reliance on economics is best demonstrated in the ways its scholarship addresses the self-serving bias. Despite this bias's clear relevance for morality and responsibility and therefore its close relationship to legal theory and enforcement, the BLE literature focuses on it instead as a deviation from rationality. For example, self-serving biases have been held responsible for people's inability to estimate correctly the probability of winning legal battles. Babcock and Loewenstein conducted the most famous study, which showed that self-serving biases operated to reduce the likelihood of people settling out of court.[23] This is a typical BLE finding because it assumes that people make rational decisions – basing their decision to pursue legal action or settle based on their probability of winning. In this case, the self-serving bias suggests a narrow deviation from rationality, causing them to over-estimate their probability of winning. But a much greater problem for the law, one that currently is mostly ignored, is the contribution of the self-serving bias to people's inability to recognize both their own wrongdoing and the dominant role that their self-interest plays in their behavior – which limits their ability to understand why legal action is being brought against them. The law and economics movement has thus limited the richness of the psychology being used in legal scholarship.

[22] For a review see Jolls et al., *supra* note 1. See also Korobkin & Ulen, *supra* note 1. See also Halpern, D. (2016). Inside the nudge unit: How small changes can make a big difference. Random House.
[23] Babcock, L., & Loewenstein, G. (1997). Explaining bargaining impasse: The role of self-serving biases. *Journal of Economic Perspectives*, 11(1), 109–126.

The proposed legal perspective is not concerned with whether people are acting rationally. Instead, it is concerned with whether they are at fault, whether their behavior can be modified, and whether something in the situation has affected their ability to recognize their wrongdoing. Understanding these processes of decision making and how they affect questions of motivation, autonomy, and responsibility, rather than how to reach the optimal outcome, should be at the core of the new behavioral analysis of law.

1.3 WHY BEHAVIORAL ETHICS HAS BEEN NEGLECTED IN LAW

As suggested earlier, both the BE and the traditional BLE literatures focus on the automatic processes that underlie people's decision making. However, they have different emphases: BE explores the automaticity of self-interest, whereas BLE examines areas in which automatic decisions undermine self-interest.[24]

Given the importance of intentionality to the law, one would expect behavioral ethics to be more central to legal scholarship than it is today. Yet BE has had less of an impact on the legal arena than has behavioral law and economics. This is primarily because of BE's structural limitations. For example, BE has a relatively large number of founding scholars, whereas BLE has two main ones: Kahneman and Tversky. As a result, BE suffers from the simultaneous development of multiple, competing paradigms, muddling the underlying points on which the literature agrees. These disagreements prevent BE from being able to propose consistent policy recommendations, which is another obstacle to its adoption within the law. Yet another limitation of BE is that it relies to a greater extent than does BLE on dual-reasoning mechanisms, whose concepts of automaticity, awareness, and controllability are difficult to explore and measure. How is it possible to prove that people are unaware or even partly unaware of their selfish intentions? By contrast, classical BLE focuses on suboptimal outcomes, which can be easily examined empirically. This focus places many of the findings of BE at methodologically inferior positions relative to those of BLE.

Finally, another limitation of BE relative to BLE is the greater inability of third parties to recognize the biases of the decision making. When it comes to BLE-related biases such as loss aversion, third parties can more easily recognize the fact that this bias undermines the ability of decision makers to treat loss and profit as similar consequences. By contrast, the main mechanisms in behavioral ethics are related to self-serving biases and motivated reasoning, which contribute to people's reduced ability to recognize their own wrongdoing. Since these mechanisms are self-driven, it is harder for third parties who look at others' bad behaviors to recognize them as

---

[24]　Kish-Gephart, J. J., Harrison, D. A., & Treviño, L. K. (2010). Bad apples, bad cases, and bad barrels: Meta-analytic evidence about sources of unethical decisions at work. *Journal of Applied Psychology*, 95(1), 1. See also Bazerman, M. H., & Gino, F. (2012). Behavioral ethics: Toward a deeper understanding of moral judgment and dishonesty. *Annual Review of Law and Social Science*, 8, 85–104.

"good" people who simply cannot recognize their own wrongdoing. To use a hypothetical example, if a public official promoted a friend, BE suggests a whole array of mechanisms that might bias her ability to recognize the impact of personal familiarity on the objectivity of her decisions.[25] However, for third parties, BE research suggests that they will have trouble believing that the public official did not favor her friends knowingly.[26] Such a gap between the decision maker and third parties also contributes to the reluctance of BLE scholars to adopt BE-based biases as part of the bounded rationality project.[27] Despite the aforementioned limitations, bringing BE into mainstream legal scholarship is both a challenging and rewarding task and it will be the primary occupation of the present book.

1.4 THE GIST OF THE BOOK

As alluded to in the previous paragraphs, in this book, I aim to create a new branch of scholarship that focuses on the rule of law in a world populated by individuals with different levels of awareness of their own unethicality. This book is based on the assumption that many of the current directions in legal enforcement research, especially with regard to 'ordinary unethicality' miss important elements of both behavioral and legal methods and theories. It challenges the ability of states to systematically account for non-deliberative, unethical human behavior given a legal system based largely on either sanctions or moral messages, both of which assume some level of calculation and deliberation. The legal literature on enforcement needs to undergo a major revision in its approach to the regulation of intellectual property, employment discrimination, conflict of interest, and many other legally relevant behaviors that people engage in for multiple reasons and with limited awareness of their full legal and moral meaning. In such contexts, the BE approach is especially potent and needs to be taken into account. This change in perception creates many new challenges from a regulation and enforcement perspective, as it is unclear to what extent current legal instruments could be seen as effective in curbing misconducts conducted by people limited awareness to the full meaning of their own behavior. The focus of the book is to explore the ability to create regulatory and enforcement tools that will be able to target people who differ in their self-awareness to wrongdoing.

As suggested, the book criticizes the behavioral-legal scholarship for overemphasizing rationality and cognitive biases at the expense of non-deliberative choice and

---

[25] See discussion in Chapter 2 on the objectivity bias.
[26] See discussion in Chapter 9 on implicit corruption.
[27] Compare with the argument made in Soltes, E. (2016). *Why they do it: Inside the mind of the white-collar criminal*. New York: PublicAffairs, where convicted white color criminals report they were unaware at the time that their behavior was unethical or illegal. The vast majority of people find it very hard to believe that those people indeed did not know what they were doing.

ethical biases. However, as is shown throughout the book, the move to dual-reasoning theories should not lead to a categorical rejection of deterrence and morality. In fact, the reverse is true: one of the arguments developed in later chapters is that traditional enforcement mechanisms have more than one type of effect on people; therefore, the current fascination with "nudges"[28] as a means of changing behavior, along with the abandonment of traditional intervention mechanisms, is misguided.

In latter chapters, I examine the new insights derived from behavioral ethics, a relatively overlooked area in current legal research, which help identify many mechanisms that prevent people from fully recognizing the wrongfulness of their behavior. At a conceptual level, the book revises some jurisprudential concepts related to choice, responsibility, and autonomy in light of growing knowledge about the role of non-deliberative choice in human behavior. Based on these insights, I revisit many of the existing behavioral paradigms of legal regulation and enforcement and conclude by presenting a multidimensional taxonomy of legal doctrines and of the various instruments that states can use to modify human behavior. I recommend certain changes that legal scholarship on enforcement needs to make to remain relevant in the face of recent behavioral research and regulatory changes.

Such a change in focus would greatly affect the design and enforcement of laws and regulations in many legal domains. For example, how can we justify the use of deterrence in light of the "blind spot" argument (i.e., ethical unawareness) advanced by scholars such as Bazerman and Tenbrunsel as well as Banaji and Greenwald?[29] How can we understand the legal responsibility of organizations given what we know about situational cues of unethicality? How should we think of nudges when our goal is to increase ethicality, rather than improving the available choices, although only the latter are in the long-term interest of individuals? How are we to understand the *Why People Obey the Law* project of Tom Tyler,[30] which is based on self-report and explicit accounts of fairness, in light of the writings on moral intuition by Haidt[31] and on moral identity by Aquino?[32] Should we ascribe a new meaning to legal ambiguity, given its contribution to such processes as the moral wiggle room and self-deception? Can

---

[28] The concept of nudges, which is discussed in Chapter 4, was advanced in the 2008 book by Richard H. Thaler and Cass R. Sunstein (2008). *Nudge: Improving decisions about health, wealth, and happiness.* New York: Penguin, 2008. A nudge is a simple intervention, such as changing the default setting in decision making, that policy makers can institute to change people's behavior with a limited need for them to make any deliberative choice.

[29] See Sunstein, *supra* note 5. See also Bazerman & Tenbrunsel, *supra* note 8; Banaji, M. R., & Greenwald, A. G. (2016). *Blindspot: Hidden biases of good people.* New York: Bantam Books.

[30] Tyler, T. R. (2006). *Why people obey the law.* Princeton: Princeton University Press.

[31] Haidt, J. (2001). The emotional dog and its rational tail: A social intuitionist approach to moral judgment. *Psychological Review,* 108(4), 814.

[32] Aquino, K., & Reed II, A. (2002). The self-importance of moral identity. *Journal of Personality and Social Psychology,* 83(6), 1423.

states use enforcement mechanisms that distinguish between intentional and situational wrongdoers?

In general, I argue that we should separate situations of specific individuals – where we need to define *ex post* the level of responsibility of a given individual who is on trial given his or her own limited awareness – from situations where we examine *ex ante* how to mobilize a given population, where our focus is on the collective. The first type of situation is the traditional view of law, but the fact that current studies show that ethical awareness is limited might not be enough to lead to a normative change without more research. However, when it comes to *ex ante* intervention, even when we cannot fully determine the strength of the non-deliberative component in people's ethical motivation, we are able to predict that this component is likely to change the behavior of an unknown proportion of the population and hence should affect the *ex ante* design of law.

In subsequent chapters, I attempt to bridge the gap between the new findings of the behavioral ethics approach to behavior and existing methods used to modify behavior. The new behavioral approaches to law enforcement assume that individuals are motivated to engage in illegal conduct by more than the pursuit of material self-interest. These approaches collide with the traditional outlook, requiring a broad theoretical and empirical comparison of both traditional enforcement mechanisms and nontraditional measures to understand how states may be able to cope with bad deeds carried out by people with a variety of motivations and levels of awareness. I explore the meaning of these variations across people, types of behavior, and legal doctrines.

This book explores the pros and cons of each regulatory tool available to government using an instrument-choice perspective based on the extensive knowledge we already have on the behavioral implications of each tool. This analysis assesses the advantages of both traditional and nontraditional approaches to legal enforcement in addressing both general enforcement dilemmas and contexts of fighting corruption and discrimination.

1.4.1 *The Challenge to Legal Enforcement Posed by Behavioral Ethics*

The underlying assumption of BE regarding the complex role played by the "self" in ethical decision making is clearly problematic for legal theory. BE proposes that many of the claims about the responsibility of individuals as moral agents for their actions neglect the impact of the situation in which the decision-making process is taking place. It may be that the main driver of the individual's behavior is the situation and not the individual's current self-view. Furthermore, the automaticity of the self-enhancement process creates a "responsibility gap" for the individual who is not completely aware of the ethicality of his or her actions and therefore cannot be held responsible for them. A possible way of bridging this gap is through nudges and by designing the situation so that it enhances moral awareness and calculated decision making.

The argument that I develop throughout the book is that the current level of knowledge that BE is able to provide is limited, especially with regard to important questions from a legal perspective; therefore, it is not able to provide policy makers with a complete list of recommendations on how laws should be changed. We lack sufficient knowledge about individuals' awareness of the unethicality of their behavior and their ability to control these ethical biases.[33] The psychological and social mechanisms, which I describe in detail in the next chapter, paint a complex picture of human character according to which people mostly seek to promote their self-interest as long as they can feel good about themselves.[34] Based on this paradigm, if we allow people to choose how to behave, many good people might resort to self-deception mechanisms, such as moral disengagement or elastic justification, and take advantage of others' trust to shirk their responsibilities, engage in dishonest behavior, or violate the law.

1.4.2 *Toward a Broader Perspective of the Regulation of Good People*

One of the most difficult challenges this book addresses is how interventions can increase ethical behaviors if most unethical actions are done unconsciously. For example, Bazerman and Banaji, two of the leading scholars of ethical decision making, argue that incentives and similar concepts fail to correct a large portion of unethical behaviors because "such measures simply bypass the vast majority of unethical behaviors that occur without full conscious awareness of the actors, who engage in them."[35] If we accept this argument, we can challenge enforcement methods that focus on external measures and incentives to control unethical behavior because they ascribe an unjustifiably key role to self-control, autonomy, and responsibility for action. One of the main shortcomings of the "good-people" literature is the gap between what we know about the dominant role of System 1 in ethical decision making and about what policy makers can do to curb thoughtless and unethical behaviors. Evidence of the automaticity of unethicality suggests that a new approach is required to create effective enforcement methods across all fields of legal regulation.

This recognition of the need for a new approach to enforcement lies at the heart of this book. I argue here that the state needs to differentiate enforcement methods: targeting "traditional" misconduct with traditional measures and nontraditional, only partially aware, misconduct with different types of interventions. Throughout

---

[33] For conflicting results with regard to physiological indications of dishonesty among people, see Hochman et al., *supra* note 14.

[34] See Mazar et al., *supra* note 8.

[35] Bazerman, M. H., & Banaji, M. R. (2004). The social psychology of ordinary ethical failures. *Social Justice Research*, 17(2), 111–115.

this book, and particularly in Chapter 2, I describe mechanisms to address the nontraditional misconduct of people.

The book examines states' and organizations' ability to prevent people from engaging in uncooperative behavior, such as wrongful conduct, breach of contracts, and eschewing of professional duties, through traditional methods and compares those methods' effectiveness and limitations to behaviorally informed enforcement mechanisms such as the nudge approach, framing, expressive law, and procedural justice. After discussing the pros and cons of the various intervention mechanisms, the book recommends practical steps for legal policy makers to optimize their regulatory and enforcement efforts to influence both the deliberative and non-deliberative components of behavior.

These practical recommendations are based on a coherent account of the person that the law tries to affect and control, as well as an integrated consideration of many unresolved theoretical questions, such as the following: How much can we know *ex ante* about the awareness, controllability, and modification of the behaviors of good people? How can we know that their goodness is genuine and not fake? Are morality and traditional enforcement practices, such as deterrence, effective in curbing behaviors that are only partly deliberative? Can states regulate good and bad people by using different enforcement methods? Should the nudge approach, which avoids direct communication between the state and the people it regulates, replace all other intervention methods? Do we know to what degree the sustainability of behavioral change and autonomy is reduced when we abandon traditional inter-vention methods?

Some of these questions have been the subject of empirical and theoretical studies, and the book draws on extensive empirical research that others and I have conducted. For example, I have studied empirically the effect of social norms on the perception of legality in the context of intellectual property, the effect of incentives on people's intrinsic and extrinsic motivations in the area of environ-mental protection and whistle-blowing laws, and the effect of legal uncertainty on the compliance and performance of people with different motivational back-grounds. The book moves one step further and fills the gaps unresolved by these and other studies by answering this key question: How much does the behavioral analysis of law (which studies deterrence, legitimacy, procedural justice, and the expressive function of the law) have to offer to improving legal compliance, as understood today, given what we know about the role of automaticity in legal compliance? Although earlier studies have contributed to the body of knowledge of the behavioral analysis of law, they fall short of offering a coherent behavioral and normative picture of the person we are trying to regulate and of answering the questions raised earlier.

1.4.3 *Behavioral Ethics and the Instrument-choice Literature*

An additional goal of the book is to integrate the growing interest in BIT with the increasing use of nontraditional measures, such as nudges, thereby addressing the debate in the literature over "legal instrument choice"[36] and experimental legislation.[37] The change in regulatory instruments follows directly from the recognition of people's bounded rationality. One response to the greater appreciation of the role of non-deliberation in decision making is a move from a command-and-control approach to softer types of regulation.[38] Traditional enforcement mechanisms used by states worldwide are based on the assumptions that people actively chose to engage in "bad" behaviors and that techniques such as incentives can be used to change those choices.

However, recent research shows that much of that behavior is engaged in unconsciously. This book proposes the most effective ways to change behavior by accounting for the effect of both traditional and nontraditional enforcement methods on public trust, legitimacy, and the perceived rule of law. In the context of instrument choice, it addresses the following questions: How do the recommendations of BITs affect people with different modes of reasoning and with different motivations regarding the law? How do modes of reasoning interact with previously shown effects of motivations on legal compliance? What are the long-term effects of BITs proposals on people's perception of responsibility and autonomy? Can we find connections between knowledge of behavioral ethics on the part of the law and legal concepts such as negligence, acting knowingly, and intentionality? Can we identify connections between people's motivations regarding the law and the likelihood of engaging in ethical biases? Can we find the optimal balance between traditional methods and nontraditional ones? Can we be sure that, when looking at the most effective legal intervention for a given situation, we measure not only short-term effects but also factors such as legitimacy, perception of the rule of law, and durability of behavioral changes?

For the interaction between behavior-based regulation and the broader concept of law to be meaningful, it is necessary to identify the steps that would allow psychological knowledge to be generalized to the societal level rather than remaining at the individual level. The ideal behavioral approach to law, advocated by this book, must be sensitive to various normative and institutional factors such as trust, legitimacy, and legal culture. Only by combining the behavioral approach with institutional and normative ones can we create a coherent theoretical framework for nontraditional instruments that states can use to achieve greater success than with earlier,

---

[36] See, for example, Bemelmans-Videc, M. L., Rist, R. C., & Vedung, E. O. (Eds.). (2011). *Carrots, sticks, and sermons: Policy instruments and their evaluation* (Vol. 1). New Brunswick, NJ: Transaction Publishers.

[37] Gubler, Z. J. (2014). Experimental rules. *BCL Review*, 55, 129; Gersen, J. E. (2007). Temporary legislation. *University of Chicago Law Review*, 74(1), 247–298.

[38] Lobel, O. (2004). The renew deal: The fall of regulation and the rise of governance in contemporary legal thought. *Minnesota Law Review*, 89, 342.

narrower approaches. Integrative behavioral research, which explores and analyzes the approaches that government should follow to regulate various types of unethicality in society, can provide policy makers with the methods they need across all legal contexts, going beyond the current focus on energy savings, pension planning, and food consumption; these methods can reach into areas where traditional enforcement methods have failed to produce sustainable change because of their limited focus.[39]

The "Law of Good People" paradigm requires revisiting many of the existing behavioral models of legal regulation and enforcement, which for the most part have relied on the assumption of deliberateness and rationality. These questions need to be answered: What is the optimal use of incentives? Should we replace traditional enforcement mechanisms with nudge interventions? What should be our attitude toward the expressive function of the law, the effect of fairness, or the interaction between incentives and fairness? Furthermore, in contrast to behavioral economics, which deals with biases that prevent people from behaving in a desirable way (e.g., saving more, eating more healthfully), from the BE perspective, many people behave in a way that they consider to be desirable, even after they have had time to reflect on their behavior; others, however, do not.

Yet the need to regulate both good and bad people long preceded the BE revolution. States deal with a world in which people have different motivations to comply with the law, mostly because of their differing levels of internalized moral and legal norms. The solution to dealing with a variety of people lies in the common denominator approach, along with a nuanced use of incentives to prevent crowding-out effects. But when it comes to differences between people's level of deliberation, it is not clear that there is a common denominator at work. And even with the spotlight aimed at the new approach, the previous dichotomies of extrinsic and intrinsic compliance motivations remain relevant, maybe even more so than before. We are now facing the need to regulate people across two dichotomies, which are not necessarily orthogonal: their internalization of norms and their mode of reasoning.

Despite our growing understanding of "good people", no one-size-fits-all policy suggests itself. For the legal policy maker to be able to use the rich knowledge about people's bounded ethicality, we need to create a multidimensional taxonomy of legal doctrines and of the various instruments that states can use in their attempt to modify human behavior. The deviation from the assumption that an actor did wrong because he or she had planned on doing so is justified only in some legal doctrines and only with regard to certain situations. Being able to recognize *ex ante* the areas in which people's lack of moral awareness is expected to be significant can change the balance of the tools that should be used.

---

[39]   Bubb, R., & Pildes, R. H. (2014). How behavioral economics trims its sails and why. *Harvard Law Review*, 127(6), 1637.

1.4.4 *Limitations in the Current Behavioral Ethics Literature*

Several limitations in the behavioral ethics literature prevent it from fully incorporating and applying the research on non-deliberative choice and then using the results to improve the ethicality of society in many important domains of life. There is almost no discussion in BE of such concepts as the controllability of non-deliberative choice and awareness of its effect on behavior. The absence of feedback from the applied behavioral sciences limits the ability of basic theoretical science to provide clear answers regarding aspects of non-deliberative choice.[40] In addition, little comparative research has been conducted on the efficacy of various intervention methods in various contexts. The absence of research leads to a lack of serious attempts in the legal and behavioral literature to understand the mechanisms on which intervention methods are based. Behavioral research does not account for trade-offs between the methods and therefore provides no normative guidelines for policy makers.[41] Finally, because of an absence of substantial interaction with legal scholarship, the fields of behavioral engineering and mechanism design treat law in a simplistic way, ignoring the normative complexities and goals embedded in each legal doctrine and painting all legal doctrines with a broad brush.[42]

There is a great need for a richer view of the interaction between law and human behavior that accounts for the effect of legal intervention on good and bad people alike. There also needs to be a deeper understanding of trade-offs, which should be taken into account when evaluating the effectiveness of government intervention in changing behavior. An example of such context sensitivity appears in this book when I address the area of ethical decision making. Empirical results show that accountability is effective in undermining unconscious biases.[43] However, this might not be the case for bad people who are looking for ways to rationalize their intentional bad behaviors. The inability to predict the effect of various legal interventions on behavior demonstrates the need for evidence-based behavioral-legal scholarship. Legal scholarship must recognize that behavioral findings are not merely on the sidelines but are at the heart of the theory and practice of legal enforcement. It must also demonstrate to scholars in the behavioral and public

---

[40] The assumption of a one-way influence is problematic on many grounds. In the area of non-deliberative choice, the book suggests that understanding what intervention methods work in what circumstances can help basic science gain clarity regarding the interplay between deliberative and non-deliberative choice.

[41] Feldman, Y., & Lobel, O. (2015). Behavioural trade-offs. In A. Alemanno & A.-L. Sibony (Eds.), *Beyond the land of nudges spans the world of law and psychology in nudge and the law.* Oxford: Hart.

[42] For example, in many economics papers about contracts or employment discrimination, the legal doctrine is presented rather naively. The nudge approach often ignores alternative solutions offered by the doctrine itself.

[43] Lerner, J. S., & Tetlock, P. E. (1999). Accounting for the effects of accountability. *Psychological Bulletin,* 125(2), 255.

policy fields that law is a unique area that cannot be overlooked.[44] To regulate behavior in a comprehensive way, legal scholarship must adopt an integrative methodological and theoretical approach to the deliberative and non-deliberative predictors of behavior.

Based on the new insights generated by BE, current research seeks to demonstrate that the methods of behavioral-legal scholarship are no longer sufficient. For example, the main studies in the "why people obey the law", mentioned above, assumes for the most part a deliberative process.[45] Likewise, experiments in which participants are required to play cooperation games assume that people readily recognize their self-interest and the public interest. At the same time, the literature on non-deliberative choice ignores the possible effect of compliance on factors such as perception of legitimacy and public trust, as well as cultural and institutional constraints. Furthermore, lab research lacks the required methodological focus of field experiments that provide external validity, which is so much more important for law than for psychology.

For example, one of the main techniques that "good people" can use to self-justify unethical behavior is to engage in a biased interpretation of the legal requirements they must follow. Research on corruption and conflict of interest has studied numerous examples of situations in which people who exhibit professional and moral responsibility have allowed their self-interest, possibly without full awareness, to prevail over fulfilling their duties.[46] The existing literature on contractual performance decisions and framing focuses on the dichotomous choice: to breach or not to breach. However, in a study coauthored with Teichman and Shur,[47] I argued that the focus should not be on whether people choose to comply with contractual obligations, but on their decision to interpret the contract in a self-serving way. This is in contrast to the work of Wilkinson-Ryan and Baron; describing to their participants the promisor's decision to breach a contract, they simply stated, "He decides to break his contract in order to take other, more profitable work."[48] Such studies implicitly assume that choices are made in reference to clear contractual

---

[44] Dagan, H., Kreitner, R., & Kricheli-Katz, T. (forthcoming). Legal theory for legal empiricists. *Law and Social Inquiry*.

[45] See discussion in Chapters 3, 4, and 5 on the expressive effect of law – where the language of the law changes the social meaning of behavior.

[46] There is a wealth of research on the prevalence of conflicts of interest in almost every field. See, for example, Rodwin, M. A. (1993). *Medicine, money, and morals: Physicians' conflicts of interest*. New York: Oxford University Press. See also Thompson, D. F. (1993). Understanding financial conflicts of interest. *New England Journal of Medicine*, 329, 573–576.

[47] Feldman, Y., Schurr, A., & Teichman, D. (2013). Reference points and contractual choices: An experimental examination. *Journal of Empirical Legal Studies*, 10(3), 512–541.

[48] Wilkinson-Ryan, T., & Baron, J. (2009). Moral judgment and moral heuristics in breach of contract. *Journal of Empirical Legal Studies*, 6(2), 405–423 at 413. See also Wilkinson-Ryan, T., & Hoffman, D. A. (2010). Breach is for suckers. *Vanderbilt Law Review*, 63, 1003, at 1029 (using precisely the same phrase to describe the decision to breach).

obligations. This book instead focuses on the arguably more common situation of how to interpret an ambiguous obligation.

Similarly, much of the current literature on morality and legal compliance examines people's moral judgment but ignores the role of moral intuition and the fact that people might engage in motivated reasoning. The classical approach assumes that people consider the situation, recognize the moral conflict, and then decide what to do. This approach ignores that fact that they decide what seems to be the right thing to do based on their highly motivated perception of the situation. Their behavior may be immoral, but they still view themselves as moral people because they frame the situation in such a way that it "allows" immoral behavior. Clearly, people's self-image of being cooperative or moral is not based on acting morally. Many studies in the social cognitive literature discuss mechanisms that either prevent people from knowing in advance that they are violating the law or enable them to develop an *ex post* approach that uses various strategies to change people's perception of the wrongfulness of their behavior. Ariely et al. have shown that people do not believe that it is legitimate to cheat more if one is financially deprived.[49] But when they were manipulated into thinking that they were deprived (by receiving a smaller amount of money in a game), they were quick to start cheating. This finding shows the importance of explicit judgment not only relative to implicit judgment but also to actual behavior. The methodological observation of Greenvald and Banaji on the power of implicit judgment may have even stronger force: because people love themselves so much, there is no reason for them to admit to themselves that they behave amorally.[50]

1.5 BRIEF OUTLINE OF THE CHAPTERS

Chapter 2: Behavioral Ethics and the Meaning of Good People for Legal Enforcement

In this chapter, I review the work of scholars such as Bazerman, Banaji, Ariely, Gino, Haidt, Bereby-Meyer, Shalvi, Rand and others on deliberative and non-deliberative mechanisms that people use to promote their self-interest and that result in good people doing bad things. I discuss the relevance to BE of several theoretical mechanisms: moral disengagement, embodiment, self-deception, moral licensing, automaticity of self-interest, moral hypocrisy, elastic justification, ethical fading, and the dishonesty of honest people. I also describe various

---

[49] Sharma, E., Mazar, N., Alter, A. L., & Ariely, D. (2014). Financial deprivation selectively shifts moral standards and compromises moral decisions. *Organizational Behavior and Human Decision Processes*, 123(2), 90–100.

[50] Greenwald, A. G., & Banaji, M. R. (1995). Implicit social cognition: Attitudes, self-esteem, and stereotypes. *Psychological Review*, 102(1), 4.

phenomena that challenge the current regulatory approach followed by most states.[51]

In the last part of this chapter, I offer a few words of caution to states that wish to use the knowledge of behavioral ethics to modify legal policy making. The field is relatively young, and it is not yet able to answer important questions with regard to ethical biases, such as their internal mechanisms, the awareness of the existence of biases, and the variation between people in their ability to overcome those biases. However, I strongly believe that legal scholarship cannot wait for a consensus to be reached on those questions. Although we do not know the percentage of good versus bad people, the extent of involvement of the automatic system in decision making, or the level of awareness of its role, the recognition that a substantial portion of the population engages in non-deliberative choices is enough to shift the normative debate. The chapter concludes that knowing the ratio of people of each type and the exact level of people's awareness is secondary in importance to the fact that such variation exists and that legal policy making has to recognize the need to adopt more than one type of intervention to deal with different modes of awareness. We cannot afford to wait until we know more before we act.

Chapter 3: Resisting Traditional Enforcement Mechanisms

In Chapter 3, I reexamine some behavioral theories that explain people's motivation to follow the law. One of the key arguments of this book is that to deal with good people, we do not need to abandon everything we know about legal enforcement; we just need to revise our current understanding of how traditional intervention methods can influence different types of people. Chapter 3 focuses on traditional enforcement methods that were not intended to take into account dual reasoning and the need to deal with non-deliberative choices. Nevertheless, many of those traditional paradigms are highly sensitive to the behavioral revolution. Among the concepts reviewed in this chapter are deterrence, morality and fairness, incentives, social norms, and the expressive function of the law.

This chapter examines the techniques that governments use to regulate behavior.[52] Traditional intervention methods discussed in the literature include incentives (all forms of penalties, fines, rewards,[53] and other external

---

[51] In the next chapter, I examine the relevancy of paradigms such as egotism (sharing first names, birthdays); embodiment (washing hands, closing one eye, carrying weight); food consumption (drinking coffee, glucose studies); priming the ten commandments, eyes, faces, money, dirty money, and various situational cues that trigger compliance (teddy bears).

[52] There is a huge literature on the typology of regulatory approaches that I do not discuss here. I review many of them in my work with Lobel, see Lobel & Feldman, *supra* note 41.

[53] For the literature on this topic, see Becker, G. S. (1968). Crime and punishment: An economic approach. *Journal of Political Economy*, 76(2), 169–217. See also Feldman, Y., & Lobel, O. (2009). Incentives matrix: The comparative effectiveness of rewards, liabilities, duties, and protections for reporting illegality. *Texas Law Review*, 88, 1151. For a comparison of the efficacy of incentives that use

measures[54]) and more intrinsic measures such as fairness-, legitimacy-, and morality-based interventions;[55] social norm-based interventions;[56] and the expressive function of the law, which shapes the social meaning of behaviors.[57] Another technique reviewed in this chapter focuses on disclosure and transparency, which assume that people engage in deliberation, so that given enough information, they will make the right decision or will avoid making the wrong one if what they do is open for everyone to see.

The theoretical and critical part of this chapter focuses on examining how formal enforcement methods should be modified, given that people are not fully deliberative in their decisions to disobey the law or breach their contracts. I show how various subliteratures in the behavioral approach to law (e.g., social norms, compliance motivation, the perceived role of self-interest, the non-instrumental effects of law) should be revised in light of the new knowledge regarding dual-system reasoning and BE. The chapter concludes with a description of the new challenges that policy makers face as a result of recent findings about ethical decision making (e.g., do people who do not want to discriminate react to penalties?) and the development of various behaviorally informed approaches to legal compliance.

The traditional line of research on the role of fairness and morality in legal research could be traced to reasoning advocated by scholars such as Kohlberg[58] on moral development or Kelman[59] on compliance. Kohlberg's ideas, which were incorporated into legal theory, maintain that people clearly recognize that they are facing a moral dilemma, and the question is only what kind of moral rule they use in any given context. By contrast, I argue that people do not regard much of the bad behavior in which they engage as bad behavior at all. Various processes, operating on various levels of self-awareness, help them interpret their behavior as being

---

different labels (e.g. fines, rewards), See Feldman, Y., & Perez, O. (2012). Motivating environmental action in a pluralistic regulatory environment: An experimental study of framing, crowding out, and institutional effects in the context of recycling policies. *Law & Society Review*, 46(2), 405–442 for a comparison of the effects of sanctions versus taxes in environmental contexts.

[54]   Gneezy, U., Meier, S., & Rey-Biel, P. (2011). When and why incentives (don't) work to modify behavior. *The Journal of Economic Perspectives*, 25(4), 191–209.

[55]   See Tyler, *supra* note 30. For a review, see Feldman, Y. (2011). Five models of regulatory compliance motivation: Empirical findings and normative implications. In D. Levi-Faur (Ed.) (2013). *Handbook on the politics of regulation* (pp. 335–347). Cheltenham: Edward Elgar.

[56]   McAdams, R. H. (2000). Law and Economics Working Papers Series. *Oregon Law Review*, 79, 339–390. See also Feldman, Y., & Nadler, J. (2006). The law and norms of file sharing. *San Diego Law Review*, 43, 577.

[57]   Sunstein, C. R. (1996). On the expressive function of law. *University of Pennsylvania Law Review*, 144(5), 2021–2053. See also Feldman, Y. (2009). The expressive function of trade secret law: Legality, cost, intrinsic motivation, and consensus. *Journal of Empirical Legal Studies*, 6(1), 177–212.

[58]   Kohlberg, L. (1981). *The philosophy of moral development: Moral stages and the idea of justice*. New York: Harper & Row.

[59]   Kelman, H. C. (1958). Compliance, identification, and internalization: Three processes of attitude change. *Journal of Conflict Resolution*, 2(1), 51–60.

either legal and ethical or justifiably illegal and unethical. Some mechanisms even prevent people from recognizing that they are facing a moral dilemma.

The BE perspective also differs from that of most of the compliance motivation literature, including Kelman's basic paradigm on compliance and Tyler's procedural fairness approach. According to Tyler's approach, the main difference is between people with an extrinsic versus those with an intrinsic commitment to obey the law. I claim instead that in many cases, people do not make an informed decision about the right way to act based on their level of commitment to the law. The approach I advocate suggests that the effect of morality on law operates in a completely different way, at least in some cases of legal noncompliance. The core argument of BE is that in a considerable number of cases, people do not engage in any form of deliberative moral reasoning before deciding whether or not to obey the law. Many bad deeds are not seen as such by the people who commit them; therefore, they are not always aware that they might be about to perpetrate a moral wrong. It follows that the focus should be on identifying both the situational and the personality characteristics that will increase the likelihood that people will recognize the moral flaw in their behavior.[60]

According to the traditional approach, certain techniques, most notably incentives,[61] can be used to change the behavior of people so that they do not act in an unethical manner in situations relevant to legal and public policy. In the past three decades, this approach, based on the neoclassical economic doctrine of rational choice, has been challenged by theories based on the behavioral approach to human judgment and decision making. Various alternatives and modifications in regulating human behavior, going beyond simple incentives, have been offered over the years, including some in my own research. For example, the following interventions have been proposed: those that change the wording of incentives (to make people more likely to consider their ethical behavior), that increase legitimacy (by mandating employee voice procedures such as pay talks and hearing prior to termination, in the workplace), that account for crowding out (e.g., when people would rather do things without being compensated for them), that increase the sensitivity to cognitive limitations (e.g., in examining how people engage in aggressive interpretation when contractual obligations are framed as a potential loss rather than a potential gain).[62] Nonetheless, the challenge to legal

[60] In this vein, a work conducted on the scale of rule conditionality is Fine, A., van Rooij, B., Feldman, Y., Shalvi, S., Scheper, E., Leib, M., & Cauffman, E. (2016). Rule orientation and behavior: Development and validation of a scale measuring individual acceptance of rule violation. *Psychology, Public Policy, and Law*, 22(3), 314.

[61] Camerer, C. F., Hogarth, R. M., Budescu, D. V., & Eckel, C. (1999). The effects of financial incentives in experiments: A review and capital-labor-production framework. In B. Fischhoff & C. F. Manski (Eds.), *Elicitation of preferences* (pp. 7–48). Dordrecht: Springer.

[62] Feldman, Y. (2011). For love or money? Defining relationships in law and life: The complexity of disentangling intrinsic and extrinsic compliance motivations: Theoretical and empirical insights from the behavioral analysis of law. *Washington University Journal of Law and Policy*, 35(1), 11–51.

enforcement posed by the BE perspective has not been explored in this context, mainly because of the dominance of economics in the interplay between law and psychology.

Chapter 4: Revisiting Non-formal Enforcement Mechanisms

This chapter examines new nontraditional, soft enforcement methods that take into account people's limited awareness and cognition; these methods include the nudge (an intervention that changes behavior without creating economic incentives or banning other possibilities),[63] de-biasing (a group of doctrines and methods used to overcome biased thinking),[64] accountability, and reflection (which requires individuals to explain why they made a certain decision after making it).[65] I also emphasize the effectiveness of these new behavioral measures, which were developed to deal with cognitive biases, in overcoming ethical biases. This chapter concludes with a description of experimental work comparing the efficacy of explicit and implicit types of interventions on how people behave in subtle conflict of interest situations.

The chapter reviews the studies that have demonstrated the limitations of each intervention when dealing with people who lack a full awareness of their behavior; these limitations are evident in the few famous failures of the nudge-based approach. For example, initially the default rule – having to opt in versus out when donating – seemed to be an effective nudge in increasing rates of organ donation; however, later studies showed that the nudge was actually much less effective.[66] The message, "Save more tomorrow," shown to be a strong nudge in pension savings, also turned out to be less effective in the long term.[67] Generally speaking, giving people full information proved to be problematic;[68] de-biasing was found to produce limited results,[69] as was disclosure of conflicts of interest, which in many contexts ended up having the opposite effect from the desired one.[70] Masking personal information in

---

[63]   See Jolls et al., *supra* note 1.
[64]   Jolls, C., & Sunstein, C. R. (2006). The law of implicit bias. *California Law Review*, 94(4), 969–996.
[65]   See Lerner & Tetlock, *supra* note 43. There are many other techniques that have been studied in recent years, such as signing first and teddy bears, reviewed and assessed in Feldman, Y. (2014). Behavioral ethics meets behavioral law and economics. In E. Zamir & D. Teichman (Eds.), *Oxford handbook of behavioral law and economics* (pp. 213–241). New York: Oxford University Press.
[66]   Orentlicher, D. (2008). Presumed consent to organ donation: Its rise and fall in the United States. *Rutgers Law Review*, 61, 295.
[67]   See Bubb & Pildes, *supra* note 39, at 1637.
[68]   Ben-Shahar, O., & Schneider, C. E. (2011). The failure of mandated disclosure. *University of Pennsylvania Law Review*, 159(3), 647–749.
[69]   Larrick, R. P. (2004). Debiasing. In D. J. Koehler & N. Harvey (Eds.), *Blackwell handbook of judgment and decision making* (pp. 316–338). Oxford: Wiley-Blackwell.
[70]   Cain, D. M., Loewenstein, G., & Moore, D. A. (2005). The dirt on coming clean: Perverse effects of disclosing conflicts of interest. *Journal of Legal Studies*, 34(1), 1–25.

hiring applications was found to be more effective in reducing biases against minorities than against women.[71] Thus predicting when and how to change behavior through non-traditional mechanisms such as nudges has proven to be more difficult than previously assumed.

Chapter 5: Social Norms and Compliance

Chapter 5 focuses on the social norms in legal compliance. This chapter was separated from Chapters 3 and 4 due to its interaction with both traditional and nontraditional means of intervention. Hence, this relatively short chapter outlines the main literature on the role of social norms, with particular focus on non-deliberative processes in how people perceive social norms and in how that affects their behavior.

Chapter 6: Are All People Equally Good?

In this chapter, I examine several factors that might explain the variations among people in their level of implicit and explicit legally relevant behaviors. Because personality scales are an important measure of such variations, I review several scales, including those relating to moral identity,[72] level of moral disengagement,[73] and moral firmness,[74] as well as context-specific measures, such as racism, which are based on the implicit association test.

Second, following a critical assessment of the relevance of data accumulated in personality research to legal compliance, given the great variation in the factors that could be correlated with that compliance, I examine the research in economics, psychology, and law concerning the differences between the intrinsic and extrinsic motivation of individuals; this is another way to differentiate among people.[75] Variations in compliance usually depend on the particular content of the law; some people may be highly motivated to obey certain laws but not have the same level of intrinsic motivation to obey other types of laws.[76]

---

[71] Krause, A., Rinne, U., & Zimmermann, K. F. (2012). Anonymous job applications of fresh Ph.D. economists. *Economics Letters*, 117(2), 441–444.

[72] Reed II, A., & Aquino, K. F. (2003). Moral identity and the expanding circle of moral regard toward out-groups. *Journal of Personality and Social Psychology*, 84(6), 1270.

[73] Bandura, A. (1999). Moral disengagement in the perpetration of inhumanities. *Personality and Social Psychology Review*, 3(3), 193–209.

[74] Shalvi, S., & Leiser, D. (2013). Moral firmness. *Journal of Economic Behavior & Organization*, 93, 400–407.

[75] For the main economic model, see Benabou, R., & Tirole, J. (2003). Intrinsic and extrinsic motivation. *Review of Economic Studies*, 70(3), 489–520. For a review of implications to legal theory, see Feldman, *supra* note 62.

[76] Although, as explained in this chapter, there are some general tendencies to obey the law. These tendencies are supported also with regard to the citizenship approach to legal compliance whereby people obey the law simply because it is the law. It is interesting to examine whether people who obey laws simply because they are laws should be seen as intrinsically committed individuals.

To understand the "law of good people" paradigm, it is necessary to examine whether there is a correlation between people's level of motivation and their personality traits. For that reason, I focus on more specific personality traits that influence people's general tendency to obey or disobey the law. I discuss the work of Glockner et al.,[77] who compared situational and individual factors related to legal compliance with a focus on self-control. In addition, I review a new scale developed by me in a joint work with Fine, Van Rooji,[78] and others on people's ability to find excuses for violating the law.

Chapter 7: Pluralistic Account of the Law: The Multiple Effects of Law on Behavior

The pluralistic account of the effect of the law on behavior is based on several assumptions developed in this chapter. Most people obey the law for multiple reasons, but people are more likely to experience and report their more noble motivations. Dual reasoning greatly reduces our ability to measure the "true" effect of the law. The law, according to this view is multi-faced and must communicate with different populations at the same time. Some aspects of the law serve multiple functions simultaneously, as for example, the expressive effects of punishments.

Chapter 8: Enforcement Dilemmas and Behavioral Trade-offs

Is it possible to use both traditional and nontraditional methods simultaneously, or are they based on conflicting assumptions? Research in other contexts suggests that it is not always possible to use approaches that combine intrinsic and extrinsic measures.[79] Research conducted by various scholars[80] suggests that the interaction between intrinsic motivation and implicit behaviors is more complex than what the legal literature assumes.[81] My research is based on the assumption that govern-

---

[77] Waubert de Puiseau, B., Glöckner, A., & Towfigh, E.V. (2016). *Comparing and Integrating Theories of Law Obedience: Deterrence, Legitimacy, and Self-control.* Unpublished manuscript, University of Hagen, Hagen, Germany.

[78] See Fine et al., *supra* note 60, at 314.

[79] Feldman, Y. (2011). The complexity of disentangling intrinsic and extrinsic compliance motivations: Theoretical and empirical insights from the behavioral analysis of law. Wash. UJL & Pol'y, 35, 11.

[80] Devine, P. G., Plant, E. A., Amodio, D. M., Harmon-Jones, E., & Vance, S. L. (2002). The regulation of explicit and implicit race bias: The role of motivations to respond without prejudice. *Journal of Personality and Social Psychology*, 82(5), 835.

[81] Legault, L., Gutsell, J. N., & Inzlicht, M. (2011). Ironic effects of antiprejudice messages: How motivational interventions can reduce (but also increase) prejudice. *Psychological Science*, 22(12), 1472–1477, for evidence of backfire effects when attempting to change people's prejudice either explicitly or implicitly.

ments must invest in improving legitimacy and morality of law even in areas that seem to involve automatic behavior. As an alternative to focusing on individual behavior, the chapter examines the contexts in which governments, organizations, and individuals engage in improving their automatic ethical behavior. I also discuss the many trade-offs that the BE literature requires us to take into account. For example, as suggested earlier, is accountability good or bad? Does it undermine some biases, but allow others? How important is legitimacy in a dual-reasoning context? To what extent is it possible to treat both good and bad people using different enforcement mechanisms? Should we let people know about the existence of the nudge?[82]

Chapter 9: The Corruption of "Good People"

Individuals often feel that they are not being treated fairly by employers, public officials, or people whom they hire to attend to their best interests in various capacities such as lawyers, physicians, architects, and accountants. Professionals whom we trust to behave responsibly and to focus primarily on our interests (when we hire them), on the interest of the public (in the case of public officials), or on the workplace (in the case of the employer) turn out instead to be influenced by personal or competing institutional interests. For example, at the workplace, an individual who may be up for promotion may develop the impression that other candidates are more likely to know the decision makers personally and thus have an unfair advantage. In the areas of corruption and discrimination, the notion of trust in the system is highly important because it affects individuals' ability to trust the professionals who are expected to attend to their interest (lawyers, physicians, etc.), public officials (municipal officers), and hiring managers (in employment situations).

Often the potential deviation from objectivity and impartiality is relatively subtle, and the professional can easily deny or ignore it based on legitimate rationales. In hiring or promotion contexts and regarding the exercise of professional duties, subtle deviations usually occur in situations in which there is more than one legitimate choice, and therefore there is room for various interpretations of what is the right thing to do. In the presence of vagueness, people have greater room for self-deception and motivated reasoning, and we expect that good people are more likely to find ways to justify their bad behavior. Some argue that such deviations are beyond the reach of classical enforcement mechanisms. Yet the focus on subtle deviations from impartiality creates a rich ground for research on the interplay between legal theory, ethical decision making, and empirical analysis of the law.

Many deviations from impartiality and professional integrity are carried out without full awareness. But because the proportion of unethical behaviors that are

---

[82] This is investigated in Ariel Tikochiski's PhD research.

carried out with full awareness in any given context is unknown in advance, it is necessary to explore a hybrid approach to modifying human behavior that allows us to address both implicit and explicit violations, with limited cross-interference. Although soft interventions are criticized because of their threat to autonomy,[83] ethical nudges – which are aimed at curbing corruption and discrimination – generate a different type of policy trade-off, as explained earlier.

In this chapter, I pay special attention to answering the following theoretical and applied policy questions: What effect does group or institutional affiliation have on bias and impartiality? How do monetary incentives affect impartiality? To what extent are people aware that such effects can change their judgment as well as that of others, and how does it affect their trust in the integrity of these processes? To what extent do people believe in the efficacy of various traditional and BIT-related legal instruments? What legal interventions are most likely to be regarded as legitimate and improve public trust both in society and in the ability of the state to change human behavior in a sustainable way?

Focusing on implicit corruption, I compare the different intervention methods, examining their effectiveness in curbing people's behavior in situations of conflict of interest. I pay special attention to subtle conflicts of interest, where many good people may not recognize that there is something unethical about their behavior.[84] This focus is needed because, globally, countries experience some degree of corruption at most levels of government,[85] and corruption arises in a different form in the private sector (e.g., in the area of corporate governance).

Research on corruption and conflict of interest contains numerous examples of situations in which people who exhibit professional and moral responsibility have allowed their self-interest, admittedly without full awareness, to prevail over fulfilling their duties.[86] One of the most studied areas in this context is the conflict of interest of physicians who conduct clinical studies financed by pharmaceutical companies or who prescribe drugs based on their relationship to such

---

[83] See, for example, Arad, A., & Rubinstein, A. (2015). The people's perspective on libertarian-paternalistic policies and nudging and choice architecture: Ethical considerations; http://arielrubin stein.tau.ac.il/papers/LP.

[84] Here are a few examples of subtle conflict of interest situations: voting on the academic promotion of a friend, consulting for a firm that may compete in the future with one's current employer, when a civil servant treats an affluent entrepreneur with greater consideration than usual, when a physician performs a procedure because he is more comfortable with it but it may not be what the patient would most benefit from, or a lawyer rejecting a plea bargain or a settlement that is in the best interests of her client.

[85] For example, a 2012 report found that all European countries suffer from political corruption at some level. Mulcahy, S. (2012). *Money, politics, power: Corruption risks in Europe.* Berlin: Transparency International.

[86] There is a wealth of research on the prevalence of conflict of interest in almost every field. See, for example, Rodwin, *supra* note 46. See also Thompson, *supra* note 46.

companies.[87] Most clinicians do not think they are doing anything wrong when they prescribe a certain course of treatment to their patients while ignoring the subtle effects of competing interests. In many similar situations, most good people may believe that the option that promotes their self-interest is also the correct one. We can include in this group lawyers dealing with their clients, executives acting on behalf of shareholders, prosecutors making plea bargains, and academics deciding whether their colleagues should be promoted.

In the context of implicit corruption, psychological processes such as self-deception, elastic justification, moral disengagement, and motivated reasoning enable people to behave unethically without recognizing their wrongdoing.[88] As in research on prejudice and discrimination, a vast literature suggests that self-interest may influence people without their recognizing its effect on their behavior.[89] Moore et al.[90] showed that people truly believed their own biased judgments and had limited ability to recognize that their behavior was affected by self-interest.[91] These conclusions are also supported by the work of Gino et al.[92] and of Shalvi et al.[93] regarding honesty and by the work of Halali et al. regarding fairness.[94] Although the debate in the literature continues,[95] from an applied perspective, making the behavior of good people more ethical requires an understanding of implicit corruption and the fact that it is difficult to manage.[96] Various

[87]   Rodwin, M. A. (2012). Conflicts of interest, institutional corruption, and pharma: An agenda for reform. *Journal of Law, Medicine & Ethics*, 3(40), 511–522.
[88]   "Much of the problem with conflicts of interest is not intentional corruption but *unintentional bias*. Bias is widespread and is a problem even for well-meaning professionals": Cain, D. M., & Detsky, A. S. (2008). Everyone's a little bit biased (even physicians). JAMA, 299(24), 2893–2895; Loewenstein, G., Sah, S., & Cain, D. M. (2012). The unintended consequences of conflict of interest disclosure. JAMA, 307(7), 669–670.
[89]   See Moore & Loewenstein, *supra* note 16.
[90]   Moore, D. A., Tanlu, L., & Bazerman, M. H. (2010). Conflict of interest and the intrusion of bias. *Judgment and Decision Making*, 5(1), 37.
[91]   "Private" evaluations were measured by giving participants incentives to be accurate in their predictions. See also Bazerman, M. H., & Sezer, O. (2016). Bounded awareness: Implications for ethical decision making. *Organizational Behavior and Human Decision Processes*, 136, 95–105, for a review of the mechanism responsible for limited awareness of unethicality.
[92]   Gino, F., Schweitzer, M. E., Mead, N. L., & Ariely, D. (2011). Unable to resist temptation: How self-control depletion promotes unethical behavior. *Organizational Behavior and Human Decision Processes*, 115(2), 191–203.
[93]   See Shalvi et al., *supra* note 13.
[94]   Halali, E., Bereby-Meyer, Y., & Ockenfels, A. (2013). Is it all about the self? The effect of self-control depletion on ultimatum game proposers. *Frontiers in Human Neuroscience*, 7.
[95]   For example, Cushman, F., Young, L., & Hauser, M. (2006). The role of conscious reasoning and intuition in moral judgment: Testing three principles of harm. *Psychological Science*, 17(12), 1082–1089.
[96]   See Lessig, L. (2011). *Republic, lost: How money corrupts congress – and a plan to stop it*. New York: Twelve. See also Feldman, Y., Gauthier, R., & Schuler, T. (2013). Curbing misconduct in the pharmaceutical industry: Insights from behavioral ethics and the behavioral approach to law. *Journal of Law, Medicine & Ethics*, 41(3), 620–628.

studies have shown that disclosure, which has been regarded as the ultimate solution for curbing corruption, does not work for implicit processes and can even have the reverse effect from that desired.[97]

Chapter 10: Discrimination by "Good" Employers

Employment discrimination is one of the most serious problems in labor markets worldwide and so has attracted more attention than other forms of discrimination (e.g., financial, residential). Anti-discrimination employment laws prohibit specific forms of employment discrimination – for example, that based on race, sex, religion, and age.[98] But usually these laws do not address each form of discrimination individually, nor do they take into account the different sociological and psychological mechanisms behind each form. In most countries, the legal approach is a general one, and similar remedies and prohibitions are applied to various forms of discrimination.

Research on the non-deliberative aspects of discrimination uses the insights of social and cognitive research in intergroup psychology,[99] which has focused on stereotyping processes.[100] Fiske's work is especially promising for legal scholars because it offers a nuanced and multidimensional approach to discrimination.[101] Psychological insights have been incorporated into the study of employment discrimination to a greater extent than in any other legal area.[102] Legal scholars, most

---

[97] See Cain et al., *supra* note 70.

[98] Civil Rights Act, Title VII (1964) prohibits employment discrimination on the basis of religion, race, and sex. The Age Discrimination in Employment Act of 1967 (ADEA) protects applicants and employees who are 40 years old and older from discrimination. Both laws are enforced by the US Equal Employment Opportunity Commission (EEOC). In the United States, the difference between the categories of discrimination is mostly due to constitutional reasons rather than behavioral ones.

[99] Tajfel, H. (Ed.). (2010). *Social identity and intergroup relations.* Cambridge: Cambridge University Press. See also Tajfel, H., & Turner, J. C. (1979). An integrative theory of intergroup conflict. *Social Psychology of Intergroup Relations*, 33(47), 74.

[100] Much of the research in this field can be attributed to the writing of Fiske and collaborators, for example, Fiske, S. T., Cuddy, A. J., Glick, P., & Xu, J. (2002). A model of (often mixed) stereotype content: Competence and warmth respectively follow from perceived status and competition. *Journal of Personality and Social Psychology*, 82(6), 878. See also Fiske, S. T. (2012). Managing ambivalent prejudices: Smart-but-cold and warm-but-dumb stereotypes. *The Annals of the American Academy of Political and Social Science*, 639(1), 33–48; Lepore, L., & Brown, R. (1997). Category and stereotype activation: Is prejudice inevitable? *Journal of Personality and Social Psychology*, 72(2), 275; Fiske, S. T., Gilbert, D. T., & Lindzey, G. (Eds.). (2010). *Handbook of social psychology* (Vol. 2). Hoboken, NJ: John Wiley & Sons.

[101] Fiske, S. T. (2000). Stereotyping, prejudice, and discrimination at the seam between the centuries: Evolution, culture, mind, and brain. *European Journal of Social Psychology*, 30(3), 299–322.

[102] Bodensteiner, I. E. (2008). The implications of psychological research related to unconscious discrimination and implicit bias in proving intentional discrimination. *Missouri Law Review*, 73, 83, on circumstantial evidence; for the shift in the burden of proof in employment discrimination cases and for a broader account, see Pedersen, N. B. (2010). A legal framework for uncovering implicit bias. *University of Cincinnati Law Review*, 79, 97.

notably Krieger, have suggested that many biased employment decisions result not from discriminatory motivations but from a variety of unintentional categorization errors.[103] Considering the richness of behavioral findings on employment discrimination, the lack of responsiveness of the law to this knowledge is frustrating. Krieger and Fiske[104] discussed the outdated nature of US laws in this area from both jurisprudential and practical aspects. For example, the law requires showing intention and finding evidence for what has occurred at the stage of discrimination,[105] but it falls short of providing a comprehensive legal alternative to implicit discrimination.

Some legal scholars have acknowledged that most acts of discrimination are the product of a variety of unintentional errors.[106] As in most other types of research on non-deliberative choice, the recent literature on discrimination reveals the problems associated with automatic reasoning, but it offers almost no suggestions for the format of a new legal policy that would address both deliberative and non-

---

[103]   Krieger, L. H. (1995). The content of our categories: A cognitive bias approach to discrimination and equal employment opportunity. *Stanford Law Review, 47*, 1161–1248; Krieger, L. H., & Fiske, S. T. (2006). Behavioral realism in employment discrimination law: Implicit bias and disparate treatment. *California Law Review, 94*(4), 997–1062. Krieger, L. H. (2000). Afterword: Socio-legal backlash. *Berkeley Journal of Employment and Labor Law, 21*(1), 476–520; Hart, M. (2004). Subjective decisionmaking and unconscious discrimination. *Alabama Law Review, 56*, 741; Cuddy, A. J., Fiske, S. T., & Glick, P. (2008). Warmth and competence as universal dimensions of social perception: The stereotype content model and the BIAS map. *Advances in Experimental Social Psychology, 40*, 61–149; Uhlmann, E. L., Brescoll, V. L., & Machery, E. (2010). The motives underlying stereotype-based discrimination against members of stigmatized groups. *Social Justice Research, 23*(1), 1–16. See Agerström, J., & Rooth, D. O. (2011). The role of automatic obesity stereotypes in real hiring discrimination. *Journal of Applied Psychology, 96*(4), 790, in the context of overweight people.

[104]   See Krieger & Fiske, *supra* note 103.

[105]   A vast body of federal employment statutes provides protection against discrimination based on group membership. See Title VII of the Civil Rights Act of 1964, *supra* note 98, for example, prohibits discrimination based on race, color, religion, gender, or national origin. The Equal Pay Act prohibits employers from paying different wages based on the gender of the employee (but does not prohibit other discriminatory employment practices). The Age Discrimination in Employment Act prohibits employment discrimination on the basis of age. The Americans with Disabilities Act (1990) prohibits discrimination by employers based on physical or mental handicaps. In recent years, the legal situation is similar in Israeli courts, although the courts are aware of the existence of unconscious discrimination and try to objectively test for discrimination (H.C.J. 104/87 Dr. Neomi Nevo v. The National Labor Court, 1987, 09-9690 Ababa v. A.A 101 Group, 2013). Nevertheless, the vast majority of misconduct in this area never reaches the courts; this is true of employment discrimination in general, see Nelson, R. L., & Bridges, W. P. (1999). *Legalizing gender inequality: Courts, markets and unequal pay for women in America* (Vol. 16). New York: Cambridge University Press; and in Israel in particular: Sharon Rabin Margaliot (2000) The slippery case of age discrimination – how does one prove its existence? *Advoc* 44, 529, 537. See also Cerullo, C. (2013). Everyone's a little bit racist: Reconciling implicit bias and Title VII. *Fordham Law Review, 82*, 127, for a review of the treatment of implicit biases by US courts.

[106]   See Krieger, *supra* note 103.

deliberative discriminatory behavior. For the most part, the law still looks for a smoking gun when identifying employers as committing acts of discrimination and prejudice.

Chapter 11: Summary and Conclusion

It is important both theoretically and practically to understand that there is no one-size-fits-all solution to incorporating considerations of the intrinsic versus extrinsic dynamic into government policies. It is difficult to predict the accumulated effect of these mechanisms without taking into account the context, and, in any case, the accuracy of predictions will always be limited. I therefore recommend that theoretical efforts be focused on creating a multidimensional taxonomy of contexts that elucidates the dynamics of intrinsic-extrinsic motivations.

First, what is the nature of the behavior we want to encourage?[107] It is important to take into account the behavior that the policy maker wishes to promote. One cannot excel in recycling or even in organ donation;[108] for the most part, policy makers care only about one's activity level and willingness to pay for engaging in recycling. In various other legal contexts, however, the quality of the behavior is more important. For example, in whistle-blowing or blood donation, it is less helpful to think about employees who do it for purely extrinsic reasons. In a legal context, where extra-role activity is desired, the cost of reducing intrinsic motivation increases, and one should be more cautious in introducing extrinsic motives.

Second, what proportion of the target population do we need to cooperate?[109] When the level of intrinsic motivation is heterogeneous, what proportion of the target population do we need to comply?

In the context of trade secrets, we need the cooperation of 100 percent of the target population, from those with the highest level of intrinsic motivation to those with the lowest. Therefore, the effect of reducing the intrinsic motivation of committed employees may be secondary to making sure that even those without intrinsic motivation remain loyal to their employers. In the case of whistle-blowing, the exact opposite is true, and we need the cooperation of only some of the employees to come forward when some illegal activity is taking place within the organization. Therefore, the policy maker can focus primarily on those who are high on intrinsic motivation.[110] For obvious reasons, we may not even want to provide incentives to those without intrinsic motivation because of fear of false reports by bounty hunters. Finally, in the context of recycling, we are interested in averaging, so that as many

---

[107] To date, I have presented data about three main types of activities (trade secrets, recycling, whistle-blowing): I use these three examples to help us think about the importance of being aware of legal contexts when policy makers attempt to decide how to provide incentives for certain behaviors without harming individuals' intrinsic motivations.
[108] But this is not the case with regard to blood donation.
[109] See Benabou & Tirole, *supra* note 75.
[110] This argument is obviously oversimplified, and fine-tuning is highly needed here.

people as possible recycle as much as possible. In this situation, we have no preference for either high or low intrinsically motivated individuals; therefore, the balancing consideration for the policy maker is whether or not to use extrinsic motivation and, if yes, determining which types of incentives to use.

Third, how important is it to think that others are being motivated by intrinsic motives? People are biased in their perceptions of what others are doing and for which reasons. It is clear, however, that the effect of knowing why other people do what they do is different depending on the context, the nature of the relationship, the level of reciprocity, the importance of others' motivation to one's evaluation of its authenticity, and more. Presumably, the closer the behavior is to areas where one would expect identity-related factors to be dominant, the greater the damage is to the other from viewing one's motivation as being extrinsically motivated. In commercial contexts, we are less likely to find that extrinsic motivation harms perceptions of authenticity in the behavior of others. A relatively straightforward aspect we may want to consider is the visibility of the behavior and the ability to measure both its quantity and quality (recycling in houses vs. loyalty to an employer in keeping proprietary information secret). It is safe to assume that with more visible and measureable behavior, the policy maker should care less about harming intrinsic motivation whose main advantage is its limited dependence on external measurement. Thinking about these context dimensions could lead the policy maker to focus efforts on protecting intrinsic motivation in the most suitable contexts.

In the next section of the conclusion chapter, I examine the ability of law to change people's implicit tendency to behave unethically, relating this discussion to the research conducted by scholars such as Devine and Inzlicht on the ability to change people's intrinsic tendency to rely on stereotypes. Furthermore, because the focus of this book is on legal enforcement, I examine whether existing mechanisms through which the law could change the social meaning of certain behaviors could end up also affecting the unethical behavior of people that is based on implicit processes.

The concluding section of this chapter summarizes the many important questions we have discussed in the book and suggests that they remain open to further research. Because some of the most important interactions between psychology and law have not yet been studied, the book cannot be expected to resolve all these issues or even address them. In this section, I focus on emerging research directions. First, I present the set of jurisprudential questions that should be addressed more extensively, such as free will, autonomy, variations among people, equality, and the role of law relative to morality. As long as these questions are being addressed mainly from a legal enforcement perspective, without extensive involvement by scholars of law and philosophy, the ability to change the field remains limited. Second, I present a series of research questions on enforcement mechanisms. For example, given what we know about good people, should we change the desired standard of behavior? How much information should the state collect on people's attitudes and preferences? Should states impose standards of behavior whereby organizations are actively required to actively engage in regulating situations? Should people's and organizations' failure to adopt certain situational procedures to prevent unethicality put them in some legal responsibility by omission?

2

Behavioral Ethics and the Meaning of "Good People" for Legal Enforcement

In his book about dishonesty, Dan Ariely cites a locksmith's axiom that locks are not used against "bad people," who can easily break into locked homes, but rather against good people who would walk through an open door when they see one.[1] Many new behavioral ethics (BE) studies share the view expressed in this axiom: we are all potentially bad people, committing ethical failures in everyday situations.[2] With regard to violent crimes, the distinction between good and bad people still makes sense, but regarding ordinary unethical behavior such as evading taxation, acting uncooperatively in civil contexts (e.g., breaching contracts or not disclosing problematic information in commercial contexts), and violating corporate and administrative duties of loyalty, the involvement of implicit processes might be greater than previously assumed.

The focus on how people can be encouraged to behave well reflects the growing recognition that many ethical decisions are the result of implicit, not explicit, choices. Simply reviewing the titles of recent works shows how central this theme has become.[3] Admittedly, none of the authors listed would suggest that there are no

* This chapter is based in part on the chapter, "Behavioral Ethics Meets Behavioral Law and Economics," in *The Oxford Handbook of Behavioral Law and Economics*, eds. Eyal Zamir and Doron Teichman (Oxford: Oxford University Press, 2014), 213–240

[1] Ariely, D. (2012). *The (honest) truth about dishonesty: How we lie to everyone–especially ourselves.* New York: HarperCollins.

[2] Mazar, N., Amir, O., & Ariely, D. (2008). The dishonesty of honest people: A theory of self-concept maintenance. *Journal of Marketing Research, 45*(6), 633–644.

[3] For example, see Bersoff, D. M. (1999). Why good people sometimes do bad things: Motivated reasoning and unethical behavior. *Personality and Social Psychology Bulletin, 25*(1), 28–39. See also Kidder, R. M. (2009). *How good people make tough choices: Resolving the dilemmas of ethical living.* New York: HarperCollins; Pillutla, M. M. (2011). When good people do wrong: Morality, social identity, and ethical behavior. In D. De Cremer, R. van Dijk, & J. K. Murnighan (Eds.), *Social psychology and organizations* (pp. 353–370). New York: Routledge; Hollis, J. (2008). *Why good people do bad things: Understanding our darker selves.* New York: Gotham Books; and Banaji, M. R., & Greenwald, A. G. (2013). *Blindspot: Hidden biases of good people.* New York: Random House. This is also the view held by Bazerman et al. in their studies on why "good" accountants conduct bad audits. See Bazerman, M. H., Loewenstein, G., & Moore, D. A. (2002). Why good accountants do bad audits.

bad people. However, the contrast between saying that people are inherently good or bad and saying that a person's individual deeds are good or bad suggests a growing recognition that many ethically relevant behaviors that were previously assumed to be choice based, conscious, and deliberative are anything but. Along these lines, Bazerman and Banaji suggest that, especially with regard to ordinary unethical behavior, "incentives and similar concepts fail to correct a large portion of ethical behaviors because "such measures simply bypass the vast majority of unethical behaviors that occur without the conscious awareness of the actors who engage in them."[4] Thus, ordinary, good people who are unaware of their misconduct engage in many instances in unethical behavior in their daily lives. This book focuses on understanding the situational, legal, and psychological circumstances that allow "good" people to behave badly.

As argued in Chapter 1, it builds on the psychological literature of BE, which examines the gap between people's actual ethical behavior and how they perceive it. Even though the BE literature is growing rapidly, with hundreds of papers published every year for at least the past five years, it is still not as advanced and mature as the behavioral law and economics (BLE) literature. This chapter reviews and evaluates both literatures to determine the strengths and weaknesses of each. In the current chapter, we revisit some of the concepts developed in Chapter 1 and further develop our understanding of the advantages and perils of using BE in the legal literature.

Over the past 40 years, the influence of psychology on economics in general and on the law and economics movement in particular has increased dramatically. Significant efforts have been devoted to mapping flaws in human cognition and situational effects and examining how they cause individuals to deviate from making optimal decisions – for example, how context, framing, or specific situations can cause individuals to make decisions contrary to their best interests.[5] The literature reviewed in this chapter focuses on how these factors affect people's decisions to engage in unethical behavior.

The concept of two systems of reasoning first gained widespread recognition in Kahneman's book *Thinking, Fast and Slow* and is at the core of both BE and BLE research.[6] System 1 is an automatic, intuitive, mostly unconscious process of

---

Harvard Business Review, 80(11), 96–103. Note that the "good people" scholarship is usually different from the type of research conducted by Zimbardo on the Lucifer effect. See Zimbardo, P. (2007). *The Lucifer effect: Understanding how good people turn evil*. New York: Random House. These works generally try to explain how ordinary people end up doing evil or engaging in gross criminal behaviors.

[4] Bazerman, M. H., & Banaji, M. R. (2004). The social psychology of ordinary ethical failures. *Social Justice Research*, 17(2), 111–115.

[5] Jolls, C., Sunstein, C. R., & Thaler, R. (1998). A behavioral approach to law and economics. *Stanford Law Review*, 50, 1471–1550. See also Ulen, T. S., & Korobkin, R. B. (2000). Law and behavioral science: Removing the rationality assumption from law and economics. *California Law Review*, 88(4), 1051–1144; Langevoort, D. C. (1998). Behavioral theories of judgment and decision making in legal scholarship: A literature review. *Vanderbilt Law Review*, 51, 1499–1540; and Jolls, C. (2007). *Behavioral law and economics*. National Bureau of Economic Research Working Paper No. 12879, available at www.nber.org/papers/w12879.

[6] Kahneman, D. (2011). *Thinking, fast and slow*. New York: Macmillan. See further discussion of the two systems in chapter 1.

thought, in contrast to the controlled and deliberative process in System 2.[7] Both the BLE and BE literatures focus on automaticity, with BE placing special emphasis on the automaticity of self-interest. Yet, BE has suffered from structural limitations that have reduced its ability to affect broad legal and academic circles.

First, it has a relatively large number of founding leaders,[8] in contrast to BLE, which rests on the shoulders of only two researchers: Kahneman and Amos Tversky. As a result, BE suffers from the simultaneous development of multiple, competing paradigms that can muddle the underlying points on which the literature agrees. These disagreements also prevent BE from being able to present consistent policy recommendations. Another obstacle to its adoption by the legal community is its much greater reliance on identifying *mechanisms* of behavioral automaticity and awareness and their relationship to self-interest, areas that are difficult to explore; for example, how is it possible to prove that people are completely unaware of their selfish intentions? In contrast, the classic BLE literature focuses on areas where automatic decisions undermine people's self-interest, leading to bad outcomes for the decision makers themselves.[9] These suboptimal *outcomes* are easily measured. These factors have placed many of the findings of BE in an inferior methodological position to those of BLE.

The field of BE is also challenged by the prosocial account of human behavior, which is based on an entirely different view of self-interest. BE believes that a broad account of self-interest reveals our tendency toward selfish action, whereas the prosocial literature argues that it makes people more altruistic.

Yet, BE research and literature offer a more complex view of what it means for a choice to be in one's self-interest and how this affects behavior than do the BLE and prosocial accounts.[10] Although BLE research on biases attributed to non-deliberative choices has made significant contributions to legal scholarship,[11] it has been primarily about the effects of framing, perception of risk, and probabilities, with almost no focus on compliance motivation. Thus, it attributes ethical bias either to the involvement of automatic reasoning

---

[7]   Stanovich, K. E., & West, R. F. (2000). Individual differences in reasoning: Implications for the rationality debate? *Behavioral and Brain Sciences* 23(5), 645–665. See also Evans, J. St. B.T. (2003). In two minds: Dual-process accounts of reasoning. *Trends in Cognitive Sciences* 7(10), 454–459.

[8]   There are definitely researchers who have contributed more than 10 papers to this literature; they include Max Bazerman, Dan Ariely, Francesca Gino, Shaul Sahlvi, Yoella Baribay Meir, and Dolly Cho Shahar Eyal.

[9]   Kish-Gephart, J. J., Harrison, D. A., & Treviño, L. K. (2010). Bad apples, bad cases, and bad evidence about sources of unethical decisions at work. *Journal of Applied Psychology* 95, 1–31. See also Bazerman, M. H., & Gino, F. (2012). Behavioral ethics: Toward a deeper understanding of moral judgment and dishonesty. *Annual Review of Law and Social Science* 8, 85–104.

[10] Zamir, E., & Sulitzeanu-Kenan, R. (forthcoming). *Explaining self-interested behavior of public-spirited policymakers. Public Administration Review.*

[11] See Ulen & Korobkin, *supra* note 5. See also Zamir, E., & Teichman, D. (Eds.). (2014). *The Oxford handbook of behavioral economics and the law.* Oxford: Oxford University Press.

through unconscious self-deception (in BE terminology, non-deliberative[12]) or to *post hoc* rationalization that justifies unethical behavior (in BE terminology, deliberative).[13]

In contrast, BE takes the broad view that many people's actions are based on self-interest in that they serve a need to maintain a positive and coherent view of the self. It accounts for the effect that self-interest has on our cognitive processes (e.g., memory, sight, and information processing) as opposed to simply looking at how self-interest affects motivation[14]. Finally, BE is more concerned with the implicit effects of self-interest, without people's admitting to themselves that such influence exists, than with how it shapes explicit choices.

Given the importance that law gives to intentionality (e.g., determining culpability in criminal law), one would expect BE to be much more central to legal scholarship than it currently is. However, its structural limitations and the fact that it developed primarily within the field of management and not legal scholarship, coupled with the nascent stage of the BE literature, have kept it from being part of mainstream legal scholarship. In addition, legal scholarship has been more open to accept behavioral economics because of the extensive interaction between law and economics.

BE analyzes how and why people are often unaware of their level of ethicality; it also uncovers the true motivations underlying their decisions. I will examine cognitive biases and situational effects that make it difficult for people to recognize beforehand what behavior is either immoral or illegal in a way that enables them to choose not to engage in it.[15] The analysis covers both the scope of the effects of these System 1 biases and their applicability to the legal context. These biases do not block people's recognition of the wrongdoing but just limit their ability to understand the true meaning of their actions to the extent that good people either engage in unethical behavior or

[12] For an example of a non-deliberative process that allows for unethical behavior of good people, see Chugh, D., Bazerman, M. H., & Banaji, M. R. (2005). Bounded ethicality as a psychological barrier to recognizing conflicts of interest. In D. A. Moore, D. M. Cain, G. Loewenstein, & M. H. Bazerman (Eds.), *Conflicts of interest: Challenges and solutions in business, law, medicine, and public policy* (pp. 74–95). Cambridge: Cambridge University Press.
[13] For an example of a deliberative process that allows for unethical behavior of good people, see Bandura, A. (1999). Moral disengagement in the perpetration of inhumanities. *Personality and Social Psychology Review* 3(3), 193–209.
[14] See Chapter 1 for further discussion of the literature of prosocial behavior as represented in the following works: Stout, L. (2010). *Cultivating conscience: How good laws make good people.* Princeton: Princeton University Press. See also Benkler, Y. (2011). *The penguin and the leviathan: How cooperation triumphs over self-interest.* New York: Crown Business.
[15] For a review of the dichotomy between ex ante strategies people will use to feel good about engaging in an immoral act such as ambiguity or considering their act as for other people vs. ex post strategies such as engaging in various cleansing rituals or in engaging in compensatory ethics, see Shalvi S., Gino, F., Barkan, R., & Ayal, S. (2015). Self-serving justification: Doing wrong and feeling moral. *Current Directions in Psychological Science,* 24(2), 125–130.

some form of unethicality.[16] In bounded awareness, there is a gap between full awareness and the intention to do a bad act.[17] This bounded effect, even if its size is hard to determine *ex ante*, is substantial enough to require different enforcement mechanisms.

For example, there has been much discussion of how US Supreme Court Justice Antonin Scalia mocked the possibility that his friendship with Dick Cheney would undermine his objectivity. Scalia was aware of the effects of close relationships on objectivity but denied that a hunting trip would affect his ability to be an objective judge.[18] Such denials are common elements of many BE contexts. When large numbers of people engage in such denials, this partial reduction in self-awareness of unethicality is likely to create a major shift in behavior of a substantial portion of the population, which policy makers need to take into account when designing enforcement mechanisms.

I will briefly discuss the design of such legal enforcement mechanisms so that they more effectively address cognitive biases and situational effects, which will be developed later in the book. In particular, I will examine the shift in assigning culpability from individuals to situations and the need to determine what serves as an incentive in a world in which unethicality is built on both implicit and explicit choices, many of which are *reactions* to a given situation or norm rather than a preference based on deliberative and calculative *choice*. This discussion lays the foundation for the following chapters that focus on legal enforcement approaches that governments should take to deal with such reaction-based behavior. It also examines to what extent debasing and nudging, which are common normative reactions to the findings of BLE, are relevant to bounded ethicality.[19] Later chapters of the book conclude with some suggestions concerning disambiguation and forced reflection, which may be able to curb the types of noncompliance uncovered by the bounded ethicality literature.

---

[16]   An example is the paradigm of half-lies in the dice-under-the-cup experiments performed by Shalvi et al., *supra* note 15.

[17]   As developed by Bazerman, for example, in his book on blind spots. See Bazerman, M. H., & Tenbrunsel, A. E. (2012). *Blind spots: Why we fail to do what's right and what to do about it.* Princeton: Princeton University Press.

[18]   See www.nytimes.com/2004/03/18/politics/scalia-angrily-defends-his-duck-hunt-with-cheney.html.

[19]   This gap will later enable us to argue that nudges are more likely to be effective in BE contexts than in BLE contexts, where people have a greater interest in overcoming their biases so they can do what's good for themselves; for example, saving more for retirement or eating healthier. When it comes to BE, people might be less likely to increase their awareness so they could be more ethical. In many BE contexts, their ignorance of their true intentions is good for them, either by protecting their self-image as ethical people or enabling them to engage in behavior that promotes their self-interest. This gap leads me to argue that the BE literature not only undermines the need for deterrence but also enhances that need while changing the function of deterrence. Deterrence is not supposed to change the price of the unethical behavior, but to force people to reflect on their unethically with more limited self-serving biases.

2.1 REVIEW OF SOME OF THE MAIN BEHAVIORAL ETHICS PARADIGMS

Many competing paradigms attempt to explain why good people engage in unethical behavior. Some focus on reframing reality to enable people to feel good about themselves and to protect their self-value, while still promoting their self-interest; others focus on ethical blind spots that reduce awareness of the unethical behavior.[20]

2.1.1 *The Approach of Bazerman and Colleagues*

A recent paper by Sezer, Gino, and Bazerman provides a good review of the major themes of behavioral ethics and bounded ethicality.[21] They suggest that three types of behavioral mechanisms are responsible for unintended unethical behavior: implicit biases, temporal distance from ethical dilemmas, and decision biases that cause people to incorrectly evaluate the unethical behavior of others. They cite research by Chugh, Bazerman, and Banaji[22] on the "illusion of objectivity," which explains why people view themselves as being more objective than others and so are unable to see themselves as corrupt. This notion relates to a broader paradigm, mostly associated with the work of Bazerman, of ethical blind spots, which prevent people from recognizing their own unethicality. Another cognitive block is the gap between "the want self" (i.e., self-interest) and "the should self" (moral imperatives). As the gains of unethical behavior become more apparent in a situation, the influence of the want self becomes more dominant. Bazerman and colleagues also discuss a post-decision process of ethical cleansing through which people tend to disengage from the ethical meaning of their behavior. Among the processes that they describe is moral forgetting,[23] a mechanism used to diminish the social threat posed by immoral behavior.[24]

Other important work in conceptualizing the larger framework of BE is the recent research done by Chugh and Kern.[25] They posit that one's *self-view* is more forceful and automatic than the role played by monetary self-interest in classic perspectives of ethical decision making. They focus on how automatic processes are all largely related to self-driven bounded ethicality processes.[26]

---

[20] See Bazerman & Tenbrunsel, *supra* note 17. See also Banaji & Greenwald, *supra* note 3; Balcetis, E., & Dunning, D. (2006). See what you want to see: Motivational influences on visual perception. *Journal of Personality and Social Psychology*, 91(4), 612.

[21] Sezer, O., Gino, F:, & Bazerman, M. H. (2015). Ethical blind spots: Explaining unintentional unethical behavior. *Current Opinion in Psychology*, 6, 77–81.

[22] See Chugh et al., *supra* note 12.

[23] Shu, L. L., Gino, F., & Bazerman, M. H. (2011). Dishonest deed, clear conscience: When cheating leads to moral disengagement and motivated forgetting. *Personality and Social Psychology Bulletin*, 37 (3), 330–349.

[24] This paradigm was recently revisited in another influential work by Kouchaki and Gino. See Kouchaki, M., & Gino, F. (2016). Memories of unethical actions become obfuscated over time. *Proceedings of the National Academy of Sciences of the United States of America*, 113(22), 6166–6171.

[25] Chugh, D., & Kern, M. C. (2016). A dynamic and cyclical model of bounded ethicality. *Research in Organizational Behavior*, 36, 85–100.

[26] See Chugh et al., *supra* note 12.

2.1.2 *Intuitive Rather than Bounded Ethicality*

Haidt's work on political psychology, which is important to all types of public discourse on the role of morality and legality, is somewhat different from the previously mentioned paradigm.[27] Most famous for his explanation of variations in the moral judgment of different political groups (e.g., Republicans vs. Democrats),[28] Haidt has developed paradigms that highlight the role of emotions in people's moral attitudes.[29] His model shows how intuitive morality is, how much morality depends on one's group affiliation, and how hard it might be for people to understand the actual reasoning used to explain their own behavior. Haidt argues that people use deliberative arguments to support their intuition, but these arguments do not in fact represent the true antecedent of the attitudes they hold. In a sense, Haidt paints a very pessimistic view of people, relative to most other behavioral ethics scholars, holding that if not for the monitoring of the environment, they would just follow their desires. Therefore, governments that attempt to regulate the behavior of people have to understand how to support the ability of people to act morally.

Furthermore, Haidt seems to hold a minority view: many of the scholars reviewed in this chapter claim that people engage in a more conscious process to justify their actions while being aware of the existence of an ethical problem in their behavior. For example, according to Bandura's moral disengagement theory,[30] people are able to find various justifications for their unethicality based on euphemisms, perceived norms, and ambiguity, but they do recognize the existence of some criteria of morality that can be evaluated objectively. In other words, Haidt's work seems to suggest in contrast to Bazerman and others that there is no explicit objective criteria of morality that people deviate from implicitly due to self-serving biases; rather, people's genuine sense of morality is their intuitive reasoning and most efforts should be put to understanding it rather than to debiasing it.

2.1.3 *The Complexity of Self-serving Biases*

Taking a different but related angle on the blind spot argument, Tenbrunsel and Smith-Crowe focus on the gap between how ethical we think we are and how ethical we actually are.[31] Their contribution to the literature is their complex approach to the role of self-serving mechanisms. Rather than focusing only on self-

---

[27]   Graham, J., Haidt, J., & Nosek, B. A. (2009). Liberals and conservatives rely on different sets of moral foundations. *Journal of Personality and Social Psychology*, 96(5), 1029.

[28]   Ibid.

[29]   Haidt, J. (2001). The emotional dog and its rational tail: A social intuitionist approach to moral judgment. *Psychological Review*, 108(4), 814.

[30]   See Bandura, *supra* note 13.

[31]   Tenbrunsel, A., & Smith-Crowe, K. (2008). Ethical decision making: Where we've been and where we're going. *Academy of Management Annals*, 2(1), 545–607.

serving biases, which are usually interpreted as aligning reality with people's self-interest, they differentiate between self-threat assessment, self-enhancement, and self-protection – all mechanisms that operate on different levels of automaticity and awareness but nonetheless affect the likelihood that an individual will engage in unethical behavior in a way that states initiated mechanisms would find hard to predict. An additional important behavioral paradigm that they identify is related to dynamic views of morality. According to this approach, people do not just react to their current situation; much of their behavior is related to experiences in previous situations.[32] Under such circumstances, a government's ability to regulate situations is even more diminished, given that it needs to know not only about who the individuals are or what the situation is but also what situations they were in before.

2.2 HOW GOOD ARE GOOD PEOPLE? A COMPLEX ANSWER TO A COMPLEX QUESTION

How aware individuals are of their own morality varies depending on when that awareness is examined and how it is defined; some scholars challenge, even beyond awareness limitations, whether an objective criterion of morality even exists. For example, Haidt's social intuitionist model argues that judgments on morality are formed spontaneously, but later, individuals build reflective support for those intuitive judgments. Thus, according to Haidt, there are no clear objective moral criteria. In contrast, Bazerman and his coauthors suggest that people are blind to their own immorality, but that there are indeed objective criteria of immorality.

Chugh and Kern[33] argue that four dimensions of automatic behavior are involved in ethical decision making: low awareness, low intentionality, high efficiency, and low controllability. They claim that few decision-making processes related to unethicality are purely automatic according to all dimensions. However, it may not even be possible to characterize ex ante or even ex post people's level of automaticity according to all four dimensions. According to Chugh and Kern,[34] moral awareness is a combination of ethical predispositions (e.g., moral identity)[35] or moral attentiveness[36] and situational factors. Tenbrunsel and Smith-Crowe suggest a taxonomy of behaviors based on the presence or absence of moral awareness.[37] In the camp of theories related to unaware processes are those that examine

[32] Effron, D. A., & Monin, B. (2010). Letting people off the hook: When do good deeds excuse transgressions? *Personality and Social Psychology Bulletin, 36*(12), 1618–1634.
[33] See Chugh & Kern, *supra* note 25.   [34] Ibid.
[35] Aquino, K., & Reed, A., II. (2002). The self-importance of moral identity. *Journal of Personality and Social Psychology 83*, 1423–1440.
[36] Reynolds, S. J. (2008). Moral attentiveness: Who pays attention to the moral aspects of life? *Journal of Applied Psychology, 93*(5), 1027.
[37] See Tenbrunsel & Smith-Crowe, *supra* note 31.

situational features, such as time pressure, and ego depletion that increase the likelihood that people will behave unethically.[38]

From a legal standpoint, the question of awareness is even more important than that of automaticity.[39] In other words, when focusing on awareness, we can ask, even if self-interest is automatic, are we at least aware that we are behaving in a self-interested manner? The material cited earlier in the chapter suggests that in all likelihood we are not aware. Indeed, most of the BE literature, in particular that on self-deception, shows that we are unaware of the effects that System 1 reasoning has on our level of awareness of these biases. However, this discussion is far from resolved, and strong dissenting voices still support the existence of conscious self-deception processes.

Whether or not we are aware of these automatic processes and of the behaviors they cause has many legal implications. For example, assuming that people are unaware might alter our approach toward criminal responsibility and lead legal policy makers to rethink what interventions may be necessary in other domains of law, such as administrative, corporate, and intellectual property law.

The notion that people act either intentionally or unintentionally is thus outdated. Yet because evidence on the level of awareness of wrongdoing is still incomplete, it might be most useful for governments to develop legal policy based on a limited awareness view. Limited awareness claims that people do not deliberatively choose to do wrong or at least they do wrong without fully grasping the meaning of their behavior. Support for this view comes from studies of various situational effects that increase wrongdoing, such as a lack of time to think, moral forgetting of rules that contradict one's self-interest, and the inability to recognize information that contradicts one's self-interest. The combination of these effects seems to be substantial enough such that we should at least recognize that people should not be seen as fully deliberative when making ethical decisions, even according to the more "aware camp" in behavioral ethics.

2.2.1 Self-awareness and Self-deception

BE largely relies on the assumption that self-interested behavior is automatic. This concept is still very controversial, both theoretically and empirically. Most of the experimental evidence is inconclusive about how automaticity operates. Even if we accept the automaticity of self-interest, we do not necessarily know

---

[38] Shalvi, S., Eldar, O., & Bereby-Meyer, Y. (2012). Honesty requires time (and lack of justifications). *Psychological Science*, 23, 1264–1270. See also Gino, F. & Margolis, J. (2011). Bringing ethics into focus: How regulatory focus and risk preferences influence (un)ethical behavior. *Organizational Behavior and Human Decision Processes*, 115(2), 145–156.

[39] There has been a recent attempt to examine people's awareness of their ethical misconducts using dilatation of the pupils as a proxy for awareness. Hochman, G., Glöckner, A., Fiedler, S., & Ayal, S. (2016). "I can see it in your eyes": Biased processing and increased arousal in dishonest responses. *Journal of Behavioral Decision Making*, 29(2–3), 322–335.

the extent to which people are aware of this predisposition and whether it is malleable or even controllable. One must carefully distinguish automaticity from the related, overlapping concepts of awareness, controllability, intentionality, and attention.

An understanding of the scope of self-deception and self-awareness is crucial to implementing the appropriate legal strategies to deal with criminality and rule breaking. A group of scholars addressed the issue from various perspectives at the Evolution and Psychology of Self-deception Symposium in 2011. Several scholars supported the notion that people can engage in self-deception without awareness. Bandura suggested that self-deception is possible whenever we strongly suspect the truth but deceive ourselves by avoiding actions that would confirm the truth of our suspicions.[40] Evans and Frankish went beyond a System 1 and System 2 analysis, arguing that individuals develop attitudes that support their ability to accept their own views as true.[41] Similarly, Kenrick and White proposed a modular self beyond System 1 and System 2, whose independent modules are capable of creating conscious self-deception.[42] Buss maintained that there is not enough empirical data to prove whether unaware self-deception is possible.[43] Huang and Bargh suggested that our ability to pursue multiple goals at once allows for conscious self-deception.[44] Johansson et al. added evidence from choice-blindness experiments supporting the possibility of conscious self-deception.[45] Lu and Chang called attention to memory systems that allow the brain to hide and retrieve information later, making conscious self-deception possible.[46] McKay et al. elaborated on the social benefits of conscious self-deception.[47] Mercier suggested that conscious self-deception is a form of confirmation bias.[48] Pretti and Miotto examined how self-deception improves people's tendency to cheat and their ability to detect cheating.[49] Meanwhile, a minority of authors argued against the concept of unaware self-deception. In separate studies,

---

[40] Bandura, A. (2011). Self-deception: A paradox revisited. *Behavioral & Brain Sciences*, 34, 16–17.

[41] Evans, J. S. B., & Frankish, K. E. (2009). *In two minds: Dual processes and beyond*. Oxford: Oxford University Press.

[42] Kenrick, D. T., & White, A. E. (2011). A single self-deceived or several subselves divided? *Behavioral and Brain Sciences*, 34(1), 29–30.

[43] Buss, D. M. (2011). The evolution and psychology of self-deception. *Behavioral and Brain Sciences*, 34 (1), 1–16.

[44] Huang, J. Y., & Bargh, J. A. (2011) The selfish goal: Self-deception occurs naturally from autonomous goal operation. *Behavioral and Brain Sciences*, 34(1), 27–28.

[45] Johansson, L., Hall, L., & Chater, N. (2011). Preference change through choice. In R. Dolan & T. Sharot (Eds.), *Neuroscience of preference and choice: : Cognitive and neural mechanisms*, pp. 121–141. New York: Academic Press.

[46] Lu, H. J., & Chang, L. (2011). Self-deceive to countermine detection. *Behavioral and Brain Sciences*, 34, 3333.

[47] McKay, R, Mijovic-Prelec, D, & Prelec, D. (2011). Protesting too much: Self-deception and self-signaling. *Behavioral and Brain Sciences*, 34(1), 34–35.

[48] Mercier, H. (2011). Self-deception: Adaptation or by-product? *Behavioral and Brain Sciences*, 34(1), 35.

[49] Preti, A., & Miotto, P. (2011). Self-deception, social desirability, and psychopathology. *Behavioral and Brain Sciences*, 34(1), 37.

Smith,[50] Pinker,[51] and Dunning[52] explained why current research cannot demonstrate that self-deception is conscious rather than unconscious.

2.2.2 *Current Research on Automaticity*

The researcher most identified with the automaticity of behavior is John Bargh.[53] In a series of experiments spanning nearly a decade, Bargh explored the meaning and significance of automatic processes, finding that the majority of daily behaviors are the product of those automatic and unconscious processes.

Automaticity is typically examined using the technique of "priming." Priming involves displaying some cue (e.g., an image) to participants in such a way that they are not consciously aware that they have been exposed to it. In a well-known study, priming stereotypes of elderly people and of African Americans caused people to adopt slower moves and aggressive behavior, respectively.[54] The effects of priming have also been observed in legally relevant behaviors such as competitiveness and cooperation.[55]

Money has also been shown to be an effective primer, both methodologically and theoretically. In a series of nine experiments, Vohs et al. show that exposing people to subtle reminders of money completely changed their level of cooperation and social interaction.[56] Aquino et al. compare the effects of priming with such stimuli as the Ten Commandments, morality, and financial incentives on such behaviors as contributions to civic causes and dishonesty.[57]

---

[50] Smith, D. L. (2004). *Why we lie*. New York: St. Martin's Griffin.

[51] Pinker, S. (2011). Representations and decision rules in the theory of self-deception. *Behavioral and Brain Sciences*, 34(1), 35–37.

[52] Dunning, D. (2011). The Dunning-Kruger Effect: On being ignorant of one's own ignorance. *Advances in Experimental Social Psychology*, 44, 247.

[53] Bargh, J. A., Chaiken, S., Govender, R., & Pratto, F. (1992). The generality of the automatic attitude activation effect. *Journal of Personality and Social Psychology*, 62(6), 893–912. See also Bargh, J. A., Chen, M., & Burrows, L. (1996). Automaticity of social behavior: Direct effects of trait construct and stereotype activation on action. *Journal of Personality and Social Psychology* 71(2), 230–244; Bargh, J. A., & Chartrand, T. L. (1999). The unbearable automaticity of being. *American Psychologist* 54(7), 462–479.

[54] See Bargh et al., *supra* note 53.

[55] Kawakami, K., Dovidio, J. F., & Dijksterhuis, A. (2003). Effect of social category priming on personal attitudes. *Psychological Science*, 14(4), 315–319. See also Kay, A. C., Wheeler, S. C., Bargh, J. A., & Ross, L. (2004). Material priming: The influence of mundane physical objects on situational construal and competitive behavioral choice. *Organizational Behavior and Human Decision Processes*, 95(1), 83–96.

[56] Vohs, K. D., Mead, N. L., & Goode, M. R. (2006). The psychological consequences of money. *Science* 314(5802), 1154–1156. See also Vohs, K. D., Mead, N. L., & Goode, M. R. (2008). Merely activating the concept of money changes personal and interpersonal behavior. *Current Directions in Psychological Science*, 17(3), 208–212. For a related study, see Kay et al., Material priming.

[57] Aquino, K., Freeman, D., & Reed, A., III. (2009). Testing a social-cognitive model of moral behavior: The interactive influence of situations and moral identity centrality. *Journal of Personality and Social Psychology*, 97, 1–123. See also Mazar et al., *supra* note 2, who provided an earlier demonstration of the effect of the Ten Commandments.

Their findings reveal an interaction between participants' level of moral identity and the situational prime.[58] People with high moral identity were more likely to change their behavior following both moral and financial primes than were those with low moral identity. Kouchaki et al. demonstrate that priming with money increases the inclination to engage in unethical behavior,[59] and Welsh and Ordonez show how priming can activate ethical standards outside of awareness.[60]

Another relevant example of automatic behavior is "embodiment." In contrast to priming, which attempts to circumvent System 2 by creating a stimulus that it cannot fully process, embodiment involves a physical stimulus that interacts with the individual's body.[61] Kouchaki et al. show, for example, that carrying heavy weights caused people to feel guiltier about a given behavior than did carrying lighter weights.[62] Washing one's hands has been shown to lessen feelings of guilt when recalling unethical behavior[63] and to reduce the severity of moral judgments against those who behaved unethically.[64] When people close one eye, they tend to act either more or less morally.[65] Lower levels of lighting caused people to cheat more, and sitting farther away from the steering wheel caused people to violate more traffic laws. Lower glucose levels increased unethicality, and hormonal levels affected misconduct.[66] Holding Teddy bears and listening to childhood melodies decreased unethicality. Naturally, such effects challenge the assumption that people are responsible for their behavior.

Although these techniques show the automaticity of some legally relevant behaviors, the more important question is how automatic processes affect our reasoning capabilities. The next section examines this question.

---

[58]   Moral identity is a self-regulation mechanism that was shown to predict moral behavior; for a review of the various approaches to moral identity and to its relationships to other self-related mechanisms, see Aquino & Reed, *supra* note 35.

[59]   Kouchaki, M., Smith-Crowe, K., Brief, A. P., & Sousa, C. (2013). Seeing green: Mere exposure to money triggers a business decision frame and unethical outcomes. *Organizational Behavior and Human Decision Processes*, 121(1), 53–61.

[60]   Welsh, D. T., & Ordóñez, L. D. (2014). Conscience without cognition: The effects of subconscious priming on ethical behavior. *Academy of Management Journal*, 57(3), 723–742.

[61]   For example, see Niedenthal, P. M., Barsalou, L. W., Winkielman, P., Krauth-Gruber, S., & Ric, F. (2005). Embodiment in attitudes, social perception, and emotion. *Personality and Social Psychology Review*, 9(3), 184–211.

[62]   Kouchaki, M., Gino, F., & Jami, A. (2014). The burden of guilt: Heavy backpacks, light snacks, and enhanced morality. *Journal of Experimental Psychology: General*, 143(1), 414.

[63]   Zhong, C. B., & Liljenquist, K. (2006). Washing away your sins: Threatened morality and physical cleansing. *Science*, 313(5792), 1451–1452.

[64]   Schnall, S., Benton, J., & Harvey, S. (2008). With a clean conscience cleanliness reduces the severity of moral judgments. *Psychological Science*, 19(12), 1219–1222.

[65]   Caruso, E. M., & Gino, F. (2011). Blind ethics: Closing one's eyes polarizes moral judgment and discourages dishonest behavior. *Cognition*, 118(2), 280–285.

[66]   Lee J. J., Gino, F., Jin, E. S., Rice, L. K., & Josephs, R. A. (2015). Hormones and ethics: Understanding the biological basis of unethical conduct. *Journal of Experimental Psychology: General*, 144(5), 891–897.

2.3 AUTOMATICITY AND ETHICALITY

2.3.1 *The Automaticity of Morality in Making Moral Judgments*

A contentious debate still rages over whether System 1 or System 2 is responsible for generating moral judgments. Haidt, whose approach to ethicality was discussed earlier, demonstrated experimentally that System 1 plays a role in moral reasoning, which is a product of System 2.[67] He concluded that moral judgments are not driven solely by moral reasoning, because the automaticity with which we evaluate targets undercuts deliberative System 2 processes. He also cited behavioral evidence of the tendency to create rationales after the fact to explain events and of the importance of moral emotions in moral judgment to suggest that System 1 is responsible for generating moral judgments.[68]

Haidt's views have been subject to a variety of criticisms. For example, Cushman et al. argue that the intuitiveness of morality cannot be assumed across the board and that the accessibility of different moral principles in people's automatic and conscious mechanisms varies.[69] Moral identity may be more central to the behavior of some people than of others. Along those lines, the dynamic view of the moral self makes it more difficult to predict the effect of social norms.[70] For example, working with others who seem to be acting morally might evoke resentment, whereas observing them from afar might elicit admiration.

2.3.2 *Is System 1 or System 2 Responsible for Unethical Behavior?*

In contrast to the lack of consensus on the automaticity of moral judgment, the majority view grants System 1 the leading role in unethical behavior. Moore and Lowenstein were among the first to show that self-interest and concern for others affect behavior through different cognitive systems and that self-interest is automatic, viscerally compelling, and often unconscious: "In many instances of conflict of interest, self-interest tends to operate via automatic processes whereas ethical and professional responsibilities operate via controlled processes."[71] By comparing private beliefs and public behavior, Moore et al. demonstrate that people truly believe their own biased judgments, not recognizing that their

---

[67]   See Haidt, *supra* note 29, at 814. See also Haidt, J., & Joseph, C. (2004). Intuitive ethics: How innnately prepared intuitions generate culturally variable virtues. *Daedalus* 133(4): 55–66.

[68]   Mikulincer, M. E., & Shaver, P. R. (2010). *Prosocial motives, emotions, and behavior: The better angels of our nature*. Washington, DC: American Psychological Association.

[69]   Cushman, F., Young, L., & Hauser, M. (2006). The role of conscious reasoning and intuition in moral judgment: Testing three principles of harm. *Psychological Science*, 17(12), 1082–1089.

[70]   Monin, B., & Jordan, A. H. (2009). The dynamic moral self: A social psychological perspective. In D. Narvaez & D. Lapsley (Eds.), *Personality, identity, and character: Explorations in moral psychology* (pp. 341–354). New York: Cambridge University Press.

[71]   Moore, D. A., & Loewenstein, G. (2004). Self-interest, automaticity, and the psychology of conflict of interest. *Social Justice Research*, 17(2)189–202, p. 195.

behavior is problematic.[72] Gino et al. advance a similar view, showing that the level of control needed to behave ethically is much higher than that required to act unethically.[73]

Because of the legal importance of self-interest, it is necessary to understand the interplay between Systems 1 and 2 in ethical decisions. Recent work by Rand et al. suggests that people in a cooperative context are more likely to be cooperative, and those in a competitive context are more likely to be competitive, when they use System 1 reasoning.[74] Providing monetary incentives and treating people as possibly dishonest might increase their likelihood of behaving badly. Thus, the dual-reasoning paradigm supports a new version of the crowding-out argument.

Epley and Caruso conclude that automatic processing leads to egocentric ethical interpretations.[75] Similarly, Van den Bos et al. find support for the notion that when appraising a situation, people prefer outcomes that benefit themselves and only later correct their views to take into account fairness toward others.[76] Using an implicit association test, Marquardt and Hoeger show that decisions are made based on implicit rather than explicit attitudes (although they also found that implicit attitudes are correlated with choices that subjects believed to be moral).[77] Berby-Mayer, and Shalvi review a series of studies that claimed that people's intuitive reasoning makes them more likely to cheat and be less cooperative.[78] For example, in one study they found that when people write in a second language (which is less intuitive and more reflective), they are less likely to cheat compared to when they write in their native language.

Time seems to play an important role in unethical behavior. When the System 1 process is operative, people even of a basically moral character engage in unethical behaviors that, given more time and reflection, they would not do. As a further proof of this notion, Shalvi et al. show time pressure effects on honesty, suggesting that people's automatic, immediate reactions tend to be more dishonest than their later

[72] Moore, D. A., Tanlu, L., & Bazerman, M. H. (2010). Conflict of interest and the intrusion of bias. *Judgment and Decision Making*, 5(1), 37–53. The measurement of "private" evaluations was done by giving participants incentives to be accurate in their predictions.

[73] Gino, F., Schweitzer, M., Mead, N., & Ariely, D. (2011). Unable to resist temptation: How self-control depletion promotes unethical behavior. *Organizational Behavior and Human Decision Processes*, 115 (2), 191–203.

[74] Rand, D. G., Greene, J. D., & Nowak, M. A. (2012). Spontaneous giving and calculated greed. *Nature* 489(7416), 427–430. See also Rand, D. G. (2017). Reflections on the *Time-pressure Cooperation Registered Replication Report*. *Perspectives on Psychological Science*, 12(3), 543–547.

[75] Epley, N., & Caruso, E. M. (2004). Egocentric ethics. *Social Justice Research* 17(2), 171–187.

[76] Van den Bos, K. S., Peters, L., Bobocel, D. R., & Ybema, J. F. (2006). On preferences and doing the right thing: Satisfaction with advantageous inequity when cognitive processing is limited. *Journal of Experimental Social Psychology* 42(3), 273–829.

[77] Marquardt, N., & Hoeger, R. (2009). The effect of implicit moral attitudes on managerial decision-making: An implicit social cognition approach. *Journal of Business Ethics*, 85(2), 157–171.

[78] Bereby-Meyer, Y., & Shalvi, S. (2015). Deliberate honesty. *Current Opinion in Psychology*, 6, 195–198. See also Kobis, N., Verschuere, B., Rand, D., Bereby-Meyer, Y., & Shalvi, S. (2017). Honesty requires time: A meta-analysis. Working paper [on file with author].

actions.[79] This is part of a larger line of research that suggests that when people are pressured to make quick decisions, they may be more likely to engage in unethical behavior,[80] though there is some evidence that the strength of this tendency could vary.[81]

Muravan and colleagues argue that self-control is the main mechanism in determining an individual's non-deliberative unethical behavior.[82] They show that people without self-control are less able to resist tempting situations and those that provide justifications to lie; as a result, they cheat more than people with self-control.

Along those lines, "cognitive depletion" is another factor that facilitates unethical behavior. Many studies argue that when, in experimental settings, people direct their cognitive energy to solving complicated assignments, they lack the cognitive resources such as self control that are needed to recognize their own wrongdoing and to properly analyze what is the right thing to do.[83] Even physical depletion has been shown to lead to more unethical behaviors.[84] This tiredness could be a product of the time of day[85] or of the week.[86]

The minority opinions on this impact of automaticity on behavior hold that people's automatic responses are, at least some of the time, more cooperative than their deliberative responses.[87] Greene shows that the decision to engage in dishonest behavior involves more control-related parts of the brain than does deciding to act honestly.[88] In a recent meta-analysis, Rand argues that there is more research to support the argument that System 1 processing makes people more cooperative in cooperative settings than that dishonesty is related to competitive settings.[89] Kahan supports this view, showing that people who score high on the cognitive reflection

[79] See Shalvi et al., *supra* note 78.
[80] Gunia, B. C., Wang L., Huang, L., Wang J., & Murnighan, J. K. (2012). Contemplation and conversation: Subtle influences on moral decision making. *Journal of Academic Management*, 55, 13–33. But see Foerster, A., Pfister, R., Schmidts, C., Dignath, D., Kunde, W. (2013). Honesty saves time (and justifications). *Frontiers of Psychology*, 4, 473 http://dx.doi.org/10.3389/fpsyg.2013.00473.
[81] Greene, J. D. & Paxton, J. M. (2009). Patterns of neural activity associated with honest and dishonest moral decisions. *Proceeding of the National Academy of Sciences of the USA*, 106, 12506–12511.
[82] Muraven, M., Pogarsky, G., & Shmueli, D. (2006). Self-control depletion and the general theory of crime. *Journal of Quantitative Criminology*, 22, 263–277.
[83] Mead, N. L., Baumeister, R. F., Gino, F., Schweitzer, M. E., Ariely, D. (2009). Too tired to tell the truth: Self-control resource depletion and dishonesty. *Journal of Experimental Social Psychology*, 45, 594–597. See also Gino et al., *supra* note 73.
[84] Barnes C. M., Schaubroeck, J., Huth, M., & Ghumman, S. (2011). Lack of sleep and unethical conduct. *Organizational Behavior and Human Decision Processes*, 115, 169–180.
[85] Kouchaki, M., & Smith, I. H. (2014). The morning morality effect: The influence of time of day on (un)ethical behavior. *Psychological Science*, 25, 95–102.
[86] Ruffle, B. J., & Tobol, Y. (2014). Honest on Mondays: Honesty and the temporal separation between decisions and payoffs. *European Economic Review*, 65, 126–135.
[87] See Rand et al., *supra* note 74.
[88] Greene, J. D. (2009). The cognitive neuroscience of moral judgment. *Cognitive Neurosciences*, 4, 1–48.
[89] Rand, D. G. (2016). Cooperation, fast and slow meta-analytic evidence for a theory of social heuristics and self-interested deliberation. *Psychological Science*, 27(9), 1192–1206.

scale (i.e., are more likely to use System 2 reasoning) are more likely to engage in motivated reasoning, which is an enabling mechanism for unethical behavior.[90] A question still to be answered is whether it is possible to reconcile these approaches, at least partially, by suggesting that being cooperative and dishonest serves people's intuitive self-interest (especially in a social context, where appearing to be moral seems to be the rational move from an evolutionary perspective). Although these studies do not suggest that self-interest is deliberative, they do suggest that automatic reasoning is superior ethically to deliberative reasoning in at least some noncompetitive situations.

2.3.3 Motivated Reasoning

Many BE paradigms are based either directly or indirectly on motivated reasoning.[91] Kunda argues that motives have a significant effect on complex reasoning skills, such as the ability to establish a causal connection between events.[92] He defines two distinct types of motivated reasoning: one is used when our motive is to arrive at an accurate conclusion, and we use the other when the objective is a desired conclusion.

Whereas Kunda suggests that motivated reasoning affects higher-level reasoning skills, Shu et al. claim that motivated reasoning also affects memory and perception, areas that are highly relevant to the law.[93] For example, within very short periods of time, people misremember both what they did and what they were told to do, when such misremembering allows them to believe that they had acted ethically. Participants who cheated in the experiment demonstrated higher moral disengagement, and those cheaters who had read an honor code before the experiment demonstrated significantly worse recall of the code than did those who did not have an opportunity to cheat. Because compliance with the law is dependent on remembering the relevant law, the notion that memory itself could be corrupted by self-interest becomes relevant to how we design laws.

Motivated reasoning also influences visual capabilities. Balcetis and Dunning[94] use physiological measurements, such as eye tracking, to show that preconscious processing of visual stimuli is affected by people's preferences, suggesting that

---

[90] Kahan, D. M. (2013). Ideology, motivated reasoning, and cognitive reflection. *Judgment and Decision Making*, 8, 407–424.

[91] Theories such as moral licensing or compensatory ethics, which focus on how people maintain their self-concept by making a change in their behavior, are an exception. But even these theories take into account some change in people's understanding of the action to maintain a positive view or receive some potential credit. See Zhong, C. B., Ku, G., Lount, R. B., & Murnighan, J. K. (2010). Compensatory ethics. *Journal of Business Ethics*, 92(3), 323–339.

[92] Kunda, Z. (1990). The case for motivated reasoning. *Psychological Bulletin*, 108(3), 480.

[93] See Shu et al., *supra* note 23.   [94] See Balcetis, *supra* note 20, at 612.

awareness is indeed highly limited when it comes to processing information that is inconsistent with one's self-interest.

2.4 ARE WE ALL POTENTIALLY BAD PEOPLE?

When we shift the focus to helping "good people" be good, the main question that arises is whether everyone can behave unethically, given the new research on the implicit effects of the situation.

2.4.1 *Behavioral Ethics and the Power of the Situation*

The BE literature suggests that situational factors are of greater importance than individual factors in causing unethical behavior; it thus builds on the growing recognition in the legal enforcement literature that the source of wrongdoing is not the "bad apples" themselves but rather the environment in which they operate. This claim flows naturally from people's limited ability to control their unethicality, which gives the situation a different and presumably stronger causative role. In fact, the nudge approach is based on recognizing the influence of non-deliberate reasoning, and its aim is to change the situation, not the individual. This situational change can be either subtle, as through nudges, or more overt, by clarifying ambiguity and reducing rationales that justify dishonesty.

BE scholars have studied the effect of situational changes on unethical behavior. For example, Tenbrunsel and Smith-Crowe conclude that the presence of an ethical infrastructure is much more important than individual factors in facilitating moral awareness.[95] Along those lines, Tenbrunsel and Messick[96] argue that formal systems, informal systems, and organizational climate are responsible for a great deal of unethical behavior, especially through the process of ethical fading that is triggered by euphemism.[97]

A different perspective is provided by Boles and Messick's research on the ultimatum game, which shows that the way people view their situation affects their behavior.[98] In their study, the order in which participants played the game determined how fairly they behaved: when they got the money first and then instructions on how to distribute it, they behaved more fairly than when they got the instructions first and the money second. The reason for these differential effects is that in most situations people cannot accurately estimate what cognitive or motivational

---

[95] See Tenbrunsel & Smith-Crowe, *supra* note 31.
[96] Tenbrunsel, A., & Messick, D. (2004). Ethical fading: The role of self-deception in unethical behavior. *Social Justice Research*, 17, 223–236.
[97] Compare with Bandura, *supra* note 13.
[98] Boles, T. L., & Messick, D. M. (1990). Accepting unfairness: Temporal influence on choice. In K. Borcherding, O. I. Larichev, & D. M. Messick (Eds.), *Contemporary issues in decision making* (pp. 375–389). Oxford: North-Holland.

processes are determining their behavior; instead, they perceive the situation in relation to "shallow rules, habitual rules and other process, that generate decision heuristics that is being used in many moral and ethical situations."[99]

Zimbardo details how extreme situational pressures and group dynamics can work in concert to make monsters out of decent men and women.[100] In his best-known study, the Stanford Prison Experiment, he replaces the long-held notion of the "bad apple" with that of the "bad barrel": the idea that the social setting and the system contaminate the individual, rather than the other way around.

In contrast to the majority of BE studies, some research suggests that much of the variance in unethical behaviors that are committed without forethought can be attributed to personal traits rather than simply to the power of the situation.[101] For example, Greene suggests that there are strong individual differences in people's basic morality that affect the likelihood that they will engage in automatic reasoning (note that automatic reasoning has been associated with dishonest responses).[102] Other studies show indirectly that there are strong individual differences associated with "moral hypocrisy"[103] and that people with low self-awareness are more likely to ignore their own bad behavior and to judge others more harshly. None of this research answers the underlying question of whether we are fully aware of, and therefore responsible for, our actions, but they call for rethinking the definition of being a good person. As discussed in more detail in Chapter 5, which focuses on individual differences, a central question for legal policy makers is whether people are indeed blameworthy for the types of misconduct that BE addresses.

2.5 TAXONOMY OF BOUNDED ETHICALITY MECHANISMS

This section examines the main processes that underlie BE that policy makers and academics should consider when evaluating the effectiveness of legal interventions. The first subsection reviews theoretical paradigms that account for the ways people act to protect their concept of themselves as good and coherent people.

---

[99] Messick, D. M. (1999). Alternative logics for decision making in social settings. *Journal of Economic Behavior & Organization*, 39(1), 11–28.

[100] See Zimbardo, *supra* note 3.

[101] Feldman, Y., & Smith, H. E. (2014). Behavioral equity. *Journal of Institutional and Theoretical Economics JITE*, 170(1), 137–159.

[102] Greene's study involved an experiment under fMRI in which participants were asked to predict the outcome of a coin flip. Participants were presorted based on a questionnaire into honest, dishonest, or ambiguous and were asked to either self-report accuracy or write down their guesses in advance. The results showed that members of the honest group generated no more brain activity when they lost money and had no opportunity to cheat than they did when they lost money but had an opportunity to cheat. This supports the "grace" hypothesis that being honest is not the result of a "choice" involving greater brain activity. See Greene & Paxton, *supra* note 81.

[103] Valdesolo, P., & DeSteno, D. (2007). Moral hypocrisy, social groups, and the flexibility of virtue. *Psychological Science*, 18(8), 689–690.

2.5.1 *Maintenance of Self-concept*

In the self-concept maintenance process, motivated reasoning is used to bridge the dissonance between one's bad deeds and the desire to view oneself as a good person. Bersoff, one of the early researchers working in the area, showed in an experiment on how unethical behavior is facilitated that people are able to develop and maintain a biased characterization of an unethical action as morally acceptable.[104] The findings of Mazar et al. and Arieli, which indicate that people cheat only to the extent that they can maintain their self-concept of being honest, are good examples of research done in this tradition.[105]

Dana et al. demonstrate people's use of one dominant strategy – defined as "moral wiggle room" – to maintain an ethical self-concept while engaging in self-interested behavior.[106] In a series of experiments, the dictator had to choose between a personal payoff of $6 or $5. Each of these payoffs was matched with an uncertain payoff (determined exogenously by a lottery and unknown to the dictator) of either $1 or $5 to the opposing player. Thus, in such a setting, the dictator could choose the selfish payoff ($6) while convincing herself that the opposing party would also receive the high payoff ($5 rather than $1). Before choosing between the payoffs, the dictators were offered a chance to see (at no cost) the lottery results, so that they would know the implications for the opposing player of their decision. Most participants chose not to receive this information. They preferred the "moral wiggle room" – that is, strategically using ambiguity to create a more favorable description of their ethical dilemma – which allowed them to believe that they had not behaved unethically when they actually picked the option that was preferable for them. In doing so, they engaged in a process of "information avoidance," leading the authors to claim that people wish to pursue their self-interest while maintaining the illusion of behaving fairly.

Within this line of research, the most coherent account for the idea that implicit unethicality is related to self-concept maintenance is that of Chugh and Kern, who differentiate between self-protection and self-enhancement.[107] Both processes have the same goal of enabling people to maintain a positive view of themselves, but they work differently. Self-protection is the deliberative process in which individuals are motivated to fix a threat to their self-esteem. Self-enhancement is the automatic process that occurs when we are not experiencing threats to our self-concept. In other words, it is the default track and the one in which unethical behavior occurs most often. People engage in self-enhancement when they automatically and unconsciously make unethical decisions without interpreting them as unethical or

---

[104]   Bersoff, D. M. (1999). Explaining unethical behaviour among people motivated to act prosocially. *Journal of Moral Education*, 28(4), 413–428.

[105]   See Mazar et al., *supra* note 2.

[106]   Dana, J., Weber, R. A., & Kuang, J. X. (2007). Exploiting moral wiggle room: Experiments demonstrating an illusory preference for fairness. *Economic Theory*, 33(1), 67–80.

[107]   See Chugh & Kern, *supra* note 25.

threatening to their positive perception of themselves. When that positive perception is threatened, they become more aware of their decisions and thus more
motivated to make decisions that will help reinstate their positive self-view.
The decision-making process then becomes more deliberative, and the decisions
themselves tend to be more moral in the self-protection process.

Moral licensing theory, which suggests that people use good deeds to excuse later
bad deeds, is another self-maintenance-based theory.[108] Monin and Miller find that
participants who believed that they had previously established their moral credentials
(in this case, a lack of prejudice) felt empowered to subsequently express views that
conflicted with moral norms.[109] These findings are contrary to the traditional view,
which holds that those who behaved badly are more likely to do so in the future.

2.5.2 *Reframing of Reality*

Another way that people act to preserve their self-concept, after they recognize they
have acted unethically, is to change the moral meaning of their misconduct by
changing their assessment of the reality in which they operated and the effects of
their actions on that reality. This reframing of reality is closely tied to other
mechanisms underlying BE; for example, the blind spot argument aligns well with
the change in reality approach. The moral forgetting paradigm originating from the
work of Shu and Gino holds that people change the perception of what kind of
behavior is required from them as a way to allow themselves to do bad things.[110]

A related theory that emphasizes the adjustment of reality is "ethical fading."[111]
According to this theory, by deceiving themselves, people allow ethical concerns to
fade into the background of the decision-making process, undermining those threats
to their positive self-image. Ethical fading also suggests that people reconcile the
dissonance in a different way: instead of thinking of themselves as objectively good
people, they focus on the fact that they are better than those around them. The need
to maintain self-concept is also central to the moral hypocrisy theory, which holds
that people can maintain their self-concept by *not* comparing their behavior to
preexisting moral standards. Support for this theory is found in the work of Batson
et al., who show that self-interested behavior decreases when participants are placed
in conditions of high self-awareness.[112]

---

[108] See Effron & Monin, *supra* note 32.
[109] Monin, B., & Miller, D. T. (2001). Moral credentials and the expression of prejudice. *Journal of Personality and Social Psychology*, 81(1), 33.
[110] Shu, L. L., & Gino, F. (2012). Sweeping dishonesty under the rug: How unethical actions lead to forgetting of moral rules. *Journal of Personality and Social Psychology*, 102(6), 1164.
[111] See Tenbrunsel & Messick, *supra* note 96.
[112] Batson, C. D., Thompson, E. R., Seuferling, G., Whitney, H., & Strongman, J. A. (1999). Moral hypocrisy: Appearing moral to oneself without being so. *Journal of Personality and Social Psychology*, 77(3), 525.

2.5.3 Moral Disengagement

Another mechanism based on cognitive dissonance is "moral disengagement," in which people change their view of how moral it is to harm a certain individual by changing their views on the morality of the intended victim.[113] It is probably the most dominant paradigm to explain how people, who have some awareness that they are doing wrong, justify doing inhuman actions such as murder. Bandura[114] described eight mechanisms by which individuals convince themselves that their actions are not immoral:

(1) Moral justification, used to explain why an immoral act actually has a moral purpose;
(2) Euphemistic labeling used to reclassify an action such as "stealing" as a more innocuous act, such as "shifting resources";
(3) Palliative comparisons, used to explain why the immoral action is a better option than its alternatives;
(4) Displacement of responsibility accomplished by blaming a superior who is believed to have ordered the immoral act;
(5) Diffusion of responsibility by stating that they were merely part of a group in which everyone was performing the immoral action or that their individual part of the action was not immoral;
(6) Trivializing the consequences of the act to make it seem more acceptable;
(7) Dehumanizing the victim to render the action acceptable;
(8) Blaming the victims to render the immoral action acceptable by claiming that they provoked it.

In a follow-up study, Moore at al. applied the eight categories to explain the use of self-deception and concluded that moral disengagement has three important effects on institutional corruption.[115] First, it can make unethical decisions easier by reducing psychological discomfort in making such decisions. Second, because moral disengagement excludes moral values from consideration, it expedites unethical behavior by freeing up cognitive resources to work on the unethical goal. Finally, since these actions promote the interests of the corporation, individuals who morally disengage rise in the corporation, perpetuating unethical behavior.

Based on a thorough literature review, Ayal and Gino[116] propose a taxonomy of mechanisms of moral disengagement. They discuss the concept of "moral

---

[113] See Bandura, *supra* note 13.   [114] Ibid.
[115] Moore, C. (2008). Moral disengagement in processes of organizational corruption. *Journal of Business Ethics*, 80(1), 129–139.
[116] Ayal, S., & Gino, F. (2011). Honest rationales for dishonest behavior. *The social psychology of morality: Exploring the causes of good and evil*. Washington, DC: American Psychological Association, pp. 149–166.

cleansing," which they describe as an attempt to rid oneself of negative feelings after committing an unethical act by mental appeasement. This controlled process enables individuals to distance themselves from transgressions by engaging in either overt practices, such as washing hands and going to confession, or more covert ones, such as moral licensing – whereby people use their morality in one occasion to justify their immorality in another.[117]

2.5.4 Creative Justifications

Another process related to reframing reality is finding creative justifications for misconduct, thereby giving permission to behave unethically. Shalvi et al.[118] explore people's view of what is a justifiable lie, finding that merely being shown an alternative outcome of a game made participants willing to lie about the outcome. In their study, participants rolled dice under a cup so that only they could see their number value. Instructed to report the results of the first roll out of two in exchange for money corresponding to the value of the dice, participants felt morally comfortable to lie by reporting the higher second, rather than the first one, to receive a higher payment. This seems to suggest that some people are willing to be more creative when it comes to violating the rules of the game, rather than to bluntly make up a number.

2.5.5 Social Norms and Fairness[119]

Finally, two concepts have the potential to limit the "damage" to society from nondeliberative unethicality – social norms and fairness. Indeed, these two concepts receive much attention in the BLE literature, which shows their effectiveness in curbing some of the negative effects of self-interest by limiting its conscious effects on behavior.[120] For example, in a seminal study based on survey data on how people behave in contexts that are supposed to focus on profit maximization, Kahneman et al. show that people's sense of fairness can overcome their desire to act selfishly.[121]

BE researchers have responded with an intuitive counterargument: fairness is a concept that is highly susceptible to self-interested interpretations, casting doubt on its ability to curb self-interest. For example, Thompson and Lowenstein show that people in a dispute are more likely to remember information related to their own

---

[117] Merritt, A. C., Effron, D. A., & Monin, B. (2010). Moral self-licensing: When being good frees us to be bad. *Social and Personality Psychology Compass*, 4(5), 344–357.

[118] Shalvi, S., Dana, J., Handgraaf, M. J., & De Dreu, C. K. (2011). Justified ethicality: Observing desired counterfactuals modifies ethical perceptions and behavior. *Organizational Behavior and Human Decision Processes*, 115(2), 181–190.

[119] The concept of social norms is being discussed in more details in chapter 5 of the book.

[120] For a review of the limitations of these notions, see Feldman, Y., & Tyler, T. R. (2012). Mandated justice: The potential promise and possible pitfalls of mandating procedural justice in the workplace. *Regulation & Governance*, 6(1), 46–65.

[121] Kahneman, D., Knetsch, J. L., & Thaler, R. H. (1986). Fairness and the assumptions of economics. *Journal of Business*, S285–S300.

position, so that their view of fairness is aligned with their interest in how a settlement should look.[122] Babcock et al. show a similar effect when people predict the judicial outcome of their cases, thus reducing the likelihood of agreeing to an out-of-court settlement.[123]

Social norms can also affect the likelihood that people will engage in unethical behavior. The effects of social norms have been incorporated into rational-choice approaches espoused by BLE, taking into account aspects such as reputation, expressive effects, shaming, and social sanctioning. Cooter,[124] for example, developed an economic theory of how the expressive values of the law can shape social norms and individual preferences. Ellickson and Ellickson[125] described the embrace by law and economics of status and social norms as mechanisms for informal enforcement. Looking at trade secret law, Feldman[126] found experimental support for the notion that the expressive function of law operates through a combination of intrinsic and extrinsic forces.

Shaming in particular has received a great deal of attention in the BLE literature. Kahan and Posner[127] examined how shaming penalties can shape preferences against crime and express social norms. Some BLE scholars have recognized the process of internalization of social norms and preference changes, rather than arguing that social norms merely account for costs and benefits of noncompliance.[128]

BE literature takes this discussion a step further by exploring which factors enhance the automatic internalization of social norms. For example, Gino et al. show that the effect of unethical group norms on people's inclination to engage in dishonest behavior strongly depends on the salience of group identity.[129] In a more thorough examination of this psychological mechanism, Gino and Galinsky studied the effect of psychological closeness on the likelihood that social norms cause people to engage in unethical behavior; they show that the likelihood that an unethical norm will lead to a change in one's ethical decision making is highly dependent on the level of psychological closeness of the participant to the unethical individual.[130]

[122] Thompson, L., & Loewenstein, G. (1992). Egocentric interpretations of fairness and interpersonal conflict. *Organizational Behavior and Human Decision Processes*, 51(2), 176–197.

[123] Babcock, L., Loewenstein, G., Issacharoff, S., & Camerer, C. (1995). Biased judgments of fairness in bargaining. *American Economic Review*, 85(5), 1337–1343.

[124] Cooter, R. (1998). Expressive law and economics. *Journal of Legal Studies*, 27(S2), 585–607.

[125] Ellickson, R. C., & Ellickson, R. C. (2009). *Order without law: How neighbors settle disputes.* Cambridge, MA: Harvard University Press.

[126] Feldman, Y. (2009). The expressive function of trade secret law: Legality, cost, intrinsic motivation, and consensus. *Journal of Empirical Legal Studies*, 6(1), 177–212.

[127] Kahan, D. M., & Posner, E. A. (1999). Shaming white-collar criminals: A proposal for reform of the federal sentencing guidelines. *The Journal of Law and Economics*, 42(S1), 365–392.

[128] See Bilz, K., & Nadler, J. (2009). Law, psychology, and morality. *Psychology of Learning and Motivation*, 50, 101–131.

[129] Gino, F., Ayal, S., & Ariely, D. (2009). Contagion and differentiation in unethical behavior: The effect of one bad apple on the barrel. *Psychological Science*, 20(3), 393–398.

[130] Gino, F., & Galinsky, A. D. (2012). Vicarious dishonesty: When psychological closeness creates distance from one's moral compass. *Organizational Behavior and Human Decision Processes*, 119(1), 15–26.

Another innovation in the BE literature on social norms is its finding of the asymmetric influence of unethical and ethical norms on behavior. Some research suggests that given the tendency for self-concept maintenance, people pay more attention to the unethical behavior of others in order to subsequently justify their own ethical missteps.[131] However, other research shows that people can be very bad at noticing the unethical behavior of others. Gino et al.[132] discuss various processes that account for that lack of awareness.

2.6 LIMITATIONS OF BE RESEARCH

The major limitation of BE research is that unethical behaviors are usually studied in a lab, and it is very difficult to draw direct and practical conclusions from the findings. Abstract experimental designs do not necessarily mimic real-life dilemmas and fail to account for individual differences: there is a great difference between the abstract conflict of interest situations experienced in a lab and the ones employees face in the workplace where they may believe their careers are on the line. In addition, the unethical behaviors that are studied are usually simple ones, such as people reporting the number value of dice, or the number of questions they answered, or the number shown on a screen. In real life, unethical behaviors are much more complex – too complex to be done without any deliberation – which raises doubts about the external validity of some of the lab studies.

A lack of consensus among researchers on basic concepts and on methodology limits the ability to develop policy from the research. The inability to determine the relative component of automaticity in unethical behavior is similar to the problem of mixed motives, which we see in areas such as taxation or in employment discrimination. For example, how can we apply findings relating to time pressures (how much time) and ego depletion (to what extent)? Would giving people more or less time to make decisions increase or decrease the likelihood that they would engage in wrongdoing?[133] Finally, the validity of methods such as the Implicit Attitudes Test,[134] which focuses on people's ease in reporting associations between

---

[131] Epley, N., & Dunning, D. (2000). Feeling "holier than thou": Are self-serving assessments produced by errors in self or social prediction? *Journal of Personality and Social Psychology*, 79(6), 861. See also Cooter, R. D., Feldman, M., & Feldman, Y. (2008). The misperception of norms: The psychology of bias and the economics of equilibrium. *Review of Law & Economics*, 4(3), 889–911.

[132] Gino, F., Moore, D. A., & Bazerman, M. H. (2008). *See no evil: When we overlook other people's unethical behavior.* Harvard Business School, Working Paper Summaries. Available at https://hbswk.hbs.edu/item/see-no-evil-when-we-overlook-other-peoples-unethical-behavior.

[133] See Rand et al., *supra* note 74. See also Shalvi et al., *supra* note 78.

[134] Greenwald, A. G., McGhee, D. E., & Schwartz, J. L. (1998). Measuring individual differences in implicit cognition: The implicit association test. *Journal of Personality and Social Psychology*, 74(6), 1464.

concepts and values, is still being debated.[135] What are needed are consistent measures that predict behavior across situations.

2.7 THE NORMATIVE IMPLICATIONS OF BEHAVIORAL ETHICS

The BE field has a great potential to shape legal policy making, but it is difficult to incorporate the data generated by BE research into public policy without the necessary adaptations. For example, many of the priming and ethical nudge effects studied are lab based and short term. Numerous problems could account for why some of these effects may get diluted in the field. Similarly, the call for a differentiated treatment of good and bad people is based on the claim that good people are genuinely unable to recognize when they are acting unethically. However, there is very little research on this topic, and it is difficult to rule out the option that they are playing dumb to avoid punishment. This limits the ability to remove responsibility from those good people.

A lack of consensus remains on many aspects of bounded ethicality, and there are competing and redundant underlying explanations of the relevant behaviors. Research is also limited on the long-term effects of many of the celebrated BE experimental manipulations. Awareness, which may dictate whether individuals engage in self-interested behaviors intentionally or unintentionally, is a crucial aspect but is notoriously difficult to measure.

Thus, the normative part of this chapter is especially challenging. Some theories, such as those related to fairness and social norms, suggest possible solutions, but the questions raised by the research are far more numerous than the answers currently offered.

It seems to be a straightforward argument that individuals' limited awareness of their bad behavior requires a substantial revision in the design of legal rules that govern them.[136] Naturally, the stronger the case that unethical acts are committed by people who do not realize they are behaving unethically, the more limited the law's ability to change their behavior. As suggested above, some of the leading scholars in BE are quick to point out that classic intervention techniques, such as penalties, are rendered ineffective if ethical decisions are produced by System 1 without awareness.[137] While the management literature is replete with studies offering various prescriptions for organizations to respond to this concern, the legal scholarship has mostly ignored this concept of automaticity.

Based on the classical dichotomy of intrinsic vs. extrinsic, motivation in law may have to be replaced by a different broader paradigm that combines the controlled

---

[135]   Blanton, H., Jaccard, J., Klick, J., Mellers, B., Mitchell, G., & Tetlock, P. E. (2009). Strong claims and weak evidence: Reassessing the predictive validity of the IAT. *Journal of Applied Psychology*, 94 (3), 567.
[136]   See Feldman & Smith, *supra* note 101.   [137]   See Bazerman & Banaji, *supra* note 4.

and automatic modes of cognition underlying ethical reasoning and motivation. In Chapters 9 and 10, I discuss two of areas of law in which BE could account for the dichotomy between the bad deeds committed by good people vs. those done by bad people and the way the law should respond to both. Clearly as suggested in Chapter 1, these concepts are highly relevant for any legal doctrine that involves ordinary unethical behavior, such as consumer protection law, corporate law, contract law, administrative law and employment law. In any of these legal doctrines it is very important to account for the behavioral ethics mechanisms through which good people can justify and downplay, either implicitly or explicitly, their own non-cooperative behavior.

2.8 CONCLUDING REMARKS

The common theme in the literature on BE is that unethical behaviors are the product not of explicit choices to do wrong but rather of System 1 non-deliberative choices. A closer look at some of the mechanisms described in the bounded ethicality literature, however, shows that in many cases, there is awareness of the misconduct. Yet we still regard the behavior as "bounded" because of mechanisms such as rationalization or lack of attention, which prevent individuals from recognizing the wrong nature of their actions. Another common theme in the literature is the need to protect our self-image, to resolve the dissonance between believing that we are good people and our desire to maximize self-interest. Many of the studies reviewed in this chapter focus on how people resolve this dissonance.

Finally, although most scholars believe that self-interest is automatic, the lack of conclusive evidence about whether we can control or at least be aware of automatic behavior (and thereby compensate for the negative effects of self-interest) casts doubt on whether those who engage in these automatic, unethical behaviors are still good people.

3

Revisiting Traditional Enforcement Interventions

In this and the following chapter, I review the array of regulatory tools that states can use to regulate human behavior. Many scholars compare the different tools and the distinction between traditional and nontraditional intervention methods is not always clear. In my view, Orly Lobel's analysis of new governance techniques that have replaced more traditional command-and-control approaches is particularly useful for my purposes.[1] The current chapter focuses on three main mechanisms of legal compliance – price, fairness, and the expressive effects[2] – that aim to change people's explicit behaviors that are the result of a deliberative process.[3] The chapter presents the implicit desirable and undesirable processes that accompany each mechanism, such as crowding out, misperception of norms and socialization, social norms and moral intuition, and egocentric interpretations of fairness, and each approach's strengths and weaknesses in regulating human behavior.

After describing these approaches, I advance several critical arguments that will lay the groundwork for the next chapter, which focuses on newer, "softer" intervention methods. I show that the traditional and the newer mechanisms are

[*] The first half of this chapter includes modified versions of text from the following papers: Feldman, Y. (2011). Five models of regulatory compliance motivation: Empirical findings and normative implications. In D. Levi-Faur (Ed.), *Handbook on the Politics of Regulation* (pp. 335–347). Cheltenham: Elgar; Cooter, R. D., Feldman, M., & Feldman, Y. (2008). The misperception of norms: The psychology of bias and the economics of equilibrium. *Review of Law & Economics*, 4(3), 889–911; and Feldman, Y. (2009). The expressive function of trade secret law: Legality, cost, intrinsic motivation, and consensus. *Journal of Empirical Legal Studies*, 6(1), 177–212.

[1] For more on the rise of regulatory governance, see Braithwaite, V., Braithwaite, J., Gibson, D., & Makkai, T. (1994). Regulatory styles, motivational postures and nursing home compliance. *Law & Policy*, 16(4), 363–394. See also Ayres, I., & Braithwaite, J. (1995). *Responsive regulation: Transcending the deregulation debate*. Oxford University Press on Demand, with a focus on the concept of pyramid of sanctions against different types of situations based on their regulatory intentions.

[2] Price refers to sanctions, fairness to mechanisms such as procedural justice, and expressive effects to the ability of the law to change the social meaning of behavior.

[3] See Cooter, R. D. (2000). Three effects of social norms on law: Expression, deterrence, and internalization. *Oregon Law Review*, 79, 1. See also Feldman, Y. (2009). The expressive function of trade secret law: Legality, cost, intrinsic motivation, and consensus. *Journal of Empirical Legal Studies*, 6(1), 177–212.

not mutually exclusive and that the separation between the mechanisms is less real than argued. Furthermore, I argue that the limitations of the different approaches in bringing about sustainable change in people's behavior partly derive from their inability to address people with differing levels of awareness of their wrongdoing and different motivations to comply with legal and ethical regulations.

As suggested earlier, behavioral scholars have challenged the traditional paradigm of legal compliance as being primarily motivated by the fear of sanctions.[4] The work of Tyler, Paternoster and Simpson, and Robinson and Darley emphasizes the role of fairness and morality in legal compliance, rather than self-interest.[5] In my earlier research on curbing deliberative misconducts, I too examined and compared the different compliance motivations such as deterrence, fairness, citizenship, and social norms – all of which assume that an individual thinks deliberately about whether or not to obey the law.[6]

The most well-known regulatory approach targets the calculative or the incentive-driven individual. According to this model, the decision about how to act is based primarily on a cost-benefit calculation; hence, the approach of the regulator should focus on deterring the bad behavior and providing incentives to engage in good behavior. The literature that discusses this approach is the richest one, given the centrality of both deterrence and incentives within legal scholarship.[7] However, the deterrence or cost-benefit model has been criticized on numerous grounds. Some have demonstrated, empirically, the limits of deterrence in explaining both self-reported and actual compliance.[8] Other scholars have suggested that deterrence does not really work, simply because people have little awareness of the law on the books.[9]

The main rival explanatory model to the deterrence rationale comes from the research on the limits of self-interest in accounting for people's motivation. Various studies have demonstrated that fairness is a dominant factor in human motivation, at

---

[4] Becker, G. S. (1968). Crime and punishment: An economic approach, in N. G. Fielding, A. Clarke, & R. Witt (Eds.), *The economic dimensions of crime* (pp. 13–68). London: Palgrave Macmillan.

[5] Tyler, T. R. (1990). *Why people obey the law: Procedural justice, legitimacy, and compliance*. Princeton: Princeton University Press. See also Paternoster, R., & Simpson, S. (1996). Sanction threats and appeals to morality: Testing a rational choice model of corporate crime. *Law and Society Review*, 632, 549–583; Robinson, P. H., & Darley, J. M. (1996). Utility of desert. *Northwestern University Law Review*, 91, 453.

[6] For a review, see Feldman, Y. (2011). The complexity of disentangling intrinsic and extrinsic compliance motivations: Theoretical and empirical insights from the behavioral analysis of law. *Washington University Journal of Law & Policy*, 35(1), 11–51.

[7] See, generally, Zimring, F. E., Hawkins, G., & Vorenberg, J. (1973). *Deterrence: The legal threat in crime control*. Chicago: University of Chicago Press, p. 58. See also Tittle, C. R. (1980). *Sanctions and social deviance: The question of deterrence*. New York: Praeger.

[8] See, for example, Braithwaite, J., & Makkai, T. (1991). Testing an expected utility model of corporate deterrence. *Law and Society Review*, 25, 7–40.

[9] Robinson, P. H., & Darley, J. M. (2004). Does criminal law deter? A behavioural science investigation. *Oxford Journal of Legal Studies*, 24(2), 173–205.

times overshadowing self-interest more than expected.[10] Perceptions of fairness have been shown to shift the behavior of people toward greater compliance with and acceptance of organizational rules in various legal contexts,[11] more sensitive environmental behavior,[12] and higher rates of reporting illegality.[13]

To analyze the difference between deterrence methods and those targeting perceptions of fairness, I first create a taxonomy of various legal interventions. Although many are context dependent and vary in their application across different legal settings, I focus on methods that are relevant to most social domains. The two main types of legal interventions are traditional ones, focusing mainly on deliberative choice, and nontraditional legal interventions, which focus on non-deliberative choice.[14] This chapter focuses on traditional interventions, based on the following three mechanisms:

1. **Incentives**, including all forms of penalties, fines, rewards, and other external measures.[15]
2. **Fairness-, legitimacy-,** and **morality**-based interventions.[16]
3. **Expressive function of the law**, which shapes the social meaning of behaviors[17] and assumes that people change their behavior to fit the prevailing social norms because of social enforcement mechanisms, signaling, and reputational costs.[18]

Many of the questions that I focus on in the second half of the book regard the efficacy of traditional intervention methods given people's limited awareness of how their motivations may vary. Clearly an approach that takes into account deliberative and non-deliberative processes must be sensitive to possible unintended effects of the law. I discuss in later chapters how to align these compliance motivation models with the focus on people's self-awareness.

[10]   See, for example, Kahneman, D., Knetsch, J. L., & Thaler, R. H. (1986). Fairness and the assumptions of economics. *Journal of Business*, 59(4), S285–S300.
[11]   Feldman, Y., & Tyler, T. R. (2012). Mandated justice: The potential promise and possible pitfalls of mandating procedural justice in the workplace. *Regulation & Governance*, 6(1), 46–65.
[12]   Feldman, Y., & Perez, O. (2012). Motivating environmental action in a pluralistic regulatory environment: An experimental study of framing, crowding out, and institutional effects in the context of recycling policies. *Law & Society Review*, 46(2), 405–442.
[13]   Feldman, Y., & Lobel, O. (2009). The incentives matrix: The comparative effectiveness of rewards, liabilities, duties, and protections for reporting illegality. *Texas Law Review* 88, 1151.
[14]   Feldman, Y. (2011). Five models of regulatory compliance motivation: Empirical findings and normative implications. In D. Levi-Faur (Ed.), *Handbook on the Politics of Regulation*. Cheltenham: Edward Elgar, pp. 335–347.
[15]   Gneezy, Meier, & Rey-Biel, P. When and why incentives (don't) work to modify behavior. *Journal of Economic Perspectives*, 25(4), 191–209. See also Feldman & Lobel, *supra* note 13, at 1151.
[16]   See Tyler, *supra* note 5. For a review, see Feldman, Y. (2011). The complexity of disentangling intrinsic and extrinsic compliance motivations: Theoretical and empirical insights from the behavioral analysis of law. *Wash. UJL & Pol'y*, 35, 11.
[17]   Sunstein, C. R. (1996). On the expressive function of law. *University of Pennsylvania Law Review*, 144 (5), 2021–2053. See also Feldman, *supra* note 3.
[18]   McAdams, R. H. (2000). An attitudinal theory of expressive law. *Oregon Law Review*, 79(2), 339–390. See also Feldman, Y., & Nadler, J. (2006). The law and norms of file sharing. *San Diego Law Review*, 43, 577.

3.1 REGULATORY APPROACHES AND COMPLIANCE MOTIVATIONS

The taxonomy of traditional legal interventions, which is not new to the psycho-legal literature, is useful in framing legislation to be responsive to people's varying motivations. It is based both on existing social influence models and on moral reasoning models that are well recognized within social psychology.[19] One of its foundational concepts is that depending on the context, people process information differently and choose a course of action using alternative modes of conduct. Within this context, another key idea in the socio-legal literature is that people differ in the dominant motivation that guides them, not just across people but also across contexts.[20]

As will be demonstrated in the book, focusing on people's motivation is the only sustainable way to ensure long-term compliance. Interventions also need to account simultaneously for people's motivations, whether intrinsic or extrinsic, and their level of awareness of their possible wrongdoing. In Chapter 1, we divided wrongdoers into three groups:[21] "erroneous wrongdoers," those whose wrongdoing can be attributed mainly to limited awareness due to errors and blind spots but they do not actively look for justification for their wrong doing; "situational wrongdoers," those whose unethicality is primarily justified by their rationalizations for doing bad in a given situation; and "bad people, or calculative wrong doers," who deliberately engage in unethical behavior (see Table 3.1). Naturally, the dividing line between these three groups is sometimes blurry. Nonetheless, where the variation across people is clear or blurry, once this variation is being recognized, there is a need to revisit the suitability of the type of enforcement effort for the type of population targeted.

TABLE 3.1 *Three Mind-sets Underlying Wrongdoing*

	Level of awareness of illegality	Motivation toward the law
Erroneous wrongdoers	Unaware, blind-spot, situational unethicality	Intrinsic motivation, genuine morality
Situational wrongdoers	Partially aware, more likely to engage in motivated reasoning to avoid recognizing their own wrongdoing	Dissonance between intrinsic motivation to obey the law and desire to enhance profit; will use ethical justifications to solve this tension
"Bad" calculative people	Aware, deliberative, calculative	Extrinsic motivation

[19] Tapp, J. L., & Kohlberg, L. (1971). Developing senses of law and legal justice. *Journal of Social Issues*, 27(2), 65–91.

[20] For a review, see Feldman, Y., & MacCoun, R. (2005). Some well-aged wines for the "new norm" bottles: Implications of social psychology to law and economics. In P. F. Vernon (Ed.), *The law and economics of irrational behavior*, pp. 358–397. Stanford: Stanford University Press. In Chapter 6, which examines individual differences in responses to law, I discuss the possibility that people's motivations differ based on their individual differences.

[21] As noted also in chapter 1, clearly there is also a spectrum between those two prototypes. Furthermore as developed in chapter 6, most people will behave differently across the different types in any given situation.

The first regulatory approach, incentives, is most suitable for individuals motivated by price considerations. According to this model, the individual's choice of behavior is based primarily on a cost-benefit calculation; thus, the regulatory approach should focus on deterring bad behavior while incentivizing good behavior. In that regard, it is most likely to resemble the calculative mindset. The second regulatory approach, focusing on people's considerations of morality and fairness, using concepts such as procedural and distributive justice when enacting and enforcing the law, is most suitable for the moral individual; its main assumption is that individuals want to be moral and helping them recognize the morality of law will increase their compliance. In that regard, this category is best suited for the genuinely moral individual. The third regulatory approach, the expressive function of the law, assumes that the dominant compliance motivation of individuals is to fit the social norm, focuses on changing the social meaning of certain behavior by changing their view of the situation as well as of the prevailing social norm. Therefore, it focuses on demonstrating to the individual that the prevailing norm, either quantitatively or qualitatively, is to obey the law. In the current context, this expressive effect of law could be said to be especially suitable for targeting the situational wrongdoers who are most sensitive to the situational and social cues about the ability not to comply in a given situation, given some assurance that such noncompliance is acceptable.

In addition, it is important to mention a fourth category that could be connected to each one of the previous categories: some people comply simply because it is the law, regardless of its content. The main theoretical body for this model is related to certain aspects of institutional legitimacy.[22]

3.2 INCENTIVES: THE PRICE-BASED REGULATORY APPROACH

3.2.1 Extrinsic vs. Intrinsic Motivation

To understand the interrelations between extrinsic motivation and self-interest, and between intrinsic motivation and morality, it is important to understand the full meaning of the difference between extrinsic and intrinsic motivations. This discussion is based on the work by Ryan and Deci.[23] *Extrinsic motivation* refers to the performance of an activity in order to gain a beneficial outcome or to avoid a negative one; *intrinsic motivation* does not depend on external incentives and

[22] Gibson, J. L. (1989). Understandings of justice: Institutional legitimacy, procedural justice, and political tolerance. *Law and Society Review,* 23(3), 469–496. But see Tyler, T. R., & Rasinski, K. (1991). Procedural justice, institutional legitimacy, and the acceptance of unpopular US Supreme Court decisions: A reply to Gibson. *Law and Society Review,* 25, 621–630.

[23] Ryan, R. M., & Deci, E. L. (2000). Intrinsic and extrinsic motivations: Classic definitions and new directions. *Contemporary Educational Psychology,* 25(1), 54–67.

can be defined as self-sustained.[24] There are two types of intrinsic motivation: *enjoyment based* and *obligation based*.[25] Obligation-based intrinsic motivation reflects a sense of moral or civic duty and is not driven by instrumental considerations; for example, people recycle because they are motivated to improve the environment.[26] This type of motivation has been associated with moral-driven legal compliance,[27] even though morality in many accounts can be seen in itself as being driven by extrinsic rationales.

3.2.2 Crowding-out of Intrinsic Motivation

The most important legal policy implication of intrinsic vs. extrinsic motivation is the crowding-out effect of the latter on the former. Intrinsic and extrinsic motivations can sometimes be in conflict. By suggesting that (in some cases) increasing monetary incentives to obey the law will reduce rather than increase socially desirable behavior, the crowding-out effect constitutes an intriguing anomaly that goes counter to the classic economic behavioral model[28]: it holds that classical price effects are sometimes reduced or even reversed and the monetary effects undermine people's intrinsic motivation to obey the law.

Frey, the economist most identified with the crowding-out effect, has conducted many experiments to show the negative effect of money on behavior.[29] For example, he found that residents were more likely to oppose a nuclear plant in their neighborhood if they were offered compensation. The tension between intrinsic and extrinsic motivation has been shown to be relevant to the question of compliance in different regulatory contexts, ranging from tax evasion[30] to labor law (whistle-blowing).[31] A nuance in the crowding-out effect is offered by Ariely et al., who showed that especially with regard to prosocial behaviors, its effect is stronger in public settings where people believed that their image would be

---

[24] Frey, B. S., & Jegen, R. (1999). *Motivation crowding theory: A survey of empirical evidence*. Zurich: University of Zurich Institute for Empirical Research in Economics.

[25] Osterloh, M., Frey, B. S., & Frost, J. (2001). Managing motivation, organization and governance. *Journal of Management and Governance*, 5(3), 231–239.

[26] Thøgersen, J. (2003). Monetary incentives and recycling: Behavioural and psychological reactions to a performance-dependent garbage fee. *Journal of Consumer Policy*, 26(2), 197–228.

[27] This also includes fairness-driven compliance, which reflects the idea that people will be more compliant when they think the law coheres with either their distributive justice intuitions (e.g., Robinson, P. H. (2008). *Distributive principles of criminal law: Who should be punished how much?* New York: Oxford University Press) or with their conceptions of procedural justice (e.g., Tyler, *Why people obey the law*).

[28] Frey, B. S., & Jegen, R. (2001). Motivation crowding theory. *Journal of Economic Surveys*, 15(5), 589–611.

[29] Frey, B. S. (1998). *Not just for the money*. Cheltenham: Edward Elgar.

[30] Wenzel, M. (2005). Motivation or rationalisation? Causal relations between ethics, norms and tax compliance. *Journal of Economic Psychology*, 26(4), 491–508.

[31] See Feldman & Lobel, *supra* note 13, at 1151.

harmed by others viewing their behavior as being motivated solely by money rather than virtue.[32]

The related mechanism of imposing fines for infractions of rules may similarly be counterproductive. Gneezy and Rustichini documented this phenomenon in the context of day care centers that assessed fines on parents who were late in picking up their children at the end of the day.[33] They found that imposing a fine on late parents actually increased the number of late pickups. Apparently, the fine led parents to feel licensed to arrive late. Gneezy and Rustichini argue that the introduction of fines can be interpreted as placing a price tag on asocial behavior, thus leading to an increase in the performance level of this behavior, contrary to the traditional deterrence model.

Another study on the potentially disruptive effect of incentives found that both rewards and punishments were shown to trigger an over-justification effect, in which external rewards were likely to cause people to question their "true motivation."[34]. A related finding is the negative effect of regulation on trust. Falk and Kosfeld demonstrated experimentally that when a principal signals distrust to an agent, the agent's performance level is reduced, as is his or her compliance with various rules.[35] Similarly, Blair and Stout showed the inadvertent effect of regulation and monitoring on the behavior of corporate executives.[36] They suggest that the mistrust signaled through harsh regulation serves as a self-fulfilling prophecy. A policy that has the threat of sanctions overlooks the possibility that threatened punishment may be perceived as a signal that noncompliance is widespread.[37] By signaling to others that few people are engaging in prosocial behavior and imposing sanctions for bad behavior, incentives can crowd out altruism because they eliminate the opportunity to demonstrate altruism and goodwill.

The crowding-out literature suggests several behavioral explanations for the potential erosion of internal motivation by external incentives. First, the cognitive evaluation theory (CET) highlights the need for individuals to feel competent and in control of a particular task.[38] External incentives may erode people's motivation by undermining their concept of competency and autonomy. Command-and-control regulations, which leave little room for discretion, negatively influence the

[32]   Ariely, D., Bracha, A., & Meier, S. (2009). Doing good or doing well: Image motivation and monetary incentives in behaving prosocially. *American Economic Review*, 99(1), 544–555.
[33]   Gneezy, U., & Rustichini, A. (2000). A fine is a price. *Journal of Legal Studies*, 29(1), 1–17.
[34]   Benabou, R., & Tirole, J. (2003). Intrinsic and extrinsic motivation. *Review of Economic Studies*, 70(3), 489–520.
[35]   Falk, A., & Kosfeld, M. (2004). Distrust: The hidden cost of control. IZA Discussion Paper No. 1203.
[36]   Blair, M. M., & Stout, L. A. (2001). Trust, trustworthiness, and the behavioral foundations of corporate law. *University of Pennsylvania Law Review*, 149(6), 1735–1810.
[37]   Depoorter, B., & Vanneste, S. (2005). Norms and enforcement: The case against copyright litigation. *Oregon Law Review*, 84, 1127.
[38]   Weibel, A., Rost, K., & Osterloh, M. (2010). Pay for performance in the public sector – Benefits and (hidden) costs. *Journal of Public Administration Research and Theory*, 20(2), 387–412.

self-concept of the regulatee as someone with decision-making ability and reduce his or her sense of autonomy.[39]

A second explanation is the over-justification theory, which suggests that when people derive pleasure from an action *per se*, and would have acted even in the absence of external rewards, the introduction of explicit incentives may "over-justify" the activity and undermine the person's intrinsic motivation to perform well.[40] A third explanation, which is more in line with the BE perspective that this book advances, focuses on the framing effect of external intervention. Intervention in the form of economic incentives may change people's perception of the social context in which their action is embedded, shifting the reference frame from the moral plane to the economic one. This frame shifting could crowd out intrinsic motivations by corrupting a purely social act with economic considerations.[41] Terbrunsel and Messick found that without a sanctioning system, 55 percent of the participants in their study viewed their own decision making as being guided by exclusively ethical factors, whereas with a sanctioning system 74 percent viewed their behavior as guided by economic considerations.[42] They also showed that when people were put into a situation that was framed as business-like, they focused on the size of the sanction. However, when the situation was presented as an ethical one, the size of the sanction had less of an effect on their decisions.

Another potential explanation associates the crowding-out effect with an image motivation – a desire to signal altruism. Benabou and Tirole argue, for example, that if blood donors are paid, the value of blood donation as a sign of generosity will be weakened, leading to reduced motivation to donate blood.[43] To avoid confusion, it should be noted that "image motivation" (i.e., how am I being perceived by others), while non-materialistic, is an extrinsic motivation.[44]

If we take seriously the idea that intrinsic and extrinsic compliance motivations are not necessarily synergetic (in contrast to the predictions of neoclassical economics), and that society is composed of people with varied levels of intrinsic motivation, the overall impact of a certain regulatory initiative then becomes sensitive to the distribution of different types within the targeted community. This social variability raises the question of how people with high and low levels of intrinsic motivation to obey and high and low levels of awareness of their wrongdoing react to different regulatory incentives. Given our distinction between situational wrongdoers, who

---

[39] See Frey & Jegen, *supra* note 24.
[40] Bowles, S., & Hwang, S. H. (2008). Social preferences and public economics: Mechanism design when social preferences depend on incentives. *Journal of Public Economics*, 92(8), 1811–1820.
[41] Anik, L., Aknin, L. B., Norton, M. I., & Dunn, E. W. (2009). Feeling good about giving: The benefits (and costs) of self-interested charitable behavior. Harvard Business School Working Paper No. 10-012.
[42] Tenbrunsel, A. E., & Messick, D. M. (1999). Sanctioning systems, decision frames, and cooperation. *Administrative Science Quarterly*, 44(4), 684–707.
[43] See Benabou & Tirole, *supra* note 34.   [44] See Ariely et al., *supra* note 32.

want to do good but will behave badly in a situation that allows them to self-justify that behavior, and genuinely good people who only engage in unethical behavior because of a blind spot that is beyond their awareness, the typology of people becomes even more complex. Replacing the assumption of uniformity with one of heterogeneity is, therefore, critical for the design of optimal social policies. It suggests a different regulatory paradigm – "differentiated regulation" – that aspires to match regulatory strategies to different types of individuals.

As mentioned earlier, the main economic treatment of the interaction between extrinsic and intrinsic motivation is that of Benabou and Tirole.[45] Their work is unusual, especially for economists, because of their willingness to account for implicit processes by addressing concepts such as image motivations and the intrinsic value of the activity, in addition to the price effects of incentives. Their model allows for various predictions of when incentives will work and in what directions. The size of the monetary incentive is obviously relevant to when the price effect of incentives will be larger than the crowding-out effect: They found that large enough incentives will overcome the crowding-out effect at least in the short run,[46] although too large incentives will cause people to "choke under pressure."[47]

In Chapter 8, which focuses on regulatory trade-offs, there is a discussion of an important difference between nudges and incentives. Although neither incentives nor nudges have long-term effects, the decline in their effectiveness differs. Whereas nudges tend to lose their effectiveness even while they are still in place because of reduced awareness, incentives' impact declines only when they are removed. However, after incentives are removed, levels of engaging in the behavior that was previously incentivized are even lower than before imposition of the incentives.[48] There seems to be no rebound effect with nudges, likely because the mechanism driving behavior is largely below awareness.

3.2.3 Is Self-interest Intuitive or Deliberative?

The earlier discussion on the disruptive effects of incentives is most relevant to the regulation of non-deliberative misconducts as demonstrated in chapter two with regard David Rand's research on intuition and cooperation.[49] It could be argued that his research posits an alternative view of the crowding-out effect: when people's view of the

---

[45] Bénabou, R., & Tirole, J. (2006). Incentives and prosocial behavior. American economic review, 96(5), 1652–1678.

[46] Gneezy, U., & Rustichini, A. (2000). Pay enough or don't pay at all. *Quarterly Journal of Economics*, 115(3), 791–810. The crowding-out paradigm also raises the question of the optimal size of monetary regulatory incentives.

[47] Ariely, D., Gneezy, U., Loewenstein, G., & Mazar, N. (2009). Large stakes and big mistakes. *The Review of Economic Studies*, 76(2), 451–469.

[48] See Gneezy & Rustichini, *supra* note 46.

[49] Rand, D. G. (2016). Cooperation, fast and slow: Meta-analytic evidence for a theory of social heuristics and self-interested deliberation. Psychological Science, 27(9), 1192–1206.

situation changes from its being cooperative to competitive, their cooperative behavior decreases.

Rand and his colleagues have contributed to our understanding of people's intuitive reasoning and its effect on self-interest. In contrast to the majority view on the relationship between System 1 and people's self-interest, they hold that people intuitively cooperate and only act selfishly when given more time to deliberate. Therefore, incentives, by encouraging careful reflection and consideration and weakening people's automatic processing, may actually encourage "bad" behavior. Rand's 2016 meta-analysis on cooperation found support for the perverse effects of incentives because of their relationship to Systems 1 and 2 thinking: when people are using the intuitive mode of reasoning (System 1), they are more likely (17.3 percent) to have cooperative behaviors than when they use System 2 deliberative thinking.[50]

In a related field experiment Artavia et al. examined the effect of distance from a stranger on the willingness to help that person and reached a similar conclusion.[51] They showed that the closer the subject was to the stranger (in this case, someone who had lost a glove), the more willing he or she was to return that glove. Thus, subjects who had less time to think (because they were closer to the person in need) displayed more willingness to help. Similarly, in a work on heroism, interviews with people who had saved the lives of others revealed that the most common element of their experiences was the lack of time to think.[52]

Thus, according to these researchers, the crowding-out effect could be simply due to the effect of incentives in creating competitive environments that evoke System 2 deliberation, thereby reducing the strength of people's intuition to be cooperative; then it will only be through deliberation on the monetary aspects of people's decisions that cooperative behavior will increase. Economic incentives thus reduce pure cooperation stemming from the intuitive mode of thinking and emphasize more calculated motives. In a related argument, Vhos et al.[53] showed that the implicit effect of being aware of money is its ability to change a situation's social meaning, making it seem more competitive and less cooperative.

Although the approach of Rand and his colleagues contributes dramatically to the ability to predict the non-calculative approach to wrongdoing – suggesting that people have an intuitive desire to be cooperative and that treating everyone as potential wrongdoers will reduce this desire and move them to strategic cooperation effects – the main problem with the intuitive cooperation argument is the variation between people. Some people will just not be cooperative and enforcement mechanisms will need to be used. Is it possible for policy makers to know ex ante

---

[50]   Ibid.
[51]   Artavia-Mora, L., Bedi, A. S., & Rieger, M. (2017). Intuitive help and punishment in the field. *European Economic Review*, 92, 133–145.
[52]   Rand, D. G., & Epstein, Z. G. (2014). Risking your life without a second thought: Intuitive decision-making and extreme altruism. *PLoS ONE*, 9(10), e109687.
[53]   Vohs, K. D., Mead, N. L., & Goode, M. R. (2006). The psychological consequences of money. *Science*, 314(5802), 1154–1156.

whether and when it is more important to use enforcement mechanisms? Resolution of these enforcement dilemmas is discussed in Chapters 7 & 8 on enforcement dilemmas and the pluralistic effect of law.

3.2.4 *Deterrence and Pluralistic Effect of Incentives in Enforcement Contexts*

The basic economic model of deterrence is that people will engage in criminal behavior only when the expected utility from the crime surpasses a certain value, based on their rational analysis of the probability of being caught and the level of punishment to be levied. This idea has been developed into a mathematical motivational model that attempts to predict precisely when people will engage in unlawful behavior based on the severity and nature of the crime, the probability of being caught, the size of the punishment,[54] and the relevant characteristics of the identity of the offender.[55]

Within the literature, much attention has been given to whether deterrence actually works. The model had such an intuitive appeal that criminologists and sociologists in the 1960s and 1970s, who on other occasions challenged the simplicity of self-interest motivations postulated by economic theorists, conducted studies on the extent to which deterrence affected individuals' decisions to do wrongful actions.[56]

Interestingly, given the importance of incentives to criminal lawyers, empirical economists have made little progress in studying their influence in the criminal justice system. Data availability has constrained their ability to pinpoint the specific effect of incentives on the crime rate. Most studies have tried to relate changes in the severity and types of punishment to the number and types of offenses committed. One well-studied example is the 1982 change in the criminal law of California. Although Kessler and Levitt originally identified a reduction in the crime rate,[57] other researchers since reanalyzed the same data to show no such reduction.[58] A broader account of the measurement problems associated with deterrence can be seen in the work of Paternoster.[59]

[54] Tittle, C. R. (1977). Sanction fear and the maintenance of social order. *Social Forces*, 55(3), 579–596.
[55] Polinsky, A. M., & Shavell, S. (2007). The theory of public enforcement of law. *Handbook of Law and Economics* (Vol. 1, pp. 403–454). Philadelphia, PA: Elsevier.
[56] See, for example, Silberman, M. (1976). Toward a theory of criminal deterrence. *American Sociological Review*, 41(3), 442–461. See also Zimring et al., *supra* note 7; See Tittle, *supra* note 7.
[57] Kessler, D., & Levitt, S. D. (1999). Using sentence enhancements to distinguish between deterrence and incapacitation. *Journal of Law and Economics*, 42(S1), 343–364.
[58] Webster, C., Doob, A. N., & Zimring, F. E. (2006). Proposition 8 and crime rates in California: The case of the disappearing deterrent. *Criminology & Public Policy*, 5(3), 417–448.
[59] Paternoster, R. (1987). The deterrent effect of the perceived certainty and severity of punishment: A review of the evidence and issues. *Justice Quarterly*, 4(2), 173–217.

Many studies have shown that perceptions of the severity and likelihood of punishment have no effect on delinquent behavior.[60] Others have demonstrated, empirically, the limits of deterrence in explaining both self-reported and actual compliance.[61] From a different perspective that is more in line with the focus of this book, some researchers have suggested that deterrence does not work simply because people have little awareness of existing laws.[62] Therefore, deterrence's ineffectiveness could be explained on the grounds of cognition rather than on the grounds of motivation.

MacCoun and Reuter conducted a cross-national study showing that increases in the severity of punishment made no difference to the rate of marijuana use.[63] In contrast, other scholars have suggested that the insensitivity to punishment is limited only to some aspects of deterrence. A common argument within this body of literature is that people are more sensitive to the probability of detection than to the severity of punishment.[64] Some researchers have claimed that expressive effects of punishment – that is, how the punishment changes the social meaning of behavior – have more effect on reducing crime than does the punishment itself.[65] Other analyses, which reviewed much of the literature for and against deterrence, concluded that, when using the right measurements, deterrence can be an important policy tool.[66] In any case, as suggested in Chapter 1, one of the main limitations of deterrence, which is completely ignored by the literature, is that, for many forms of misconduct, people do not even recognize that their behavior is subject to punishment. Chapters 8, 9, and 11 revisit this limitation, proposing that we rethink the concept of deterrence by increasing the focus on detection, rather than punishment.

3.2.5 *Economic Incentives: The Example of Educational Achievement*

In addition to the effectiveness of detection and punishment as deterrents, there has been much discussion in the literature of the price effect of incentives in encouraging desirable behavior. This is in contrast to the focus of BE on misbehavior and its limited attention given to positive behaviors that states might be interested in

[60] Paternoster, R., & Iovanni, L. (1986). The deterrent effect of perceived severity: A reexamination. *Social Forces*, 64(3), 751–777.

[61] See Braithwaite & Makkai, *supra* note 8.   [62] See Robinson & Darley, *supra* note 9.

[63] MacCoun, R. J., & Reuter, P. (2001). *Drug war heresies: Learning from other vices, times, and places.* Cambridge: Cambridge University Press.

[64] Doob, A. N., & Webster, C. M. (2003). Sentence severity and crime: Accepting the null hypothesis. *Crime and Justice*, 30, 143–195.

[65] Gibbs, J. P. (1975). *Crime, punishment, and deterrence.* New York: Elsevier, p. 58.

[66] Nagin, D. S. (1998). Criminal deterrence research at the outset of the twenty-first century. *Crime and Justice*, 23, 1–42. See also the discussion in Chapter 7 on how meting out harsh punishment to fewer people can also create a process through which good people can find a justification to continue to feel good about themselves.

promoting. An arena in which one can readily assess the impact of economic incentives is educational achievement. Studies can measure quantitatively the long-term effects of incentives through the continuous measurement of students' progress. Gneezy et al. wrote the most rigorous analysis, which we examine here, paying particular attention to their findings that account for people's level of awareness of the incentives.[67] They found that incentives are effective in encouraging relatively simple behaviors that can be easily measured. For example, they report that incentives seem to yield stronger results in math achievement than in reading, although the difference may be because it is easier to measure progress in math. In addition, Rodriguez-Planas demonstrated that incentives alone are not enough to bring about major changes in grades but must be combined with additional regulatory tools such as monitoring.[68]

One way to reduce the crowding-out effect of price incentives is to aim them at the family as a whole, rather than only at the students. Focusing on the family reduces the possibility of students' paying increased attention to their schoolwork solely because of the individual rewards they will receive.[69]

Another important caveat is related to the differential effect of incentives on different population segments. This aligns with one of the most fundamental arguments of the book – the damage from a one-policy-fits-all approach. Leuven et al. showed that incentives are more effective with students who were successful in their first year than with students who performed poorly in their first year.[70] Similarly, Bettinger found that incentives work best for students who were already doing well in school.[71]

Along those lines, research by Levitt et al. found that, for effects of incentives on academic achievement to be sustainable, they need to address multiple aspects of the relevant behavior.[72] Gneezy et al. concluded their analysis of the effect of incentives on academic achievement by noting, "The current evidence on the effects of financial incentives in education indicates moderate short-run positive effects on some subgroups of students, at least while the incentives are in place."[73]

[67] See Gneezy et al., *supra* note 15.
[68] Rodríguez-Planas, N. (2010). Mentoring, educational services, and economic incentives: Longer-term evidence on risky behaviors from a randomized trial. Available at http://ftp.iza.org/dp4968.pdf.
[69] Behrman, J. R., Sengupta, P., & Todd, P. (2005). Progressing through PROGRESA: An impact assessment of a school subsidy experiment in rural Mexico. *Economic Development and Cultural Change*, 54(1), 237–275. See also Schultz, T. P. (2001). School subsidies for the poor: Evaluating the Mexican Progresa Poverty Program. Center Discussion Paper.
[70] Leuven, E., Oosterbeek, H., & Klaauw, B. (2010). The effect of financial rewards on students' achievement: Evidence from a randomized experiment. *Journal of the European Economic Association*, 8(6), 1243–1265.
[71] Bettinger, E. P. (2012). Paying to learn: The effect of financial incentives on elementary school test scores. Review of Economics and Statistics, 94(3), 686–698.
[72] See Gneezy et al., *supra* note 15. See also Levitt, S. D., List, J. A., & Sadoff, S. (2016). *The effect of performance-based incentives on educational achievement: Evidence from a randomized experiment* (No. w22107). National Bureau of Economic Research.
[73] See Gneezy et al., *supra* note 15.

This concept of the durability of the effect of incentives is indeed a major policy concern that affects the choice of legal instrument. For example, in an analysis of the effects of incentives on smoking cessation, Donatelle et al. argue, "Studies on incentives for smoking cessation suggests that extrinsic motivation can enhance short-term cessation and reduction."[74] Their overall conclusion is that "large enough, well-specified and well-targeted incentives have documented support in changing the effect of behavior in both the short and medium term but with somewhat less clear effect on the long term."

3.3 BEYOND SELF-INTEREST: FAIRNESS, MORALITY, AND LEGITIMACY

Until now, this chapter has focused on understanding incentives and deterrence, taking into account the crowding-out effect and the impact of limited awareness of "good people" of the moral and legal meaning of their behavior. The main "beyond self-interest" alternative to deterrence, which we examine in the context of its effectiveness with regard to good people, is related to concepts of morality, legitimacy, and fairness and alternative compliance motivations.[75]

The question of whether humans are fundamentally good or evil dates back to the Book of Genesis in the Hebrew Bible and continues to this day. In social psychology, Batson[76] and Cialdini[77] have been engaged in an ongoing debate over the motivations for prosocial behavior. According to Bateson's empathy-altruism hypothesis, prosocial behavior emanates from genuine empathy toward the target of the behavior, whereas the experience of personal distress leads to self-protective behaviors and disengagement from the target. Cialdini et al.[78] have challenged this model, claiming that, to some extent, many if not all prosocial behaviors are based on egotistical motivations. Some of these motivations are more apparent, such as an immediate material gain from the behavior, and others are more implicit, such as self-expansive motivations and the motivation to uphold important social values.

---

[74]   Donatelle, R. J., Hudson, D., Dobie, S., Goodall, A., Hunsberger, M., & Oswald, K. (2004). Incentives in smoking cessation: Status of the field and implications for research and practice with pregnant smokers. *Nicotine & Tobacco Research*, 6(Suppl 2), S163–S179, quote at S167.

[75]   Cummings, R. G., Martinez-Vazquez, J., McKee, M., & Torgler, B. (2009). Tax morale affects tax compliance: Evidence from surveys and an artefactual field experiment. *Journal of Economic Behavior & Organization*, 70(3), 447–457.

[76]   Batson, C. D. (1987). Prosocial motivation: Is it ever truly altruistic? *Advances in Experimental Social Psychology*, 20, 65–122.

[77]   Cialdini, R. B. (1991). Altruism or egoism? That is (still) the question. *Psychological Inquiry*, 2(2), 124–126.

[78]   Cialdini, R. B., Brown, S. L., Lewis, B. P., Luce, C., & Neuberg, S. L. (1997). Reinterpreting the empathy–altruism relationship: When one into one equals oneness. *Journal of Personality and Social Psychology*, 73(3), 481.

A similar debate about the sources of resentment toward injustice has emerged in the sociology literature between scholars such as Mansbridge[79] and Sugden.[80] This scholarship has also drawn attention to implicit processes involved in people's attitudes toward various social institutions. For example, according to Mansbridge, the main proof that preferences cannot be explained solely on instrumental grounds is that certain unjust activities seem to intuitively trigger emotions of resentment. Sugden, in contrast, has argued that there is no need to incorporate vague, abstract concepts, because values and frustration of expectations are sufficient to explain feelings of resentment.

One of the richest areas of research into people's motivations to obey the law is payment of taxes.[81] Schwartz and Orleans randomly assigned a group of taxpayers to a treatment that made salient the fear of punishment (in our terminology, deterrence).[82] Another group was assigned to a treatment that made salient elements of morality, in which they were reminded of the good purposes to which tax revenues are put in the United States (in our terminology, most closely related to justice and fairness). The dependent variable was the change in reported income taxes paid between the year before and the year after the treatment. Although they showed that both conditions did have a positive effect (compared to a control group), those in the second treatment had a greater increase in the amount of taxes paid. Although this study showed the positive impact of compliance by convincing people that their actions are socially beneficial, as opposed to just frightening them,[83] Kagan has shown that the most important factor predicting tax compliance was the ability of authorities to monitor individuals' income on which they were required to pay taxes.[84] These studies, while increasing the ability to compare different compliance motivations, have done little to explore the effect of different motivations on people's awareness of the meaning of what they do. In other words, it is not clear from such research whether the different compliance approaches have any effect on how people understand what they do. Chapters 7 and 11 further explore the connection between compliance motivation and legal awareness.

[79] Mansbridge, J. J. (Ed.). (1990). *Beyond self-interest.* Chicago: University of Chicago Press.

[80] Sugden, R. (1989). Spontaneous order. *Journal of Economic Perspectives*, 3(4), 85–97.

[81] Kagan, R. A., Why do we pay our taxes? Revisiting Red Schwartz's "On Legal Sanctions." Unpublished Manuscript [file with the author].

[82] Schwartz, R. D., & Orleans, S. (1967). On legal sanctions. *University of Chicago Law Review*, 34(2), 274–300.

[83] Obviously while the demonstration here is high in its external validity, the comparison between the two treatment groups is problematic, since it might be easier to build the case for social duty in the context of an interview than to frighten people about the possibility of punishment.

[84] Kagan, R. A. (1989). On the visibility of income tax law violations. In J. A. Roth & J. T. Scholz (Eds.). *Taxpayer Compliance*, Vol. 1: *An Agenda for Research.* Philadelphia: University of Pennsylvania Press, pp. 76–125.

3.3.1 The Limited Discussion of "Self" in Self-interest

To continue the discussion of the works of Sugden, Mansbridge, Bateson, and Cialdini and given that the focus of this book is on noncompliance triggered by non-calculative individuals, it is important to understand how economists have discussed the role of the self in self-interest. The assumptions underlying their research are that people know what is good for them and what is good for others and that they choose their actions based on a cost-benefit analysis that sometimes factors in the well-being of others in the benefit.

For the most part, behavioral economics has focused on self-interest as representing the materialistic opposite motivation to fairness, which is shown to be intrinsic and non-instrumental. However, the behavioral approach to law has ignored the possibility that non-materialistic self-interest might make people more corrupt rather than less and that non-materialistic self-interested mechanisms are responsible for various modifications in the ethical behavior of people. To protect their self-view, people might end up doing more harm than good.[85]

For example, the study by Guth et al. on ultimatum games is one of the earliest experimental accounts of people behaving not according to a sense of fairness, but rather out of self-interest.[86] They showed that people usually offer only 40–50 percent of the overall reward to their partner, even though the lower the offer, the increased likelihood of its rejection.[87] Fehr also has suggested that much of the variation in the effect of other-regarding behaviors (ORBs) could be explained by context. For example, in competitive markets, people do not seem to demonstrate ORBs, whereas they do in simple experimental contexts such as the dictator and the ultimatum games. In addition, there is still a great deal of evidence to show that some people will not promote the well-being of others, even in settings that are not competitive. Much of the cooperation in various important societal institutions is due to the threat of sanctions.

In their review of various games, Fehr and Schmidt found little evidence for the effect of demographic variables on trust games, making results obtained from student samples as reliable as results from the general population. However, studies done by Roth et al.[88] and many others have suggested an aggregate variation among populations in different countries in behavior in ultimatum games, in preferences

---

[85] See development of this point in the work on the corrupting but different self-interest of the scientists vs. executives: Feldman, Y., Gauthier, R., & Schuler, T. (2013). Curbing misconduct in the pharmaceutical industry: Insights from behavioral ethics and the behavioral approach to law. *Journal of Law and Medical Ethics*, 41(3), 620–628.

[86] Güth, W., Schmittberger, R., & Schwarze, B. (1982). An experimental analysis of ultimatum bargaining. *Journal of Economic Behavior & Organization*, 3(4), 367–388.

[87] Camerer, C. (2003). *Behavioral game theory: Experiments in strategic interaction*. Princeton: Princeton University Press.

[88] Roth, A. E., Prasnikar, V., Okuno-Fujiwara, M., & Zamir, S. (1991). Bargaining and market behavior in Jerusalem, Ljubljana, Pittsburgh, and Tokyo: An experimental study. *American Economic Review*, 81(5), 1068–1095.

on the individual level – for example, between altruistic and spiteful – and between reciprocal or inequity-averse individuals. Interestingly, they view such individuals as conditional cooperators who will cooperate to the extent that they think that the other will cooperate.

Fehr and Gachter showed that the partners' ability to punish increases cooperation dramatically.[89] This suggests that although self-interest might predict that no participant would pay the price needed to punish, people still choose to punish, and consequently, individuals will act more cooperatively. To explain this behavior, they have proposed the concept of *altruistic punishment*: people will engage in costly activity just to punish others who behave in an unfair way. This research assumes that once it can be shown that the punishment is not promoting the self-interest of the punisher, then it is being done for altruistic purposes. Thus, if an individual engages in costly activity or punishment that does not serve his or her own self-interest, no other unconscious motive is looked at to explain motives, and the behavior is defined as interest free or as having an altruistic motivation.[90]

The main problem with these studies of people's decisions to punish or to cooperate is that they assume that people are fully aware of when they are being cooperative. The "Law of Good People" paradigm seems to suggest that, in many cases, the opposite is true. Even the meanings of being cooperative and of being objective are far from clear. For example, consider researchers who review papers of fellow academics as part of their job. Do they know how objective they are being in their assessment? Are those assessments influenced by considerations of their own career and advancement prospects? When being cooperative means giving an objective evaluation, do people know how cooperative they are, given the objectivity bias?

3.3.2 *Awareness of Fairness*

As suggested above, fairness is widely recognized as an important determinant of human behavior that can sometimes overcome self-interest.[91] The first step in discussing fairness is to clarify the nature of the concept, especially with regard to the relationship between procedural and distributive justice.[92] *Distributive justice* focuses on the substance of the law and claims that people will comply more when they think

[89] Fehr, E., & Gachter, S. (2000). Fairness and retaliation: The economics of reciprocity. *Journal of Economic Perspectives*, 14(3), 159–181.

[90] Fehr, E., & Falk, A. (2002). Psychological foundations of incentives. *European Economic Review*, 46 (4), 687–724. See also again, this article does not mention fear at all as the source for prosocial behavior but as the opposite perspective of human motivation.

[91] Fehr, E., & Schmidt, K. M. (1999). A theory of fairness, competition, and cooperation. *Quarterly Journal of Economics*, 114(3), 817–868. See also Kahneman, D., Knetsch, J. L., & Thaler, R. (1986). Fairness as a constraint on profit seeking: Entitlements in the market. *American Economic Review*, 76 (4), 728–741.

[92] For a recent critical theoretical discussion of the interaction between fairness and the actual power of law, see Schauer, F. (2015). *The force of law*. Cambridge, MA: Harvard University Press.

the law provides what they are entitled to or that guilty individuals get the punishment they deserve.[93] Thus, there is a marked similarity between the effect of morality and a belief in distributive justice on one's motivation to comply.

In contrast, *procedural justice* focuses on how decisions are made in terms of neutrality and voice, regardless of the content of the decision or the law. It is one of the most-studied concepts in the psycho-legal scholarship. Starting from the work of scholars such as Thibaut and Walker[94] and Lind and Tyler,[95] a list of requirements has been developed for people to perceive procedural justice; among them are consistency, accuracy, and representativeness. Even without reference to its effect on legitimacy, the concept of procedural justice can be seen as having an effect on both extrinsic and intrinsic motivations to obey the law. One of the leading scholars to explore the contribution of procedural justice to legal compliance is Tom Tyler. In his widely cited book, *Why People Obey the Law*, he suggested that procedural fairness, the way in which people are treated by authorities, is the main motivation for legal compliance.[96]

Another conception of fairness in psychology and organizational behavior scholarship (in contrast to economics[97]) is *interactional justice*.[98] Hamilton argued that many studies in organizational settings suggest that, in fact, both procedural justice and distributive justice predict general notions of fairness and that they are substitute factors.[99] That is, when the outcome is seen as fair, the fairness of the process becomes less important, and where the outcome is not seen as fair but the procedure

[93]   Darley, J. M., Carlsmith, K. M., & Robinson, P. H. (2001). The ex ante function of the criminal law. *Law and Society Review*, 165–190.

[94]   Thibaut, J. W., & Walker, L. (1975). *Procedural justice: A psychological analysis*. Hillsdale, NJ: Erlbaum Associates.

[95]   Lind, E. A., & Tyler, T. R. (1988). *The social psychology of procedural justice*. New York: Springer Science & Business Media.

[96]   See Tyler, *supra* note 5. *See also* Darley, J. M., Tyler, T., & Bilz, K. (2003). Enacting justice: The interplay of individual and institutional perspectives. In M.A. Hogg & J. Cooper (Eds.), *Sage Handbook of Social Psychology* (pp. 458–476). Thousand Oaks, CA: Sage.

[97]   This is not to say that economists do not differentiate between distributive and procedural fairness. Due to influence from social psychology, this type of research is fairly common. For an example of a paper focusing solely on the distributive aspect of fairness, see Corchón, L. C., & Iturbe-Ormaetxe, I. (2001). A proposal to unify some concepts in the theory of fairness. *Journal of Economic Theory*, 101(2), 540–571. For an example of a paper that focuses on the procedural aspect of fairness in economics, see Anand, P. (2001). Procedural fairness in economic and social choice: Evidence from a survey of voters. *Journal of Economic Psychology*, 22(2), 247–270. Nonetheless, economists, especially in the context of game theory, focus on a general notion of fairness that is sometimes referred to as reciprocity or morality. Those views of fairness are neither distributive nor procedural. See, for example, Fehr, E., & Schmidt, K. M. (2000). Fairness, incentives, and contractual choices. *European Economic Review*, 44(4), 1057–1068.

[98]   This is a concept attributed to the work of Bies. The meaning of the concept could be seen as being relevant to issues such as respect and kind treatment by the other party or authority. Bies, R. J. (1997). The predicament of injustice, the management of moral outrage. In E. Romanelli, L. L. Cummings, & B. M. Staw (Eds.), Research in organizational behavior (Vol. 9, pp. 289–319). Cheltenham: Edward Elgar.

[99]   Hamilton, R. W. (2006). When the means justify the ends: Effects of observability on the procedural fairness and distributive fairness of resource allocations. *Journal of Behavioral Decision Making*, 19(4), 303–320.

is, people are still satisfied overall with the process, and their general notion of fairness remains positive.

Fairness is a concept of interest not only in psychology but also in economics. In recent years, economists have studied fairness extensively,[100] recognizing its importance to many domains of market behavior.[101] Nonetheless, the enthusiasm of economists for the predictive power of fairness has been constantly challenged.[102]

3.3.3 Fairness and Compliance

Research on why people obey the law demonstrates the importance of non-instrumental motivations, such as individuals' desire for fairness, in accounting for compliance. Frank recognized moral motivation as a force that encourages people to defy narrow versions of rational choice theory and to make decisions that are either neutral or contrary to their material self-interest.[103] Much of the original behavioral economics literature examined how concepts of fairness may be employed to encourage individuals to overcome their own self-interest (see also Shavell[104]). More broadly, economists such as Cooter have argued that the law can cultivate social norms, which in turn serve as intrinsic motivation for compliance with the law.[105] Cooter's work demonstrates the growing recognition among law and economics scholars of the superiority of compliance triggered by intrinsic motivation, thereby reducing reliance on monitoring and enforcement.[106] The unique contribution of morality to legal compliance has been demonstrated in various legal contexts, even in areas that are usually viewed as economic, such as paying taxes.[107]

Of the tools that give states their legitimacy, some rationales are more useful from an informative perspective than from a moral one. When states implement laws with the aim of causing people to change their behavior, people sometimes comply not because they believe that the state is enforcing morality but rather because they

---

[100]　See Jones, D. N., & Mann, P. C. (2001). The fairness criterion in public utility regulation: Does fairness still matter? *Journal of Economic Issues*, 35(1), 153–172.

[101]　See Fehr & Schmidt, *supra* note 91.

[102]　See, for example, Kagel, J. H., & Wolfe, K. W. (2001). Tests of fairness models based on equity considerations in a three-person ultimatum game. *Experimental Economics*, 4(3), 203–219. See also Rutström, E. E., & Williams, M. B. (2000). Entitlements and fairness: An experimental study of distributive preferences. *Journal of Economic Behavior & Organization*, 43(1), 75–89, demonstrating a use of a distribution games setting in which almost all individuals chose the income distribution that maximized their own income.

[103]　Frank, R. H. (1988). *Passions within reason: The strategic role of the emotions*. New York: W. W. Norton.

[104]　Shavell, S. (2002). Law versus morality as regulators of conduct. *American Law and Economics Review*, 4(2), 227–257.

[105]　Cooter, R. (2000). *The strategic constitution*. Princeton: Princeton University Press.

[106]　See Feldman, *supra* note 6.

[107]　Wenzel, M. (2005). Misperceptions of social norms about tax compliance: From theory to intervention. *Journal of Economic Psychology*, 26(6), 862–883.

believe that the state has superior knowledge than they have, either regarding scientific facts or the prevailing practices in a given region. The informational account's primary assumption about human motivation is that individuals look to regulators to be convinced of the wisdom of engaging in constructive and efficient behavior while abstaining from destructive behavior. Thus, the legislative process aggregates information to produce a decision that is superior to the opinion of any individual legislator. As a result, if a legislative body prohibits public smoking, people may be less likely to smoke publicly because the process of enacting the legislation leads people to update their beliefs.[108] Kagan et al. take a somewhat different view of informative functioning in an environmental context.[109] They show how the law clarifies the boundary between activity that is harmful to the environment and activity that should be tolerated. For example, to encourage behavior that combats global warming, informative campaigns are waged that use scientific knowledge to increase people's propensity to engage in protective actions.[110] An additional context in which the substantive focus of the policy maker is aimed at information processing is in traffic laws. Here, too, as with deterrence, the procedures through which law gains legitimacy mostly focus on deliberative processes such as information, voice, and transparency, rather than on more nuanced processes through which people might come to sense that a certain institution is fair. The next section presents non-deliberative aspects of fairness that might decrease situational wrongdoing but may not be salient to people responding to survey-based questions in projects such as Tyler's *Why People Obey the Law*, in which people actively remember how they were treated by the authorities.

3.3.4 *Moral Judgment and Moral Identity*

As suggested earlier, one of the limitations of the research about the role of morality (in its current view that focuses on choice) is the notion that moral identity is mostly a non-deliberate process. For example, Reynolds and Ceranic have suggested that the predictive power of moral judgment, which more closely relates to explicit reasoning, and of moral identity, which relates to implicit measures of reasoning, is independent.[111] Furthermore, in areas where moral consensus was low, moral identity was found to be a better predictor of moral behavior. Indeed, there is an

---

[108] This model also targets the socially oriented individual discussed in the next section. Dharmapala, D., & McAdams, R. H. (2003). The Condorcet jury theorem and the expressive function of law: A theory of informative law. *American Law and Economics Review*, 5(1), 1–31.

[109] Kagan, R. A., Gunningham, N., & Thoronton, D. (2003), Explaining corporate environmental performance: how does regulation matter?. *Law & Society Review*, 37 (1), 51–90.

[110] LaTour, M. S., & Zahra, S. A. (1988). Fear appeals as advertising strategy: Should they be used? *Journal of Services Marketing*, 2(4), 5–14. See also Tay, Richard (2005), The effectiveness of enforcement and publicity campaigns on serious crashes involving young male drivers: Are drink driving and speeding similar? *Accident Analysis & Prevention*, 37 (5), 922–929.

[111] Reynolds, S. J., & Ceranic, T. L. (2007). The effects of moral judgment and moral identity on moral behavior: An empirical examination of the moral individual. *Journal of Applied Psychology*, 92(6), 1610.

increased recognition that to understand the effect of morality and fairness, one needs to account not only for explicit but also for implicit measures of reasoning. This is usually seen as being related to implicit reasoning (even though in studies on moral identity, both the identity and measured behavior were self-reported and thus relied on deliberative thinking).

An important attempt to conceptualize the role of morality was made by the economists Griffith and Goldfarb.[112] Their threefold model of fairness, norms, and morality suggests the following function of morality: (1) morality works as a decision rule[113] that influences decisions in complex environments[114]; (2) as imposed by society, morality constrains the individual's abilities to maximize self-interest[115]; and (3) morality manifests as preferences through the concept of interdependent utility functions.[116]

3.3.5 *Legitimacy*

The legitimacy of the law is distinct from the moral content of the law. When an individual believes that the sovereign authority is entitled to create rules, he or she will obey these rules because this is what good citizens do, regardless of the law's content.[117] According to many accounts of legitimacy, the content of the law seems to be secondary to the perception that the law was formulated and executed with full authority. Given that procedural justice is seen by many as the main indicator of legitimacy, there is room to make the distinction between the content of the law and the procedure through which it is enacted and enforced. Many accounts claim that when people obey the law due to an obligation, rather than because of a belief in its morality, they are more likely

[112]   Griffith, W. B., & Goldfarb, R. S. (1991). Amending the economist's rational egoist model to include moral values and norms, Part 1: The problem. In K. J. Koford, & J. B. Miller (Eds.), *Social norms and economic institutions*, pp. 85–95. Ann Arbor: University of Michigan Press.

[113]   Though, see, for example, Platow, M. J., Mills, D., & Morrison, D. (2000). The effects of social context, source fairness, and perceived self-source similarity on social influence: A self-categorisation analysis. *European Journal of Social Psychology*, 30(1), 69–81, which argues that fairness of the source itself could not explain a change in behavior without taking into account aspects of social categorization.

[114]   Ullmann-Margalit, E. (2015). The emergence of norms (Vol. 11). New York: Oxford University Press. Griffith and Goldfarb treat morality and fairness interchangeably. In psychology, morals, norms, and fairness are defined differently; however, the rationale behind this taxonomy seems to hold true for both concepts.

[115]   See Kahneman et al., *supra* note 91. See also Mueller, D. C. (1986). Rational egoism versus adaptive egoism as fundamental postulate for a descriptive theory of human behavior. *Public Choice*, 51 (1), 3–23.

[116]   Sen, A., & Körner, S. (1974). Choice, ordering and morality. In S. Korner (Ed.), *Practical reason*. Oxford: Blackwell. Interesting qualitative work was conducted by Monroe, K. R. (1998). *The heart of altruism: Perceptions of a common humanity*. Princeton: Princeton University Press. She demonstrates that entrepreneurs were less likely to discuss non-materialistic incentives than were philanthropists and World War II heroes. Naturally these differences might be attributed to some social expectations – of what your main motivations for giving charity could be, and so on. Nonetheless, it raises an interesting perspective that the law might need to consider the likelihood that these particular target populations will use internal motivations.

[117]   Scholz, J. T., & Pinney, N. (1995). Duty, fear, and tax compliance: The heuristic basis of citizenship behavior. *American Journal of Political Science*, 490–512.

to obey the law, even when they do not fully agree with its content.[118] However, other scholars make a stronger claim for the role of values in legitimacy,[119] noting the few differences between the demands of morality and of citizenship.[120]

3.4 ARE DIFFERENT COMPLIANCE MODELS MUTUALLY EXCLUSIVE?

In a discussion of the interplay of the different enforcement mechanisms to address erroneous and situational wrongdoers, it is important to ask what the interaction is between the two primary models of compliance: deterrence and nonmaterial motivations. Clearly, if deterrence is likely to change not only the costs of doing wrong but also the meaning of wrongdoing, then its effect on the two types of wrongdoers could be understood in more than one way.

Non-formal models of enforcement are gaining increasing prominence for two reasons: limitations in the ability of law enforcement agencies to monitor compliance with the law and the high costs associated with the law enforcement process. There is a growing recognition that formal enforcement alone cannot explain why people obey the law.[121] In other words, if law enforcement agencies cannot monitor the behavior of each individual, why do the great majority of people obey the law?

Many empirical studies show that informal controls play a greater role in explaining human behavior than previously thought. Several studies by Meier and Johnson show the increased effectiveness of non-formal controls compared to formal legal threats in yielding compliance.[122] For example, they found that social approval is a stronger

[118]   Kelman, H. C. (2001). The role of national identity in conflict resolution. *Social Identity, Intergroup Conflict, and Conflict Reduction*, 3, 187.

[119]   Strauss, D. A. (2005). Reply: Legitimacy and obedience. *Harvard Law Review*, 118(6), 1854–1866. See also Tyler, T. R., & Fagan, J. (2008). Legitimacy and cooperation: Why do people help the police fight crime in their communities. *Ohio State Journal of Criminal Law*, 6, 231.

[120]   Tyler, T. R., & Darley, John M. (2000). Building a law-abiding society: Taking public views about morality and the legitimacy of legal authorities into account when formulating substantive law. *Hofstra Law Review*, 28, 707.

[121]   For a seminal empirical work discussing the limits of deterrence in explaining both self-reported and actual compliance, see Braithwaite & Makkai, Testing an expected utility model of corporate deterrence. A more recent theoretical discussion is suggested by Posner, E. A. (2000). Law and social norms: The case of tax compliance. *Virginia Law Review*, 86, 1781–1819, discussing the "problem of tax compliance" – how can it be that such a high percentage of taxes are collected while the probability* size of sanction is so low. In attempting to answer this question, he returns to his famous model of signaling. By paying taxes, individuals signal to their surroundings that they belong to the good type of people. A range of alternative explanations account for tax compliance, such as citizenship and legitimacy of government that we refer to in the following sections. See also MacCoun, R., & Reuter, P. (2001). Evaluating alternative cannabis regimes. *British Journal of Psychiatry*, 178(2), 123–128. for a cross-national study that demonstrates, among other things, that increase or decrease in the punishment makes no difference to the rate of marijuana use.

[122]   Meier, R. F., & Johnson, W. T. (1977). Deterrence as social control: The legal and extralegal production of conformity. *American Sociological Review*, 42(2), 292–304. See also Hollinger, R. C., & Clark, J. P. (1983). Deterrence in the workplace: Perceived certainty, perceived severity, and employee theft. *Social Forces*, 62(2), 398–418. There are studies that suggest that in some contexts non-formal controls are doomed to fail; see MacKenzie, D. L., & Li, S. D. (2002). The impact of formal and informal social controls on the criminal activities of probationers. *Journal of Research in Crime and Delinquency*, 39(3), 243–276.

predictor of intention to engage in criminal activity than formal controls such as the likelihood of being punished. In a study of prison inmates, Anderson has shown that, for the most part, prisoners were unaware of the punishment they could receive for their crimes before they were apprehended and therefore concluded that severity of punishment could not be a deterrent to criminal behavior.[123] As Griffith and Goldfarb argue, "it is impossible to imagine that morality is being supportive solely by economic incentives,"[124] As suggested in chapter 1, the law of good people theme suggests that another reason for the limited effect of punishment size, is related to behavioral ethics mechanism which prevent many people to even recognize themselves as doing anything which deserves punishment.

3.4.1 *Top-Down Social Enforcement*[125]

Using experimental surveys, Lobel and I examined the behavior of individuals when confronting unlawful conduct in the workplace.[126] By further exploring the interplay between internal and external enforcement motivations, these experiments provide novel insights into the comparative advantages of systems that incentivize compliance and social enforcement. Our findings offer important practical and theoretical advances, including establishing the existence of the "holier than thou" effect in the legal context, illuminating gender differences among social enforcers, and explaining the importance of framing misconduct and legal mechanisms for better compliance.

The significance of social enforcement and regulatory incentives to encourage reporting of noncompliance is clear, yet there is little knowledge of the comparative effectiveness of the myriad of regulatory tools that provide such incentives. Bringing together the various developments in incentivizing social enforcement, our study of whistle-blowing provides an ideal context for studying the interplay between individual compliance behavior, the organizational setting in which it is detected, and the regulatory regime that defines the contours of legality.[127]

---

[123]   Anderson, D. A. (2002). The deterrence hypothesis and picking pockets at the pickpocket's hanging. *American Law and Economics Review*, 4(2), 295–313. There is some problem of adverse selection here, since there are an unknown number of people who did not commit any crime whom he did not put in his sample (he mentioned that on p. 297). On the other hand, he rightly says that most people have no idea what the fine for jaywalking is, let alone whether there have been any changes in the amount of the fine.

[124]   Amending the economist's "Rational Egoist," model to include moral values and norms in K. J., & Miller, J. B. (Eds.). (1991). *Social norms and economic institutions*, pp. 39–50 Ann Arbor: University of Michigan Press. See also Gondwe, D. K. (1986). Neoclassical political economy: The analysis of rent-seeking and DUP activities. *Southern Economic Journal*, 52(3), 883–885. Nowhere is this statement truer than in the case of trade secrets, in which the employer's ability to supervise the behavior of his employees in his new company is very limited

[125]   This section focuses on the formal framework of social norms and is based on my work with Lobel on the role of social enforcement as supplementary to formal enforcement.

[126]   See Feldman & Lobel, *supra* note 13.

[127]   Miceli, M. P., & Near, J. P. (1992). *Blowing the whistle: The organizational and legal implications for companies and employees*. New York: Lexington Books.

Surprisingly, despite the widespread recognition of the importance of social enforcement and the potential application of different incentives in regulatory policy, questions about these fundamental interactions between individual and organizational factors have received relatively little research attention.[128] If policy makers knew which legal mechanisms trigger reporting action, a more tailored approach could be designed to provide employees with the needed motivation.

More broadly, the ongoing debate about the desirability and effectiveness of self-regulatory approaches and their ability to replace traditional command-and-control regulation is central to socio-legal theory and practice. At the broadest level, more knowledge about the behavior of individuals in a social enforcement context is an important scholarly contribution to the interdisciplinary study of motivation, cooperation, norms, and institutional design.

3.4.2 *Interaction of Deterrence and Other Motivational Models*

Even though the models discussed thus far differ from one another in many ways, it is difficult to separate their effects. Adding to this complexity is the variation in people's mind-sets with regard to the law, which reduces even more the ability to provide guidance to policy makers on the approach they should take. Deterrence models focus on the framing of the law: legal policy makers only need to prime certain aspects of the regulations that would trigger compliance, but no real change in legal policy is required. Other models require that the law be perceived by the public as legitimate, and hence a broader institutional change is required. Finally, some models, such as the informative and the social models, tend to be context specific; therefore, the required behavior by the regulator will more likely apply only to a specific law or group of laws. Thus, legal policy makers who are interested in being responsive to different compliance motivations must not only emphasize and communicate different aspects of the law but may also need to bring about a broader institutional adjustment. This task becomes even more complex given the wealth of empirical research that suggests crossover between the models. Clearly when the law can affect behavior motivated by more than one mechanism, its effects are harder to predict. To take into account several motivations when shaping regulation, the legal policy maker may need to speak with many voices. Because there is a limited ability to predict ex ante the compliance motivations of specific individuals, designing responsive regulation is especially difficult. The question remains whether legal policy can really react to each of these motivations without altering the efficacy of the other motivations.

Deterrence, which seems to be a clear-cut regulatory tool that is supposed to interact solely with the calculative individual, has been shown to interact with other models as well. Paternoster et al. showed that perceived punishment is a significant

---

[128] Miceli, M. P., & Near, J. P. (2005). Standing up or standing by: What predicts blowing the whistle on organizational wrongdoing? In J. J. Martocchio & H. Liao (Eds.), *Research in personnel and human resources management* (pp. 95–136). Bingley, UK: Emerald Group Publishing.

predictor of an act's perceived morality.[129] This suggests that formal deterrence is needed to maintain the credibility of informal sanctions. Similarly, in the previously mentioned experimental setting, Schwartz and Orleans demonstrated in the context of tax compliance that people in a "fear-of-punishment" group were more likely to feel a moral duty to pay taxes than those in a control group.[130]

One of the most intuitive demonstrations of mutual influence among the compliance models is the interrelationship between the informative model and other models. For example, the information expressed in the substance of the law (i.e., smoking is unhealthy) is likely to be relevant to individuals who are socially driven (because most people want to be healthy), morally driven (harm of secondary smoking), and citizenship oriented (the government has legitimacy to protect the health of its citizens). According to many accounts, legitimacy is related not only to justice principles[131] but is also embodied in the reason-driven individual's recognition of the importance of compliance to the social order of society, regardless of the content of the law.[132]

Kelman and Hamilton have suggested a typology of compliance motivations that illustrates the mutual influences of legitimacy and non-materialistic models.[133] A classical type of mutual influence is rule orientation, in which the fear of punishment is the main legitimizing power of government sovereignty. Rule-oriented legitimacy is also related to identification with authority. Lastly, value-oriented legitimacy is related to shared morality and therefore requires examination of the moral content of the law.

De Pauiseau et al. recently conducted a series of experiments with both students and laypeople that compared the main theories of legal compliance and found evidence for the work of both intrinsic and extrinsic motivations.[134] Both detection probability and self-control had significant effects, whereas legitimacy was reduced to an insignificant effect. This work adds more evidence that formal mechanisms are not mutually exclusive. For example, they found an interaction effect between legitimacy and detection probability: those for whom the salience of legitimacy considerations was high did not have an increased probability to obey the law when the probability of being detected decreased.[135] However, when measured separately, self-control, legitimacy, and probability of detection were shown to each affect

[129]   Paternoster, R., Saltzman, L. E., Waldo, G. P., & Chiricos, T. G. (1983). Perceived risk and social control: Do sanctions really deter? *Law and Society Review*, 17(3), 457–479.

[130]   See Schwartz & Orleans, *supra* note 82.

[131]   Mueller, C. W., & Landsman, M. J. (2004). Legitimacy and justice perceptions. *Social Psychology Quarterly*, 67(2), 189–202.

[132]   Suchman, M. C. (1995). Managing legitimacy: Strategic and institutional approaches. *Academy of Management Review*, 20(3), 571–610.

[133]   Kelman, H. C., & Hamilton, V. L. (1989). *Crimes of obedience: Toward a social psychology of authority and responsibility.* New Haven: Yale University Press.

[134]   Waubert de Puiseau, B., Glöckner, A., & Towfigh, E. V. (2016). Comparing and Integrating Theories of Law Obedience: Deterrence, Legitimacy, and Self-control. Unpublished manuscript, University of Hagen, Hagen, Germany.

[135]   Compare with the work Feldman & Lobel, *supra* note 13, at 1151. See also Feldman & Perez, *supra* note 12.

people's self-reported intention to comply.[136] The effect of the likelihood of detection was much stronger than that of the severity of punishment, which was very small. This last finding goes well with the argument developed both in chapter 1 and 11 regarding the greater importance of detection for "good" people.

A similar mixture of influences can be shown with regard to procedural justice, which is also related to several models, in addition to its obvious association with legitimacy and the moral individual, as suggested earlier. According to Van Den Bos et al., procedural justice is a proxy used to evaluate the likelihood of one's achieving positive results, thus suggesting its relevance to the calculative individual.[137] Other accounts suggest that people use procedural justice considerations to evaluate their social role in the group, hinting toward their use by the socially sensitive individual.[138]

In sum, although these motivations can be separated conceptually, confining legal intervention to just one model is close to impossible. The dependency of the models on one another and their mutual influence make the regulatory challenges much greater.

3.5 A MULTIDIMENSIONAL APPROACH TO LEGAL COMPLIANCE

As reviewed in this chapter, theories of legal compliance and moral development have undergone an evolution in recent years. Beginning with the assumption that egotistic self-interest underlies social behavior, they are placing increasing emphasis on considerations of social responsibility, fairness, and altruistic motivations. This shift has moved self-interest, fear, and punishment to the sidelines of human motivation and suggests that when people are treated fairly by the authorities, they will be motivated to behave in a fair and equitable manner. Fear and punishment, according to this view, are counterproductive tools that hamper people's internal motivation and signal to them that they are not trustworthy.[139] As will be developed in later chapters, this argument is exacerbated when adopting the "Law of Good People" paradigm.

This view of moral and legal behavior tends to equate self-interest with fear and punishment-avoidant behaviors, which I argue is a very narrow and limited definition of self-interest that may lead to lower levels of legal compliance.[140] A more

---

[136]   Gottfredson, M. R., & Hirschi, T. (1990). *A general theory of crime*. Stanford: Stanford University Press.

[137]   Van den Bos, K. (2001). Fairness heuristic theory. *Theoretical and Cultural Perspectives on Organizational Justice*, 63.

[138]   Tyler, T. R., & Lind, E. A. (1992). A relational model of authority in groups. *Advances in Experimental Social Psychology*, 25, 115–191.

[139]   "Much of the existing literature on compliance focuses on the problem of deterrence. The goal of deterring evasion is usually sought through methods that create fear, for example, through increasing the probability of an audit or increasing the magnitude of a fine." Forest, A., & Sheffrin, S. M. (2002). Complexity and compliance: An empirical investigation. *National Tax Journal*, 55(1), 75–88.

[140]   Sethi, R., & Somanathan, E. (1996). The evolution of social norms in common property resource use. *American Economic Review*, 86(4), 766–788.

productive approach holds that social responsibility, fairness, and altruistic motivations operate in conjunction with self-interest because they seem to satisfy fundamental human needs. Although this book focuses on the "Law of Good People" paradigm, its aim is to create a new approach to encouraging legal compliance that focuses on a mind-set with regard to a particular legal context, rather than the personality of the individual.

In the shift from the recognition that people care only about themselves to the recognition that they also care about the fairness and the welfare of others, an important question has yet to be addressed: Why are people altruistic and why do they care about the welfare of others? According to many accounts in social psychology, altruistic behavior and social responsibility are mechanisms that validate important social values and maintain the cohesiveness of the in-group. Fairness and social responsibility also serve fundamental egotistical needs as psychological defense mechanisms. The dual-process models of behavior that differentiate explicit and implicit motivations and sources of behavior that are more immediate or proximal to one another show that the relationship between fear and compliance may be more complex than previously thought.

One of the premises underlying the pluralistic account of the law, as developed in chapter 7, is that upholding the law and social norms serves as a buffer of death anxiety and is therefore consistent with one's self-interest. One criticism of this assumption is that there is no evidence that self-interest is involved in the mechanism proposed. Moreover, one may argue that unconscious defensive processes cannot be considered to emanate from self-interest because people's awareness of what they need and desire is a conscious process. This view of self-interest is pervasive in both the economic and legal literatures, which have primarily focused on the rational and deliberate processes of decision making. However as discussed in Chapters 1 and 2, the psychological literature has long questioned the role of the conscious processes in goal-directed behaviors in general and in the promotion of self-interest in particular. Many studies show how the self operates through various focused and directed ways. For example, Wegner discusses the process through which people tend to infer a causal path between their own intention and behavior.[141] These studies demonstrate that the illusion of will is so strong that people engage in false inferences even when there is no logical way for the intention to contribute to the action. This finding strengthens the point that people are usually unaware of their true motivations and are likely to attribute their motivations to noble reasons when they are in reality based on selfish motives.[142]

---

[141] Perring, C. (2003). Review: Daniel M. Wegner, The Illusion of Conscious Will. *Philosophy in Review*, 23(4), 299–301. See also Dijksterhuis, A., & Bargh, J. A. (2001). The perception-behavior expressway: Automatic effects of social perception on social behavior. *Advances in Experimental Social Psychology*, 33, 1–40.

[142] Sanderson, C. A., & Darley, J. M. (2002). "I am moral, but you are deterred": Differential attributions about why people obey the law. *Journal of Applied Social Psychology*, 32(2), 375–405.

3.5.1 Relying on Intrinsic Motivations Can Be Problematic

The classical argument for the importance of understanding motivation in legal compliance is that intrinsic motivations for compliance have advantages over extrinsic motivations. It suggests that when people are motivated by intrinsic motivation and are aware to the meaning of their behavior, enforcement is not only cheaper but also might lead people to behave in ways that could not be achieved by mere deterrence. In many areas where behavior beyond compliance is desirable, there seems to be a clear advantage in activating intrinsic or non-instrumental motivations of human behavior.[143] Designing a law that will be viewed as just, reasonable, or legitimate by those who are its targets is likely to cause them to rely on their intrinsic motivation when complying with the law.[144] This classical view suffers, however, from several problems that are briefly addressed in this section.

First, individual and situational differences exist in the context of compliance motivation, as suggested earlier. Although it may be possible to adapt the regulation to the likely dominant motivation in any given situation, it is much harder to adapt the regulation *ex ante* to the motivations of different individuals. As long as some of the people are expected to be calculative, one cannot really avoid the use of instrumental sanctions, even if they are more costly.

Second, there is a gap between what people say motivates their compliance (mostly internal factors) and their perceptions of what motivates others (the fear of punishment) to obey the law.[145] According to the expressive model, people are willing to comply if they think that others will similarly comply; thus, policy makers have to take into account not only what motivates the individual but also what he or she *thinks* motivates others. This creates a paradoxical situation in which deterrence may need to be used not to motivate people, but rather to make them believe that others will obey, even when they themselves could have been motivated by internal factors.

These challenges might suggest that the safest regulatory approach is to focus on the common denominator – the fear of punishment – thereby avoiding the need to target a specific motivation. The use of incentives as either the primary or the sole approach might be seen as the lesser evil in comparison to the complexity and uncertainty associated with targeting the presumed motivation of the individuals we wish to regulate. Although this approach has some value and is well established within the legal scholarship ("The bad man of Holmes"),[146] playing it safe and focusing only on the calculative model of reasoning are likely to harm, at least theoretically, the functioning of most other models reviewed thus far.

---

[143] Tyler, T., Dienhart, J., & Thomas, T. (2008). The ethical commitment to compliance: Building value-based cultures. *California Management Review*, 50(2), 31–51.

[144] Admittedly, there is a reason to suspect that being motivated by morality is not the same intrinsic motivation as being motivated by citizenship or reason. On many accounts, such as willingness to pay, endurance, and consistency, these models are not expected to trigger similar levels of motivation in accounting for legal motivation on most aspects.

[145] See Feldman & Lobel, *supra* note 13, at 1151. See also Sanderson & Darley, *supra* note 142.

[146] Holmes, O. W. (1897). The path of the law. *Harvard Law Review*, 10, 457.

3.6 A REGULATORY DESIGN RESPONSIVE TO DIFFERENT MODELS OF MOTIVATION

This concluding section briefly outlines a regulatory design that would be responsive to the different models of human motivation and at the same time is sensitive to the specific context and likely audience of the regulation in question. For example, when the regulated activity carries great potential for immediate harm to others, taking the safest approach and focusing on deterrence is justified.[147] In contrast, if the regulated behavior is such that it requires the goodwill of the people and that they engage in actions beyond those motivated by compliance, then it is not useful to rely on deterrence, and emphasis should be placed on attempting to target people with the regulatory measure that supports their dominant motivation. Additional considerations that could be taken into account include enforceability of the targeted behavior. When enforcement is less costly, there is less need to focus on models other than those supporting deterrence. Furthermore, when the quality of regulated behavior is more important than ensuring that it occurs, then the harm that may arise from ignoring the other models or even lessening their impact through various crowding-out mechanisms increases. Finally, given the differences among individuals in their motivations, preliminary analysis of the attitudes of target population could shed light as to the likely effect of each of the models on aggregated compliance behavior.[148]

A responsive regulatory system could be based on the preventive approach, which shares with the deterrence approach the instrumental view of compliance motivation but is less likely to crowd out other compliance motivations.[149] Cheng proposed a structural law approach that makes socially undesirable behavior more costly by design rather than by enforcement.[150] Thus, the approach to reduce mail theft would not be the imposition of fines, but rather making mailboxes less accessible to unauthorized individuals. The system of tax withholding is a structural approach to deterring tax evaders; using technological modifications to prevent file sharing rather than penalizing individuals for sharing files is another example.[151] Thus, although this approach does not focus on enforcement, it is based on the instrumental assumption that the individual would have broken the law if not for the costs of the violation.

As seen in the preventive approach, although many have questioned the effectiveness of deterrence, abandoning it as a sole regulatory tool does not imply rejection of the assumption of the calculative individual. Various modern methods of governance are

---

[147] In later chapters, the addition of the problem of self awareness to the current question of what motivates one to comply with law will be be discussed further.

[148] Feldman, Y., & Lobel, O. (2011). Individuals as enforcers: The design of employee reporting systems. In C. Parker & V. L. Nielsen (Eds.), Explaining compliance: Business responses to regulation (chap. 12, pp. 263–286). Cheltenham: Edward Elgar.

[149] Katyal, N. K. (2002). Architecture as crime control. *Yale Law Journal*, 111(5), 1039–1139.

[150] Cheng, E. K. (2006). Structural laws and the puzzle of regulating behavior. *Northwestern University Law Review*, 100, 655.

[151] The importance of the preventive approach which focuses on ex-ante regulation will be discussed further in chapters 7, 9 and 11

based on that assumption. In that regard, the environmental field has been an especially interesting context, where deterrence has been used in a more sophisticated way through regulations that force organizations to publicize their emission levels and face sanctions from the public.[152] In addition, various forms of self-governance programs that do not always carry direct sanctions[153] are based on deterrence, but they also account for various social factors and sanctions that may make deterrence more effective.[154]

Finally, a responsive regulatory design[155] should focus on the traditional but non-instrumental models reviewed in this chapter that are less likely to interfere with other models or to have inadvertent effects on compliance, as was demonstrated with regard to sanctions or incentives. For example, the concept of procedural justice, widely studied by scholars such as Tyler and others, is likely to increase perceptions of legitimacy and compliance with less likelihood of interfering with the effective functioning of deterrence. Similarly, informing people of the harm associated with their behavior might increase compliance without causing them to resent the imposed regulations. Nevertheless, some scholars have suggested the possibility that focusing on aspects such as morality might give people the impression that the state is unable to enforce the law and therefore might backfire, resulting in reduced compliance.[156] Furthermore, the literature on self-serving interpretations of fairness[157] as well as the various mechanisms discussed in Chapter 2 with regard to people's ability to reinterpret the moral aspect as being irrelevant for them, naturally argues against the ability to use fairness and morality as an alternative to self-interest. Thus, legal policy makers should create those policies that will target as many motivations as possible, while recognizing the impossibility of complete success in this mission. The next chapter discusses an additional set of legal interventions – nontraditional ones – which will increase the options that legal policy makers can rely on in their enforcement efforts, especially when taking into account people's limited awareness to their own unethically.

[152] Feldman, Y., & Perez, O. (2009). How law changes the environmental mind: An experimental study of the effect of legal norms on moral perceptions and civic enforcement. *Journal of Law and Society*, 36(4), 501–535.

[153] King, A. A., & Lenox, M. J. (2000). Industry self-regulation without sanctions: The chemical industry's responsible care program. *Academy of Management Journal*, 43(4), 698–716.

[154] Kahan, D. M. (1996). Between economics and sociology: The new path of deterrence. *Michigan Law Review*, 95, 2477. See also McAdams, *supra* note 18.

[155] See Ayres & Braithwaite, *supra* note 1. I discuss the concept of responsive regulation in further detail in Chapter 11.

[156] Bardach, E. (1989). Moral suasion and taxpayer compliance. *Law & Policy*, 11(1), 49–69.

[157] Thompson, L., & Loewenstein, G. (1992). Egocentric interpretations of fairness and interpersonal conflict. *Organizational Behavior and Human Decision Processes*, 51(2), 176–197.

4

Revisiting Non-formal Enforcement Interventions

4.1 INTRODUCTION

Chapter 3 focused on the effectiveness of traditional forms of state interventions in responding to the revised agency model that we explored in the first two chapters of the book. The current chapter evaluates the effectiveness of nontraditional interventions – which assume that the legal assumptions about human agency are inadequate – in changing the behavior of people. This critical overview of nontraditional methods, which for the most part do not focus on ethical issues but rather on changing behavior based on cognitive concepts of bounded rationality, examines several important questions: to what extent are those nontraditional methods able to supplement the traditional ones change ethical motivation as well as ethical behavior? To what degree can they offer differentiated approaches to segments of the population who vary in their approach to ethicality? And to what extent do the differences between the methods (e.g., between nudges and debiasing) and between traditional and nontraditional approaches (e.g., between monetary incentives and reframing of the legal or ethical dilemma) align with the dual-reasoning approach to ethical decision making? I argue that for analytical reasons it is useful to distinguish between approaches that focus on changing the individual by influencing his or her deliberative choices directly and those that attempt to change the situation and so bypass System 1 reasoning. As will be clear from the literature review in the first part of the chapter, little attention has been given to *ex ante* approaches to behavior regulation of ethical behavior. For that reason, the rest of the chapter focuses on various nontraditional approaches to handling ethical biases based on the targeted population and the type of ethical behavior regulated. The need for using various approaches is further discussed in Chapters 7 and 8, which incorporate a pluralistic view of the multifaceted behavioral impacts of the law on different people, behavioral trade-offs, and a taxonomy pairing intervention techniques and situations.

In this chapter, I include modified versions of texts that appeared in Feldman, Y., & Lobel, O. (2015). Behavioural trade-offs: Beyond the land of nudges spans the world of law and psychology. In A. Alemanno & A.-L. Sibony (Eds.), *Nudges and the law: An European perspective* (chap. 13). Oxford: Hart.

4.2 MAIN NONTRADITIONAL APPROACHES

There are few main nontraditional approaches to regulating behavior. The most classic approach is *debiasing*, a group of cognitive methods used to overcome biased thinking and non-deliberative choice.[1] It uses various techniques, such as consideration of the opposite approach, reflection on one's choices, and taking an alternative view. An important form of debiasing is *accountability*, which informs individuals prior to their making a decision that they will need to explain after the fact why they made that choice.[2] *Framing*, which is based on research showing how a shift in one's reference point affects subsequent perceptions of gains and losses,[3] is another technique that can be used to alter behavior.[4] An additional approach is the use of *nudges* – an intervention that changes behavior by changing the situation, but not by creating economic incentives.[5] Whereas the nudge approach aims to directly affect the individual's System 1 by changing the situation, debiasing, for the most part, attempts to encourage the person to use System 2 thinking. Nonetheless, in recent years there have been various examples of System 2 nudges.[6] According to this choice architecture approach, rather than attempting to curb people's biases, it uses this knowledge to shift their non-deliberative choices toward the desired direction. The best-known examples of choice architecture with a nudge mind-set derive from the default rule relating to organ donation[7] or saving for retirement.[8]

4.2.1 *Debiasing*

Debiasing techniques, especially in the cognitive context, are designed to help people overcome their biases by making them re-evaluate their errors.[9] Many

---

[1] Jolls, C., & Sunstein, C. (2005). Debiasing through law. *National Bureau of Economic Research*, No. W11738.

[2] Lerner, J. S., & Tetlock, P. E. (1999). Accounting for the effects of accountability. *Psychology Bulletin*, 125(2), 255–275.

[3] For example, I have examined the relevancy of loss aversion to people's ethical choices in contractual contexts. Feldman, Y., Schurr, A., & Teichman, D. (2013). Reference points and contractual choices: An experimental examination. *Journal of Empirical Legal Studies*, 10(3), 512–541.

[4] Levin, I. P., Schneider, S. L., & Gaeth, G. J. (1998). All frames are not created equal: A typology and critical analysis of framing effects. *Organizational Behavior and Human Decision Processes*, 76(2), 149–188 for the most comprehensive analysis of these approaches.

[5] Sunstein, C., & Thaler, R. (2008). *Why nudge: The politics of libertarian paternalism*. New Haven: Yale University Press.

[6] Jung, J. Y., & Data, B. A. M. (2016). American attitudes toward nudges. *Judgment and Decision making*, 11(1), 62 for a review of different nudges and how they are being viewed.

[7] Johnson, E. J., & Goldstein, D. G. (2003). Do defaults save lives? *Construction of Preference*, 302(5649), 1338–1339. Another example of choice architecture, which takes advantages of biases as a way to improve the lives of people, addresses status quo and inaction biases; rather than changing them, they use them to push behavior toward a desired direction, as in encouraging people to save more money or to donate organs.

[8] Thaler, R., & Benartzi, S. (2004). Save More Tomorrow™: Using behavioral economics to increase employee saving. *Journal of Political Economy*, 112(S1), S164–S187.

[9] For a theoretical and applied analysis of debiasing in such fields as litigation, employment, and consumer protection, see Jolls & Sunstein, *supra* note 1.

interpretations exist as to how to taxonomize biases; one of the most useful is related to Arkes, whose taxonomy is described next.[10]

The first technique is to ask people to consider evidence of an opposing outcome.[11] According to Koriat and Fischoff, this technique is effective in reducing the overconfidence people have in their answers to general-knowledge questions;[12] Lord et al. show that it works by changing people's focus and the stimuli they have access to when making decisions.[13] The second technique is to change the reference points and meaning of gains and losses; Arkes suggests that this strategy of reframing is effective in reducing biased reasoning.[14] The third technique encourages people to draw on their professional training: Lehman et al. show that when professionals consciously draw on their graduate training, they make increased and more accurate use of statistical reasoning.[15] Overall, it seems there is a limited ability to extend this taxonomy to ethical contexts, since the focus is on people's limited ability to draw sound conclusions from data rather than on their self-serving biases, as described in Chapter 2.

An approach that could be more easily extended to ethical contexts is found in the work of Devine, who focuses on debiasing techniques – which she refers to as "training" – aimed to reduce people's likelihood to demonstrate racial biases and stereotyping.[16] This method's primary mechanism is to make people aware of their biases, thus, in a sense, moving them from relying on automatic cognitive strategies to more reflective and deliberate ones. In another study, Schur et al. suggest that engaging people in planning for the future and broadening the scope of those decisions make it difficult for them to engage in self-deception, which justifies

[10]   Arkes, H. R. (1991). Costs and benefits of judgment errors: Implications for debiasing. *Psychological Bulletin*, 110(3), 486–498.

[11]   Mussweiler, T., Strack, F., & Pfeiffer, T. (2000). Overcoming the inevitable anchoring effect: Considering the opposite compensates for selective accessibility. *Personality and Social Psychology Bulletin*, 26(9), 1142–1150.

[12]   Koriat, A., Lichtenstein, S., & Fischoff, B. (1980). Reasons for confidence. *Journal of Experimental Psychology: Human Learning and Memory*, 6(2), 107–118.

[13]   Lord, C. G., Lepper, M. R., & Preston, E. (1984). Considering the opposite: A corrective strategy for social judgment. *Journal of Personality and Social Psychology*, 47(6), 1231–1243.

[14]   See Arkes, *supra* note 10.

[15]   Lehman, D. R., Lempert, R. O., & Nisbett, R. E. (1988). The effects of graduate training on reasoning: Formal discipline and thinking about everyday-life events. *American Psychologist*, 43(6), 431–442. See also Arlen and Tontrup, who have studied the use of professional training, have examined the effectiveness of institutional characteristics (such as use of an agent) in reducing biases like the endowment effect. Arlen, J., & Tontrup, S. W. (2015). Does the endowment effect justify legal intervention? The debiasing effect of institutions. *Journal of Legal Studies*, 44(1), 143–182; Arlen, J., & Tontrup, S. (2015). Strategic bias shifting: Herding as a behaviorally rational response to regret aversion. *Journal of Legal Analysis*, 7(2), 517–560.

[16]   Devine, P. G., Forscher, P. S., Austin, A. J., & Cox, W. T. (2012). Long-term reduction in implicit race bias: A prejudice habit-breaking intervention. *Journal of Experimental Social Psychology*, 48(6), 1267–1278. See also Amodio, D. M., & Devine, P. G. (2005). Hanging prejudice: The effects of persuasion on implicit and explicit forms of race bias; Shavitt, S. E., & Brock, T. C. (1994). *Persuasion: Psychological insights and perspectives* (pp. 249–280). Boston: Allyn & Bacon.

decisions made on the basis of self-interest.[17] Sezer et al. argue that encouraging people to reflect on their behavior might cause them to move from using System 1 to System 2 thinking.[18]

4.2.2 Accountability

The crown jewel of debiasing techniques seems to be accountability: The process by which people reduce the impact of biases upon their decisions by consciously thinking before they make those decisions and how they would justify them later. The most influential paper on accountability, written by Lerner and Tetlock, proposes a taxonomy of the biases for which accountability may or may not be effective.[19] First, they argue that accountability is most effective when the biases stem from a lack of attention to information that is available. To avoid looking foolish later, people who use the accountability technique search for a wider range of conceivably relevant cues, pay greater attention to the cues they use, anticipate counterarguments and factor some of them into their overall opinion or assessment of the situation and regularly monitor the cues that influence judgment and choice. However, accountability is not able to reduce biases when no alternative line of reasoning is being offered. Second, they suggest that the accountability strategy actually increases bias when the most easily justifiable option is also the one that goes in the same direction as the bias. As discussed in the next sections, this debiasing approach seems to be a much better fit for dealing with ethical biases than the other biases reviewed by Arkes.

4.2.2.1 Relevancy to Ethical Biases

Overall, the approaches offering mechanisms that could be relevant for ethical biases (e.g., reflection, taking a different perspective, and accountability) were not studied in that context. Indeed, only a few studies use debiasing to overcome ethical biases, and most adopt similar techniques as used in reducing cognitive debiasing. Milkman et al. review some classic examples of debiasing techniques that attempt to create rigorous changes in the ethical decision-making process, with mixed results in reducing people's biases.[20] They find that these techniques, which make the use of System 2 reasoning explicit, enable people to pay greater attention to attribution

---

[17] Schurr, A., Ritov, I., Kareev, Y., & Avraham, J. (2012). Is that the answer you had in mind? The effect of perspective on dishonest behavior. *Judgment and Decision Making*, 7(6), 679–688. See the discussion on the limitation of ethical nudges on p. 100.

[18] Sezer, O., Gino, F., & Bazerman, M. H. (2015). Ethical blind spots: Explaining unintentional unethical behavior. *Current Opinion in Psychology*, 6, 77–81.

[19] See Lerner & Tetlock, *supra* note 2.

[20] Milkman, K. L., Chugh, D., & Bazerman, M. H. (2009). How can decision making be improved? *Perspectives on Psychological Science*, 4(4) 379–383. See also Sunstein, C. R. (2015). On interesting policymakers. *Perspectives on Psychological Science*, 10(6), 764–767.

errors, rather than process, and reduce the overconfidence of decision makers in their choices.[21]

4.2.3 Debiasing Unethicality through Law?

Since in this book we focus on changes that could be made by the state itself rather than solely by organizations, we need to think about changes in laws and regulations. There is a clear and natural difference between the effectiveness of debiasing techniques used in research studies and of those incorporated into the law for various institutional, ethical, and practical reasons. Debiasing strategies may prove ineffective in real life simply because people have little incentive to adopt them; in many contexts of ordinary unethicality, people do not want to be made aware of the implications of their behavior and would prefer to act as they wish, ignoring uncomfortable notions of ethicality. In addition, how people behave in research studies may be very different from how they ordinarily behave. Hence, for debiasing strategies to curb mindless unethical behavior, the state needs to administer them. The suggestion that the law itself could operate either by design or indirectly as an ethical debiasing mechanism is currently being explored; however, to date, behavioral economic biases are the main focus of this ongoing discussion and research.

The most influential paper on debiasing in the legal literature is by Jolls and Sunstein, who coined the concept of "debias through law," which is the incorporation in law of debiasing strategies that move people in more rational directions.[22] Even though Sunstein also developed the concept of "nudges," he and Jolls suggest a strategy that opposes the nudge. Whereas nudges are designed to eliminate System 1 irrational thinking from the decision-making process, the goal of debiasing through law is to encourage people to make more use of System 2 reasoning.

Jolls and Sunstein first provide examples of strategies to achieve that goal. To overcome optimism bias, for instance, they suggest providing people with concrete instances of its occurrence. Another example is what they call "debiasing through framing."[23] Jolls and Sunstein then examine various debiasing techniques incorporated into laws on the books. For example, a mandate that requires companies to disclose various types of safety information to consumers is aimed at curbing the optimism bias. However, the authors recognize that even if consumers receive accurate information, they might ignore it because of that same optimism bias.[24]

---

[21] Kahneman, D., & Lovallo, D. (1993). Timid choices and bold forecasts: A cognitive perspective on risk taking. *Management Science*, 39(1), 17–31. See also Gigerenzer, G., Hoffrage, U., & Kleinbölting, H. (1991). Probabilistic mental models: A Brunswickian theory of confidence. *Psychological Review*, 98(4), 506–528.

[22] See Jolls & Sunstein, *supra* note 1.

[23] Meyerowitz, B. E., & Chaiken, S. (1987). The effect of message framing on breast self-examination attitudes, intentions, and behavior. *Journal of Personality and Social Psychology*, 52(3), 500–510.

[24] See Hanson, J. D., & Kysar, D. A. (1999). Taking behavioralism seriously: Some evidence of market manipulation. *Harvard Law Review*, 112(7), 1420–1572.

In the context of corporate law, they suggest removing optimistically biased inside directors from the board or adding outside directors as a way to reduce the impact of optimism biases. In the context of property law, they focus on the work of Rachlinski and Jourden, which examines ways to use the endowment effect to encourage people to value their homes in line with rational predictions.[25] In addition, they highlight the findings of Arlen et al. on ways to reduce the endowment effect through the use of agents.[26] It is interesting to note that the behavioral ethics perspective would predict that using agents would produce the exact opposite effect-as people are more likely to engage in unethical behavior when they are doing so for others.[27]

In another paper, Jolles and Sunstein focus less on functionality of the law and more on behavioral mechanisms that it can utilize.[28] They compare techniques that will "insulate the outcomes from the problems created by heuristics and biases" and techniques that will "reduce people's level of bias." Relying on the work of Kang and Banaji,[29] they suggest that "antidiscrimination law's framework for assessing the legality of affirmative action plans can be understood as enabling employers, educational institutions, and other organizations to use such plans to break the connection between implicit bias and outcomes."[30] However, their dichotomy ignores the fact that if one cannot predict the effect of implicit biases and hence bypassing them might lead to overcorrection.

4.2.4 *The Nudge as an Alternative to Debiasing*

The limited effect of debiasing has led scholars to look for alternative approaches, specifically, approaches that acknowledge the use of intuitive reasoning and focus rather than approaches that change the situation and take biases into account. For example, designing the situation so that when people make choices based on their biases that favor inaction or value the present, those choices will lead to desirable behavior.[31] The nudge approach is now used widely, relying on the assumption that people are often unable to use System 2 thinking and that change needs to occur on the situational level with limited need for deliberation.

---

[25] Rachlinksi, J. J., & Jourden, F. (1998). Remedies and the psychology of ownership. *Vanderbilt Law Review*, 51, 1541–1582. They found a reduction in the disparity between willingness to accept and willingness to pay when liability rules rather than property rules protect the entitlement, which was studied.

[26] Arlen, J., Spitzer, M. L., & Talley, E. L. (2002). Endowment effects within corporate agency relationships. *Journal of Legal Studies*, 31(1), 1–37.

[27] As developed in chapter 9.

[28] Jolls, C., & Sunstein, C. R. (2006). The law of implicit bias. *California Law Review*, 94, 969–996 at 978 and 977.

[29] Kang, J., & Banaji, M. R. (2006). Fair measures: A behavioral realist revision of "affirmative action". *California Law Review*, 94(4), 1063–1118.

[30] See Jolls & Sunstein, *supra* note 28, at 980.

[31] Larrick, R. P. (2015). Debiasing. In G. Keren & G. Wu (Eds.), *The Wiley Blackwell handbook of judgment and decision making* (pp. 316–338). Chichester: John Wiley & Sons.

This form of behavioral engineering – the nudge – first received widespread attention in Thaler and Sunstein's 2008 bestseller.[32] They argue that individuals' preferences are often incoherent and affected by biases of which they are unaware, thereby requiring a paternalistic redesign of the situation. However, paternalistic interventions should "nudge" individuals without restricting their choices and toward what they would have chosen had they not been subject to specific limitations of rationality. Although some of the normative suggestions outlined in this chapter could be seen as related to the nudge approach, there is a limit to the ability of these tactics that lead to sustainable change. This approach has been implemented most widely in the context of health and finance – areas where people's short-term decisions and long-term interests are not always aligned.[33] In these contexts of behavioral economics, people prefer to save money, quit smoking, choose the best schools for their children, enroll in health programs, lose weight, and avoid taking expensive loans, but they may find it hard to take action to achieve those aims. In other words, the nudge, at least in those more paternalistic contexts, works in part because it helps people achieve the goals they have already formulated.

A fascinating body of interdisciplinary studies in law, economics, and psychology addresses the use of nudges in other contexts. Kahan wrote one of the first papers applying nudges to legal enforcement.[34] It deals with situations that shortly follow the criminalization of new norms, when some of those responsible for enforcing the law display resistance. Kahan finds that the use of small punishments increases the enforcers' willingness to enforce the law, which gradually leads to changes in norms.[35]

4.2.5 Criticisms of the Nudge Approach

As mentioned in Chapter 1, the nudge approach has been criticized on various grounds, mostly in terms of limiting individual autonomy and imposing a form of paternalism.[36] This criticism of contemporary behavioral policy is predominantly philosophical in nature, exploring the implications of using insights from psychology to limit individual autonomy and choices. For example, Mitchell argues that the nudge approach misuses the concept of libertarianism, subjugating "the liberty of irrational individuals to a central planner's paternalistic welfare judgments." He warns that nudges are designed to capitalize on irrational tendencies of private

[32] Thaler, R. H., & Sunstein, C. R. (2008). *Nudge: Improving decisions about health, wealth, and happiness.* New Haven: Yale University Press.
[33] Marteau, T. M., Ogilvie, D., Roland, M., Suhrcke, M., & Kelly, M. P. (2011). Judging nudging: can nudging improve population health?. BMJ: British Medical Journal (Online), 342.
[34] Kahan, D. M. (2000). Gentle nudges vs. hard shoves: Solving the sticky norms problem. *University of Chicago Law Review,* 67(3), 607–645.
[35] Schurr, A., Rodensky, D., & Erev, I. (2014). The effect of unpleasant experiences on evaluation and behavior. *Journal of Economic Behavior & Organization,* 106, 1–9.
[36] For a discussion of the problems associated with this, see Rebonato, R. (2012). *Taking liberties: A critical examination of libertarian paternalism.* London: Palgrave Macmillan.

citizens and so enable paternalistic planners to direct their lives.[37] A related line of research in recent years has examined public perceptions of the legitimacy of the government's use of nudges; it has found some positive attitudes toward nudges in areas seen as legitimate for state intervention.[38]

In examining the limited effectiveness of using nudge-like approaches to solve policy issues, Amir and Lobel's work criticizes the lack of a clear distinction between nudges and debiasing.[39] In their review of Ariely and Sunstein's books on irrationality and nudges, they argue that for policy makers to successfully implement policy solutions, they need to do a more thorough job of classifying the mechanisms underlying behavioral biases and modify the implementations accordingly. For example, they should determine whether bounded ethicality or bounded rationality is at issue. If bounded rationality is the problem, the focus should be on simplifying the choices available to the individual. In contrast, if bounded ethicality is at issue, the focus should be on eliminating justifications for inappropriate behavior.

Others argue that the nudge produces an opposite result of its initial intention. In their study, Madrian and Shea find that switching to an automatic retirement savings plan actually reduces the average amount of pension savings.[40] Similar results have been found with other health and energy-savings nudges.

Amir and Lobel argue that in the attempt to attain bipartisan support for policy changes, some implemented nudges fail to account fully for the range of regulatory solutions that could be employed, given the insights of behavioral economics.[41] Instead, policy makers and thought leaders tend to narrow the scope of regulatory tools used, to a small set of iconic choice architecture modules. Amir and Lobel, as well as Feldman and Lobel,[42] argue that a more suitable approach would be to

[37] Gregory, M. (2005). Libertarian paternalism is an oxymoron. *Northwestern University Law Review*, 99 (3), 1–42. Mitchell, G. (2004). Libertarian paternalism is an oxymoron. *Northwestern University Law Review*, 99, 1276.

[38] Arad, A., & Rubinstein, A. (2015). The people's perspective on libertarian-paternalistic policies. Unpublished Manuscript. http://arielrubinstein.tau.ac.il/papers/LP.Pdf. See also Sunstein, C. R. (2015). Nudging and choice architecture: Ethical considerations. *Yale Journal on Regulation*; available at SSRN: https://ssrn.com/abstract=2551264. For two studies on the areas that the public recognize as legitimate for state intervention, Sunstein, C. R. (2015). Do people like nudges? http://nrs.harvard.edu/urn-3:HUL .InstRepos:16147874; and Reisch, L. A. & Sunstein, C. R. (2016). Do Europeans like nudges? *Judgment and Decision Making*, 11(4), 310–325. For a more elaborate recent review of most of the relevant issues see Sunstein, C. R. (2016). The ethics of influence: Government in the age of behavioral science. Cambridge University Press.

[39] Amir, O., & Lobel, O. (2009). Stumble, predict, nudge: How behavioral economics informs law and policy. *Columbia Law Review*, 108, 6–9.

[40] Madrian, B., & Shea, D. (2001). The power of suggestion: Inertia in 401(k) participation and savings behavior. *Quarterly Journal of Economics*, 116, 1149–1184. See also Bubb, R., & Pildes, R. H. (2014). How behavioral economics trims its sails and why. *Harvard Law Review*, 127(6), 1637.

[41] Amir, O., & Lobel, O. (2012). Liberalism and lifestyle: Informing regulatory governance with behavioural research. *European Journal of Risk Regulation*, 3(1), 17–25. See also Amir & Lobel, *supra* note 39.

[42] Feldman, Y., & Lobel, O. (2015). Behavioural trade-offs: Beyond the land of nudges spans the world of law and psychology. In A. Alemanno & A.-L. Sibony (Eds.), *Nudges and the law: An European perspective* (chap. 13). Oxford: Hart.

understand behavioral economics as aiding the regulator in expanding the regulatory toolbox, drawing on the broad spectrum of measures from command-and-control, through collaborative regulation, and to self-regulation that are offered by the new governance school of thought.[43]

In a related critique, Bubb and Pildes characterize nudge-style prescriptions as being too narrowly focused on choice architecture and on a "trimming of the sails," thereby eliminating a range of options because of behavioral law and economics (BLE) researchers' ideological preference for seemingly noninterventionist proposals.[44] They argue that the "two seductive dimensions [of behavioral law and economics] – its appeal as a social science and as politics" – are in tension, because the insights that come out of behavioral social science often require more stringent regulatory solutions than behavioral law could offer.[45] The problem with focusing on one policy tool is exacerbated in ethical contexts and is further discussed in Chapters 7 and 8. However, it is clear that without a parallel focus on modalities such as ethical training and effective enforcement; it will be very hard for any one tool to improves people ethicality. Chapter 6, which focuses on individual variations in ethicality, makes an even stronger claim for more nuanced attention to people who differ in their level of ethical awareness and motivation.

4.2.6 *Choice Architecture Approach*

Although seen by some scholars as a subset of the nudge approach, choice architecture places less emphasis on designing the situation and more on determining the set of choices and the way in which they are presented. The work of Johnson et al. is seminal in that regard; they recommend the optimal number of choices to be presented.[46]. Schwartz and others discuss the "tyranny" of choice posed by providing too many choices.[47] Other scholars have addressed technology-based decision aids to steer consumers toward choosing desirable products, services, and activities, without restricting their freedom to choose[48], and the use of defaults settings or

[43] On new governance, see generally, Lobel, O. (2004). The renew deal: The fall of regulation and the rise of governance in contemporary legal thought. *Minnesota Law Review*, 89, 7–27.

[44] See Bubb & Pildes, *supra* note 40, at 1637.   [45] Ibid. at p. 1595

[46] Johnson, E. J., Shu, S. B., Dellaert, B. G., Fox, C., Goldstein, D. G., Häubl, G., & Weber, E. U. (2012). Beyond nudges: Tools of a choice architecture. *Marketing Letters*, 23(2), 487–504.

[47] Schwartz, B. (2016). *The paradox of choice: Why more is less*. New York: Ecco. In this book Schwartz calls too many options "the tyranny of choice". See also Iyengar, S. S., & Lepper, M. R. (2000). When choice is demotivating: Can one desire too much of a good thing? *Journal of Personality and Social Psychology*, 79(6), 995–1006; Jacoby, J. (1984). Perspectives on information overload. *Journal of Consumer Research*, 10(4), 432–435. Both articles call too many options "choice overload."

[48] Häubl, G., & Trifts, V. (2000). Consumer decision making in online shopping environments: The effects of interactive decision aids. *Marketing Science*, 19(1), 4–21.

choices.[49] The choice architecture approach has been used most widely with regard to the framing of loss and gain and its effect on people's economic and legal decision making.[50]

4.2.7 *Differences among the Three Approaches*

The literature on nontraditional enforcement techniques distinguishes among debiasing, nudges, and choice architecture, though not always clearly. Generally, debiasing attempts to reduce people's reliance on System 1 and shifts them to System 2 thinking, whereas nudges redesign the situation such that even if people's choices are motivated by System 1, their behavior will change to align with the interests of the state. The choice architecture approach suggests certain contexts in which empowering people and causing them to reflect are more effective than nudges (Grüne-Yanoff and Hertwig describe these contexts in their article on the nudge versus the boost approach[51]).

In a sense, the debiasing in comparison to nudges as well as the choice architecture distinction can be conceptualized as one between a focus on regulating the situation versus regulating the individual's cognitive and emotional biases. Debiasing focuses on the individual and on nudges; while choice architecture focuses on the situation. In the next section, we take a broader perspective that focuses on situational design as an approach to increasing the likelihood of "good people" engaging in ethical behavior.

4.2.8 *Regulating Situations Rather than People: From Behavioral Economics toward Behavioral Ethics*

Most of the preceding analysis has been based on interventions to modify cognitive and social cognition biases (mainly stereotypes). Now, let us examine the use of these tools to produce behavioral change in ethical contexts.

Behavioral ethics (BE) recognizes that changing the underlying situations faced by individuals can shape both their explicit and implicit choices, whereas

---

[49] Cronqvist, H., & Thaler, R. H. (2004). Design choices in privatized social-security systems: Learning from the Swedish experience. *American Economic Review*, 94(2), 424–428. See also Madrian & Shea, The power of suggestion; Johnson, E. J., Hershey, J., Meszaros, J., & Kunreuther, H. (1993). Framing, probability distortions, and insurance decisions. *Making Decisions about Liability and Insurance*, 35–51; Johnson, E. J., & Goldstein, D. G. (2003). Do defaults save lives? *The Construction of Preference*, 682–688; Goldstein, D. G., Johnson, E. J., Herrmann, A., & Heitman, M. (2008). Nudge your customers toward better choices. *Harvard Business Review*, 86(12), 99–105.

[50] See Zamir, E. (2015). *Law, psychology, and morality: The role of loss aversion.* Oxford: Oxford University Press.

[51] Grüne-Yanoff, T., & Hertwig, R. (2015). Nudge versus boost: How coherent are policy and theory? *Minds and Machines*, 26(1–2), 149–183. This line is further developed in Chapter 8 on behavioral trade-offs.

changing the pertinent incentives only affects their conscious decisions.[52] Yet, changing the social cues, as nudge-like approaches do, is not sufficient; it is also necessary to shape and curtail the biases that determine the way in which people approach dilemmas, even before they consciously explore how to solve them. People often engage in unethical behavior because they are unaware that it is not ethical. The recommended BE approach causes people to recognize when they are engaged in bad behavior; this recognition will then help curtail this type of behavior.

In the 1980s, Trevino, one of the pioneers of business ethics research, focused on how business environments facilitate unethical behaviors above and beyond any characteristics of the individuals themselves.[53] The BE literature has built on Trevino's work. In a comprehensive review, Bazerman and Gino outline characteristics of situations that are likely to increase unethical behavior.[54] One key feature is the extent to which the situation facilitates the rationalization of unethical behaviors. Situational factors that increase bad behavior include role playing (as in the Stanford Prison Experiment), visual elements such as the presence of graffiti on walls, and social factors such as a relationship with a wrongdoer. People also are more likely to behave dishonestly when they face loss,[55] especially if behaving unethically can help them turn the loss into a gain.[56]

In a world that pays attention only to deliberate unethicality, behavioral law and economic (BLE) models based on incentives are more than enough to change behavior in ethical contexts. However, the more we understand that people's conscious choices drive only part of their bad behavior, the more regulatory resources must be allocated to create situations that reduce all forms of unethicality and legal noncompliance.

4.2.9 *Ethical Debiasing*

Tenbrunsel and others coined the concept of "ethical mirage," the biases responsible for the gaps in awareness between the ethicality of what people actually do, what they want to do, and what they think they are doing.[57] In particular, they discuss

---

[52]   Aquino, K., Freeman, D., Reed, A., Lim, V. K., & Felps, W. (2009). Testing a social-cognitive model of moral behavior: The interactive influence of situations and moral identity centrality. *Journal of Personality and Social Psychology*, 97(1), 123–141.

[53]   Trevino, L. K. (1986). Ethical decision making in organizations: A person-situation interactionist model. *Academy of Management Review*, 11(3), 601.

[54]   Bazerman, M. H., & Gino, F. (2012). Behavioral ethics: Toward a deeper understanding of moral judgment and dishonesty. *Annual Review of Law and Social Science*, 8(1), 85–104.

[55]   Kern, M. C., & Chugh, D. (2009). Bounded ethicality: The perils of loss framing. *Psychological Science*, 20(3), 378–384.

[56]   Shalvi, S. (2012). Dishonestly increasing the likelihood of winning. *Judgment and Decision Making*, 7 (3), 292–303.

[57]   Tenbrunsel, A. E., & Diekmann, K. A. (2007). When you're tempted to deceive. *Negotiation*, Jg(5), 9–11. See also Tenbrunsel, A. E., Diekmann, K. A., Wade-Benzoni, K. A., & Bazerman, M. H. (2008). *Why we aren't as ethical as we think we are: A temporal explanation.* Harvard Business School.

the concept of a "should self," which is capable of describing level-headedly how we ought to act, and they try to understand why it does not play a greater role in actual decision making. The authors suggest cognitive practices that will enable better communication between the various parts of the self. These include detailed planning of the situation, practicing how to deal with potential sources of biases, and active listening to the should self during the decision-making process. Finally, along similar lines, a recent a review paper has focused on the ability of using debiasing techniques as well as nudges to encourage ethical decisions.[58]

4.2.10 Ethical Training

A different type of intervention that has been attracting attention with the growing understanding of human behavior is training intervention, a form of intervention that is more popular in organizational contexts. More specifically, many forms of ethical training address people's associations and stereotypes.[59] As suggested earlier, training people with the goal of producing long-term behavioral change is based on outdated assumptions about people's behavior. Although many researchers are skeptical about the effectiveness of ethical training, there are some signals in the research that it can work on modifying short-term behavior.[60] As previously mentioned, Devine's work has shown how training enables people to overcome their racial biases.[61]

4.2.11 Changing People's Intrinsic Motivation

BE research suggests that increasing people's motivation to act ethically might reduce the chance of their being affected by implicit biases.[62] Blair reviews some

---

[58] For a review see Haugh, T. (2017). The ethics of intracorporate behavioral ethics. *California Law Review Online*, www.californialawreview.org/the-ethics-of-intracorporate-behavioral-ethics.

[59] See Devine et al., *supra* note 16. See also Phills, C. E., Kawakami, K., Tabi, E., Nadolny, D., & Inzlicht, M. (2011). Mind the gap: Increasing associations between the self and blacks with approach behaviors. *Journal of Personality and Social Psychology*, 100(2), 197–210. Training in approaching blacks increases associations between the self and blacks that in turn reduce implicit prejudice against blacks.

[60] Warren, D. E., Gaspar, J. P., & Laufer, W. S. (2014). Is formal ethics training merely cosmetic? A study of ethics training and ethical organizational culture. *Business Ethics Quarterly*, 24(1), 85–117. This study showed both short-term and long-term (two years) improvement in bank employees' intent to behave ethically.

[61] Devine, P. G. (2001). Implicit prejudice and stereotyping: How automatic are they? Introduction to the special section. *Journal of Personality and Social Psychology*, 81(5), 757–759. See also Devine et al., *supra* note 16. Devine, P. G., Plant, E. A., Amodio, D. M., Harmon-Jones, E., & Vance, S. L. (2002). The regulation of explicit and implicit race bias: The role of motivations to respond without prejudice. *Journal of Personality and Social Psychology*, 82(5), 835–848.

[62] Bartlett, K. T. (2009). Making good on good intentions: The critical role of motivation in reducing implicit workplace discrimination. *Virginia Law Review*, 95, 1893–1972.

of the techniques based on individuals' motivation to maintain a positive self-image.[63] She reports the well-known finding that people display fewer stereotypes, both explicitly and implicitly, when the experimenter is from a minority group.[64] Leagault et al. conducted research on the contribution of intrinsic motivation to changing people's stereotypical views.[65]

Interestingly, some studies show that a change in intrinsic motivation is more effective than extrinsic motivation in reducing or eliminating implicit biases.[66] This finding has important implications for the intrinsic-extrinsic dichotomy with regard to people's ability to fight bias. However, at the same time it is important to remember research that suggests that attempting to change biases by changing motivation can sometimes backfire.[67]

4.2.12 *The Problem with Ethical Nudges*

Haugh reviews the area of ethical nudges in corporations and reports that in certain corporations, various types of nudge interventions such as pictures of alarms or deliberate delay in the computers of stock exchange traders that would allow for a reflection that would prevent various ethical biases were tested.[68] It is important to remember that cognitive nudges and ethical nudges differ in one fundamental respect: cognitive nudges push people to behave in ways that reward their self-interest, whereas ethical nudges encourage them to act in ways that are morally correct but may not have any concrete benefits or be in their self-interest. In the classical behavioral economics context, once people are reminded that there is a problem with their behavior – for example, they are not saving enough money or not eating healthfully enough – they will use this added awareness to improve their behavior. This is not necessarily the case in ethical contexts, where people may enjoy being blind to the ethical complexity of their behavior because this blindness serves their interest. For example, they may benefit financially from cutting corners, avoiding taxes, and underperforming in a contract, while deluding themselves into

[63]   Blair, I. V. (2002). The malleability of automatic stereotypes and prejudice. *Personality and Social Psychology Review*, 6(3), 242–261.

[64]   Lowery, B. S., Hardin, C. D., & Sinclair, S. (2001). Social influence effects on automatic racial prejudice. *Journal of Personality and Social Psychology*, 81(5), 842–855.

[65]   Legault, L., Gutsell, J. N., & Inzlicht, M. (2011). Ironic effects of antiprejudice messages: How motivational interventions can reduce (but also increase) prejudice. *Psychological Science*, 22(12), 1472–1477.

[66]   "Using control to motivate prejudice reduction backfired, and was more detrimental than not motivating participants at all. The support of autonomous motivation to regulate prejudice, however, caused a reduction in prejudice." Conversely, activating autonomous motivation reduced prejudice. In the studies described in the paper, explicit race bias was moderated by internal motivation to respond without prejudice, whereas implicit race bias was moderated by the interaction of internal and external motivation to respond without prejudice. Specifically, high internal, low external participants exhibited lower levels of implicit race bias than did all other participants Ibid. at p. 1473.

[67]   Ibid.   [68]   See Haugh, *supra* note 58.

believing that they have not misbehaved; this behavior is more likely to occur when enforcement is weak. Thus, if the objective is to drive them away from meeting their self-interest, we are likely to encounter resistance to the softer nudge-like approaches.

Another difference between the two types of nudges in health and financial contexts is that people know there are concrete consequences if they do not alter their actions. If they do not lose weight, they may get diabetes; if they do not save money, they may face an impoverished retirement. These outcomes are objective and can be measured. Ethical nudges do not produce such clear-cut consequences. Let's imagine the situation in which a supervisor wants to hire her friend rather than another candidate. The supervisor's self-interest is to hire her friend, and her goal in deceiving herself is to allow herself to feel that her decision was neither corrupt nor nepotistic but rather, was made in the best interests of the organization. With the exception of being subject to formal or informal penalties for nepotism, the supervisor does not have objective criteria to guide her ethical decision making. Ethical nudges should be accompanied by such criteria.

Nudges were first designed to cope with bounded rationality, but their use later expanded to the context of behavioral ethics. For example, Shu et al. show that people are more honest and less likely to engage in "moral forgetting" and "moral disengagement" if they sign an agreement at the beginning of the document, which makes the need to be honest salient.[69] The rationale is that the act of signing itself triggers morally desirable behavior; when a signature is not required until the end of the document, the individual would have already decided whether to fill out the form honestly or to lie, and it is too late to change this behavior. The strong effects demonstrated in this study might be attributed to the fact that participants saw the "sign first, write later" as an unusual practice, rather than simply altering the timing of the signature; therefore, making such a practice into a state law might undermine its efficacy. Nonetheless, the study does suggest the potential for nudge-related innovation in legal policy making to curb ordinary unethicality of "good people."

There is an additional concern regarding the facial validity of nudge approaches. Some studies have found that ethical shifts are produced by atypical cues, not by the interventions. For example, Gino and Desai find that cues from childhood, such as soft toys and nursery rhymes, have the power to decrease unethical behavior in participants.[70] Although such studies contribute greatly to understanding how

---

[69] Shu, L. L., Gino, F., & Bazerman, M. H. (2011). Dishonest deed, clear conscience: Self-preservation through moral disengagement and motivated forgetting. *Personality and Social Psychology Bulletin*, 37(3), 330–349.

[70] Gino, F., & Desai, S. D. (2012). Memory lane and morality: How childhood memories promote prosocial behavior. *Journal of Personality and Social Psychology*, 102(4), 743.

people make ethical decisions, there are obvious limitations to their applicability in the legal context. However, facial validity issues are less of a concern in the corporate or nonprofit context; those organizations are more likely to engage in soft nudge-based enforcement of unethical behaviors than government bodies, which need to maintain their legitimacy. Thus, for example, employers might see the use of teddy bears or priming the Ten Commandments to enhance honest behavior as a clever ethical nudge; however, that intervention is unlikely to be seen as such when done by a government agency such as the IRS.

4.3 ADDITIONAL NONTRADITIONAL INTERVENTIONS

4.3.1 *Disambiguation*

Many of the BE theories of bounded ethicality reviewed earlier suggest that legal ambiguity causes people to engage in wrongdoing.[71] This is the opposite conclusion reached by the BLE assumptions underlying rational choice, which hold that ambiguity and uncertainty increase compliance because people tend to be risk averse.[72]

Moral disengagement, as presented in Bandura's theory (see Chapter 2), is one of the principal techniques that people use to justify unethical behavior. It allows them to construct self-serving interpretations of legal and organizational requirements. For example, joint work with Teichman shows that people use legal ambiguity strategically to generate a self-serving interpretation of what is required from them by laws or contracts.[73] It is possible to speculate that these types of interpretations of legal imperatives will be sensitive to the individual's motivation (monetary vs. status), level of awareness, and amount of cognitive resources available (following pressures of ego depletion and time). Since people need to believe that they are following the letter of the law and yet are motivated by self-interest, the existence of ambiguity facilitates their routinely engaging in self-serving interpretation of legal norms.

A similar strategic use of ambiguity may be found in other contexts, where reducing the fear of behaving unethically may sometimes produce more, rather than less, unethical behavior. For example, the situations with the greatest conflict of interest should produce the most unethical behavior according to rational choice predictions. BE suggests that the opposite may be true. When there is ambiguity

[71]   Feldman, Y., & Harel, A. (2008). Social norms, self-interest and ambiguity of legal norms: An experimental analysis of the rule vs. standard dilemma. *Review of Law & Economics*, 4(1), 81–126.
[72]   Garoupa, N. (2003). Behavioral economic analysis of crime: A critical review. *European Journal of Law and Economics*, 15(1), 5–15; Logue, K. D. (2007). Optimal tax compliance and penalties when the law is uncertain. *Virginia Tax Review*, 27, 241–196.
[73]   Feldman, Y., & Teichman, D. (2009). Are all legal probabilities created equal? *NYU Law Review*, 84, 980–1022; Feldman, Y., & Teichman, D. (2011). Are all contractual obligations created equal? *Georgetown Law Journal*, 100(1), 5–52.

about the existence and impact of a conflict, individuals will be tempted to convince themselves that no such conflict exists and will act in a way that disregards the conflict. In clear-cut situations, individuals do not have such an excuse; therefore, they are less likely to misbehave. Thus, the law should seek to avoid the creation of ambiguous solutions that solve only part of a problem, for example, the mandate to disclose the conflict of interest but not to eliminate it.

Along the same lines, although much of the research on conflict of interest and corruption tends to suggest that money is more easily transferable and therefore more dangerous to the integrity of society than other sources of conflict, such as prestige and loyalty, some research on self-deception suggests that the opposite may be true. Most people recognize that taking money from various entities limits their ability to remain objective[74]. In contrast, the influence of non-monetary interests such as prestige, esteem, loyalty, and competence is less likely to trigger an alert by System 2; therefore, they are more likely to have an automatic effect on people, who are unconstrained by System 2.

4.3.2 *Reflection*

Bazerman and Tenbrunsel's examination of blind spots highlights the limited awareness process that facilitates unethical behaviors.[75] The classic response to the limited awareness problem is to force people to reflect on what they do, making sure they cannot brush aside the unethicality of their behavior using any of the numerous rationales reviewed earlier. Indeed, research on the interplay between System 1 and System 2 suggests that accountability may prevent people from relying on their automatic reasoning.[76] Unfortunately, in many legal contexts, in which some reporting is necessary, the opposite occurs. Forms are constructed to promote quick, hasty binary decisions, leaving little room for open-ended reflection and thought (e.g., forms relating to taxation, disclosures made when selling a car or a house, customs declarations, financial reports by businesses, and reports by oil and gas companies of payments to foreign countries related to processing minerals). In many cases, the information that individuals or corporations may decide not to report is never detected; if it is subsequently revealed, its omission is usually seen as

---

[74] This argument could be learned from the type of research conducted by Dan Ariely on how people are far better able to see the wrongness of taking someone else's money but can't see the same problem in taking things that money can buy such as a soda. Ariely, D. (2012). *The (honest) truth about dishonesty: How we lie to everyone especially ourselves.* New York: Harper.

[75] Bazerman, M., & Tenbrunsel, A. (2011). *Blind spots: Why we fail to do what's right and what to do about it.* Princeton: Princeton University Press.

[76] Tetlock, P. E., & Lerner, J. S. (1999). The social contingency model: Identifying empirical and normative boundary conditions on the error-and-bias portrait of human nature. In S. Chaiken & Y. Trope (Eds.), *Dual process theories in social psychology* (pp. 571–585). New York: Guilford.

an honest mistake.[77] Creating situations that encourage people to explicitly report information that may be related to ethical dilemmas may make it possible for people to reflect on the need to be honest. For example, it may be possible to include open-ended rubrics on tax forms, where taxpayers would indicate the areas about which they feel uncertain.

4.3.3 *The REVISE Approach*

Finally, Aval et al.'s approach is a great example of a nontraditional intervention to curb unethicality that recognizes that effective policy making in this area must address several parallel mechanisms at the same time. Their approach incorporates three main principles to encourage people's ethical behavior: reminders, visibility, and self-engagement.[78] To remind people not to use gray areas to justify dishonesty, they suggest setting subtle cues to the importance of ethical criteria or displaying hints at critical points and switching them from time to time; for instance, to encourage tax compliance, provide moral reminders in different sections of the tax return or use cues to highlight the moral uses of tax money. Because moral responsibility is diminished by anonymity, one should include procedures that strengthen people's perception that they are seen and recognized by other people who know them; regarding tax compliance, make the reporting process more personal or personalize the correspondence with the individual. Finally, the gap between people's abstract perception of their moral self-image and their actual behavior allows them to do wrong while still feeling moral. Therefore, they suggest creating and maintaining a self-commitment to act ethically before engaging in action; again to increase tax compliance, a recommendation is to survey people before tax time about their ethical and moral values and to ask specific questions about tax cheating. Another technique is to redesign the form to require signing an honor code at the beginning of the document.

The next chapter focuses on the role of social norms in changing people's ethical behavior. Norms are discussed in a separate chapter because of their enormous theoretical and practical relevance to the ethical behavior of good people.

---

[77] Compare with Kahan, D. M. (1997). Ignorance of law is an excuse: But only for the virtuous. *Michigan Law Review*, 96(1), 127–154, showing how the normative treatment of mistakes is beneficial for differentiating between people based on their approach to law and morality.

[78] Ayal, S., Gino, F., Barkan, R., & Ariely, D. (2015). Three principles to REVISE people's unethical behavior. *Perspectives on Psychological Science*, 10(6), 738–741. See discussion in Chapter 9 about how the REVISE approach could be relevant for curbing implicit corruption.

5

Social Norms and Compliance

Social norms are relevant for the ability of states to regulate ethically related behaviors: they play an important role in the efficacy of deterrence[1] and social enforcement[2] – traditional tools of intervention – and in influencing what people perceive to be fair.[3] They can both increase and reduce compliance by good people. This chapter focuses on cognitive and motivational limitations in relation to social norms that play an important role in the ability of states to trigger informal controls and other enforcement tools. An important component that underlies social norms' impact on behavior is individuals' misperception of them, which encourages them to violate the law in accordance to what they perceive incorrectly as the prevailing social norm. Due to the importance of social norms to both traditional and nontraditional approaches to legal compliance, and to the combination of cognitive misperceptions in recognizing what is the norm, in a way that supports our argument for the need to focus on good people, we dedicate a special chapter to the topic of social norms. The main case study that I use in this chapter analyzes the effects of social norms on the behavior of Silicon Valley employees with regard to divulging trade secrets when they move from one company to

---

This chapter include some modified texts from the paper coauthored with Michal Feldman and Bob Cooter: Cooter, R. D., Feldman, M., & Feldman, Y. (2008). The misperception of norms: The psychology of bias and the economics of equilibrium. *Review of Law & Economics*, 4(3), 889–911. It also draws insights from my dissertation field study, which was done on the effect of perceived social norms on Silicon Valley employees' divulgence of trade secrets as they move from one company to another. Y. Feldman. (2004). *Confidential know-how sharing and trade-secrets laws: Studying the interaction between legality, social norms and justice among high-tech employees in Silicon Valley.* PhD dissertation, University of California–Berkeley.

[1] For a behavioral perspective see Wenzel, M. (2004). The social side of sanctions: Personal and social norms as moderators of deterrence. *Law and Human Behavior*, 28(5), 547–567. For a rational choice perspective (mostly through signaling theory), see Posner, E. A. (2009). *Law and social norms.* Cambridge, MA: Harvard University Press.

[2] Kandori, M. (1992). Social norms and community enforcement. *Review of Economic Studies*, 59(1), 63–80.

[3] Elster, J. (1989). Social norms and economic theory. *Journal of Economic Perspectives*, 3(4), 99–117.

another. This case study, which was the subject of my dissertation research, is an apt illustration of the types of ordinary unethicality engaged in by many "good people," who pay limited attention to the legal and moral aspects of what their behavior actually means. The chapter first presents theories underlying behavioral perspectives toward social norms and then moves to the context of trade secrets to demonstrate how social norms operate to enable hi-tech employees to self-justify their behavior.

Some regulatory approaches assume that social norms are the dominant mechanism underlying compliance. It therefore focuses almost entirely on communicating the prevailing norm and information about the proportion of others who engage in law-abiding behavior, rather than the wisdom of the law itself. When people perceive that many others are misbehaving, they are more likely to misbehave as well.[4] Conversely, individuals' perceptions that they can rely on others to cooperate with them are a major factor in the promotion of cooperation.[5] In all social dilemmas, people tend to cooperate more when they think that others will also do so.[6]

Social norms define the unspoken psychological contract that guides behavior. The context of trade secrets, which I explored in my dissertation, with particular focus on the gap between formal law and social norms regarding information sharing, illustrates many of the mechanisms through which social norms can enable noncompliance. If people think that most of their friends are sharing confidential information, then they will perceive their own unwillingness to disclose the information in question as useless to the employer (because the information has already been shared) and even harmful to their own careers. It will cause them to question whether it even makes sense to keep information in confidence if everyone around them will disclose it anyway. Moreover, if people believe that many others are using confidential information to get hired, they will realize that not disclosing information may decrease their marketability when it comes time to compete for their next job.[7] If the social norm is to share information, then it communicates to people that they are entitled to do so as

---

[4]   The effect that the perceived number of people engaging in a particular behavior has on people's willingness to engage in that behavior is recognized as one of the main mechanisms in juvenile delinquency. This phenomenon, usually referred to as "social modeling," is a process by which observation of others' enactment of a behavior (e.g., heavy drinking) is thought to increase the likelihood of the observer adopting that behavior. Wood, M.* D., Read, J. P., Palfai, T. P., & Stevenson, J. F. (2001). Social influence processes and college student drinking: The mediational role of alcohol outcome expectancies. *Journal of Studies on Alcohol*, 62(1), 32.

[5]   See, for example, Van Vugt, M. (2013). Solving natural resource dilemmas through structural change: The social psychology of metering water use. In M. Foddy, M. Smithson, S. Schneider, & M. A. Hogg (Eds.), *Resolving social dilemmas: Dynamic, structural, and intergroup aspects* (pp. 121–133). New York: Psychology Press. See also Fischbacher, U., Gächter, S., & Fehr, E. (2001). Are people conditionally cooperative? Evidence from a public goods experiment. *Economics Letters*, 71(3), 397–404.

[6]   Keser, C., & Van Winden, F. (2000). Conditional cooperation and voluntary contributions to public goods. *Scandinavian Journal of Economics*, 102(1), 23–39.

[7]   For a discussion of the notion that following others' behavior could also be the most efficient step to take in an organizational setting, see Kraut, R. E., Rice, R. E., Cool, C., & Fish, R. S. (1998). Varieties

well. In many cases, when people internalize such norms of divulgence, they no longer even pay any attention to the legal or moral question. Such a blind spot is especially plausible when the trade secrets are not tangible and are part of people's skill sets, even though they are still legally defined as trade secrets.[8]

In this chapter, we use the social norms of Silicon Valley to understand the contribution of social norms to the creation and maintenance of the "good people rationale." Behaving as others do provides people with strong explicit and implicit signals that their noncompliance does not define their character.

5.1 HOW DO SOCIAL NORMS MATTER?

What is interesting from the perspective of this book about social norms is that they seem to have a different impact on people's deliberative decisions to comply than on their non-deliberative decisions to obey the law. The economic models of behavior focus on calculative decisions and suggest that formal enforcement such as deterrence and punishment fosters good behavior. Other models based on informal enforcement suggest that the effect of social norms on compliance is mediated by the social meaning of the situation and social identity. These factors are far more likely to have an effect on situational wrongdoers whose behavior this book attempts to capture.

Yet models of informal enforcement cannot explain why people behave when it is not necessarily in their self-interest to do so. It has been demonstrated that people follow societal rules, even under the condition of anonymity and in one-shot games.[9] In these cases, the mechanisms of social signaling, coordination, and reciprocity that underlie informal control models seem to be irrelevant, since no monitoring or tracking of the individuals is taking place. Yet these people are still "good," even when doing so does not necessarily maximize what appears to be their own self-interest. Informal control models also do not explain why people behave in ways that are beyond the call of duty – indeed, why they engage in anything more than minimal compliance.

In response to these shortcomings of informal control models, a growing number of legal economists have been attempting to revise the understanding of how rationality, self-interest, and values are related to law enforcement.[10] One

---

of social influence: The role of utility and norms in the success of a new communication medium. *Organization Science*, 9(4), 437–453.

[8] See Feldman, Y. (2006). The behavioral foundations of trade secrets: Tangibility, authorship, and legality. *Journal of Empirical Legal Studies*, 3(2), 197–235, for experimental evidence for the effect of people's intuitions of what types of information could be defined as trade secrets.

[9] For a review of people sensitive to fairness in the context of ultimatum games, see Güth, W. (1995). On ultimatum bargaining experiments – A personal review. *Journal of Economic Behavior & Organization*, 27(3), 329–344.

[10] See Korobkin, R. B., & Ulen, T. S. (2000). Law and behavioral science: Removing the rationality assumption from law and economics. *California Law Review*, 88(4), 1051.

explanation for why people are compliant in the absence of monitoring is that people have an internal respect for the law.[11] A trend in the legal theory of regulation and enforcement is to discuss voluntary compliance as necessary for maintaining social order.[12] Cooter adds that, ultimately, self-enforcing mechanisms are only ensured when people internalize the social norm.[13]

5.1.1 Social Norms and Group Identity

The importance of group identity and the individual's need to belong is beyond debate.[14] The motivation to fit in and belong to a group is widely recognized as a way to counteract the self-interest of the individual.[15] Tyran and Feld have demonstrated through a series of experiments that people are conditional cooperators in the context of public goods, and they want to engage in legal compliance when they have a reason to believe that others would do the same.[16] Kahan has suggested a somewhat different explanation, not based on identity, as to why people would care about what others are doing. He argues that the individual needs to believe that other members of society share his or her commitment to the law to maintain his or her own commitment to society and to its rules.[17] According to this approach, the focus is neither on reputation nor on identity, but rather on the fear of being the only "sucker" who obeys the law.[18]

5.1.2 Social Norms and the Expressive Function of the Law

A fast-growing body of literature focuses on the expressive function of the law and emphasizes social norms' mediated approach to legality.[19] McAdams's attitudinal

[11]   This argument is one of the main arguments of Hart, H. L. A. (1961). *The concept of law.* Oxford: Oxford University Press.
[12]   Ryesky, K. H. (1998). Of taxes and duties: Taxing the system with public employees' tax obligations. *Akron Law Review*, 31(3).
[13]   Cooter, R. (2000). Do good laws make good citizens? An economic analysis of internalized norms. *Virginia Law Review*, 86(8), 1577.
[14]   Baumeister, R. F., & Leary, M. R. (1995). The need to belong: Desire for interpersonal attachments as a fundamental human motivation. *Psychological Bulletin*, 117(3), 497.
[15]   Brewer, M. B., & Kramer, R. M. (1986). Choice behavior in social dilemmas: Effects of social identity, group size, and decision framing. *Journal of Personality and Social Psychology*, 50(3), 543.
[16]   Tyran, J. R., & Feld, L. P. (2002). Why people obey the law: Experimental evidence from the provision of public goods. CESifo Working Paper No. 651.
[17]   Kahan, D. M. (2001). Trust, collective action, and law. *Boston University Law Review*, 81, 333.
[18]   Scholz, J. T., & Lubell, M. (1998). Trust and taxpaying: Testing the heuristic approach to collective action. *American Journal of Political Science*, 42, 398–417. See also Biel, A., Von Borgstede, C., & Dahlstrand, U. (1999). Norm perception and cooperation in large scale social dilemmas. In In M. Foddy, M. Smithson, S. Schneider, & M. Hogg (Eds.), *Resolving social dilemmas: Dynamic, structural, and intergroup aspects* (pp. 245–252). Philadelphia: Taylor & Francis.
[19]   Sunstein, C. R. (1996). Social norms and social roles. *Columbia Law Review*, 96(4), 903–968; Cooter, R. D. (2000). Three effects of social norms on law: Expression, deterrence, and internalization. *Oregon Law Review*, 79, 1.

theory of expressive law suggests that enacting a law solves the pluralistic ignorance problem by signaling the underlying attitudes of a community or society. This approach assumes that people's main legal motivation is to seek the approval of others, so the information signaled by legislation provides a guide for engaging in socially approved behavior.[20]

While many legal economists share the view that the content of the prevalent social norm is crucial in determining the motivation to engage in legal compliance, their view of why that content is important to the individual is obviously different from that of psychologists. For example, Posner, returning to his famous model of signaling, discusses why such a high percentage of taxes are collected despite the low probability of being caught and the small size of sanctions.[21] By paying taxes, individuals signal to others that they are law abiding; this view is along the same lines as the various models of using shaming to increase compliance.[22] Thus, while such economic approaches focus on the approval of others, many of them relate this approval to reputation maintenance (resembling the calculative model discussed earlier), rather than to an endogenous desire to belong.

A somewhat hybrid type of intrinsic motivation–based model of social norms is related to social values, which extend beyond considerations of fairness and morality.[23] In direct contradiction to theoretical models in economics, which explain social order as a mechanism of coordinating the various interests of various actors in society,[24] more and more voices within the economics literature now recognize the impossibility of maintaining social order without social values.[25]

[20] McAdams, R. H. (2015). *The expressive powers of law: Theories and limits*. Cambridge, MA: Harvard University Press. See also Dharmapala, D., & McAdams, R. H. (2003). The Condorcet jury theorem and the expressive function of law: A theory of informative law. *American Law and Economics Review*, 5(1), 1–31.

[21] Posner, R. A. (1997). Social norms and the law: An economic approach. *The American Economic Review*, 87(2), 365–369.

[22] See also Kahan, D. M., & Posner, E. A. (1999). Shaming white-collar criminals: A proposal for reform of the federal sentencing guidelines. *The Journal of Law and Economics*, 42(S1), 365–392.

[23] For an excellent review, see Ben-Ner, A., & Putterman, L. (1999). Values and institutions in economic analysis. In A. Ben-Ner & L. Putterman (Eds.), *Economics, values, and organization* (pp. 3–70). Cambridge: Cambridge University Press.

[24] Leading voices among them are Sugden, R. (1989). Spontaneous order. *Journal of Economic Perspectives*, 3(4), 85–97. See also Hardin, R. (1990). *Morality within the limits of reason*. Chicago: University of Chicago Press.

[25] A very famous example is Kahneman, D., Knetsch, J. L., & Thaler, R. H. (1986). Fairness as a constraint on profit seeking: Entitlements in the market. *Journal of Business*, 76(4), 728–741. See also Alvi, E. (1998). Fairness and self-interest: An assessment. *Journal of Socio-Economics* 27(2), 245–261, who generally support the view that fairness and self-interest have independent explanatory power.

They recognize the importance of norms,[26] morality,[27] and social values to social order.[28]

A related line of research explores social virtue and social capital. Coleman's[29] and Putnam's research[30] has focused on the existence of networks of civic engagements and a set of functioning and efficient norms underlying them. They find that regulating behaviors operating under a set of social norms might counterintuitively lead to incompliance. Such misconduct may be related not to the various models of social influence but rather to a macro perspective of what society will look like when norms are replaced by regulation.

A non-deliberative process related to socialization can also affect how social norms interact with the "good" people model. In contrast to scholars such as Kelman,[31] who views compliance and internalization as mutually exclusive processes, wherein compliance is based on fear and internalization is based on understanding and rational acceptance, socialization models see these two processes as steps in a developmental sequence. Accordingly, the regulation of social behavior may begin with an experience of fear from an external source. However, throughout the socialization process, norms and laws become internalized and incorporated in the self to the extent that social control becomes self-regulated.[32]

---

[26] Symposium, Law, economics, and norms. (1996). *University of Pennsylvania Law Review, 144,* 1643. See also Symposium, The legal construction of norms (2000). *Virginia Law Review, 86,* 1577; for an interesting analysis of how the scholars of this movement perceived themselves, see Bernstein, L. (1998). The New Chicago School: Myth or reality? *University of Chicago Law School Roundtable, 5,* 1; Symposium, Social norms, social meaning, and the economic analysis of law. (1998). *Journal of Legal Studies, 27,* 537.

[27] As opposed to the more instrumental/self-related concepts of justice, the literature on moral norms relates to the internalization aspects of social norms and was shown to have a predictive value, even when attitudes and social norms were present; Manstead, A. S. (2000). The role of moral norm in the attitude–behavior relation. In D. J. Terry & M. A. Hogg (Eds.), *Attitudes, behaviour, and social context: The role of norms and group membership.* Mahwah, NJ: Erlbaum. Thus, for example, I have a moral obligation to do so and so increased more than 20 percent the predictive value of attitudes in the context of tax returns. For an overview of the role of morality in economic life, especially its role as a constraint on profit making, see McLeary, J. W. (1991) *Morality, economic justice, and profits.* New York: Vantage Press. For an example of an empirical demonstration of the role of morality in ethical decision making in organizations, see Paolillo, J. G., & Vitell, S. J. (2002). An empirical investigation of the influence of selected personal, organizational and moral intensity factors on ethical decision making. *Journal of Business Ethics, 35*(1), 65–74.

[28] Frey, B. S. (1997). *Not just for the money: An economic theory of personal motivation.* Cheltenham: Edward Elgar, regarding the crowding-out effect; he relies on theories of locus of control and self-esteem. See also Frank, R. H. (1988). *Passions within reason: The strategic role of the emotions.* New York: W. W. Norton.

[29] Coleman, J. S. (1988). Social capital in the creation of human capital. *American Journal of Sociology, 94,* S95–S120.

[30] Putnam, R. D. (1995). Bowling alone: America's declining social capital. *Journal of Democracy, 6*(1), 65–78.

[31] Kelman, H. C. (1958). Compliance, identification, and internalization: Three processes of attitude change. *Journal of Conflict Resolution, 2*(1), 51–60.

[32] Zimring, F. E., Hawkins, G., & Vorenberg, J. (1973). *Deterrence: The legal threat in crime control.* Chicago: University of Chicago Press, 58.

5.2 SOCIAL NORMS AND DUAL REASONING

Insights developed from the large literature on social norms have succeeded in changing the perspective of law and economic research on compliance.[33] Based on the behavioral economics[34] and the behavioral ethics literatures, there seems to be a need to reevaluate how social norms shape "good people's" intention to obey laws, given the cognitive and motivational limitations that hinder their ability to view themselves as behaving badly.

Naturally, social norms are not a concept of interest only for law and economics; sociologists, whose focus is society itself, have made important contributions to the effect of social norms on behavior.[35] For a more behavioral account from the field of psychology of how social norms change the behavior of people, see Wood's account containing a description of the dual processing through which people learn to adopt new social norms.[36]

Theories in cognitive psychology that focus on mechanisms such as anchoring, selective accessibility, and representation are celebrated in the judgment and decision-making contexts that are highly relevant to our concept of good people Yet, as with regard to the ignorance of behavioral ethics, these same theories, when applied by psychologists to understand the cognitive (e.g., assimilation vs. contrast) and affective impacts of social comparison standards[37] and social norms, have received no attention from behavioral law and economics – an astonishing omission given that some of the key scholars in that field are also the leading scholars in the law and economics of social norms.[38]

Law and economics scholars assume that norms affect behavior in a deliberative way. However, the preponderance of research on social influence, such as that supporting Cialdini's focus theory and Latene's social impact theory,[39] demonstrates that much of the impact of social norms on the behavior of people is done through non-deliberative processes, which in turn could change the likelihood of noncompliance, by good people. The possible inadvertent effect of social norms on the unethical behavior of good people is exacerbated by taking into account the over-estimation of unethical social norms, as explained in the next section.

---

[33] See Sunstein, *supra* note 19.

[34] Kahneman, D., & Tversky, A. (1984). Choices, values, and frames. *American Psychologist*, 39(4), 341–350. See also Tversky, A., & Kahneman, D. (1981). The framing of decisions and the psychology of choice. *Science*, 211(4481), 453–458.

[35] Etzioni, A. (2000). Social norms: Internalization, persuasion, and history. *Law & Society Review*, 34 (1), 157–178.

[36] Wood, W. (2000). Attitude change: Persuasion and social influence. *Annual Review of Psychology*, 51 (1), 539–570.

[37] Mussweiler, T., & Strack, F. (2000). Consequences of social comparison. In J. Suls & L Wheeler (Eds.), *Handbook of social comparison* (pp. 253–270). New York: Plenum Publishers.

[38] Tversky, A., & Kahneman, D. (1974). Judgment under uncertainty: Heuristics and biases. *Science*, 185 (4157), 1124–1130. If your comparison standard was a heavy user, you would tend to estimate that you are a heavier user than you would if you had first been asked to compare yourself to a light user. See also Mussweiler, T., & Strack, F. (2000). The "relative self": Informational and judgmental consequences of comparative self-evaluation. *Journal of Personality and Social Psychology*, 79(1), 23–38.

[39] Latane, B. (1981). The psychology of social impact. *American Psychologist*, 36(4), 343–356.

5.3 MISPERCEIVING SOCIAL NORMS AS A MEANS TO JUSTIFY "BAD" BEHAVIOR BY GOOD PEOPLE

This section presents psychological research on the misperception of norms, which relates to the rationales "good people" use to self-justify noncompliance and still feel good about themselves. Then findings from my dissertation research on the misperception of engineers in Silicon Valley concerning divulging trade secrets are presented.

5.3.1 Research on Misperception of Norms

Research on tax evasion has investigated the connection between the willingness of people to pay taxes and their perception of the extent of tax evasion committed by others.[40] A longitudinal panel study of Australian taxpayers found that many individuals think that more people evade taxes than actually do.[41] The "others-are-bad" bias could produce this discrepancy.[42]

The same investigation found that taxpayers' personal views of the morality of tax compliance affect their perception of the levels of tax compliance by others. Those with high personal standards of tax compliance perceived relatively more compliance by others, and those with low personal standards perceived relatively less tax compliance by others. These results are consistent with the "just-like-me" bias.

Discrepancies between self vs. other perceptions of drinking, using drugs, and smoking have also been researched. A series of studies show that college students perceive their peers as less critical of heavy drinking than they actually are, which suggests others-are-bad bias. One of the studies tracked how attitudes developed over the course of two months among first-year college students and discovered gender differences. Male students adjusted their personal attitudes over time to match the perceived consensus more closely. Among female students, attitudes remained stable.[43]

---

[40] For a discussion of the concept of conditional cooperation and experimental evidence of its relevancy for legal compliance, see Tyran, J. R., & Feld, L. P. (2006). Achieving compliance when legal sanctions are non-deterrent. *Scandinavian Journal of Economics*, 108(1), 135–156. For an illustration of the importance of conditional cooperation in the context of tax compliance, see Scholz & Lubell, *supra* note 18.

[41] Wenzel, M. (2005). Misperceptions of social norms about tax compliance: From theory to intervention. *Journal of Economic Psychology*, 26(6), 862–883.

[42] Although in that study, the psychological cause they focused on was the pluralistic ignorance phenomenon.

[43] Subjects' ratings of personal comfort with Princeton drinking norms, as well as estimates of their perceptions of the average students' comfort level, were taken at two points separated by two months. The results indicated that men behaved in accordance with the expectation of social influence theorists in that they changed their own attitudes in the direction of the social norm. Indeed, personal average comfort among men in September was 5.84 with the perceived average student at 7.48. By December, men's personal comfort with drinking norm had jumped to 7.08, with perceptions of average student comfort level remaining relatively stable at 7.58. Women, on the other hand, showed

In a classic study on drugs, a sample of adolescents was divided into three groups: nonusers, cannabis users, and cannabis and amphetamine users.[44] The perceptions of drug use among members of the three groups differed significantly.[45] Compared to nonusers, drug users gave relatively high estimates of the number of users. These results are consistent with the just-like-me bias.

Turning to smoking, researchers surveyed 916 junior high school students in seventh grade and two years later in ninth grade regarding their personal smoking habits and their perception of others' smoking habits.[46] Those seventh graders who smoked thought that relatively more people smoked, and those seventh graders who did not smoke thought that relatively fewer people smoked.[47] Specifically, adolescents who were most involved with smoking believed that half or more than half of all adults or peers smoked, whereas those least involved believed that fewer than half of adults or peers smoked. The just-like-me bias could explain this data.

Similar results were found regarding cooperation in a social dilemma situation. When a tropical storm caused a water shortage in the eastern United States in 1999, Princeton University imposed a ban on showering for the first three days of the water crisis.[48] Princeton psychologists then surveyed students for self-reported and perceived showering.[49] During the ban, students estimated that others took more showers than implied by self-reports: 47 percent versus 33 percent on day two, and 56 percent versus 47 percent on day three. The others-are-bad bias would have produced this gap.

As soon as the ban was lifted, other students were seen as taking fewer showers than implied by self-reports: 70 percent versus 77 percent on day four, 72 percent versus 84 percent on day five. These results are consistent with the theory that the others-are-bad bias only applies to morally relevant behavior. During the ban, not showering was altruistic. After the ban was lifted, showering ceased to be morally relevant (or, perhaps, showering became altruistic).

no change in personal attitudes over time, save for a slight inflation of perceived average student comfort from 7.16 to 7.74.

[44] Wolfson, S. (2000). Students' estimates of the prevalence of drug use: Evidence for a false consensus effect. *Psychology of Addictive Behaviors*, 14(3), 295.

[45] Nonusers: M = 37.23%, cannabis users: M = 44.38%, and amphetamine users: M = 54.22%.

[46] Bauman, K. E., Botvin, G. J., Botvin, E. M., & Baker, E. (1992). Normative expectations and the behavior of significant others: An integration of traditions in research on adolescents' cigarette smoking. *Psychological Reports*, 71(2), 568–570.

[47] The use of longitudinal and cross-sectional designs allows the authors to speak of causality, although they use correlation-based analysis.

[48] Monin, B., & Norton, M. I. (2003). Perceptions of a fluid consensus: Uniqueness bias, false consensus, false polarization, and pluralistic ignorance in a water conservation crisis. *Personality and Social Psychology Bulletin*, 29(5), 559–567.

[49] For the relationship between self-reported behavior and actual behavior, see Epley, N., & Dunning, D. (2000). Feeling "holier than thou": Are self-serving assessments produced by errors in self- or social prediction? *Journal of Personality and Social Psychology*, 79(6), 861.

In a joint work with Cooter and M. Feldman,[50] based on the findings suggesting a perceptual bias in the estimation of the proportion of wrongdoers in society, we created two types of biases: the "others-are-bad" bias and the "just-like-me" bias.

5.3.2 Causes of Perceptual Bias

In the paper by Cooter and Feldman, we focused on possible cognitive and motivational causes of the others-are-bad bias, and this section reviews each one in turn. Media attention provides one of the simplest cognitive explanations for overestimating wrongdoing[51]: immoral acts, such as lying, adultery, robbery, and fraud get much more media coverage than moral acts.[52] Lichtenberg and MacLean demonstrate that much of what the media report is bad news.[53] Prentice and miller analyzed four types of TV news programs (national network news, local news, independent news, and cable network news) for violence, conflict, and suffering content.[54] They reviewed more than 100 individual news programs among those four types over a six-month period – finding an emphasis on news that is bad and violent.[55]

In psychology, "salience" refers to the ease of recalling events that are vivid and have occurred recently. Psychologists have found that people tend to overestimate the probability of salient events and underestimate the probability of non-salient events.[56] The media give salience to wrongdoing, which causes people to overestimate its frequency.

---

[50] Cooter, R. D., Feldman, M., & Feldman, Y. (2008). The misperception of norms: The psychology of bias and the economics of equilibrium. *Review of Law & Economics*, 4(3), 889–911.

[51] While psychology research on TV violence tends to focus on entertainment TV, the daily news is watched even more widely and also contains extreme and realistic violent content. See Miller, D. T., & Prentice, D. A. (1994). Collective errors and errors about the collective. *Personality and Social Psychology Bulletin*, 20(5), 541–550 for a discussion of the role of the media in this phenomenon.

[52] Jones, D. 1997. "48% of Workers Admit to Unethical or Illegal Acts," April 4, 1997, *USA Today*.

[53] Lichtenberg, J., & MacLean, D. (1992). Is good news no news? *Geneva Papers on Risk and Insurance. Issues and Practice*, 362–365. Koren and Klein (1991) also show the greater coverage of bad news in their comparison of news coverage of two scientific studies that investigated the relationship between radiation exposure and cancer. The bad news study showed an increased risk of leukemia in white men working at the Oak Ridge National Laboratory. The good news study failed to show an increased risk of cancer in people residing near nuclear facilities. Koren and Klein found that subsequent newspaper coverage was far greater for the study showing increased risk. Koren, G., & Klein, N. (1991). Bias against negative studies in newspaper reports of medical research. *JAMA*, 266(13), 1824–1826.

[54] Johnson, R. N. (1996). Bad news revisited: The portrayal of violence, conflict, and suffering on television news. *Peace and Conflict: Journal of Peace Psychology*, 2(3), 201. See also Prentice, D. A., & Miller, D. T. (1996). Pluralistic ignorance and the perpetuation of social norms by unwitting actors. *Advances in Experimental Social Psychology*, 28, 161–209.

[55] On parameters of time allocation and amount of featured news stories, more than half (53.4%) of the news displayed violence, conflict, and suffering. Bad news was also given greater emphasis in that it was featured earlier in the programs. While local news broadcast the most bad news, all four program types were found to emphasize bad news.

[56] Tversky, A., & Kahneman, D. (1973). Availability: A heuristic for judging frequency and probability. *Cognitive Psychology*, 5(2), 207–232.

Why do the media give disproportionate attention to negative news? Media outlets compete for people's attention, and human beings apparently pay more attention to bad news than good news.[57] According to the theory of *automatic vigilance*, individuals who respond to undesirable social stimuli gain an evolutionary advantage.[58] Thus, we are primed to pay more attention to undesirable stimuli than to desirable social stimuli.[59] We are especially attracted to undesirable behavior by others.[60]

Another possible cause of the others-are-bad bias is the way in which people explain others' behavior. Many psychological studies support the conclusion that people incorrectly attribute too much of the cause of undesirable behavior to fixed traits of character in the actor and too little to the social situation.[61] Buckley et al. suggest that this "fundamental attribution error" plays a role in overestimating the amount of wrongdoing by others.[62] According to the authors, most people are ethical with occasional lapses. Thoroughly unscrupulous people are an exceptional minority. Because of the fundamental attribution error, a person who witnesses wrongdoing will conclude that the actor usually misbehaves, whereas the correct

---

[57] Slovic, P. (1993). Perceived risk, trust, and democracy. *Risk Analysis*, 13(6), 675–682.
[58] Pratto, F., & John, O. P. (2005). Automatic vigilance: The attention-grabbing power of negative social information. *Social Cognition: Key Readings*, 250.
[59] There is a fundamental asymmetry in people's evaluations of gains and losses, of joy and pain, and of positive and negative events. A considerable body of research, in fields as diverse as decision making, impression formation, and emotional communication, has shown that people exhibit loss aversion (See Kahneman & Tversky, *supra* note 34.): they assign relatively more value, importance, and weight to events that have negative, rather than positive, implications for them. In decision making, potential costs are more influential than potential gains (e.g., Kahneman, D., & Tversky, A. (1979). Prospect theory: An analysis of decision under risk. *Econometrica: Journal of the Econometric Society*, 47(2), 263–291). In impression formation, negative information is weighted more heavily than positive information (e.g., Fiske, S. T. (1980). Attention and weight in person perception: The impact of negative and extreme behavior. *Journal of Personality and Social Psychology*, 38(6), 889.). In nonverbal communication, perceivers are more responsive to negatively toned messages than to positive ones. Frodi, A. M., Lamb, M. E., Leavitt, L. A., Donovan, W. L., Neff, C., & Sherry, D. (1978). Fathers' and mothers' responses to the faces and cries of normal and premature infants. *Developmental Psychology*, 14(5), 490.
[60] Skowronski, J. J., & Carlston, D. E. (1989). Negativity and extremity biases in impression formation: A review of explanations. *Psychological Bulletin*, 105(1), 131. This concept is related to impression formation: the fact that unfavorable characteristics are weighted more heavily than favorable ones in initial formation of an assessment of an object. Results showed that likableness ratings of a person associated with an unfavorable attribute varied significantly more from a neutral impression than did ratings of a person associated with a desirable attribute. Additionally, subjects were more confident in their likableness ratings of the negative stimulus persons. It is certainly plausible to equate unethical traits/information with negative traits/information when it comes to impression formation.
[61] Gilbert, D. T., & Malone, P. S. (1995). The correspondence bias. *Psychological Bulletin*, 117(1), 21.
[62] Halbesleben, J. R., Buckley, M. R., & Sauer, N. D. (2004). The role of pluralistic ignorance in perceptions of unethical behavior: An investigation of attorneys' and students' perceptions of ethical behavior. *Ethics & Behavior*, 14(1), 17–30. The fundamental attribution error is the basis of the pluralistic ignorance phenomenon, implying that people might fail to account for others' true motivations for engaging in various behaviors.

conclusion in most cases is that the actor only occasionally commits misconduct and usually in situations that are conducive to wrongdoing.[63]

The others-are-bad bias could also result from a tendency to believe that the behavior of others is instrumentally driven. The overestimation of unethical behavior could follow from a common belief that self-interest is the most important factor in explaining the behavior of individuals in society.[64]

Another possible cause is mostly emotional. Wrongdoers may protect their self-esteem by exaggerating how frequently others commit the same wrong.[65] Relevant concepts invoked by psychologists include social validation, self-enhancing biases, and constructive social comparison.[66]

This moves us to the "just-like-me" bias: individuals who project their own behavior onto society overestimate how many others behave like as they do. This bias is closely related to what the psychology literature calls the false consensus effect (FCE), which refers to a situation where people mistakenly think that others agree with them. According to the FCE, people tend to overestimate the social support for their own views and underestimate the social support for people who hold opposing views.[67] Evidence from the studies in the original research by Ross demonstrates a false consensus about the relative commonness not only of views but also of behavior; people tend to overestimate the number of others behaving in a manner

---

[63] For an economic model that develops the effect of attribution biases, see Dharmapala, D., & McAdams, R. H. (2005). Words that kill? An economic model of the influence of speech on behavior (with particular reference to hate speech). *Journal of Legal Studies*, 34(1), 93–136.

[64] Miller, D. T. (1999). The norm of self-interest. *American Psychologist*, 54(12), 1053.

[65] See Wenzel, *supra* note 41.

[66] Avoiding or inventing social reality when one suspects that the social practice might prevent one from following his or her own self-interest: Suls, J., & Wan, C. K. (1987). In search of the false-uniqueness phenomenon: Fear and estimates of social consensus. *Journal of Personality and Social Psychology*, 52(1), 211. See also Wheeler, L. (1966). Toward a theory of behavioral contagion. *Psychological Review*, 73(2), 179.

[67] For the false consensus effect, see generally Newman, L. S., Duff, K. J., & Baumeister, R. F. (1997). A new look at defensive projection: Thought suppression, accessibility, and biased person perception. *Journal of Personality and Social Psychology*, 72(5), 980. If someone tends to violate trade secrets, social consensus alone is not likely to lead him to understand that he is disclosing more secrets than the norm allows; see Ross, L., Greene, D., & House, P. (1977). The "false consensus effect": An egocentric bias in social perception and attribution processes. *Journal of Experimental Social Psychology*, 13(3), 279–301. But see also de la Haye, A. M. (2000). A methodological note about the measurement of the false-consensus effect. *European Journal of Social Psychology*, 30(4), 569–581, demonstrating the mistakes that Ross et al. made in their measurements. In addition, Dawes, R. M., & Mulford, M. (1996). The false consensus effect and overconfidence: Flaws in judgment or flaws in how we study judgment? *Organizational Behavior and Human Decision Processes*, 65(3), 201–211, also question the existence of the false consensus effect – basically showing the opposite – that the more people thought others were like them, the more accurate they were in their estimations of their behavior. Marks, G., & Miller, N. (1987). Ten years of research on the false-consensus effect: An empirical and theoretical review. *Psychological Bulletin*, 102(1), 72, for a reconciliation of the uniqueness and the false consensus effect. It is important to note that some have argued that the false consensus is not at all a bias, but could rather be explained according to Bayesian analysis.

similar to themselves.[68] These results were obtained both from questionnaires that presented subjects with hypothetical situations and by placing them in actual conflicts where they were presented with choices.

Several psychological mechanisms could cause just-like-me bias. One such mechanism is cognitive: people may attend to positions with which they agree and dismiss those with which they disagree. Selective attention allows people's preferred position to dominate their consciousness. People also tend to associate with others who share their general beliefs, attitudes, and values, thereby increasing their perceived validation of just-like-me bias. The number of arguments that we hear in favor of or against something affects our attitude toward it; since we hear more arguments from people inside our group than from outsiders, the sorting of people reinforces selective attention. The association could be voluntary, as when people select their friends, or involuntary, as when people are segregated. If like associates with like, then recalling instances of similar behavior to your own will be easier than recalling dissimilar behavior.[69]

Instead of cognition, emotion could cause this bias. Most people presumably need to see their own acts, beliefs, and feelings as morally appropriate.[70] Finding similarities between oneself and others may validate the appropriateness of behavior, sustain self-esteem, restore cognitive balance, enhance perceived social support, and reduce anticipated social tensions.[71]

5.3.3 *Motivationally Driven Constructive Social Comparison*

The larger problem, which some consider to encompass all the previously mentioned biases, is a form of "constructive social comparison." This social phenomenon describes the situation wherein people make false presumptions about how others behave to preserve their own self-esteem.[72] With less salient and firm social sanctions, people are more likely to invent false realities to preserve their own sense of dignity without giving up their own self-interests.

---

[68] Thus, if someone tends to violate trade secrets, social consensus alone is not likely to lead him to understand that he is disclosing more secrets than the norm allows for.

[69] Walster, E., Walster, G. W., & Berscheid, E. (1978). *Equity: Theory and research*. Boston: Allyn & Bacon. See also Ross et al., *supra* note 67.

[70] Sherman, S. J., Presson, C. C., & Chassin, L. (1984). Mechanisms underlying the false consensus effect: The special role of threats to the self. *Personality and Social Psychology Bulletin*, 10(1), 127–138.

[71] See Marks & Miller, *supra* note 67, at 72

[72] Avoiding or inventing social reality when one suspects that the social practice might prevent him from following his own self-interest. Suls & Wan, In search of the false-uniqueness phenomenon. See also Wheeler, L. (1966). Motivation as a determinant of upward comparison. *Journal of Experimental Social Psychology*, 1, 27–31.

The notion of esteem as a motivating force in obedience to norms and laws has captured the attention of many legal scholars, as well as social scientists.[73] McAdams's widely cited paper examining people's motivation for obeying social norms focuses on what he calls "competition for esteem."[74] Similarly, Kahan has used concepts of shaming and shunning as important factors in the social enforcement of laws[75] and social norms.[76] Obviously, constructive social comparison does not eliminate the impact of *actual* social comparison on people's behavior; however, given that in most cases people will act based on their *perceived* social norms, it is important to be aware of the limits of esteem-based sanctions.

First, the concept of constructive social comparison suggests that if people are interested in self-validation they are likely to envision changes in how other people behave.[77] Therefore, competition for esteem does not ensure that people will compete to engage in socially desirable behaviors. Second, the assumption that people will always look at society for cues is far from accurate, especially with regard to situations that might trigger embarrassment when such a comparison is made[78]: in both adolescence and adult life, people look to socially reward themselves. Third, that people might actually engage in a downward rather than an upward comparison could jeopardize the competition for esteem.[79] In this scenario, people's need for high self-esteem might cause them to seek out others who behave worse than they do.

5.3.4 *Divulging Trade Secrets in Silicon Valley*

In my dissertation research, subjects were asked whether they would violate trade-secret laws and then what was the frequency with which other people, both in their company and in the Silicon Valley community, would violate those laws.

[73]   Harsanyi, J. C. (1969). Rational-choice models of political behavior vs. functionalist and conformist theories. *World Politics*, 21(4), 513–538. People's behavior can be largely explained in terms of two dominant interests: economic gain and social acceptance as discussed in Pettit, P. (1990). Virtus normativa: Rational choice perspectives. *Ethics*, 100(4), 725–755.

[74]   See McAdams, R. H. (1997). The origin, development, and regulation of norms. *Michigan Law Review*, 96(2), 338–433.

[75]   Kahan, D. M. (1997). Social influence, social meaning, and deterrence. *Virginia Law Review*, 38, 349–395.

[76]   See also Fershtman, C., & Weiss, Y. (1998). Why do we care what others think about us? *Economics, Values, and Organization*, 133–50, for a formal analysis of people's quest for status.

[77]   Goethals, G. R., & Klein, W. M. (2001). Interpreting and inventing social reality. In Wheeler, L., & Suls, J. (Eds.), *Handbook of social comparison: Theory and research*, 12th ed., Vol. 5. New York: Springer.

[78]   For example, Batson et al. show the limitations of non-instrumental self-control by focusing on what they call moral hypocrisy: Batson, C. D., Thompson, E. R., Seuferling, G., Whitney, H., & Strongman, J. A. (1999). Moral hypocrisy: Appearing moral to oneself without being so. *Journal of Personality and Social Psychology*, 77(3), 525; they show that 70 to 80 percent of their subjects gave themselves the better assignment, though only 10 percent thought that this was the moral thing to do.

[79]   Taylor, S. E., & Lobel, M. (1989). Social comparison activity under threat: Downward evaluation and upward contacts. *Psychological Review*, 96(4), 569.

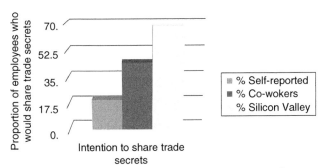

FIGURE 5.1 Gap between self-reported divulging of trade secrets and perception of other employees' engaging in divulging trade secrets.
Source: Figures 5.1 & 5.2 are taken from my dissertation: Y. Feldman. (2004). Confidential know-how sharing and trade-secrets laws: Studying the interaction between legality, social norms and justice among high-tech employees in Silicon Valley. PhD dissertation, University of California–Berkeley.

Of the study participants, 44.8 % said that they were more likely than not to violate trade-secret laws, but they estimated on average that 57 % of the employees in their company would violate such laws. When asked about the proportion of employees in Silicon Valley in general who would violate the trade-secrets laws, the average answer was 68 %. The others-are-bad bias would produce such a gap in results (see Figure 5.1).

The overestimation was also significant regarding trade secrets intentionally downloaded to one's personal computer. Only 20 percent said that they would download trade secrets and use them in a different company. They estimated that 43 percent of their peers would do so, and that 62 percent of the employees in Silicon Valley would do so as well. In an ANOVA analysis, all gaps between the measures of the co-workers and Silicon Valley employees were found to be significant.

In the study, employees who were likely to violate the law were more likely to believe that most other employees in Silicon Valley would do likewise. Employees who were less likely to violate the law were more likely to think that very few people in the Valley in fact violate trade secrets (see Figure 5.2). This finding is not conclusive evidence for overestimation, because the causal effect might be reversed: the perceived norm may affect behavior, rather than one's behavior affecting the perceived norm.[80]

This perception gap seems to demonstrate that with less information about the actual behavior of people, it is more likely that one will exaggerate the prevalence of unethical behavior. The more people know about the target group (people know more about themselves than co-workers and more about their co-workers than the general population of Silicon Valley), the less likely they are to attribute unethical behavior to that group. Hence, the cause of this type of normative failure might be

[80]   In general, the effect of false consensus and the means of measuring it are somewhat controversial. See, for example, Dawes & Mulford, The false consensus effect and overconfidence.

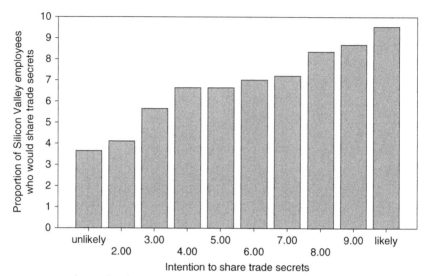

FIGURE 5.2 Relationship between participant's own likelihood of violating trade secrets and his or her estimation of the proportion of employees in Silicon Valley who would violate the law.

more than simply the tendency to overestimate the amount of support for unethical behavior in a population.[81]

5.3.5 *Biases and the Overestimation of Others' Disclosure of Trade Secrets*

To build the argument that, lacking institutional guidance, employees will overestimate the proportion of colleagues who disclose trade secrets, I briefly review two of the social-psychological effects related to the misperception of norms.[82] Pluralistic ignorance has been invoked to explain people's inability to accurately estimate both the level of acceptability that is enjoyed by a given norm in a given population and the private beliefs of their fellow employees relative to that norm.[83] Miller and

[81]   This gap could be related to in-group–out-group relations, in which the individual will tend to see her group as superior to the members of the out-group; or it might be related some commitment of secrecy that the individual has made to her own co-workers (i.e., not to report their unethical behavior).

[82]   Mcadams, R. H. (2000). An attitudinal theory of expressive law. *Oregon Law Review*, 79, 339, 349–356 for a discussion of pluralistic ignorance in the context of approval patterns. For a discussion of the characteristics of events that are likely to be more easily accessible, see Slovic, P., Fischhoff, B., & Lichtenstein, S. (1980). Facts and fears: Understanding perceived risk. *Societal risk assessment: How safe is safe enough*, 4, 181–214. See also Kahneman, D., Slovic, P., & Tversky, A. (Eds.). (1982). *Judgment under uncertainty: Heuristics and biases*. Cambridge: Cambridge University Press; and Kuran, T., & Sunstein, C. R. (1999). Availability cascades and risk regulation. *Stanford Law Review*, 51 (4), 683. These authors develop the idea that because a certain behavior might seem riskier than others, there is a danger that efforts by citizens and government will be moved in the wrong direction.

[83]   Another less innocent type of ignorance might occur in the context of trade secrets, and that is strategic ignorance. Darley, J. M. (1996). How organizations socialize individuals into evildoing.

Prentice have drawn on this theory to explain why college students overestimated the amount of alcohol consumed by their fellow students.[84] The main reason for this overestimation seems to be that over-drinking is much more vivid and salient than average drinking.

The same rationale and pattern that apply to the pattern of over-consumption of alcohol could apply to the excessive disclosure of trade secrets. To detect a norm regarding information sharing from watching others' behavior, an employee needs to deduce what types of information he or she can take after leaving the current employer. Situations in which fellow employees take jobs with competitors or create spin-off companies that produce similar products can make the attribution of motives fairly simple.[85] Moreover, the greater the violation of the trade secret-law, the greater is the vividness of the behavior and the clarity of the attribution. No such clarity exists in the opposite scenario of observing legal obedience.[86] Thus, individuals are more likely to make inferences about descriptive norms of legal disobedience than about descriptive norms of legal obedience.[87] They will thereby tend to underestimate the effect that trade-secret laws have on people's decisions about whether or not to disclose trade secrets.

The extent of overestimating others' violations might be related to the differences between the interests of trade-secret accepting firms and trade-secret producing firms. Assume that know-how information travels with a departing employee from Firm A to Firm B. Colleagues in Firm B are very likely to hear about this new information that has arrived, since it could change their current methodology. The newcomer might not feel a need to conceal the disclosure because his action

---

Codes of Conduct: Behavioral Research into Business Ethics, 13(43), 13 describes how individuals in organizations who wish to prevent the organizational pressures associated with certain organizational ethical codes might intentionally choose ignorance when these codes contradict the individual's self-interest. See also Miller, D. T., & McFarland, C. (1991). When social comparison goes awry: The case of pluralistic ignorance. In J. Suls & T. A. Wills (Eds.), *Social comparison: Contemporary theory and research* (p. 287). Hillsdale, NJ: Erlbaum, suggest that pluralistic ignorance is "a state characterized by the belief that one's private thoughts, feeling and behavior are different from those of others, even though one's public behavior is identical."

[84] See Miller & Prentice, *supra* note 51.

[85] Since there is no gap between public behavior and private attitude when someone is violating the law, it is possible to infer what they think about the law; however, if someone does not violate the law, this inference is no longer possible.

[86] Baumhart found that more than half of his subjects thought that businessmen in the United States are not ethical. Baumhart, R. (1961). How ethical are businessmen? *Harvard Business Review*, 156. Overall, pluralistic-ignorance theorists argue that individuals underestimate other people's adherence to social motives.

[87] A similar hypothesis is suggested with regard to ethics in business by Buckley, M. R., Harvey, M. G., & Beu, D. S. (2000). The role of pluralistic ignorance in the perception of unethical behavior. *Journal of Business Ethics*, 23(4), 353–364. They suggest that there is an actual ethical majority in the world but a perceived ethical minority, and that society should inform young people about this fact since they will not be able to infer it without such help.

is benefiting his new company.[88] His new peers in Firm B might not be able to determine how protected the information was in the previous company or how important it was to it, so the social status of "theft" is not salient in the social interaction.[89] Hence, because the activity of disclosure occurs in the information-accepting firm, the activity will not be disguised and is likely to be widely diffused.

Consequently, individuals with no deliberate intention to violate the law might end up behaving far more badly through different processes, deliberate and non-deliberate, that emerge with a view of the prevailing norms. Such a bias is even more likely to occur because of the social influence element of learning from success.[90]. Hence, employers' reputational cost from going after their departing employees diminishes with the increase in the perceived number of employees who obey the norm.[91] Overestimation of the number of employees who take more information than the law/norm allows will both decrease the perceived social costs and change employees' perception of what is expected from them socially and normatively.

People whose own views favor the disclosure of trade secrets might engage another type of bias when trying to discern the trade-secret norms in the Silicon Valley. An opportunistic employee might imagine that a greater number of colleagues would act as she herself has chosen to act, thus reducing the efficacy of acceptable norms that are designed to curb opportunistic behavior.

Another factor contributing to the perception that certain negative norms are more salient than positive norms is evident in research showing that deviant behaviors were twice as likely to be publicly shared, especially regarding "borderline" activities (e.g., marijuana use).[92] Given the private nature of trade secrets, the existence of a "spiral of silence" might cause people to overestimate the degree to which public expressions reflect the distribution of the private behavior.

[88] Cooter, R., & Eisenberg, M. A. (2001). Fairness, character, and efficiency in firms. *University of Pennsylvania Law Review*, 149(6), 1717–1733, for a discussion of firm-specific fairness – that is, norms that benefit only the firm.

[89] Kerr, N. L. (1999). Anonymity and social control in social dilemmas. In M. Foddy, M. Smithson, S. Schneider, & M. A. Hogg (Eds.), *Resolving social dilemmas: Dynamic, structural, and intergroup aspects* (pp. 103–120). Philadelphia: Psychology Press, suggesting that lacking monitoring by those who can sanction the individual, the fact that the individual can be identified does not ensure compliance to the norm.

[90] Cialdini concludes that, given the informative function of descriptive norms, we are much more likely to follow the steps of successful others than of those for whom the behavioral outcome is unknown. Cialdini, R. B., & Trost, M. R. (1998). Social influence: Social norms, conformity and compliance. In D. T. Gilbert, S. T. Fiske, & G. Lindzey (Eds.), *The Handbook of Social Psychology* (pp. 151–155). New York: McGraw-Hill.

[91] Cooter, R. D. (1996). Decentralized law for a complex economy: The structural approach to adjudicating the new law merchant. *University of Pennsylvania Law Review*, 144(5), 1671: increase in the proportion of enforcers of norms → decrease in the cost of punishment. In our case, it seems reasonable to assume that the cost of punishment will decrease if employers believe that fewer employees will see their move of filing a lawsuit in a negative light.

[92] Brown, J. W., Glaser, D., Waxer, E., & Geis, G. (1974). Turning off: Cessation of marijuana use after college. *Social Problems*, 21(4), 527–538. In my view one might wonder whether volunteering to participate in a study amounts to "publicly sharing one's views".

In addition to the pluralistic ignorance theory, another type of documented bias that might lead to employees overestimating the number of trade-secret violations in Silicon Valley is the "uniqueness" bias.[93] It holds that people have a tendency to underestimate the consensus of desirable behaviors; Goethals et al. found it to have the strongest impact with regard to moral reasoning.[94] Legal theories built on using norms as a tool to support engaging in socially beneficial behaviors might therefore face a huge informational obstacle, because the uniqueness bias undermines the ability of norms to draw people away from self-interested behaviors. Uniqueness bias also causes people to view their good behaviors as unique and their bad behaviors as common.[95] In the trade-secret context, this could mean that those who would not normally share trade secrets might feel that the consensus is less moral than it actually is, thereby underestimating the social costs of engaging in immoral acts and making them more likely to violate secrecy.[96] These theories all provide grounds, then, for a market failure in the perception of the norm: employees are more likely to exaggerate, rather than underestimate, the amount of wrongdoing in Silicon Valley, and hence might change their behavior to meet an even greater level of violation.

5.3.6 *The Limits of Fairness in Curbing Ordinary Unethicality*

The biases described thus far in the perception of social norms are exacerbated in the context of fairness. In large-scale social dilemmas in which communication is less likely, one of the most important informal social forces constraining opportunistic behavior is fairness.[97] It has been shown that fairness has a positive effect on people's decision to cooperate with the collective interest,[98] and many economists now realize that Becker's original model of compliance is limited.[99] In the context of my work in Silicon Valley, it is not clear that employees can tell exactly what knowledge they are allowed to take with them when they leave their jobs, since clearly all departing employees use some information when moving from one

---

[93] Goethals, G. R., Messick, D. M., & Allison, S. T. (1991). The uniqueness bias: Studies of constructive social comparison. See also Suls & Wills, *supra* note 83.

[94] Ibid., p. 37.

[95] Marks, G. (1984). Thinking one's abilities are unique and one's opinions are common. *Personality and Social Psychology Bulletin*, 10(2), 203–208.

[96] See Figure 5.1 for empirical support of this point.

[97] See Kahneman et al., *supra* note 25. See also Biel, A. (2000). Factors promoting cooperation. In Biel, A., Snyder, M., Tyler, T. R., & Van Vugt, M. (Eds.), *Cooperation in modern society: Promoting the welfare of communities, states and organisations.* London: Routledge.

[98] Van Dijk, E., & Wilke, H. (1993). Differential interests, equity, and public good provision. *Journal of Experimental Social Psychology*, 29(1), 1–16.

[99] Becker, G. S. (1968). Crime and punishment: An economic approach. In *The Economic Dimensions of Crime* (pp. 13–68). Palgrave Macmillan UK. See, for example, Dowell, R. S., Goldfarb, R. S., & Griffith, W. B. (1998). Economic man as a moral individual. *Economic Inquiry*, 36(4), 645.

company to another. The use of sensitive information seems to be a classic example of a situation in which the ability to evaluate what is fair needs a reference point. As Miller and Prentice put it: "there is nothing either good or bad but comparison makes it so."[100]

The effect of fairness will kick in only when there are clearly defined boundaries placed around the legitimate and illegitimate usage of information.[101] In the Silicon Valley context, we can expect that an employee will define the fairness of information usage in terms of the standard psychological contract that exists in each industry. Uncertainty as to what information employees can take with them upon departure is likely to make it very hard for fairness to serve as an efficient constraint.[102] Thus, the egocentric perception of fairness suggests that people's motivated reasoning prevents them from evaluating fairness as it is. In such cases, clearly fairness could not be seen as a normative constraint on good people as people would use it even mindlessly as a way to justify their own behavior.

---

[100]   Miller, D. T., & Prentice, D. A. (1996). The construction of social norms and standards. In E. T. Higgins & A. W. Kruglanski (Eds.), *Social psychology: Handbook of basic principles* (pp. 799–829). New York: Guilford Press.

[101]   A similar line of arguments is made by Shavell, S. (2002). Law versus morality as regulators of conduct. *American Law and Economics Review*, 4(2), 227–257 at 235, when he discusses the advantage of regulating behavior through law as opposed to morality given the fact that it is harder to apply morality to more complex situations. On p. 254, he argues that when morality is not intuitive, it is better to use laws. On p. 242, he discusses another limitation that arises when the regulation of behavior relative to morality occurs in firms where the relationship between morality and the regulation is more complex. On p. 247, he points out that in cases where the profit to the wrongdoer is considerable, morality is unlikely to be able to regulate behavior without assistance from the law. Thus, it seems that, according to his rationale, the ability of fairness to monitor such behavior is limited. In Chapters 7, 8, and 11 the focus is on changing the problematic role that social norms can play in providing good people justifications for their wrongdoing.

[102]   See Jones, T. M., & Ryan, L. V. (1997). The link between ethical judgment and action in organizations: A moral approbation approach. *Organization Science*, 8(6), 663–680. When discussing the elements of moral responsibility (at p. 671), they argue that moral certainty about the immorality of the action in question is empirically significant in attempting to predict the ability of morality to have any effect on one's decision making. Thus, uncertainty reduction is important from a policy perspective not only in an informative cognitive context but also in social normative context.

6

Are All People Equally Good?

6.1 INTRODUCTION

As suggested in Chapter 1, the main contribution of behavioral ethics (BE) to legal regulation is the growing recognition of the importance of situational factors – rather than internal factors of responsibility and morality – in accounting for individual behavior. BE has shown that some situations are likely to cause many people who do not intend to do harm to engage in situational wrongdoing through a combination of deliberative and non-deliberative reactions to the context or social factors (such the prevailing social norm in a given situation). However, it is crucial to understand that the strength of a situation's impact on people may vary both across types of situations and types of people in a way that could be meaningful for the legal policy maker. In other words, even though the goal of this book is to draw attention toward situational wrongdoers, there remains the need to examine whether it is possible to set them apart from intentional wrongdoers on the one hand and from individuals who are less likely to engage in situational wrongdoing on the other. From an enforcement perspective, it is clear that adopting a blanket perspective toward a given regulated population might harm good people, who are intrinsically motivated to behave in a prosocial way but may fail to do so because an extrinsic motivation crowds out their intrinsic motivation[1] – which according to the traditional "fine is a price" argument[2] changes the meaning of the situation into a competitive one, according to the dual-reasoning approach to human cooperation.[3]

---

[1] See my joint works with Perez and Lobel on the interaction between the type of people and the effect of incentives: Feldman, Y., & Perez, O. (2012). Motivating environmental action in a pluralistic regulatory environment: An experimental study of framing, crowding out, and institutional effects in the context of recycling policies. *Law & Society Review*, 46(2), 405–442. See also and Feldman, Y., & Lobel, O. (2009). The incentives matrix: The comparative effectiveness of rewards, liabilities, duties, and protections for reporting illegality. *Texas Law Review*, 88, 1151.

[2] Gneezy, U., & Rustichini, A. (2000). A fine is a price. *Journal of Legal Studies*, 29(1), 1–17.

[3] For example, Rand, D. G., Greene, J. D., & Nowak, M. A. (2012). Spontaneous giving and calculated greed. *Nature*, 489(7416), 427–430.

Thus, while in earlier chapters of the book, I have argued that regulators need to recognize that situational effects are often more important than individual factors in determining misbehavior, individual variation cannot be ignored. Misconducts continue to be committed deliberately by those individuals who intend to do harm, and there is likely a variation in how situations affect good people's likelihood to engage in uncooperative behavior. Thus, policy makers in charge of compliance face a complex challenge: they are not dealing just with people who commit harm in a calculated manner but also with wrongdoing done by good people who want to feel moral while still enhancing their self-interest (situational wrongdoers) as well as misconduct committed by genuinely moral people who do bad things unintention-ally (the blind spot argument). Recognizing and understanding this variation are hence crucial to any normative recommendation we make with regard to the situation. Thus as suggested in chapters 1 and 3, for the purposes of this book, it is useful to consider three types of people: (1) calculated wrongdoers, who resemble those described by the "bad man of " approach[4]; (2) situational wrongdoers, who engage in wrongdoing in situations (e.g., those characterized by ambiguity or by following social norms) that allow them to rationalize their misconduct, either *ex ante* or *ex post* and thereby reduce their motivation to do good; and (3) genuinely good people who actively want to do good things but end up violating the law or behaving unethically because of reduced awareness of the wrongdoing (e.g., blind spot, motivated reasoning/seeing) or internal justifications that reduce their motiva-tion to do good (e.g., moral licensing, moral forgetting).

A good illustration of these different types of people is found in Gachter and Schulz's seminal paper on intrinsic honesty and variance in commission and types of violations across societies.[5] The results of the dice in the cup experiment, in which people choose whether to report as instructed or to deviate from the rule to maximize their profit, is especially helpful in showing how participants fall into three categories, which correspond to our three groups.[6] Those who reported "5," which gives the highest payoff, are defined as profit maximizers or, in our terminol-ogy "calculative wrongdoers" (group 1). The people who reported "3-4-5" follow the bending-the-rule paradigm of justified unethicality and take advantage of a given situation to do wrong; we term them "situational wrongdoers" (group 2). Finally, those who report "6" as instructed are described as honest, because they received no rewards; in our terminology, they are called "genuinely moral people" who do wrong mostly in the context of limited cognition (group 3).

[4]   In later sections, I also discuss the possibility of calculative individuals who could not be seen as "bad" people.
[5]   Gachter, S., & Schulz, J. F. (2016). Intrinsic honesty and the prevalence of rule violations across societies. *Nature*, 531(7595), 496–499.
[6]   Shalvi, S., Dana, J., Handgraaf, M. J., & De Dreu, C. K. (2011). Justified ethicality: Observing desired counterfactuals modifies ethical perceptions and behavior. *Organizational Behavior and Human Decision Processes*, 115(2), 181–190.

The aim of the current chapter is to advance our understanding of the differences between calculative and situational wrongdoers and those between the subclassifications of situational wrongdoers: those who wish to promote their self-interest and feel good about themselves and those who are genuinely interested in complying with the law. Clearly, to be able to advocate for specific instruments that are more suitable for situational wrongdoers and others that are more suitable for calculative wrongdoers, we must determine, even in crude terms, the proportions of calculative wrongdoers in a given population, a ratio that is likely to change based on culture and in relation to a given behavior (that states want to change).[7]

For that reason, we will also examine some paradigms that might explain which people are more likely to engage in situational wrongdoing.[8] The factors that cause people to be more likely to engage in situational wrongdoing are not only related to intentionality and moral development, as traditional behavioral law and economics (BLE) scholars have assumed. Naturally, people also vary in the likelihood that a situation will influence their ethical behavior.

With regard to intentional wrongdoing, we start with the familiar dimensions of the classical calculative wrongdoer that are related to risk, respect for the law, and moral decision making.[9] For those likely to be affected by situational dimensions, we examine personality scales, which carry the potential for measuring variation among people's characters with regard to the likelihood that they will engage in misconduct. However, established scales that measure the impact of attitudes toward risk, self-control, the level of moral development, and the level of deontological reasoning on this likelihood do not seem to find large enough differences to justify a differentiated approach to ordinary unethicality likely to be performed by good people.[10] Thus, we need new measures to help account for the likelihood of non-deliberative misconduct.

Nonetheless, while we show that there are some stable differences between the levels of "goodness" of people that correlate with the likelihood that they will engage in non-calculated misconduct, we suggest that the situational factor is much more influential than the personal factor in causing wrongdoing. Hence, from the state's perspective there should be a dual focus: using traditional methods to prevent misconduct that is likely to be conducted by calculative wrongdoers and shaping situations in ways that will make most non-calculative wrongdoers less likely to do wrong.

---

[7] Pascual-Ezama, D., et al. (2015). Context-dependent cheating: Experimental evidence from 16 countries. *Journal of Economic Behavior and Organization* 116, 379–386.

[8] Rosenbaum, S. M., Billinger, S. & Stieglitz, N. (2014). Let's be honest: A review of experimental evidence of honesty and truth-telling. *Journal of Economic Psychology*, 45, 181–186.

[9] See, for example, Rest, J. R. (1986). *Moral development: Advances in research and theory*. New York: Praeger; and Trevino, L. K. (1992). Moral reasoning and business ethics: Implications for research, education, and management. *Journal of Business Ethics* 11, 445–459.

[10] For example, see Gino, F. (2015). Understanding ordinary unethical behavior: Why people who value morality act immorally. *Current Opinion in Behavioral Sciences* 3, 107–111. See also Bazerman, M. H., & Tenbrunsel, A. E. (2011). *Blind spots: Why we fail to do what's right and what to do about it*. Princeton: Princeton University Press.

We thus advocate for a differentiated approach based on the type of likely misconduct and the expected intrinsic motivation to obey the relevant law or regulation. In contexts where expected misbehavior is clearly calculative, the best approaches are traditional enforcement instruments based on traditional considerations (e.g., the limits of money, likelihood of detection, level of intrinsic motivations). However, in contexts where the expected harm is created by non-deliberative misconduct, which even good people who usually avoid calculated wrongdoing might engage in, the focus should be on designing situations that reduce people's ability to maintain their self-perception as moral while still doing bad things. Such context-shaping measures include reducing ambiguity, reducing excuses for wrongdoing, and increasing accountability.

Current research on non-deliberative choices presents a variety of challenges, many of which were explored in earlier chapters. The most important finding, from a policy perspective, is that if people do not think they are being corrupt – if they are biased by self-interest or by a discriminatory stereotype – command-and-control approaches are less likely to work without proper modifications that are discussed in the concluding chapters of the book. To manage and curb these types of implicit misconduct, an optimal combination of new and traditional enforcement mechanisms should be tailored toward both calculated and non-calculated wrongdoing. This chapter examines how to develop a differentiated approach based on the likelihood of people engaging in deliberate versus non-deliberative behaviors.

While traditional enforcement literature focuses on bad people who will do everything in their power to overcome the constraints of the government, behavioral ethics looks at people who are either unaware or partially aware of the wrongdoing of their behavior. Raskolnikov is one of the dominant scholars who attempt to differentiate between people based on their willingness to engage in wrongdoing (in tax evasion).[11] In his typology, Raskolnikov speaks about "gamers"[12] who would do everything in their power to pay less tax and, in that sense, are not reacting to the situation but are instead planning to disobey the law.[13] The "gamer" type is similar to

---

[11] Raskolinkov, A.(2009). Revealing choices: Using taxpayer choice to target tax enforcement. *Columbia Law Review*, Columbia Law and Economics Working Paper No. 337. Available at SSRN: https://ssrn.com/abstract=1267622.

[12] Raskolnikov, A. (2006). Crime and punishment in taxation: Deceit, deterrence, and the self-adjusting penalty. *Columbia Law Review*, 106(3), 569–642. See also the analysis by Stone from a more jurisprudential perspective. Rebecca Stone differentiates between various type of people based on their motivation to comply with the law. She tries to compare different types of individuals based on their commitment to obey the law. Stone, R. (2016). Legal design for the "good man." *Virginia Law Review*, 102(7). Another example of a differentiated treatment of different people toward the law could be demonstrated in the work of Bell and Parchomovsky on copyrights infringement. According to their model, there will be different types of remedies to willful infringement vs. good faith infringement. Bell, A., & Parchomovsky, G. (2016). The dual-grant theory of fair use. *University of Chicago Law Review*, 83, 1051–1118.

[13] Trevino, L. K. & Youngblood, S. A. (1990). Bad apples in bad barrels: A causal analysis of ethical decision-making behavior. *Journal of Applied Psychology*, 75(4), 378.

the calculated wrongdoer in our model. However, Raskolnikov fails to account for the fact that even the people who are not calculative could engage in some levels of wrongdoing: good people are those who may act engage in wrongdoing in situations that allow them to do bad things without making them worry too much about the consequences to their self-image or standing in society. These are not people who understand that their action is wrong and then calculate how much they are willing to pay for it. In fact, it is likely that the price they need to pay might affect their implicit choices, but those are not the types of unethical actions that they are conscious of or able to identify in advance.

6.2 DELIBERATIVE VS. NON-DELIBERATIVE WRONGDOING

The discussion of non-deliberative misconduct adds another dimension to the extrinsic-intrinsic scale: the explicit-implicit dimension. In this chapter as well as in the next, which focuses on enforcement trade-offs, we examine how to reframe legal policy to combine the two dimensions.

The situation is more complex because as we have outlined earlier, even with regard to non-deliberative dishonesty, there are two types of good people: those who engage in justified dishonesty in a given situation that allows for such justifications and those who engage in a blind-spot type of justification. These two types of individuals are complemented by the calculative individual who is a profit maximizer; from a rational choice perspective, law traditionally focuses on deterrence or legitimacy when it tries to prevent that person's bad deeds. The disadvantage of this command-and-control approach is that for the most part it assumes that people are calculative (i.e., "bad" in the terminology of the book) and ignores the fact that many people act unethically because of limited awareness: "Such measures simply bypass the vast majority of unethical behaviours that occur without the conscious awareness of the actors, who engage in them."[14] In addition, the use of incentives could be challenged in that they are extrinsic measures that do not lead to a change in people's intrinsic motivation or, even worse, might reduce people's motivation to do good due to crowding-out and commodification processes.

The two questions that we ask in this chapter focus on individual differences. Can we know, ex ante, if we are likely to be dealing with a behavior committed in a deliberate manner by a calculated individual or by a "good" person whose misconduct is facilitated by the situation? And are we able to predict whether some people are more likely than others to engage in situational wrongdoing?

Throughout the chapter, we examine two main ways to distinguish between people, based on their level of "goodness." The first uses relevant personality scales to predict whether people are likely, first, to be calculated wrongdoers and, second,

[14] Bazerman, M. H. & Banaii, M. R. (2004). The social psychology of ordinary ethical failures. *Social Justice Research*, 17(2), 111–115.

to engage in unethical behavior in a context where situational wrongdoing is likely to occur (e.g., when there is a conflict of interest, when deciding to hire candidates from different social groups, when a new company must decide whether or not to divulge trade secrets, or when thinking of whether or not to report a wrongdoing that goes against the institutional interest of the individual). The major individual difference seems to be in the locus of self-control: people who have a high external locus of control are more likely to see their action as a product of their circumstances and hence are more likely than others to engage in unethical choices. While attempting to map people on the good-bad spectrum, I discuss several personality scales but am not able to offer a comprehensive personality-based model.

The second approach is to divide people not based on their predisposition, but rather by their likely level of intrinsic motivation to engage in the behavior that the state tries to regulate. The advantage of focusing on intrinsic motivation is that it can vary across different legal contexts. The disadvantage of this approach is that it requires the legal policy maker to map the motivation of people in a given situation.

Clearly, for misconduct that is less deliberative, the situational context provides more of the variance and is easier to regulate for states than people. This chapter differentiates between the type of misconducts intentionally committed by people and those attributed to the power of the situation. However, it does not address the misconduct engaged in by genuinely moral individuals and triggered by blind spots that occurs when they fail to recognize that what they are doing is wrong, rather than recognizing it as such and simply rationalizing it for themselves.

6.2.1 *Variation in Modes of Reasoning*

Kish Gephart et al.'s work on the difference between what they term "ethical impulse misconduct" and "ethical calculus misconducts" is also highly relevant here.[15] They suggest that the former type of wrongdoing is enabled by the operation of various non-deliberative mechanisms. However, their list of predictors seems to be quite extensive, including both individual aspects and moral and environmental issues. The individual aspects refer mainly to cognitive moral development,[16] locus of control, and propensity to morally disengage.[17] Regarding moral development factors, they review characteristics such as moral intensity[18], proximity, and social consensus regarding the immorality of the act. With regard to environment, they review concepts such as the moral climate, social norms, organizational norms, and

---

[15]   Kish-Gephart, J. J., Harrison, D. A, & Trevino, L. K. (2010). Bad apples, bad cases, and bad barrels: Meta-analytic evidence about sources of unethical decisions at work. *Journal of Applied Psychology*, 95(1).

[16]   Kohlberg, L. (1971). Stages of moral development. *Moral Education*, 1, 23–92.

[17]   Bandura, A. (1999). Moral disengagement in the perpetration of inhumanities. *Personality and Social Psychology Review*, 3(3), 193–209.

[18]   Jones, T. M. (1991). Ethical decision making by individuals in organizations: An issue-contingent model. *Academy of Management Review*, 16(2), 366–395.

code of conduct enforcement. While this elaborated model indeed pays attention to both individual and situational factors, the exact process of predicting non-deliberative misconduct, relative to intentional conduct, remains somewhat unclear. Given that lack of causal connection, it is hard to connect those concepts and the type of misconducts that need to be addressed.

6.2.2 Dual Reasoning and Individual Variation

When accounting for the role of non-deliberative choice in human behavior, the variation among compliance motivations across people and situations becomes more important and complex. As suggested in Chapter 2, in recent years there has been an increase in the research on and conceptualization of non-deliberative choices, and numerous experiments have grown into competing paradigms describing various aspects of behavior that are not regulated by full consciousness.[19] One of the paradigms that has gained widespread popular recognition through Kahneman's book, *Thinking, Fast and Slow*, is that of two systems of reasoning: this paradigm now stands at the core of much research in behavioral law and economics.[20] Kahneman differentiates an automatic, intuitive, and mostly unconscious process of decision making, *System 1*, from a controlled and deliberative process, *System 2*.[21] Thousands of papers have been published in this tradition, as well as many edited volumes,[22] although some scholars have criticized the paradigm.[23]

Kish-Gephart et al.[24] provide a unique "big picture" perspective on unethicality. They develop a model, based on a meta-analysis of the literature that examines the interaction between the individual ("bad apple"), moral issues ("bad case"), and organizational environments ("bad barrel") as antecedents of unethical choices. They argue for the need to emphasize the "ethical impulse" perspective, described earlier. Another approach comes from the work of Trevino and Youngblood on personal factors that affect individual decision making, including social learning, the stage of cognitive moral development (CMD), and locus of control (LC).[25] A more applied analysis of character traits and their contribution to unethicality in organizations comes from the field experiment–based work of Dunlop and Kibeom that examines the contribution of deviant employees to the unethicality of the

[19] Haidt, Jonathan. (2001). The emotional dog and its rational tail: A social intuitionist approach to moral judgment. *Psychology Review*, 108(4), 814.

[20] Kahneman, D. (2011). *Thinking, fast and slow*. New York: Macmillan.

[21] Evans, J. S. B. (2008). Dual-processing accounts of reasoning, judgment, and social cognition. *Annual Review of Psychology*, 59, 255–278.

[22] For the most recent collection of works in this area, see Teichman, D., & Zamir, E. (2014). Judicial decisionmaking: A behavioral perspective. In E. Zamir (Ed.). *The handbook of behavioral economics and the law*. New York: Oxford University Press.

[23] Kruglanski, A. W., & Gigerenzer, G. (2011). Intuitive and deliberate judgments are based on common principles. *Psychology Review*, 118(1), 97.

[24] See Kish-Gephart et al., *supra* note 15.   [25] See Trevino & Youngblood, *supra* note 13, at 378.

workplace unit as a whole.[26] Such an approach naturally suggests that greater focus should be placed on understanding the makeup of the more deviant employees, rather than on the effect on average people. The lab experiments of Gino et al. demonstrate that bad behavior, combined with activation of a shared norm (e.g., the outgroup), could increase unethicality – emphasizing from a different methodological and theoretical perspective the importance of signaling ex ante the wrongdoers in a society.[27]

6.3 ROLE OF MORALITY

As can be seen, our approach to the role of morality in individual decision making is very different from its classical treatment in legal enforcement. Rest's work represents the traditional, deliberative approach to ethical decision making, whereby certain people are simply more likely to be defined as bad people if they choose to do bad things.[28] Tyler's scenario-based research, in which people are asked explicitly what the likelihood is that they will obey a law in a certain way in a certain situation, falls into the traditional approach.

However, if indeed people are unable to understand that their ethical behavior is mostly affected by situational heuristics, can they actually tell us something about their future ethical behavior?[29] In other words, what emerges from this growing research on automaticity in moral reasoning is the limitation of the current usage of moral reasoning in law.[30] This is especially true with the self-reported scenarios line of research, which has been highly influential on current behavioral analysis of legal research. Such research can only capture the motivation of people with regard to behaviors that they fully recognize as being in violation of the law. As BE research suggests, this approach does not include behaviors that they do not recognize as fully or partly illegal.

Jones was one of the first to recognize the important impact of automaticity of thinking on behavior, claiming that people need to recognize the moral issue at hand to use moral rules.[31] One of the new lines of research stemming from his work is termed "unintended unethicality," where people believe that their decisions are

---

[26]   Dunlop, P. D., & Kibeom, L. (2004). Workplace deviance, organizational citizenship behavior, and business unit performance: The bad apples do spoil the whole barrel. *Journal of Organizational Behavior*, 25(1), 67–80.

[27]   Gino, F., Ayal, S., & Ariely, D. (2009). Contagion and differentiation in unethical behavior the effect of one bad apple on the barrel. *Psychological Science*, 20(3), 393–398.

[28]   Rest, J. R. (1986). Moral development: Advances in research and theory.

[29]   Shu, L. L., Mazar, N., Gino, F., Ariely, D., & Bazerman, M. H. (2012). Signing at the beginning makes ethics salient and decreases dishonest self-reports in comparison to signing at the end. *Proceedings of the National Academy of Sciences*, 109(38), 15197–15200.

[30]   For an excellent review of much of the current research on morality and law, see Zamir, E. & Medina, B. (2010). *Law, economics, and morality*. Oxford: Oxford University Press.

[31]   See Jones, *supra* note 18.

moral even when they are not. This line of research basically creates a typology of dependent variables, where the decision's outcome is unethical and the process could be either intentional or unintentional.

What is important for our argument is the role of automatic behavior in certain types of ethical decision making – what Kish-Gephardt et al. call the "ethical impulse" perspective, as described earlier. This perspective focuses on how individuals recognize the required ethical behavior for a given situation.[32] It holds that there is something in the situation that needs to trigger people's reflexive judgment for them to avoid engaging in automatic processing. Behavioral ethics replicates the focus of the biases and heuristics literature, which triggered the creation of the behavioral law and economics movement, and integrates it into the arena of ethics and morality.

6.3.1 *Moral Identity*

Moral identity, as defined by Aquino et al., is the role that morality plays in one's self-definition; their studies based on measures of this concept found that people's likelihood of doing harm, even implicitly, could vary across different situations based on their level of moral identity.[33]

Aquino and Reed[34] attempted to create the most comprehensive approach to identifying the characteristics and traits that constitute a moral person that is relevant to the "Law of Good People" paradigm. Through a series of experiences measuring both explicit and implicit accounts of morality, they validated the following list of traits: *caring, compassionate, conscientious, considerate, dependable, ethical, fair, forgiving, friendly, generous, giving, hardworking, helpful, honest, kind, loyal, religious, trustworthy,* and *understanding.*

In the second stage of their research, they studied people's self-definition of their own moral identity through self-reports regarding voluntary ethical behaviors and the actual donation of food to needy people. Using a sample of students, they found a strong correlation between the participants who rated high on the different traits of the morality scales and those who were more likely to engage in volunteer work and to donate food to the needy when such a request was made by their university.

Reynolds and Ceranic went a step further in attempting to understand the difference between moral identity and moral judgment.[35] The most significant

[32] See Kish-Gephart et al., *supra* note 15.

[33] Aquino, K., Freeman, D., Reed II, A., Lim, V. K., & Felps, W. (2009). Testing a social-cognitive model of moral behavior: the interactive influence of situations and moral identity centrality. *Journal of Personality and Social Psychology,* 97(1), 123.

[34] Aquino, K., & Reed II, A. (2002). The self-importance of moral identity. *Journal of Personality and Social Psychology,* 83(6), 1423.

[35] Reynolds, S. J., & Ceranic, T. L. (2007). The effects of moral judgment and moral identity on moral behavior: An empirical examination of the moral individual. *Journal of Applied Psychology,* 92(6), 1610.

finding in their paper is that moral identity is mostly predictive of behaviors that are part of the moral consensus. This is not the case with regard to moral judgment. Thus, this variation between people in acting morally is highly dependent on the presence of a clear consensus of what is the moral thing to do, thereby limiting the ability of states to be confident that people will act morally when faced with new behaviors around which there is no strong societal norm.

According to several scholars, the main expressive contribution of the law is to signal consensus to people, which these studies show is clearly important to good people's behavioral choices. The law could help signal to people that they are dealing with a context of moral consensus, which would increase the likelihood of their moral identity kicking into gear.[36]

Another angle on the difference between moral identity and judgment is found in a study done by Gino et al.[37] where they examined the extent to which moral behavior is predicted by moral identity. When participants were depleted of their cognitive resources through daunting tasks, their moral identity was still predictive of their moral behavior. This suggests that the scale of moral identity, although dependent on social norms (the need for moral consensus), is not dependent on deliberative reasoning. According to this somewhat contradictory approach, when people are being cognitively depleted and are less likely to have self-control, they are more likely to behave unethically.[38]

Another scale related to implicit predictors of ethical behavior is the propensity to morally disengage. It is based on Bandura's well-known concept of moral disengagement, which is related to people's ability to justify their immoral behavior. Moore used this concept to create a typology of people based on the likelihood that they would engage in ordinary unethicality in the workplace.[39] She focused on the ability of people to find excuses for causing harm to others (e.g., he had it coming, it would have happened even without me). A related concept is moral firmness.[40] This scale differentiates people's propensity to engage in misconduct based on their likelihood of exploiting some ambiguity.

---

[36] See Feldman, Y. (2009). The expressive function of trade secret law: Legality, cost, intrinsic motivation, and consensus. *Journal of Empirical Legal Studies*, 6(1), 177–212, for a review of the different approaches of Cooter, MacAdams, Posner, and Scott to consensus signaling.

[37] Gino, F., Schweitzer, M. E., Mead, N. L., & Ariely, D. (2011). Unable to resist temptation: How self-control depletion promotes unethical behavior. *Organizational Behavior and Human Decision Processes*, 115(2), 191–203.

[38] Rand, D. G. (2016). Cooperation, fast and slow: Meta-analytic evidence for a theory of social heuristics and self-interested deliberation. Psychological Science, 27(9), 1192–1206.

[39] Moore, C., Detert, J. R., Klebe Treviño, L., Baker, V. L., & Mayer, D. M. (2012). Why employees do bad things: Moral disengagement and unethical organizational behavior. *Personnel Psychology*, 65(1), 1–48.

[40] Shalvi, S., & Leiser, D. (2013). Moral firmness. *Journal of Economic Behavior and Organization*, 93, 400–407.

6.4 PERSONALITY-BASED INDIVIDUAL DIFFERENCES SCALES

As hinted earlier, there are numerous accounts of the relevant differences between people. The leading scales that gauge personality-based individual differences are will and grace,[41] moral identity,[42] level of moral disengagement,[43] and moral firmness.[44] In addition, context-specific measures, such as racism, are based on the implicit association test (IAT). Furthermore, other relevant measures of people's behaviors include variation in self-control, risk attitudes, and selfishness in games, as well as new findings regarding the relevancy of the "Big Five" personality theory to dishonesty.

6.4.1 *The Proportion of Liars in a Given Population*

A possible approximation of the proportion of "good/bad" people in society could be derived from a study that focuses on mapping people's ethical behaviors based on their personal makeup, rather than situational factors.[45] Gneezy et al. analyzed the aversion to lying by giving participants the option to maximize their financial gain in an experimental game. The researchers found that close to 30 percent of their samples always lied ("economic people" in their study – in our terminology, "calculative individuals"). Close to 30 percent never lied ("ethical"), and the group in between lied as a function of the amount of money they gained from lying and of the loss their lie imposed on others. For our analysis, this "middle" group, the "situational wrong-doers" the most important one because it is most likely to react to various interventions, which is why throughout the book we refer to them as situational wrongdoers. Importantly, both the honest individuals and the occasional liars demonstrated an aversion to lying.

However, a competing paper by Gibson et al. challenged this dichotomy between ethical and economic types.[46] Their experimental setting was not a two-person game; instead, they posed the dilemma to participants of whether they would report higher earnings that were attained according to the rules but dishonestly. They show that in this context there was no clear division between types of people who lie and those who do not lie, but rather heterogeneity of preferences. However, 32 percent of their participants opted to take the ethical option, which is around the same percentage found by Gneezy et al.

---

[41] Greene, J. D., & Paxton, J. M. (2009). Patterns of neural activity associated with honest and dishonest moral decisions. *Proceedings of the National Academy of Sciences*. 106(30), 12506–12511.

[42] Reed II, A., & Aquino, K. F. (2003). Moral identity and the expanding circle of moral regard toward out-groups. *Journal of Personality and Social Psychology*, 84(6), 1270.

[43] See Bandura, *supra* note 17.   [44] See Shalvi & Leiser, *supra* note 40.

[45] Gneezy, U., Rockenbach, B., & Serra-Garcia, M. (2013). Measuring lying aversion. *Journal of Economic Behavior and Organization*, 93, 293–300.

[46] Gibson, R., Tanner, C., & Wagner, A. F. (2013). Preferences for truthfulness: Heterogeneity among and within individuals. *American Economic Review*, 103(1), 532–548.

6.4.1.1 Variation in Implicit Attitudes

Should we assume that all people, in their choice of behavior, are influenced by their self-interest and various stereotypical biases in a similar way? Is it really the case that all employers engage in implicit levels of discrimination in the same way? Are they all more likely to use ambiguity to their own advantage or ignore cues from reality that contradict their self-interest?

The answers to these questions are elusive. On the one hand, as some of the research suggests, implicit measures can identify variation across people. For example, the Implicit Attitudes Test (IAT), which has become the gold standard in the area of implicit employment discrimination, shows the impact of biases on behavior.[47] The IAT provides a score that predicts, to some extent, people's explicit behavior based on implicit attitudes. For example, in the legal context, the IAT scores of judges correlated with their discriminatory behavior against black defendants.[48] Similarly, the IAT has been used as a screening mechanism for hiring new employees at Walmart.

6.4.1.2 Variation in Reliance on System 1 Reasoning

In light of the role of implicit attitudes in people's unethicality and the general view that people's System 1 reasoning is less ethical,[49] another important dimension is related to their reliance on automatic reasoning. Frederick's cognitive reflective test (CRT) is a measure of the use of automatic reasoning.[50] This scale rates people based on the likelihood that they will use System 2 to overcome System 1 thinking. The main aim of the research on this scale is to find correlations between people's CRT scores and various behavioral measures.[51] In related research on how the dual-reasoning model could explain the differences between how most people and inherently "bad" people violate laws, it was shown that people who were criminally

---

[47]   Greenwald, A. G., McGhee, D. E., & Schwartz, J. L. (1998). Measuring individual differences in implicit cognition: The Implicit Association Test. *Journal of Personality and Social Psychology*, 74(6), 1464. See also Greenwald, A. G., Poehlman, A.T., Uhlmann, E. L. & Banaji, M. R. (2009). Understanding and using the implicit association test: III. Meta-analysis of predictive validity. *Journal of Personality and Social Psychology*, 97(1), 17.

[48]   Rachlinski, J. J., Johnson, S. L., Wistrich, A. J., & Guthrie, C. (2009). Does unconscious racial bias affect trial judges? *Notre Dame Law Review*, 84(3), 9–11.

[49]   As suggested before regarding the "honesty requires time" approach, see Shalvi, S., Eldar, O., & Bereby-Meyer, Y. (2012). Honesty requires time (and lack of justifications). *Psychological Science*, 23 (10), 1264–1270.

[50]   Frederick, S. (2005). Cognitive reflection and decision making. *Journal of Economic Perspectives*, 19(4), 25–42. See also Toplak, M. E., West, R. F., & Stanovich, K. E. (2011). The Cognitive Reflection Test as a predictor of performance on heuristics-and-biases tasks. *Memory & Cognition*, 39(7), 1275.

[51]   Paxton, J. M., Ungar, L., & Greene, J. D. (2012). Reflection and reasoning in moral judgment. *Cognitive Science*, 36(1), 163–177.

convicted were less likely to experience internal conflict when engaging in delib-erative rule violation.[52]

In a series of works, Devine and her colleagues were able to map individual differences with regard to racial biases.[53] They were able to connect people's level of intrinsic motivation not to be prejudiced with their implicit and explicit expressions of racial bias, showing that higher degrees of intrinsic motivation were related to reduced implicit and explicit of expression of prejudice.[54]

6.4.2 Occupation Variation

Although personality traits are relevant in some *ex ante* employment situations or in an *ex post* treatment in criminal law,[55] from a larger regulatory perspective, their variation is only meaningful if we know in advance the relevant personality traits of people whose behavior we attempt to change. In addition, assuming that we could identify the people *ex ante*, even with the studies that aim to identify relevant personality traits as reviewed earlier, the effects are mostly small and tend to be moderated by other factors. Let us now examine different factors that may be indirectly related to personality traits but are related to behavior in the workplace, particularly implicit corruption.

As suggested in Chapter 3, some scholars argue that moral judgments and decisions are the results of reasoning and deliberation, whereas others argue that self-interest is an automatic primary motive that needs to be constrained by appropriate inhibitory mechanisms.[56] It has been shown that people truly believe their own biased judgments and have a limited ability to recognize that their behavior was affected by their own self-interest.[57] Similarly the level of control needed to behave ethically is much higher than the level needed to behave unethically.[58] Although the

[52] Jusyte, A., Pfister, R., Mayer, S. V., Schwarz, K. A., Wirth, R., Kunde, W., & Schönenberg, M. (2017). Smooth criminal: Convicted rule-breakers show reduced cognitive conflict during deliberate rule violations. *Psychological Research*, 81(5), 939–946.

[53] Plant, E. A., & Devine, P. G. (1998). Internal and external motivation to respond without prejudice. *Journal of Personality and Social Psychology*, 75(3), 811. See also Amodio, D. M., Harmon-Jones, E., & Devine, P. G. (2003). Individual differences in the activation and control of affective race bias as assessed by startle eyeblink response and self-report. *Journal of Personality and Social Psychology*, 84 (4), 738.

[54] Plant, E. A., Devine, P. G., & Peruche, M. B. (2010). Routes to positive interracial interactions: Approaching egalitarianism or avoiding prejudice. *Personality and Social Psychology Bulletin*, 36(9), 1135–1147.

[55] Both aspects are discussed in the relevant chapters on employment.

[56] For example, see Moore, D. A., & Loewenstein, G. (2004). Self-interest, automaticity, and the psychology of conflict of interest. *Social Justice Research*, 17(2), 189–202.

[57] The measurement of "private" evaluations was done by giving participants incentives to be accurate in their predictions. See Moore, C., Stuart, H. C., & Pozner, J. E. (2010). Avoiding the consequences of repeated misconduct: Stigma's license and stigma's transferability. *Institute for Research on Labor and Employment*.

[58] Gino, F. (2015). Understanding ordinary unethical behavior: Why people who value morality act immorally. *Current opinion in behavioral sciences*, 3, 107–111.

literature in this area is still debated,[59] clearly, from an applied perspective, regulating the behavior of "good people" attests to the need for understanding implicit corruption.[60]

For example, in the medical field, we described the fertile ground for conflicts of interest, where even scientists who believe they are doing what is best for public health might end up engaging in behaviors favoring the entities that pay them.[61] A frequent example is a clinical study financed by a pharmaceutical company that provides an incentive for physician-researchers to reach certain results.[62]

In a joint work with Schuler and Gauthier on pharmaceutical corruption,[63] we focused on the different roles played by scientists and executives in the type of corruption that plagues the industry, as well as relevant interventions. Executives are likely to carry out typical acts of misconduct in pharmaceutical companies. Many of these acts are calculated, such as marketing, branding, and labeling techniques used for the purpose of enriching the corporation. We argue that interventions should be differentiated to address the specific mechanisms underlying scientists' and executives' misconduct. Scientists may have motivated reasoning biases that cause them to exaggerate evidence for the success of their companies' drugs in clinical trials. Such scientific misconduct is more effectively targeted with accountability- and reputation-driven interventions. In contrast, incentives are highly likely to affect the executives whose misconduct is calculated. Targeting interventions to professional role, which is known *ex ante,* can increase their effectiveness in reducing wrongdoing. This approach is admittedly crude, but in the balance between a one-policy-fits-all approach and a differentiated approach based on personality traits, it might be a good-enough compromise for addressing intentional vs. situational misconduct.

Another situation ripe for corruption is the transition of professionals from the public to the private sector. This can be highly problematic for public sector employees who have been trained to focus exclusively on the public interest.[64]

---

[59]   For example, Cushman, F., Young, L., & Hauser, M. (2006). The role of conscious reasoning and intuition in moral judgment: Testing three principles of harm. *Psychological Science, 17*(12), 1082–1089.

[60]   Lessig, L. (2011). *Republic, lost: How money corrupts Congress – and a plan to stop it.* London: Hachette UK. See also Feldman, Y., Gauthier, R. L., & Schuler, T. H. (2013). Curbing misconduct in the pharmaceutical industry: Insights from behavioral ethics and the behavioral approach to law. *SSRN Electronic Journal, 41*(3).

[61]   See Feldman, *supra* note 36.

[62]   For example, Rodwin, M. A. (1989). Physicians' conflicts of interest: The limitations of disclosure. *New England Journal of Medicine, 321*(1), 1405. See also Rodwin, M. A. (2012). Conflicts of interest, institutional corruption, and pharma: An agenda for reform. *Journal of Law, Medicine & Ethics, 40*(3), 511–522; Friedberg, M., Saffran, B., Stinson, T. J., Nelson, W., & Bennett, C. L. (1999). Evaluation of conflict of interest in economic analyses of new drugs used in oncology. *JAMA, 282*(15), 1453–1457; Hillman, A. L. (1987). Financial incentives for physicians in HMOs. *New England Journal of Medicine, 317*(27), 1743–1748.

[63]   See Feldman et al., *supra* note 60.

[64]   Che, Y. K. (1995). Revolving doors and the optimal tolerance for agency collusion. *The Rand Journal of Economics,* 378–397.

This transition, referred to as the "revolving doors phenomenon," facilitates possible conflicts of interest if officials abuse their position to attain personal benefit within the private sector.[65] However, the problem is much greater. The anticipation that they will later work in regulated firms at high salaries may cause regulators to be less aggressive when administering regulatory policy, even without full awareness of their actions.[66] In many other situations – including lawyers vis-à-vis their clients, executives vis-à-vis shareholders, prosecutors in plea bargains, and academics involved in the promotion of their colleagues – most good people may believe that the option that promotes their self-interest is also the correct one. Thus, in such situations, threatening people with punishments for being corrupt, when they do not view themselves as doing anything different from what others do, is not wise.

6.4.3 A Cross-cultural Approach to Variance in Ethicality

It is much easier to assess demographic traits than personality traits ex an*te* and then to develop studies and targeted interventions accordingly.[67] However, from the review done by Tenbrunsel et al., it seems that demographic factors do not carry a strong enough predictive value. They found no to little relationship between ethicality and factors such as gender and education level. With regard to culture, conflicting studies fail to present a clear picture. Tenbrunsel et al. challenged the studies that find moral differences between Brazilians and Americans, because this finding was not replicated in later studies.[68] Thus, for organizations to avoid hiring "bad apples," demographic strategies are not likely to be useful.

In an impressive cross-societal study, Gachter and Schulz used cross-national samples of younger individuals to address the direct correlation between the quality of institutions in a given state and people's honesty behavior.[69] Overall, their argument is that there are more people who are honest in countries with stronger rule of law institutions. Countries with strong institutions are more likely to have lower values of justified unethicality. Weak institutions have not only a direct effect

---

[65]   *General Motors Corp.* v. *City of New York*, 5oi F.2d 639, 650 n.20 (2d Cir. I974).

[66]   See Che, *supra* note 64.

[67]   Although see Porat, A., & Strahilevitz, L. J. (2013). Personalizing default rules and disclosure with big data. *Michigan Law Review*, 112, 1417, in the context of form contract. See also Ben-Shahar, O., & Porat, A. (2009). Foreword: Fault in American contract law. *Michigan Law Review*, 107(8), 1341–1348, in the context of personalized negligence; Feldman, Y., & Smith, H. E. (2014). Behavioral equity. *Journal of Institutional and Theoretical Economics*, 170(1), 137–159. Their work focuses on how legal ambiguity could be used to create an *ex post* acoustic separation between good and bad people.

[68]   For example, see Haidt, J., Koller, S. H., & Dias, M. G. (1993). Affect, culture, and morality, or is it wrong to eat your dog? *Journal of Personality and Social Psychology*, 65(4), 613. See also Pascual-Ezama et al., *supra* note 7; See Rosenbaum et al., *supra* note 8.

[69]   See Gachter & Schulz, *supra* note 5.

on the incidence of corruption and on productivity but may also actually directly cause dishonesty.

The researchers generalized these findings from their cup in the dice experiment described at the beginning of the chapter. The researchers found variation between countries in the percentage of honest versus dishonest claims. The range across countries of high claims was from 61 percent to 84.3 percent; thus, no country had only honest people, but some countries had only justified dishonest people, 71.8 percent on average.[70]

It is interesting that, how strong the institution was, had no effect on the maximal cheating ratio, suggesting that this type of behavior is less likely to be related to social capital and the strength of the institution. In contrast to common beliefs, gender was not predictive of honesty. Based on these findings and some of the research that followed,[71] it might be possible to assess cultural effects on the likely proportion of situational wrongdoers in a given country and plan rules accordingly. Increasingly, such knowledge is important in new types of self-regulation that require one to know in advance how much to trust citizens to decide how strict the regulation should be.

6.5 VARIANCES IN THE LEVEL OF INTRINSIC COMPLIANCE MOTIVATION

The variation between "good" and "bad" people can also be assessed by examining, ex ante, the variation in people's intrinsic motivation toward compliance with a specific legal doctrine. This section examines the main concepts from the literature on intrinsic versus extrinsic motivation and then presents my findings regarding the regulatory challenges of addressing the level of intrinsic motivation. I also discuss how these challenges would change in a system of law that focuses on both deliberative and non-deliberative views of people.

Research in economics, psychology, and law has examined the differences in the level of intrinsic and extrinsic motivation among individuals.[72] Such variations usually depend on the particular content of the law; some people may be highly motivated to obey certain laws, but not be intrinsically motivated to obey other types of laws.[73] Interestingly, the variation between people's level of intrinsic motivation is relatively malleable, as discussed in Chapter 4.

Focusing on motivation is particularly important, given that more and more studies have found that motivation can reduce the impact of automatic biases.

---

[70]   Saying they had 3, 4, 5 where by chance their proportion should be only 50 percent.

[71]   Hugh-Jones, D. (2016). Honesty, beliefs about honesty, and economic growth in 15 countries. *Journal of Economic Behavior & Organization*, 127, 99–114.

[72]   For the main economic model, see my work with Perez and Lobel, as well as Benabou, R., & Tirole, J. (2003). Intrinsic and extrinsic motivation. *Review of Economic Studies*, 70(3), 489–520.

[73]   As this chapter shows, there are some general tendencies to obey the law. This tendency is supported also with regard to the citizenship approach to legal compliance where people obey the law because it is the law. It is interesting to examine whether people who obey laws simply because they are laws should be seen as intrinsically committed individuals.

Additionally, according to the REVISE model, some recent studies suggest the importance of the motivation to maintain one's positive self-image in changing people's behavior.[74] According to this view, increasing the relevancy of obeying a certain law to maintaining one's self-image as a moral and law-abiding individual reduces the likelihood that one will engage in automatic processes that are responsible for reduced law compliance.

Given the focus on individual variation in this chapter, we are interested in evaluating variations in the intrinsic motivation of people with different levels of commitment to the law. The goal is to create differentiated processes of regulation based on this variation and to use incentives without triggering the crowding-out effect. Given our typology of three groups of people, it is essential to create policies that address the intrinsic and extrinsic motivations of each group. For example, in earlier work I found that financial instruments are highly effective incentives for people with low intrinsic motivation to behave appropriately, but they could be counterproductive for people with high intrinsic motivation because of crowding out. One can think of the relationship of incentive variation to behavior as parallel to the effect of morality: some people are more likely to react to moral language than to other approaches.

6.5.1 Motivation, Incentives, and Recycling

In my joint work with Oren Perez, we examined the ability of states to use individuals' variation in intrinsic motivation to engage in recycling as a way of improving environmental compliance behavior.[75] Our study addressed the link between the choice of regulatory instrument and institutional framework, people's intrinsic motivation, and various attitudinal measures. We examined the behavioral repercussions of several instruments that are widely used in recycling regulation, using an experimental survey on a representative sample of the Israeli population. Our findings suggest the potential value of using differentiated regulatory policies to incentivize recycling in societies characterized by broad heterogeneity in levels of intrinsic motivation toward recycling.

Our rationale for treating people with different levels of motivation differently related to the crowding-out effect. We found that we did not need to do a general evaluation of each individual, which would have been prohibitive in terms of both time and money. Instead, we could focus on the commitment of the individual to a specific doctrine. It is possible to speculate that people with high intrinsic motivation toward a particular doctrine might be more likely to have high intrinsic

---

[74] Ayal, S., Gino, F., Barkan, R., & Ariely, D. (2015). Three principles to REVISE people's unethical behavior. *Perspectives on Psychological Science*, 10(6), 738–741.

[75] See Feldman & Perez, *supra* note 1. The two figures presented below are taken from this paper.

motivation toward other legal doctrines, especially when taking into account obliga-tion-based intrinsic motivation, as described next.

First, we conducted two regressions to examine whether participants' levels of environmental attitudes predicted their pro-environmental behavior and their sen-sitivity to distance from the nearest recycling bin.[76] As expected, environmental attitudes were strongly related to self-reported pro-environmental behavior.[77] Environmental attitudes were also inversely correlated to sensitivity to distance: participants who valued the environment to a larger degree were less sensitive to their distance from the recycling bin.[78] Both findings highlight the correlation between environmental values and pro-environmental behavior, consistent with the findings of the psychological literature on pro-environmental behavior.[79] Drawing on an additional regression, we also found an inverse correlation between pro-environmental behavior and sensitivity to distance.[80] Participants who reported acting in an environmentally friendly way were also less sensitive to their distance from the recycling containers.

Since environmental attitudes, pro-environmental behaviors, and sensitivity to distance were significantly interrelated, we decided to focus on sensitivity to distance as a proxy for intrinsic environmental motivation. Sensitivity to distance is a good proxy for intrinsic motivation because it focuses on the personal effort associated with recycling, rather than on values or more general forms of pro-environmental behavior; in addition, other studies demonstrated the critical role of perceived inconvenience in people's willingness to participate in recycling schemes.[81] We characterized people with low sensitivity to distance as people with *high intrinsic motivation* and people with high sensitivity to distance as those with *low intrinsic motivation*.

---

[76] The regression analyses reported in this section were based on the complete sample, including the organizational and academic institution conditions. Since the different conditions were not entirely balanced with regard to demographics, several background variables (age, gender, education, reli-giosity, income, living place) were inserted to the regression analyses in the first step, while the relevant independent variables were inserted in the second step.

[77] (R^2=19.4%, β=0.45, p<0.01)   [78] (R^2=5.2%, β=−.23, p<0.001)

[79] Kahn, M. E. (2007). Do greens drive Hummers or hybrids? Environmental ideology as a determinant of consumer choice. *Journal of Environmental Economics and Management*, 54(2), 129–145. See also Nordlund, A. M., & Garvill, J. (2002). Value structures behind proenvironmental behavior. *Environment and Behavior*, 34(6), 740–756. There is still debate in the literature about the exact psychological mechanism underlying pro-environmental behavior. Three prominent and competing models are the norm-activation theory, the value-belief-norms, and theory of planned behavior. Howarth, R. B., & Borsuk, M. E. (2010). Pro-environmental behavior. *Annals of the New York Academy of Sciences*, 1185(1), 211–224; Steg, L., & Vlek, C. (2009). Encouraging pro-environmental behaviour: An integrative review and research agenda. *Journal of Environmental Psychology*, 29(3), 309–317. The psychological literature recognizes also the sensitivity of pro-environmental behavior to external factors, such as economic considerations.

[80] (R^2=15.0%, β=−.40, p<0.001)

[81] Hansmann, R., Bernasconi, P., Smieszek, T., Loukopoulos, P., & Scholz, R. W. (2006). Justifications and self-organization as determinants of recycling behavior: The case of used batteries. *Resources, Conservation and Recycling*, 47(2), 133–159.

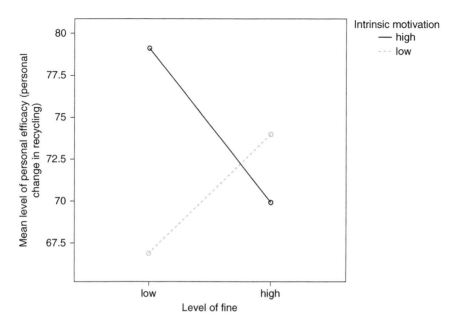

FIGURE 6.1 The adjusted mean scores of personal efficacy as a function of intrinsic motivation and the magnitude of the monetary incentive (fine).

We added a monetary incentive: imposing a high/low fine for lack of recycling as well as another condition, whereby people were told that the governing regime was high/low deposits that people got back for recycling. Finally, we examined another condition, whereby people were exposed to a code that encouraged them to engage in recycling.

We found that assigning participants who had high intrinsic motivation to the *Low Fine*[82] condition had a larger effect on their intended behavior than assigning high intrinsic motivation participants to conditions we defined as *High Deposit, High Fine,* and *Low Deposit. Ethical Code* was ranked second to the *Low Fine,* In terms of its efficacy. By contrast, among participants with low intrinsic motivation, the *High Deposit* instrument generated a higher perceived effect in comparison to the *Ethical Code, Low Fine,* and *Low Deposit* scenarios. *High Fine* was ranked second to *High Deposit condition.* As seen from Figure 6.1, all of the regulatory measures were associated with some increase in the level of recycling[83]; however, the effect of the fine was reversed for individuals with high and low intrinsic motivation. Within the high intrinsic motivation subgroup, *Low Fine* had

[82]   Values used are as follows: Low Fine: 250 NIS; High Fine: 1,000 NIS; Low Deposit 0.25 NIS; High Deposit 1 NIS.
[83]   The personal efficacy measure had a scale from 1 ("would decrease the amount to a very large degree") to 100 ("would increase the amount to a very large degree") with 50 in the middle ("would not influence at all"). Therefore, a value higher 50 in the personal efficacy scale indicated an increase in recycling intentions following the regulatory intervention, whereas a value of below 50 indicated a reduction in recycling intentions.

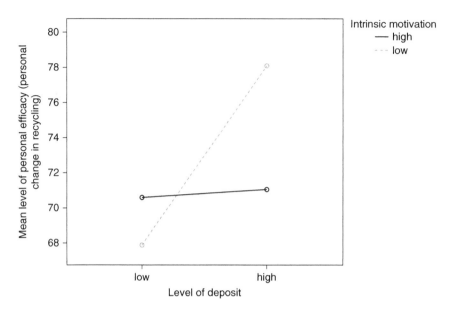

FIGURE 6.2 The adjusted mean scores of personal efficacy as a function of intrinsic motivation and the magnitude of the monetary incentive (deposit).

Source: Figures 6.1 & 6.2 are taken from Feldman, Y., & Perez, O. (2012). Motivating environmental action in a pluralistic regulatory environment: An experimental study of framing, crowding out, and institutional effects in the context of recycling policies. Law & Society Review, 46(2), 405–442.

a greater effect than *High Fine* on the measure of personal efficacy.[84] In contrast, within the low intrinsic motivation subgroup, *High Fine* generated a greater effect than *Low Fine*.[85] The results of this interaction effect are presented in Figure 6.1.

In other words, within the class of people with high intrinsic motivation, the behavioral effect of the fine decreased as the level of the fine increased. In contrast, within the class of people with low intrinsic motivation, the effect of the fine increased as its level increased. From a general policy perspective, the choice of intervention is far more important when focusing on people with limited intrinsic motivation. Identifying them in advance is highly important for the efficacy of the law.

A different pattern developed with regard to the interaction between the size of the deposit and the level of intrinsic motivation.[86] Within the low intrinsic motivation group, the pattern of results was similar to the *Fine* context: the behavioral effect of the deposit increased as the size of the deposit increased.[87] However, within the high

[84] $(F(1,288)=7.87, p<.01, \eta^2=.03)$. These tests are based on linearly independent pairwise comparisons among the estimated marginal means.

[85] $(F(1,288)=4.94, p<.05, \eta^2=.02)$

[86] We conducted the same ANCOVA analysis; the interaction between the amount of the deposit and intrinsic motivation was significant $(F(1,293)=4.19, p<.05, \eta^2=.01)$.

[87] $(F(1,293)=8.34, p<.01, \eta^2=.03)$

intrinsic motivation group, raising the deposit size was not significantly associated with behavioral effect.[88] That is, highly motivated participants reacted to deposits differently than to fines. Results are shown in Figure 6.2.

6.5.2 *Variation in Intrinsic Motivation and the Choice of Legal Instrument to Encourage Whistle-blowing*

The same pattern, whereby the choice of legal instrument is more important when intrinsic motivation is low could be seen in my work with Lobel. We examined the effectiveness of the law in dealing with variation in people's level of intrinsic motivation; our focus was how to incentivize whistle-blowing.[89] As with the work on environmental enforcement, we argued for the need to tailor the incentive design to the intrinsic motivation of people we wanted to encourage to engage in whistle-blowing. Using an experimental survey of a sample of 2,000 employees in the United States, we examined their attitudes toward certain types of misconduct and manipulated the type of incentives to which they were exposed.

We assessed the respondents' level of internal motivation and found significant differences among their evaluations of organizational misconduct.[90] As expected intuitively, the more outraged respondents felt about the illegal behavior, the more likely they were to report it and to predict reporting by others. Conversely, the less severe the misconduct and hence the lower degree of outrage, the less willing were respondents to take action. To test these predictions, we then divided the participants into two subgroups based on their evaluations of the misconduct. The first group included the respondents who evaluated the severity and immorality of the misconduct highly. The second group included those respondents who gave lower evaluations of the severity of the misconduct.[91] The first group, the perceived high-severity group, included those individuals who were internally motivated to report (*High internal*). Conversely, the second group, the low-severity group, can be understood as the group with lower levels of internal motivation (*Low internal*).[92] As expected, participants with *High internal* motivation were more likely than

---

[88] $(F_{(1,293)}=.21,\ p>.05,\ \eta^2=.00)$ [89] See Feldman & Lobel, *supra* note 1, at 1151.

[90] In evaluation of the misconduct, we refer to a factor that is based on questions 19–26; within it we include factors such as moral outrage, perception of risk to the public government from the misconduct, legitimacy, and acceptability. Multivariate $(F_{(3,1808)}=54.14,\ p<.001,\ \eta^2=.08)$.

[91] Based upon the median value of the *evaluation of the misconduct*. A two-way MANCOVA test was then conducted. The type of legal mechanism and the evaluation of the misconduct subgroups were entered as independent variables. The actions taken against the company were entered as three dependent variables and background factors were held constant.

[92] The association between internal motivation to report (as opposed to reporting due to external rewards) and perception of the misconduct's severity is clear given that the items measuring perceived severity included moral and legitimacy concerns.

Actions taken against the company by self as a function of the
legal mechanism and perceived severity of the misconduct

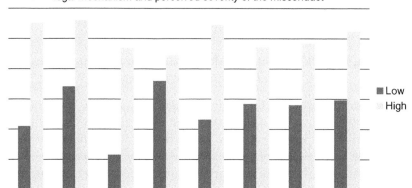

FIGURE 6.3 Responses of participants across the different experimental conditions and
perceived severity of the misconduct.
Source: Figures 6.3+6.4 are taken from Feldman, Y., & Lobel, O. (2009). The incentives
matrix: The comparative effectiveness of rewards, liabilities, duties, and protections for
reporting illegality. *Tex. L. Rev.*, 88, 1151.

participants with *Low internal* motivation to report misconducts[93] and to predict
higher reporting rates for both peers[94] and the general population.[95]

To examine the interplay between internal motivation and external legal
mechanisms, we further tested the interaction between evaluation of the misconduct and intention to report. Among our two evaluation groups, a significant
interaction was found between the type of legal mechanism and the perceived
severity of the misconduct.[96] In other words, the choice of legal mechanisms
was important for those who viewed the misconduct as relatively insignificant;
however, those who viewed the misconduct as severe reported misconduct
regardless of the legal mechanism. The findings suggest that when individuals
recognize an ethical stake in an issue, the impact of policy design variances is
diminished.

To illustrate the interplay between internal and external motivation, Figure 6.3
presents the responses of participants across the different experimental conditions
and in relation to the perceived severity of the misconduct. It demonstrates the
sharp contrast between the effect of incentive mechanisms once the moral
impulse to report is removed as a potential source of motivation. When internal

93 Univariate tests: $(F(1,1890)=159.10$, p<.001, $\eta^2=.08$); *Low Evaluation of the Misconduct*: M=7.83,
    SD=2.35; *High Evaluation of the Misconduct*: M=9.03, SD=1.72.
94 $(F(1,1890)=3.86$, p<.05, $\eta^2=.00$); *Low Evaluation of the Misconduct*: M=5.41, SD=2.45; *High
    Evaluation of the Misconduct*: M=5.64, SD=2.71.
95 $(F(1,1890)=3.86$, p<.05, $\eta^2=.00$); *Low Evaluation of the Misconduct*: M=5.41, SD=2.45; *High
    Evaluation of the Misconduct*: M=5.64, SD=2.71.
96 $(F(7,1890)=2.89$, p<.01, $\eta^2=.01$)

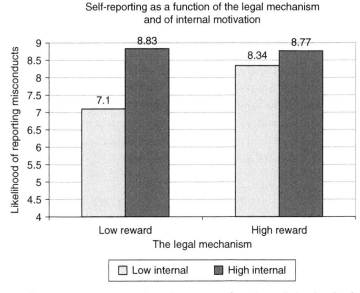

FIGURE 6.4 Intention to report misconducts as a function of the level of intrinsic motivation and the size of the reward.

motivation is missing (i.e., the severity of the misconduct is perceived as low), external incentives matter much more in deciding whether or not to report misconduct. Respondents least likely to report were those offered a low reward while having a low perception of misconduct severity. Reporting in those circumstances was even lower than in those situations where no incentive was present. Moreover, the perceived severity of the misconduct produced the greatest disparity in the reporting levels for respondents in the *Low reward* category, while it had the smallest effect on the *High reward* category. These findings suggest that the introduction of an external reward interferes with the moral dimension of reporting.

The following analysis provides another way to look at the importance of differentiated regulation as could be seen from the questionable effectiveness of using high rewards, when there is a fear that some of the workers (and hence potential enforcers) might have low internal motivation. Conducting a two-way analyis of variance (ANCOVA) revealed a significant interaction effect between the legal mechanisms (*Low reward/High reward*) and the internal motivation subgroups, indicating that the monetary reward reduced the self-reporting differences between the subgroups.[97] Within the *Low reward* condition, participants with a *High internal* motivation were more likely to report than those with a *Low internal* motivation.[98] However, within the *High reward* condition, there was no significant difference between the internal motivation subgroups.[99] As shown in Figure 6.4, paying a high reward decreases the differences between high and low

[97] $(F_{(1,474)}=10.60, p<.001, \eta^2=.02)$ [98] $(F_{(1,474)}=35.00, p<.001, \eta^2=.07)$ [99] $(p>.05)$

internally motivated individuals.[100] While there is no measure of quality of reporting in this paper, which might point out the inferiority in terms of overall efficacy of monetary-driven reporting,[101] it is clear that high rewards are able to overcome internal motivation impediments to social reporting.

In conclusion, since knowing ex ante whether a certain behavior required by the law enjoys some moral consensus and hence is likely to be intrinsically supported by a larger proportion of the population, policy makers should recognize the interaction between level of intrinsic motivation and the choice of legal instrument to optimize the efficacy of the law. This approach is hence superior to measuring the "goodness" of people based on their personality.

6.6 VARIATION IN PEOPLE'S ABILITY TO JUSTIFY NONCOMPLIANCE

Most regulatory approaches still focus on people who are deliberative with regard to the law but have varying motivations to comply. However, is people's behavior with regard to the law always as deliberative and planned as games-based methodology assumes? Fishbacher et al. measured people's level of cooperativeness by their choice to either cooperate or free-ride, in a context in which their choices between doing "good" or "bad" were clearly defined.[102] Similarly, in much of the research claiming that compliance motivation is explicit, people were given vignettes and researchers then tried to determine which factors interacted with their decision to obey the law; the assumption was that people know when they are violating the law and the question is just why they would do it. Yet, in many legally relevant situations, it is not always clear to people that when they act, they are indeed choosing between being cooperative or uncooperative. In many situations, they make choices not necessarily related to their preferences in the conventional meaning of the term, but other processes – situational and personal, some deliberative and some not – affect the likelihood that people view their behavior as cooperative or noncooperative. Next, we outline some of the main mechanisms underlying those processes.

Recently I collaborated with Fine, Von Rooji, and others[103] on identifying and measuring a new individual difference that encapsulates many of the findings of BE: the concept of *rule conditionality*. It concerns the extent to which individuals believe it is acceptable to violate legal rules – that is, the extent to which one thinks about rules in a rigid, rule-oriented manner or in a manner that recognizes exceptions. However,

---

[100] A three-way ANCOVA revealed that there was no significant interaction effect between gender, the legal mechanisms (*Low Reward/High Reward*), and the internal motivation subgroups, indicating that the same pattern of results was found among women and men.

[101] Both in terms of motivation (e.g., honesty of the report) and the quality of the report.

[102] Fischbacher, U., Gächter, S., & Fehr, E. (2001). Are people conditionally cooperative? Evidence from a public goods experiment. *Economics Letters*, 71(3), 397–404.

[103] Fine, A., van Rooij, B., Feldman, Y., Shalvi, S., Scheper, E., Leib, M., & Cauffman, E. (2016). Rule orientation and behavior: Development and validation of a scale measuring individual acceptance of rule violation. *Psychology, Public Policy, and Law*, 22(3), 314.

there was no specific measure for this internal element of legal decision making and offending. We therefore developed, validated, and tested the Rule Orientation Scale. In our first study, we developed the scale, demonstrated its convergent and divergent validity with key legal and moral reasoning scales, and found that it relates to hypothetical offending behavior across a variety of low-level crimes. In the second study, we examined whether the Rule Orientation Scale score predicts the propensity to engage in digital piracy both with and without the explicit threat of punishment. The results indicate that the score does predict offending behavior and, importantly, across different enforcement contexts. The findings suggest that an individual with low rule orientation may be able to justify offending, regardless of (1) whether a system explicitly runs an enforcement campaign, (2) how he or she perceives the severity of the threatened sanction, and (3) whether he or she believes that social norms support law violation. Identifying such individual variation is crucial in understanding ethical decision making, criminal decision making, and other strands of legal decision making.

The items that make up this scale were validated in a way that allowed us to understand what kind of people are more likely to think about legal rule violation in gray terms (i.e., seeing more acceptable conditions) versus those who see violations in black-and-white terms (i.e., a rule is a rule and there are no acceptable conditions to break it). The distribution of scores on this scale follows a normal distribution, suggesting that there is a spectrum of rule conditionality in perceiving general and acceptable circumstances for violating the law.[104] However, in contrast to the procedural justice argument, which is based on an explicit measurement of people's evaluation of different legal and governmental institutions, rule conditionality is not necessarily tied to nor derived from one's experiences with the justice system. For example, one is not expected to be more or less rule conditioned based on perceptions of how laws were created, whether they are enacted fairly, or how one perceives the legitimacy of the legal system and its actors.

6.7 CAN STATES DEAL WITH BOTH CALCULATED AND SITUATIONAL WRONGDOERS AT THE SAME TIME? OR HOW NOT TO HELP THE BAD AT THE EXPENSE OF THE GOOD

Recognizing that people have different motivations and cognitive modes that affect their wrongdoing is important not only in finding the most effective ways to increase compliance; it is also essential to preventing attempts to increase compliance by calculative individuals from decreasing compliance of good people and situational wrongdoers.

---

[104] In that paper, which relied on the work of Shalvi & Leiser (moral firmness) and that of Bandura (moral disengagement in the perpetration of inhumanities), it was shown that there is an individual variation in how people view the morality of unethical behavior. When we apply the concept of moral variation in both firmness and disengagement to the legal realm, we also see that individuals may vary in the extent to which they see circumstances under which violating legal rules would be acceptable.

Henry Smith and I propose an acoustic separation argument based on the concept of ambiguity.[105] We argue that different types of people will react differently to legal ambiguity: for some people, ambiguity may reduce their ability to find legal loopholes, whereas for others it may allow various self-deception mechanisms associated with the concept of moral wiggle room.[106] Another approach to deal with the two populations of calculated and situational wrongdoers is to increase the focus on punishment or detection, respectively. Presumably, with good people who do not believe that they are doing anything wrong, the focus should be on detection: they will not see an increase in punishment as relevant to them because they do not know they have done anything wrong. Conversely, calculated wrongdoers, because of various perceptual biases, are less likely than others to think that they will ever be caught, even when they know their behavior is either illegal or against organizational rules. Therefore, even for the calculative individuals, the size of punishment is less important.

Another approach is to strengthen or add enforcement techniques aimed at good people, but that are less likely to affect or crowd out the calculated wrongdoers. For example, the requirement to add a declaration to a tax form that one has filled it out honestly might cause some situational wrongdoers to be more careful in their reporting. It is not, however, likely to change the calculated wrongdoer's behavior. Similar points could be said about other ethical nudges, such as affixing one's signature on financial forms before filling them out.[107]

As will be developed in chapter 9 in more details, non-monetary forms of self-interest might have a greater corrupting effect on good people than on bad people, because it might be easier for good people to rationalize doing bad things for non-monetary reasons than for monetary ones. It might also be easier for good people to block out the allure of monetary influence because such influence is more easily seen as being corrupt. For calculated wrongdoers, the stronger the financial ties, the greater the fear from inappropriate influence. For situational wrongdoers, conversely, partial dependency might have a greater effect on increasing noncompliance because they might be less likely to recognize the wrongdoing associated with that influence. Furthermore, in such situations it might be easier to find room for rationalizations and for self-deception, thereby enabling situational wrongdoers to lower their guard against such influences.

An additional context, in which we might find differential effects on calculated versus situational wrongdoers, is engaging in corruption for the sake of others.[108] From a rational choice perspective, a calculated wrongdoer is expected to do more wrong

[105] See Feldman & Smith, *supra* note 67.
[106] In the next chapter – chapter 7 – this accoustic separation model is developed in more details.
[107] See Shu et al., *supra* note 29.
[108] Gino, F., Ayal, S., & Ariely, D. (2013). Self-serving altruism? The lure of unethical actions that benefit others. *Journal of Economic Behavior and Organization*, 93, 285–292.

when he will personally gain more from the misconduct. However, from a behavioral ethics perspective, the situational wrongdoer is expected to engage in more misconduct when the benefit from the harm is going to others, and not him- or herself.[109]

Some incentives offered by the state may reduce, not increase, compliance. For example, states sometimes offer tax amnesties to those who have not paid their taxes: they announce that whoever pays off before a certain date will avoid interest fees and penalties. However, who are the people who would know to take advantage of such initiatives: those who were calculated about their noncompliance in the first place. Hence, those who are more likely to know that what they did was wrong are more likely to take advantage of such measures. However, those who did not pay their taxes because they mistakenly thought they did not need to do so are less likely to remember that decision and hence less likely to use such opportunities offered by the states. Thus, the haves-come-ahead classical argument could be realized not just because of status and wealth but also with regard to people's state of mind.[110]

In this chapter, we have shown various approaches to differentiate between people based on the likelihood of their engaging in calculated vs. situational wrongdoing. We first examined various personality approaches to determining the likelihood of people engaging in unethical behavior without feeling immoral. After showing the limited ability to use those personality scales in a legal policy, we proceeded to examine other alternatives to understanding the variation between people, such as demographics and occupations. Such categories seem to be more relevant for legal policy makers, because it is much easier to use these differences *ex ante*. Finally, we examined the possibility of differentiating between people based on their level of intrinsic motivation toward the specific legal doctrine. Using some of my previous empirical work, I showed how it is possible to use such knowledge to improve the efficacy of different legal instruments. While those studies used a method that aimed at explicit intentions, the concept seems to apply also to implicit behaviors. As discussed in more detail in Chapter 11, people's intrinsic motivation is likely to affect also the likelihood that they will ignore the legal requirements implicitly.[111] The next two chapters will use the theoretical groundwork of the preceding six chapters to examine the new type of dilemmas that regulators and enforcers face regarding the effect of law on the type of unethical behaviors that could be committed by both "bad" and "good" people.

[109] Danilov, A., Biemann, T., Kring, T., & Sliwka, D. (2013). The dark side of team incentives: Experimental evidence on advice quality from financial service professionals. *Journal of Economic Behavior and Organization*, 93, 266–272.

[110] Galanter, M. (1974). Why the "haves" come out ahead: Speculations on the limits of legal change. *Law & Society Review*, 9(1), 95–160. Compare also with the work of Oren Gazal Eyal and his collaborators on the innocence effect, in which mostly guilty people are likely to use the benefits offered by the criminal justice system. For example, see Bar-Gill, O., & Gazal Eyal, O. (2006). Plea bargains only for the guilty. *Journal of Law and Economics*, 49(1), 353–364.

[111] Compare also with the work of Acquino on moral identity in this chapter.

7

Pluralistic Account of the Law: The Multiple Effects of Law on Behavior

In this chapter, I apply the theories reviewed earlier – regarding the interactions between people's modes of reasoning, between traditional and nontraditional enforcement mechanisms, and between different segments of the population – to my own empirical work on compliance and legal enforcement. In doing so, I highlight some of the inconsistencies found in my own research on the likely effect of a legal action in a given situation on people's behavior. I show that the multiple processes that underlie compliance behavior, as shown in the earlier chapters, require us to account both descriptively and normatively for the multiple effects of law on behavior. The good people approach presented thus far emphasizes the non-deliberative components of unethical behavior. It is not surprising that the ability to predict when law will induce compliance is limited. We need both a broader understanding of the behavioral processes through which people react to law and the broader perspective on the law itself.

In previous chapters, I presented a typology of three types of people – calculative individuals, situational wrongdoers, and genuinely moral individuals – and how the law needs to address each group differently and sometimes simultaneously[1]. It needs to make the wrongdoing costlier for the calculative people. For situational wrong-doers, the law needs to create situations that will weaken the justification to engage in misconduct. And for those who are genuinely committed to obeying the law, the law must reduce the likelihood that, due to a blind spot, they will fail to recognize their own wrongdoing. We need to assume that all three types of people are found in most situations and that the same law will have very different effects on the behavior of each type; this makes it hard to predict what the overall effect of the law would be. Furthermore, the elements of law – awareness, intrinsic motivation, and price – interact with one another and with the type of person. For example, for the variables of morality and prices to have an impact on compliance, people must be aware that their behavior is even relevant for the law. The situation becomes even more

---

[1] As explained in chapters 1 and 3, these three prototypes are not mutually exclusive and most people can adopt different modes in different contexts.

complex, because it is not always clear that prices affect only the calculative function and that morality focuses only on the justification function. Variations in both morality and price could also increase the likelihood that people will recognize that a given situation should be dealt with more cautiously and deliberately. Lacking the ability to know beforehand an individual type and his or her circumstances, it is hard to suggest the use of one legal approach rather than others. Chapter 8, which focuses on trade-offs and taxonomies, suggests ways to determine which legal approach to use.

7.1 LEGAL DETECTION VS. PUNISHMENT

The relative effectiveness of likelihood of detection versus severity of punishment in deterring misbehavior is still the subject of fierce debate.[2] Most studies suggest that the size of punishment has only a marginal deterrent effect on the behavioral choices of people. We propose that this might be related to our argument with regard to good people, because they do not think that they will be subject to punishment.[3] In contrast, bad people know that if they are caught they are much more likely to be punished; hence, they are more sensitive to the size of the punishment.

Instead, good people of both types – situational wrongdoers and blind-spot wrongdoers – are more likely to be affected by the likelihood of enforcement, since they are less likely to think of themselves as wrongdoers whose behavior is punishable. Enforcement that is more frequent creates more reminders to people in a way that would both reduce their justifications and increase their awareness that their behavior may lead to wrongdoing. It is also likely to reduce the uncertainty that might make it easier for people to deceive themselves as to the true legal meaning of their behavior.

In other words, the relative deterrent value of frequent detection vs. punishment size depends on people's mind-set. Raising the cost of wrongdoing mainly affects the decision-making process of calculative people who think about costs. For genuinely

[2] Becker, G. S. (1968). Crime and punishment: An economic approach. In N. G. Fielding, A. Clarke, & Robert Witt (Eds.), *The economic dimensions of crime* (pp. 13–68). London: Palgrave Macmillan.

[3] Chiricos, T. G., & Waldo, G. P. (1970). Punishment and crime: An examination of some empirical evidence. *Social Problems*, 18(2), 200–217. See also Antunes, G., & Hunt, A. L. (1973). The impact of certainty and severity of punishment on levels of crime in American states: An extended analysis. *Journal of Criminal Law and Criminology* (1973–), 64(4), 486–493; Von Hirsch, A., Bottoms, A. E., Burney, E., & Wikstrom, P. O. (1999). *Criminal deterrence and sentence severity: An analysis of recent research*. Oxford: Hart: "the studies reviewed do not provide a basis for inferring that increasing the severity of sentences generally is capable of enhancing deterrent effects" (p. 63); Nagin, D. S., & Pogarsky, G. (2001). Integrating celerity, impulsivity, and extralegal sanction threats into a model of general deterrence: Theory and evidence. *Criminology*, 39(4), 865–892; for a review of much of the literature on the advantage of certainty over severity, see Doob, A. N., & Webster, C. M. (2013). The "Truth in Sentencing" Act: The triumph of form over substance. *Canadian Criminal Law Review*, 17(3), 365.

moral individuals whose wrongdoing is mainly related to their blind spots, clearly raising the expected price might not reduce that behavior.[4]

Imposing harsh punishments does have value in clearly illustrating the government's approach and commitment to enforcing morality. Yet, harsher punishment may actually reduce good people's compliance. The process of imposing this punishment is a lengthy one, which may allow time for a backlash to set in.[5] For example, Erev et al., who examined enforcement of safety regulations in factories, found that more frequent enforcement with small fines was more effective than less frequent punishment with large fines.[6] A longer process also enables good people to create justifications to engage in smaller-level misconduct. Thus, criminal law sanctions that might deter calculative people might do the opposite for the other two types of people who engage in noncompliance with limited awareness.

7.2 ACOUSTIC SEPARATION AND LEGAL UNCERTAINTY

An additional important dimension in the ways laws affect behavior is related to legal uncertainty. In my work with Henry Smith[7] on behavioral equity, we examined whether uncertainty about the meaning of the law may have a different effect on good and bad people; it was through this analysis that we first developed the concept of the law trying to address both good and bad types of people separately.

Sometimes when the same law addresses multiple audiences, each group can receive a different message, without excessive interference between them, even if the messages are in tension. This concept has been dubbed "acoustic separation" by Meir Dan-Cohen,[8] who has explored the idea in criminal law. In Dan-Cohen's model, the law can in principle send two separate messages to two separate audiences: conduct rules directed at primary actors (the public) and decision rules aimed at guiding legal decision makers (especially judges). For example, "let no man steal" is a conduct rule, whereas "let the judge cause whoever is convicted of stealing to be hanged" is a decision rule. According to Dan-Cohen, the linguistic form of a rule does not determine its function, and the two functions of law can be served as long as there is not too much cross-talk. In other words, if there is acoustic separation

---

[4] In a work with Doron Teichman, I have focused on a different approach to this dilemma. See Feldman, Y., & Teichman, D. (2009). Are all legal probabilities created equal? *New York University Law Review*, 84, 980.

[5] Dickens, W. T., Katz, L. F., Lang, K., & Summers, L. H. (1989). Employee crime and the monitoring puzzle. *Journal of Labor Economics*, 7(3), 331–347.

[6] Part of their argument is that with smaller fines, enforcers feel far more comfortable to engage in enforcement. Schurr, A., Rodensky, D., & Erev, I. (2014). The effect of unpleasant experiences on evaluation and behavior. *Journal of Economic Behavior & Organization*, 106, 1–9.

[7] Feldman, Y., & Smith, H. E. (2014). Behavioral equity. Journal of Institutional and Theoretical Economics JITE, 170(1), 137–159.

[8] Dan-Cohen, M. (1984). Decision rules and conduct rules: On acoustic separation in criminal law. *Harvard Law Review*, 97, 625–677.

between the two audiences, the law could signal to judges when leniency is called for without the notice of the general public.

In the above mentioned work with Smith on Behavioral Equity, we argued that both groups – "good" people and bad-faith actors – receive the same literal message, but what they derive from it depends on their motivation, awareness and focus. When we separate the public into three types of people, there is the potential for many types of rules and audiences, with the greater attendant danger of acoustic non-separation.

We assumed that some actors are aware of both the conduct rule and the decision rule,[9] whereas others are aware of only the conduct rule. In the extreme situation, evasion is a problem where bad-faith actors are aware not only of the conduct rule but also of the consequences of behavior as far as the decision rule is concerned, yet they still commit wrongdoing. They are ready to game the system as a whole, and they have the requisite knowledge to enable such gaming.

In contrast, good people can be afforded a good deal of leniency without upsetting the system because they are not evaders. The legal system should provide a safe harbor for these actors, who generally sense that by following their moral inclinations they are not likely to violate of the law

To the case of classic acoustic separation, Smith and I suggested a new twist that makes the legal system better able to juggle the two audiences: the same literal message can serve as an anti-evasion device for bad-faith actors while not interfering with (or even promoting) the intrinsic motivation of good-faith actors. As we have seen, equity is couched in moral terms (clean hands, not profiting from one's own wrongdoing, equity as a court of conscience). To the evaders, the system sends a message that it is reserving a second move to counteract evasive behavior, even if it appears in a new guise. The same moral norms will have an appeal to the good-faith people, not as a legal message but as a reinforcement of existing moral norms. Thus, equity avoids crowding out intrinsic motivation and in some cases can even promote moral deliberation.[10] The model developed with Smith focused on good people as a whole. However, in this book we show that there is more than one type of good people, which makes the acoustic separation more complex.

7.3 THE INADVERTENT EFFECT OF MORALITY WHEN ACCOUNTING FOR SELF-DECEPTION

Regulating behavior in private contexts often relies on morality, and we tend to resist the usage of law in such situations. However, sometimes the intrusion of legalism can protect people from themselves. Thus, another possible new role for law, under the book's approach to human morality, is to examine its ability to make it less likely for good people to self-deceive.

---

[9] That is how you need to behave vs. what will happen to you, legally, once you behave in a certain way.

[10] Shiffrin, S. V. (2009). Inducing moral deliberation: On the occasional virtues of fog. *Harvard Law Review*, 123, 1214.

Consider this thought experiment. A father goes to an amusement park with his own child and that child's friend. From a moral perspective, he is likely to take more care of his own child than of the friend. Yet, anecdotal experience tells us that it is more likely that the parent would allow his child on a ride that is unsafe for his size; say the child is 5 cm shorter than the height requirement demands. However, because this situation appears to the parent in a legalistic framework rather than a moral one, he is less likely to violate the rule with regard to his child's friend than his own. It is not that the fear of disapproval or of a legal suit is scarier than the thought that one's own child would die; the father's greater compliance with the height requirement for the child's friend, despite the greater moral commitment to his own child, occurs because it is less likely that one would cut corners when it comes to the law with acquaintances than with family members. Thus, according to the "Law of Good People" paradigm, law has a new advantage over morality, especially in contexts where a third party might be able to use legal means against that decision.

The function of the law is to reduce self-deception and justified ethicality. In contrast to the law, considerations of morality and fairness, because they are vague and thus more likely to be interpreted differently by different actors, are far more likely to be subject to self-deception. Such considerations are limited in their ability to stop people from pursuing their self interest in high-stakes situations, and their norms vary greatly across people and situations. Fairness is not relevant to all forms of behaviors, and we cannot only rely on individual's notions of fairness; we also need the law to remind people of what not to do and to prevent self-serving decisions. However, at the end of the day the main operating component of decision making needs to be intrinsic motivation. Extrinsic intervention should not be used to motivate people but rather to make sure that they will not use various biases to reshape what is moral. According to this view, the crowding out of intrinsic motivation might have a positive effect, because we want people to worry about the law more than we want them to focus on their own morality.

Another limitation in the current treatment of morality in legal scholarship is related to the work of Dan Kahan.[11] We have discussed the advantages of morality in general legal theory. In contrast to arguments made by scholars such as Kahan about mistakes of law and the need to align law with morality, we suggest the opposite. Kahan argues against the Holmesian view of the law through an analysis of the mistake doctrine in criminal law. He essentially argues that legislatures are indeed interested in the moralizing effect of law. According to Kahan, when people make mistakes of law, we try to see if this is the type of mistake that can teach us something about the nature of the law. If a mistake tells us nothing about people's character, we will usually excuse them from responsibility. Kahan argues that in a sense the state believes that morality provides a better guide to behavior than the law itself

---

[11]   Kahan, D. M. (1997). Ignorance of law is an excuse: But only for the virtuous. *Michigan Law Review*, 96(1), 127–154.

and therefore, in contrast to Holmes – who spoke about the law without morality – Kahan maintains that the state seeks to obscure the law so people will instead focus on their own personal morality. Thus, the state does not wish to encourage people to learn about law as much as it wishes them to learn about morality. The question that we need to examine is how to view this moralizing effect of law, given what we know about people's moral biases. Is it really true that people who make mistakes about morality are worse than people who make mistakes about the law? Consider the dice under the cup experiment, which we examined in Chapter 2; it suggests that people feel that dishonesty about a rule is more likely to be deemed acceptable than lying about reality (e.g., making up the number that they did not have).

Dan Kahan was unaware of the discussion of behavioral ethics and hence was certain that if people make mistakes it is because they are following their sense of morality. The problem presented in these paragraphs is that people's own sense of morality might serve their purposes and hence cannot be viewed as some independent moral conviction people have with regard to their behavior.

7.4 LAW AS A REMINDER

One of the most tragic phenomena today is that of parents exiting their cars and leaving their children inside.[12] A classic question is whether parents should be punished for this behavior. This is probably the most extreme version of the "Law of Good People" paradigm, because very few parents would want their kids to get hurt; therefore, the challenge of law, as in many other negligence contexts,[13], is whether it is possible to use it to change the behavior of the unaware individual. The answer to this question touches on issues such as how authentic the blind spot is and to what extent failing to pay attention is an unconscious behavior. Clearly the calculative and justified mind-sets are not relevant to such decisions, because they are simply a lapse in memory that causes the mistake.[14] How would the punishment of a fine or jail time compare to the horrific tragedy of losing a child? Would sending parents to jail change the likelihood that they would forget their children in the car?

The more important issue is whether the law can be designed to shift the situation, *ex ante*, so these tragedies will not happen. Would making most parents adopt technological solutions that would minimize the chance of their forgetting their kids help actually prevent this tragedy? In many ways, the law could be shaped to penalize parents who do not implement such a technological device. Alternatively, would a situation in which parents who simply leave their kids in the car unattended are committing a punishable act reduce the chance that they would do that in the first place?

[12] Armagost, S. (2001). An innocent mistake or criminal conduct: Children dying of hyperthermia in hot vehicles. *Hamline Journal of Public Law & Policy*, 23, 109.

[13] Brady, J. B. (1980). Recklessness, negligence, indifference, and awareness. *Modern Law Review*, 43(4), 381–399.

[14] Cooter, R., & Porat, A. (2014). Lapses of attention in medical malpractice and road accidents. *Theoretical Inquiries in Law*, 15(2), 329–358.

7.5 THE COMPLEX EFFECT OF SPECIFICITY ON COMPLIANCE

Another example for a concept which could have conflicting effects on the interaction between law and behavior is specificity. Specificity can have both positive and negative effects on compliance. It is important in helping people understand their goals and use their cognitive resources in a focused manner. Yet, theories of crowding out, trust, and cooperation suggest that increased specificity can create resentment and lead to under-compliance and under-performance. Conversely, ambiguity in the law can encourage good people to engage in creative interpretations of legal requirements, allowing them to justify unethical behavior, with limited awareness of the meaning of that behavior.

To tease out the effects of specificity, in a joint work with Bousasalis and Smith, we examined its impact on compliance (when a person either does or does not follow a directive) compared to performance (when a person acts above and beyond a minimum threshold).[15] Second, we distinguished the controlling, limiting effects of specificity from its instructive, informative effects by monitoring the interaction between specificity and good faith. We hypothesized that the combination of specificity and monitoring enhances the effect of specificity on compliance but reduces levels of performance and trust, whereas the combination of specificity and good faith enhances both the informative goal-setting aspects of specificity and people's sense of commitment. To test these hypotheses, we used a 2x2x2 experimental design in which participants were instructed to edit a document under a combination of three conditions: with general or detailed instructions, with a reference to good faith or without it, and with monitoring (through sanctioning) or without it. The assignments were designed in such a way that people could engage in various levels of editing (both required and above what was required, with reasonable and more-than-reasonable care), allowing us to measure distinctly both compliance and performance. When participants require information and guidance, as in the case of editing a document, we found that specificity increases performance beyond what was required of them compared to the standard condition.

The combination of specificity, monitoring, and good faith in a factorial design, using a variety of incentive-compatible behaviors and psychological measures as dependent variables, enables us to explore a spectrum of effects of legal specificity across a range of contexts. Understanding how specificity affects each dimension, both alone and in tandem with monitoring and a good-faith requirement, guides us in optimizing the language of the law to encourage compliance and performance. Furthermore, the behavioral dependent variable chosen for this project is language editing, which gives us the freedom to vary the level of specificity. Although we

---

[15] Boussalis, C., Feldman, Y., & Smith, H. E. (2017). Experimental analysis of the effect of standards on compliance and performance. *Regulation & Governance*. doi:10.1111/rego.12140. The description of this study is partly based on that paper.

assume that most participants have some notion of what editing means, the task of editing still makes it possible for the study design to vary the emphasis of certain aspects without undermining the overall meaning of the activity. This design does not compare two extreme conditions, as is done in some studies on specificity[16] but rather the effect of a general instruction versus a more specific guideline, to which we have added specific examples (out of many other categories) of what the vague editing standard could mean (e.g., correcting spelling or punctuation errors).

We operationalized compliance and performance as the number of attempted corrections of a text document that contains nine types of errors: verb tense, punctuation, subject-verb agreement, missing words, word meaning, pronoun usage, article usage, singular/plural, and apostrophe usage. There was a total of 54 mistakes in this 1,592-word document. The experiment was conducted online in October 2012, with a sample of 339 respondents who were recruited from Amazon Mechanical Turk, a crowd-sourcing Internet labor market.[17]

Respondents were first shown a page with information about the study and a statement of informed consent. After a respondent agreed to participate, he or she was then randomly assigned to one of eight experimental conditions that primed them with different combinations of specificity, good faith, and monitoring

The empirical results suggest a nuanced impact of specificity on editing effort. Our findings dovetail with the earlier literature review, which emphasized the complexity of understanding how law affects behavior because it activates multiple processes. In contrast to most current views of specificity, which focus either on its informative value[18] or on its effect on people's self-perception of autonomy,[19] our study attempted to explore both the motivational and the informative functions of specificity, using one integrative design featuring a few incentive-compatible behavioral measures. Furthermore, we took a pragmatic and moderate approach that did not focus on the extreme high and low values of specificity but rather on a realistic hybrid version, in which vague standards are reinforced with some detailed examples.

First, we found that respondents who were given specific instructions related to the editing task were significantly more likely to attempt to correct errors found in the document than those who were given ambiguous instructions. They also attempted significantly more corrections for error types that were not mentioned in the instructions. Of the "unmentioned" errors, we found a significant main effect

---

[16] Chou, E. Y., Halevy, N. & Murnighan, J. K. (2010). The hidden cost of contracts on relationships and performance, IACM 23rd Annual Conference Paper, available at SSRN: http://papers.ssrn.com/sol3/papers.cfm?abstract_id=1612376 (Date posted: May 21, 2010).

[17] Respondents were paid $1.50 for participating in the study (58% female, mean age=32.48, SD=11.23).

[18] Kaplow, L. (1992). Rules versus standards: An economic analysis. *Duke Law Journal*, 42, 557. See also Sunstein, C. R. (1995). Problems with rules. *California Law Review*, 83, 953–1026; Schlag, P. (1985). Rules and standards. *UCLA Law Review*, 33, 379.

[19] See Shiffrin, *supra* note 10, at 1214.

on all content-related types that approximate performance (missing words and word meaning) as well as on one of five grammatical types (e.g., subject-verb agreement), which conforms with broad compliance. Of the nine error types, we found a statistically significant interaction effect of specificity only for punctuation errors, an error type mentioned in the specific instructions. However, we found that among those in the specificity treatment, respondents who were *not* given a monitoring treatment did *better* at detecting punctuation errors than subjects who were given a monitoring treatment. To further illustrate the mixed results, we found no significant interaction effect for verb-tense errors, which was the second error type mentioned in the specific instructions.

The significant increase in both corrections for error types that were mentioned and for those that were not mentioned in the instructions suggests that the main effect is some type of spillover. We attribute the spillover effect to an increase in the level of attention and not necessarily to heightened intrinsic motivation. Offering examples of error types to these respondents made them more careful and thus more likely to identify errors of all types. These results may reflect more of the instructional aspect of specificity than notions of morality/specificity. That is, for certain tasks, such as editing, the provision of specific instructions may not necessarily affect the intrinsic motivation of respondents. In certain contexts, specific instructions may indeed be sought after and welcomed by agents who otherwise would perceive the task as prohibitively ambiguous.

A second lesson is that providing detailed examples gives more information to the participant, making the motivational role of specificity more indirect. In addition to specificity's contribution to compliance, it enhanced performance in areas beyond those that were requested. Thus, specificity can serve an informative function not only in the details it gives but also in its ability to help people focus on better performance, including in other categories of behavior.

Increased specificity can also reduce, rather than boost, negative motivational effects, as shown both in earlier studies on specificity and our own work. This is in contrast to Chou et al. who argued that specificity increased resentment and consequently decreased performance.[20] Our study (which, as described earlier, focused on different circumstances) found that specificity, when phrased in an informative way, does not trigger resentful feelings. Nevertheless, it still might be the case that when legal instructions are framed using highly constraining language, the effect of specificity is indeed negative. Furthermore, it is possible to apply specificity using examples rather than a closed list, thereby avoiding many of the problems associated with over-focusing and lack of flexibility. Finally, to optimize specificity in contracts, as well as in law and regulation, multiple factors need to be taken into account, such as the relative costs of over- and under-performance, the consequences of mistakes, the cost of monitoring, and the information that both the principal and the agent are

---

[20] See Chou et al., *supra* note 16.

expected to have about the task. The different mind-sets and different motivations with regard to every legal requirement create a far greater complex challenge to regulators. The main way to meet this and the other regulatory challenges created by the "Law of Good People" paradigm is to engage in more sophisticated empirical legal research that will be sensitive enough to detect the nuanced effects of law on the behavior of the regulates.

7.6 THE COMPLEX EFFECT OF LAW ON PROCEDURAL JUSTICE

Another take on the complex relationship between law and morality can be seen in my joint work with Tom Tyler on how mandating fair procedures can be theorized to affect compliance in two opposite ways.[21] Enacting a fair procedure can enhance the expressive effects of fairness, or it can undermine its social value by reducing its voluntary nature. Using empirical findings we can see that some functions of the law have more impact on behavior than others in given contexts. In asymmetric conditions, such as the workplace, people may believe that being entitled to a right overcomes the feeling that an action is being done voluntarily.

Tyler and I explored empirically how the influence of the perceived procedural justice of employee pay and promotion procedures on employee adherence to workplace rules differs depending on whether those fair procedures are enacted within companies voluntarily or mandated by state law. In other words, was the voluntary/mandated distinction important when people were making judgments about overall justice in issues concerning pay and benefits in the workplace? This question was addressed using both a survey of employers and an analysis of employees' reactions to an experimental vignette. The two relevant findings from that study show the differentiated effect of law on the behavior of people. One can only predict that effect by understanding the numerous interactions that could alter its direction. Again, rigorous empirical research is needed to account for the various factors that might moderate the effect of law.

A regression analysis indicates that having one's voice heard during performance evaluations when employees perceived that they had a legal entitlement for such voice had a greater positive influence on ratings of overall procedural justice[22] and of distributive justice[23] than when they perceived the procedure to be voluntary. These effects were additive in nature; however, they did not interact. In other words, at any given point, the level of voice that employees shared during performance assessments strongly influenced their overall justice judgments, and this effect was not dependent on whether employees believed that level of voice to be mandated.

---

[21] Feldman, Y., & Tyler, T. R. (2012). Mandated justice: The potential promise and possible pitfalls of mandating procedural justice in the workplace. *Regulation & Governance*, 6(1), 46–65. The description of this study is based in part on that paper.
[22] (beta=0.08, p<.05)   [23] (beta=0.09, p<.01)

Conversely, people thought the workplace was more just if voice was mandated, but this effect did not vary depending on the level of voice that they had.

Finally, the study revealed another interesting finding about the complex effect of law. When workers believed that procedural changes enhanced their level of procedural justice, the changes were more influential on their fairness perception when they believed those actions were mandated by law. However, for employees who were already experiencing high levels of procedural justice in their workplace, changes only enhanced legitimacy when they were viewed as voluntary.

7.7 THE COMPLEX EFFECT OF SOFT LANGUAGE

The complex effect of legal language on behavior is illustrated in a joint study conducted with Koachaki and Gino on the optimal language of an ethical code.[24] Research in social psychology demonstrates that subtle factors in one's environment affect how one interprets a situation, which, subsequently, influences one's choices.[25] For instance, changing the name of a game from the "Wall Street Game" to the "Community Game" substantially influenced individuals' choice of actions and anticipation of their counterparts' actions. Interestingly, participants did not anticipate the extent to which this simple labeling or naming affected their responses.

The choice of language is particularly important in documents for which people could reach more than one understanding of the text, not because of its ambiguity, but rather because of their relatively limited attention to it. For example, when completing various government forms, most people only glance at their many instructions and warnings. Furthermore, organizational settings, ethical codes, sexual harassment codes, and safety codes are so ubiquitous that people rarely read them. Conventional wisdom might suggest that there is little importance to the choice of words used because people pay no heed to them. However, if the goal is to have people read and understand the forms, the nudge rationale suggests that rather than focusing on the choice of words, it would be more effective to alter the situation in which the documents are being read. Our perspective is that rather than assuming the text does not matter, it makes most sense to explore how it affects people in various situations. Only an approach that targets the interaction between the various modes of reasoning and the different intervention methods can fully analyze how much people really understand the texts around them.

[24] Kouchaki, M., Feldman, Y., & Gino, F. (2015). Expressive effects of ethical codes: An experimental survey of US employees' interpretation, understanding and implementation of institutional ethical policies. Unpublished study, on file with the author.

[25] Kay, A. C., & Ross, L. (2003). The perceptual push: The interplay of implicit cues and explicit situational construals on behavioral intentions in the Prisoner's Dilemma. *Journal of Experimental Social Psychology, 39*(6), 634–643. See also Liberman, V., Samuels, S. M., & Ross, L. (2004). The name of the game: Predictive power of reputations versus situational labels in determining prisoner's dilemma game moves. *Personality and Social Psychology Bulletin, 30*(9), 1175–1185.

Our study examined how employees perceive and interpret ethics codes, particularly the relationship between the codes' language cues and individuals' levels of dishonesty. Such codes are viewed as an important form of organizational discourse and documentation that is crafted, implemented, and interpreted within particular social and organizational systems. We compared the behavior of employees who were hired by an organization with a less formal and more family-like code of conduct (employees were addressed as "we") with that of employees hired to work in a company with a more formal code (in which they were addressed as "employees"), where the expectations for them to behave ethically were based on notions of rule. Trust and group identity are signaled by the "we" condition, and deterrence and strong power are signaled in the "employees" condition.

Two field experiments and several few laboratory studies all replicated the same effect with regard to dishonesty. We presented participants with unsolvable matrix problems and used the number of unsolvable matrices that participants reported as solving as our measure of unethical behavior. We gave participants the opportunity to overstate their performance on a next round of data entry and thus earn undeserved money, as well as to lie about their performance if they wanted. More workers in the "we-code" condition lied about their performance than in the "employees" condition.

It is also the fact that the same word may have conflicting effects. It was shown that the use of "we" increases both unethicality and positive attitudes toward their employer. Thus, this project suggests not only that minor language choices, which do not have any instrumental importance, affect behavior in unexpected directions but also have conflicting effects on people's behavior (e.g., level of unethicality vs. positive attitudes toward employers). Legal policy makers will have to decide ex ante, therefore, which direction they want to take for the people whose behavior they try to change. Careful data collection and sensitivity to the nuanced effects of law on behavior are again essential.

7.8 CONTRADICTORY EFFECT OF LOSS AVERSION ON CONTRACTUAL PERFORMANCE

The last example of the complex effect of law on behavior, given the more complex account of the people the law tries to regulate, comes from my collaboration with Schurr and Teichman on the impact of loss aversion on contract interpretation.[26] The traditional approach to studying this effect is found in studies by Brooks et al., who showed that loss aversion increased efforts by both parties to agree to a contract.[27] In contrast to this finding, which can be explained by good people's search for justifications, we showed that loss aversion is likely to decrease

[26] Feldman, Y., Schurr, A., & Teichman, D. (2013). Reference points and contractual choices: An experimental examination. *Journal of Empirical Legal Studies*, 10(3), 512–541. Figure 7.1 is taken from that paper.
[27] Brooks, R. R., Stremitzer, A., & Tontrup, S. (2012). Framing contracts: Why loss framing increases effort. *Journal of Institutional and Theoretical Economics*, 168(1), 62–82.

performance, since it highly incentivizes people to interpret the contractual requirements in a more favorable way for them.

A large body of both psychological and economic studies suggests that people treat
payoffs framed as gains and payoffs framed as losses differently. Prospect theory
suggests that the process of interpretation is reference dependent. More specifically,
people's choices are expected to be influenced by whether they view the interpretive
dilemma they face as one that involves enhancing their gains or reducing their
losses. Given that people exhibit loss aversion, it is expected that they will tend to
interpret their obligations more selfishly when they perceive that they are in the
domain of losses. However, loss aversion effects could go in different directions in
legal contexts.

Building on these studies, we hypothesized that contract interpretation decisions would be affected by the way in which they are framed. More specifically,
we expected that promisors would tend to adopt a more self-serving interpretation
when they make decisions about losses than when they make them about gains.[28]
To test this prediction, we ran a series of three experiments using a between-
subject design. The first two studies used experimental surveys that measured and
compared participants' attitudes toward a contract interpretation dilemma.
The third study was an incentive-compatible lab experiment, in which participants' actual interpretive decisions determined their payoff. All three experiments confirmed our basic hypothesis, showing that framing contractual
payoffs as losses rather than gains raises parties' tendency to interpret their
obligations selfishly.

It also contributed to the "Law of Good People" paradigm in the context of
contracts. The existing literature on contractual performance decisions and
framing focuses on the dichotomous choice: to breach or not to breach. For
example, when Wilkinson-Ryan and Baron described the promisors' breach
decision to their subjects, they simply stated, "He decides to break his contract
in order to take other, more profitable work."[29] Thus, such studies implicitly
assume clear contractual obligations in the shadow of which choices are made.
We, in contrast, focused on the arguably more common situation of how people
interpret an ambiguous contractual obligation and form a decision on what will
be seen as performance of the contract. That is, the interpreting party needs to
decide whether to assume the risk of legal liability and adopt an interpretation
that will serve its interests or opt for an interpretation that serves the interests of
the opposing party. The behavioral ethics perspective that advocates for people's

[28]   Kern, M. C., & Chugh, D. (2009). Bounded ethicality: The perils of loss framing. *Psychological
       Science*, 20(3), 378–384.
[29]   Wilkinson-Ryan, T., & Baron, J. (2009). Moral judgment and moral heuristics in breach of contract.
       Journal of Empirical Legal Studies, 6(2), 405–423 at 413. See also Wilkinson-Ryan, T., &
       Hoffman, D. A. (2010). Breach is for suckers. *Vanderbilt Law Review*, 63, 1001–1029 (using precisely
       the same phrase to describe the decision to breach).

need to maintain their self-image suggests that under that legal ambiguity is a moral wiggle room that people might use to enhance their self-interest while maintaining their self-esteem.[30] Indeed, in some of my other research on legal uncertainty,[31] I have shown, experimentally, how people can use uncertainty as self-deception to convince themselves that their behavior is within the boundaries of the law and of the prevailing norms and moral conventions.

To test the relationship between gain/loss reference points and actual behavior, participants in the third study played a computerized version of a trivia game that included both easy and difficult questions.[32] Fifty-one students, 31 men and 20 women, at the Hebrew University of Jerusalem participated in the experiment. They were recruited through ads inviting them to participate in a "fun experiment." Participants were told that the purpose of the game was to reevaluate a pool of questions that had been used in experiments in the past and would be used in future experiments.

We employed a between-subject design that included two conditions: gains and losses. Participants in the gains group were told that they would be asked to answer 20 trivia questions and that for each correct answer, whether the question was easy or difficult, they would receive 1 NIS. Participants in the loss group, in contrast, were told that they would receive 20 NIS for their participation in the experiment, but for each mistake, whether in answer to a difficult or easy question, they would lose 1 NIS. Note that although the two groups differed with respect to the frame, they were indistinguishable from an objective perspective.

To create an interpretive dilemma for the participants, the instructions stated that the university rules prohibited us from mandating the number of easy versus difficult questions that they had to answer in the experiment. Therefore, before each question they would be asked to choose whether they wanted it to be easy or difficult. The instructions then stated, "Participants are asked to answer a reasonable number of difficult questions, so that we have a good mix of both types of questions." Since the probability of answering a difficult question correctly was significantly lower, interpreting the "reasonable amount" obligation such that it required a smaller number of these questions reflected a selfish interpretation, because it raised participants' expected payoff. Thus, this design enabled us to use the number of difficult questions that participants chose to answer as a dependent variable that measured

---

[30] Mazar, N., Amir, O., & Ariely, D. (2008). The dishonesty of honest people: A theory of self-concept maintenance. *Journal of Marketing Research, 45*(6), 633–644.

[31] Feldman, Y., & Harel, A. (2008). Social norms, self-interest and ambiguity: An experimental analysis of the rule vs. standard dilemma. *Review of Law & Economics, 4*(1), 81–126. See also Feldman Y., & Lifshitz, S. (2011). Behind the veil of legal uncertainty. *Journal of Law & Contemporary Problems, 74* (2), 133–174.

[32] See Feldman et al., *supra* note 26. In this paper, we used a pool of 60 multiple-choice, general-knowledge questions in topics such as sports, music, geography, and science that had been used in previous experiments over the past four years. The questions were divided into easy and difficult categories. On average, the chance of answering a difficult question correctly was 30 percent, whereas that of answering an easy question was 60 percent. These estimates are based on series of previous experiments in which 170 students answered the questions.

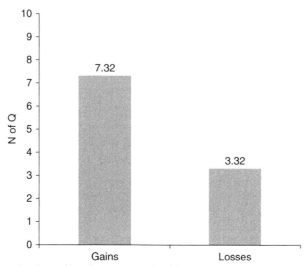

FIGURE 7.1 Number of hard question solved by participants in the gain and losses conditions.
Source: Figure 7.1 is taken from Feldman, Y., Schurr, A., & Teichman, D. (2013). Reference points and contractual choices: An experimental examination. *Journal of Empirical Legal Studies*, 10(3), 512–541.

their interpretation strategy. Figure 7.1 summarizes the main results. It shows that on average participants in the gains condition chose to answer 7.32 difficult questions compared to only 3.32 such questions in the loss condition.[33]

Our results extend the legal literature on gains, losses, and breach decisions. Much like the economic literature on the topic, the legal literature has also viewed breach decisions as not involving any interpretive dilemmas. In other words, it has focused on the unique case of willful breaches, with all of the normative uniqueness associated with such cases.[34] The current focus of the book on behavioral ethics and good people suggests also that there is a need to pay attention to much more subtle patterns that might give rise to distinctive normative intuitions among both promisors and those judging their choices. The reported results thus allow for a broader analysis of the influence of framing on a more realistic type of breach decisions, which tend to be subtler with greater room for self-deception.

[33]   Simple comparison revealed that the difference between the means was significant ($t(48)=2.265$, $p<0.05$, Cohen's $d=0.98$).

[34]   For several articles discussing and trying to justify the unique treatment of willful breach, see Thel, S., & Siegelman, P. (2009). Wilfulness vs expectation: A defense of wilful breach doctrine. *Michigan Law Review*, 107. See also Craswell, R. (2009). When is a willful breach "willful"? The link between definitions and damages. *Michigan Law Review*, 107, 1501–1515; Bar-Gill, O., & Ben-Shahar, O. (2009). An information theory of willful breach. *Michigan Law Review*, 107, 1479–1499.

SUMMARY

To summarize, since there is more than one mind-set that laws need to address and because law affects behavior in many more ways than the legal policy makers, legal policy makers face a great challenge when designing laws, as the consequences of the law seem to be much harder to account for when taking a broader perspective of the law as well as on the mechanisms through which law changes the behavior of people. In addition, when the focus on people's behavior is more nuanced, then we need to account also for the type of influences of the law on behavior. Clearly when the focus is on calculative individuals, the effects are clearer, there are less behavioral trade-offs, and people react mostly to the price function of the law.

Indeed, the empirical studies reviewed here demonstrate these complex effects of the different components of law on behavior, uncertainty, language choices, loss aversion, and legal regulation. The interesting aspect of many of these studies is that there are competing predictions of how the law would affect behavior in any particular context. In later chapters, we offer a few alternative approaches for how the law could deal with these complexities. One approach is adopting a combination of empirical research on the likely effect of law and an evidence-based approach to every particular case. Another approach could be using taxonomies and recognizing the behavioral trade-offs and the relevancy of each consideration to a particular context. These approaches will be developed both in Chapter 8, which focuses on enforcement dilemmas, and in the concluding chapter (11).

8

Enforcement Dilemmas and Behavioral Trade-offs

8.1 INTRODUCTION

In Chapters 3 and 4, we examined the traditional and nontraditional instruments that policy makers can use to change human behavior. We reviewed the pros and cons of both approaches: traditional methods address the motivation to comply (e.g., deterrence and sanctions) and nontraditional methods target cognition (e.g., nudges and debiasing). Chapter 7 focused on the multiple predicted and inadvertent effects of law on human behavior, highlighting the fact that once human behavior is being looked at in a more nuanced way, in many cases one aspect of the law might lead to conflicting effects on people, especially when the taking the variation in people's reaction to the law, as developed in Chapter 6. In this chapter, we focus on the enforcement dilemmas arising from the different interventions, given people's complex behavioral reaction to law. Its aim is to enable policy makers to design the optimal mix of behavioral change methods, given all of these complexities, while recognizing the trade-offs between competing policy goals.

Before examining enforcement dilemmas, a discussion of that nature of behavioral trade-offs is in order. When designing regulations and rules, policy makers need to make normative decisions about which goals they want those regulations to achieve. Rarely does one policy affect all types of behavior in the same way in all contexts. Much more often the same policy will facilitate one type of desired behavioral change while discouraging another type of welcomed change. Some policies produce long-term change at the expense of short-term change. Others encourage more sustainable behavioral change but at the cost of being more restrictive. Some regulations make the desired behavioral change more explicit (the expressive effect of the law), while others rely on nudges, which work without

Some of the text in this chapter is based on a chapter written with Orly Lobel, Feldman, Y., & Lobel, O. (2015). Behavioural trade-offs: Beyond the land of nudges spans the world of law and psychology. In A. Alemanno and A.-L. Sibony (Eds.), *Nudges and the Law: An European perspective*. Oxford: Hart. Some of the other text is modified from chap. 2 of my PhD dissertation.

people's full awareness. Policy makers need to be aware of all of these effects and decide which are the most important to target and when.

In addition, people's reasons for compliance may affect trade-offs and the resulting enforcement dilemmas. In some contexts, it is not important to know people's motivations – for example, whether they pay taxes out of patriotism or fear; the important thing is that they pay their taxes. Indeed, the nudge intervention does not even address motivation. The targeted behavior is likely to determine how much we should care about reasons for compliance. The level of attention paid to reasons why people obey the law might be one of the distinguishing factors between corporations and states; for example, in the area of hiring discrimination, corporations may simply want to ensure that their workforce is diverse enough to meet legal requirements, whereas the state may want employers not only to hire more minorities but also to actively overcome their biases and consciously respect the contribution of minorities to the workforce. Possibly, nudges should be saved for behaviors such as driving, where automaticity is needed and civic virtue is less critical.

As suggested in Chapter 4, which discussed interventions such as deterrence and incentives to legitimacy and fairness, we need to align the type of legal incentives used with methods aimed at increasing people's intrinsic motivation to comply, such as legitimacy, procedural justice, and morality – a well as with the deliberative model. Ideally, the state should know what the intrinsic motivation of the individual is, so it can determine which legal instruments to use in targeting that type of motivation. More importantly, however, it must know people's state of awareness in a given situation. By knowing both people's intrinsic motivation and their likely level of awareness, the state will be most effective in creating behavioral change through processes of education and increasing awareness of the consequences of behavior. It needs to know the trade-offs inherent in each intervention and strike the ideal balance in each situation.

When crafting regulations or legal doctrine, policy makers need to recognize these trade-offs because it is their presence that creates behavioral enforcement dilemmas. Thus, policy makers need to weigh the behavioral consequence of each legal intervention relative to other relevant legal interventions. For example, let us consider the policy mix and the attendant trade-offs that would encourage organ donation. Developing the most effective mix would begin with an examination of the relative efficacy of using nudges, which might affect behavior even without people's full awareness, or of interventions such as incentives that require deliberation. Default rules might be less effective from a System 2 perspective in facilitating long-term commitment but might increase the number of people who decide to engage in a desirable behavior and vice versa.[1] The enforcement dilemma is how to increase the willingness to donate while recognizing that the decline in long-term commitment might have some inadvertent effects on the quality of the donation.

---

[1] This argument is based on George Lowenstein's words at a conference at Harvard University, May 2015.

8.2 BEHAVIORAL TRADE-OFFS

To understand the enforcement dilemmas, one needs to recognize the particular behavioral trade-off that accompanies almost any type of legal intervention. Various scholars have identified dimensions of important trade-offs in the regulation of behavior.[2] In the following paragraphs, I will outline the main factors that need to be taken into account:

8.2.1 *Specificity and Complexity*

One area of great research interest has been the optimal number of options given to participants. More options are generally thought to increase autonomy, but reduce the ability of the individual to make an effective choice.[3] Yet, this effect has been shown to be dependent on age: Reed et al. found that older people care less than younger adults about choice and autonomy.[4]

Researchers have studied the competing effects that complexity has on people[5] and have found that when people have fewer choices, they are more likely to be happy later about the decisions they do make.[6] There is general agreement that most people would prefer not having many options, but instead would like to be given only several options, which will allow them to feel more confident that they are making a reasonable choice.

Others have examined the optimal amount of information needed for people to make sound health plan choices.[7] This notion is closely related to the concept of simplicity advocated by Sunstein and more recent books on simplicity as a major focus of government's regulation.[8]

8.2.2 *Outcome vs. Process*

Behavioral economics research has clearly demonstrated the great influence of default rules in steering people's choices in the contexts of the marketing literature,[9]

---

[2] Johnson, E. J., Shu, S. B., Dellaert, B. G. C., Fox, C., Goldstein, D. G., Häubl, G., Larrick, R. P., Payne, J. W., Peters, E., Schkade, D., Wansink, B., & Weber, E. U. (2012). Beyond nudges: Tools of a choice architecture. *Marketing Letters*, 23(2), 487–504.

[3] Schwartz, B. (2004). *The paradox of choice: Why more is less.* New York: Harper.

[4] Reed, A., Mikels, J. A., & Simon, K. I. (2008). Older adults prefer less choice than young adults. *Psychology and Aging*, 23(3), 671–675.

[5] Scheibehenne, B., Greifeneder, R., & Todd, P. M. (2010). Can there ever be too many options? A meta-analytic review of choice overload. *Journal of Consumer Research*, 37(3), 409–425.

[6] Iyengar, S. S., & Lepper, M. R. (2000). When choice is demotivating: Can one desire too much of a good thing? *Journal of Personality and Social Psychology*, 79(6), 995–1006.

[7] Kling, J. R., Mullainathan, S., Shafir, E., Vermeulen, L., & Wrobel, M. V. (2011). *Misprediction in choosing Medicare drug plans.* Cambridge, MA: Harvard University Press.

[8] Sunstein, C. R. (2014). *Simpler: The future of government.* New York: Simon & Schuster.

[9] Johnson, E. J., Bellman, S., & Lohse, G. L. (2002). Defaults, framing and privacy: Why opting in–opting out. *Marketing Letters*, 13(1), 5–15.

contribution to a pension fund,[10] organ donation,[11] and buying adequate amounts of insurance.[12] However, such an approach completely ignores people's motivations to comply. Yet, if we focus on making the process as meaningful as possible to increase the autonomous and expressive rationales for compliance, we might end up reducing the chance that people will make the choice we want them to make.[13]

Sunstein examined this outcome vs. process dilemma in a famous 2013 paper with regard to default rules; he concluded, "In part for that reason, any kind of default rule, including a highly personalized one, may not create the kinds of motivation that can come from active choosing."[14] As discussed in more detail later in the chapter, this trade-off is in many respects the key one faced by policy makers, and the balance between outcome and process should be based on the type of behavior that is targeted.

With short-term or relatively simple behaviors that follow from people's initial choices, there is no real need to build in any process of deliberation to enhance the endurance and sustainability of compliance. However, in behaviors that require intrinsic motivation, qualitative performance, and long-term commitment, there is greater need for explicit intervention to enhance people's deliberation and ideally a change in intrinsic motivation toward the behavior in question. Greater focus on the durability of an intervention naturally leads to a preference for process-oriented interventions that allow for reflection by people, which is more likely to lead to sustainable change.

8.2.3 *Long-term vs. Short-term Behavioral Change*

A related trade-off is that between the long- and short-term effects of regulatory interventions. This nudge approach ignores a choice's subsequent impact on an individual's long-term perceptions of that behavior and the sustainability of the policy goal in question.

Clearly, any attempt to change people's intrinsic motivation will require a lengthier process of deliberation, which might face resistance. Yet, when people's

---

[10] Madrian, B. C., & Shea, D. F. (2001). The power of suggestion: Inertia in 401(k) participation and savings behavior. *Quarterly Journal of Economics*, 116(4), 1149–1187.

[11] Johnson, E. J., & Goldstein, D. G. (2003). Do defaults save lives? Science, 302, 1338–1339.

[12] Johnson, E. J., Hershey, J., Meszaros, J., & Kunreuther, H. (1993). Framing, probability distortions, and insurance decisions. *Journal of Risk and Uncertainty*, 7(1), 35–53.

[13] I explored this dilemma in an earlier paper on the optimal freedom of contract, which is summarized toward the end of this chapter.

[14] Sunstein, C. R. (2013). Deciding by default. *University of Pennsylvania Law Review*, 162, 53. "In addition, passive choice will, almost by definition, decrease choosers' feelings of identification with the outcome. In part for that reason, any kind of default rule, including a highly personalized one, may not create the kinds of motivation that can come from active choosing. Suppose that choice architects seek to promote healthy behavior. They might use something akin to default rules of certain kinds (involving, for example, portion size and easy availability of certain foods). Such an approach may be effective, but it may not have certain benefits associated with active choosing, such as increased self-monitoring and stronger intrinsic motivations".

intrinsic motivation changes, there is a greater chance that behavioral change will be sustainable. In contrast, once nudges are removed, their influence on behavior will decrease.

8.2.4 *Invisible vs. Expressive Law*

Another trade-off derived from the outcome vs. process argument relates to the optimal level of exposure of the general public to the legal instrument itself. [15] The expressive law approach holds that making the law visible and public will trigger various expressive mechanisms to change behavior to more closely reflect the norms and values of a given society. In contrast, the nudge approach is built on the invisibility of the law, arguing that it should operate behind the scenes to facilitate people's non-deliberative choices in the direction of compliance.

The literature on expressive law and on social meaning argues that law's language and visibility to the public are among the most important tools to ensure compliance.[16] Laws influence people both by making statements on what is good behavior and by reproaching them for engaging in bad behavior through the language of the law.[17] In other words, laws affect social norms and change judgments and behavior.[18] Making certain behaviors into a law can shape the meaning of key aspects of social and family life, such as parenthood, safe driving, and good citizenship. The expressive function of the law can help people determine what the prevailing social norm is,[19] how their behavior will be viewed if they violate the law, the best course of action for coordinating their behavior with that of others,[20] and the reputation costs for engaging in certain behaviors.[21]

---

[15] The discussion on the expressive function of the law is based in part on my dissertation research.

[16] Sunstein, C. R. (1996). On the expressive function of the law. *University of Pennsylvania Law Review*, 144(5), 2021–2053. He defines the expressive function of the law as follows: "At least for purposes of law, any support for a statement should be rooted not simply in the intrinsic value of the statement, but also in plausible judgment about its effect on social norms" (emphasis added). It should be recognized that there are scholars who adopt a language-based approach to the meaning of the expressive function of the law.

[17] Fox, D., & Griffin Jr., C. L. (2009). Disability-selective abortion and the Americans with Disabilities Act. *Utah Law Review*, 845.

[18] See Sunstein, *supra* note 16, at 2025.

[19] McAdams, R. H. (2000). An attitudinal theory of expressive law (new and critical approaches to law and economics). *Oregon Law Review*, 79, 339–390. See also Dharmapala, D., & McAdams, R.H. (2003). The Condorcet Jury theorem and the expressive function of law: A theory of informative law. *American Law & Economic Review*, 5(1), 1–31.

[20] See McAdams, R. (2001). A focal point theory of expressive law. *Virginia Law Review*,86(8), 1649, 1650–1663. For empirical evidence, see McAdams, R. H., & Nadler, J. (2005). Testing the focal point theory of legal compliance: Expressive influence in an experimental hawk/dove game. *Journal of Empirical Legal Studies*, 2(1), 87–96.

[21] A typical example of the cost-related account of social norms can be found in Cooter's analysis: "With group pressures, an increase in an act's popularity lowers its cost. Imposing a non-legal sanction on someone often involves a risk of retaliation, which decreases as more people obey the norm. The risk of a non-legal sanction often increases as more people obey the norm, thus *lowering the relative costs of*

Much of the literature on law and society focuses on the symbolic effects of law on society. It takes a macro perspective on legality's role in shaping cultural and societal changes, using terms such as "social change," "symbolic politics," "evolution of social values," and "legal consciousness," as advocated by scholars such as Anderson and Pildes[22] and Adler.[23] Language plays an essential and creative role in social change, and legal language has an important role in the "struggle over power" in the law.[24] Recognizing the declarative and constitutive cultural powers of law, many legal scholars have suggested that in crafting laws, one should focus not only on their operational functions but also on their declarative purpose and responsibilities.[25]

In contrast to the expressive law literature, the nudge-based approach to regulation tends to focus on simplifying and flattening policy messages. Its advocates argue that the law should be almost unnoticed and that it is not necessary for people to even know that a given action is illegal. Thus, according to the nudge approach, the role of law is not to shape people's values, but rather to lead them to make the right choices, limiting maximally their deliberation, their awareness that they are making a choice, and their awareness that the law is behind these initiatives. For example, to reduce cigarette smoking, the first step in the nudge approach is to spread information as widely as possible that cigarettes are bad for one's

---

conforming to the norm" (emphasis added). See also Cooter, R. (2000). Do good laws make good citizens? An economic analysis of internalized norms. *Virginia Law Review*, 86(8), 1577, 1585; Kahan, D. M. (1997). Social influence, social meaning, and deterrence. *Virginia Law Review*, 83(2), 349, 352–361.

[22] In a comprehensive attempt to define the expressive function of the law, Anderson and Pildes propose that "expression refers to the ways that an action or a statement (or any other vehicle of expression) manifest a state of mind". Anderson, E. S., & Pildes, R. H. (2000). Expressive theories of law: A general restatement. *University of Pennsylvania Law Review*, 148(5), 1506.

[23] See Adler, M. D. (1999). Expressive theories of law: A skeptical overview. *University of Pennsylvania Law Review*, 148(5), 1364–1493 for a thorough discussion of the expressive function of the language of the law. Adler thinks that the work of the law and economic scholars on norms cannot be defined as expressive, since they do not focus on the language of the law.

[24] Mertz, E. (1994). Legal language: Pragmatics, poetics, and social power. *Annual Review of Anthropology*, 23(1), 435–455.

[25] This approach has been used in a wide variety of legal doctrines. See Anderson & Pildes, *supra* note 22, at 1532. Its most practical relevance is in the contexts of employment and constitutional law where courts strike down laws that express unconstitutional purposes or attitudes. Other notable areas in which the expressive functions of the law have been taken into account include voting rights; Pildes, R. H., & Niemi, R. G. (1993). Expressive harms, "bizarre districts," and voting rights: Evaluating election-district appearances after *Shaw v. Reno. Michigan Law Review*, 92(3), 483–587; and laws regarding homosexuality; see Van Der Burg, W. (2001). The expressive and communicative functions of law. *Law & Philosophy*, 20(1), 31–59; especially with regard to signaling moral standing of the state through existing, though not enforced, laws and anti-discrimination laws. Another interesting and important area in which expressive theories of law have been featured is criminal punishment. Significant in this field is the work of Kahan, Social influence, social meaning, and deterrence, regarding the expressive meaning of criminal sanctions. For a historical perspective, see Feinberg, J. (1965). *The expressive function of punishment*. Oxford: Oxford University Press. This book highlights the importance of shaming in criminal punishment. According to the shaming theory, fines and community service are problematic as criminal punishments because they carry no shaming factors.

health – through pamphlets, posters, and TV advertisements. The second step is to screen cigarettes from public view so that no one would see them or be tempted to smoke them. The distinction between nudges and expressive law is sometimes blurred; it is possible that nudges, by leading to a behavioral change (e.g., everyone donates organs), might gradually lead to an internalization process (e.g., donating organs is good) even without full deliberation.[26]

Yet the simpler nudge approach advocated by Sunstein and others not only limits the process of people's participation in decision making but also changes the function of law from shaping the social meaning of people's behavior to simply influencing their decisions, without their even knowing that the law is operating in the background, and sometimes even without their knowing that they have made a decision at all.

One way to blend the expressive law and nudge approaches is to create a public discourse on the usage of certain nudges close to the time they are implemented. This would not only satisfy the expressive function of law by having a public discussion, but it would also achieve the effect of hiding the law because it would occur soon before the nudge is to be implemented, thereby limiting awareness of it. Indeed, recently scholars have addressed the question whether informing people about the presence and use of nudges might harm their efficacy.[27] On the face of it, telling someone that unhealthy food is purposefully being put in a less accessible place in a cafeteria might reduce the efficacy of such a move. In areas such as health and consumerism, publicizing that the law is behind their choices might even cause people to make harmful decisions or those that are not in their best interests. Current research suggests a very complex picture of the impact on efficacy of providing information about the nudge.[28]

8.3 ENFORCEMENT DILEMMAS

Having described the trade-offs, let us proceed to the next stage of the analysis, which examines how regulators balance the pros and cons of each regulatory and enforcement tool. These trade-offs create enforcement dilemmas that legal policy makers need to address when accounting for the complex nature of the interaction between law and people's behavior.

---

[26] For a review of the literature on social norms and the effect of law on intrinsic motivation, see Feldman, Y. (2009). The expressive function of trade secret law: Legality, cost, intrinsic motivation, and consensus. *Journal of Empirical Legal Studies*, 6(1), 177–212.

[27] Steffel, M., Williams, E. F., & Pogacar, R. (2016). Ethically deployed defaults: Transparency and consumer protection through disclosure and preference articulation. *Journal of Marketing Research*, 53(5), 865–880. http://doi.org/10.1509/jmr.14.0421. See also Loewenstein, G., Bryce, C., Hagmann, D., & Rajpal, S. (2015). Warning: You are about to be nudged. *Behavioral Science & Policy*, 1(1), 35–42.

[28] Ibid.

8.3.1 *Moving from Common Non-deliberative Unethical Decisions to Deliberative but Uncommon Unethical Decisions*

The key enforcement dilemma, which derives from the trade-off between process and outcome, is determining we want the enforcement strategy to achieve. Do we want it to change the behavior of the situational wrongdoing engaged in by the larger population of "good" people or target the deliberative, and presumably more severe, misconduct associated with the smaller number of "bad" people? For example, states might decide to prioritize their enforcement practices so they either target harsher forms of misconduct or more benign misbehavior. Presumably, the more serious misconduct is more likely to be engaged in intentionally; minor and less blatant misconducts are more plausibly done by people without full awareness of the wrongdoing of their behavior. Thus, an implicit legal instrument is more likely to be effective when dealing with subtle unethical behaviors that are likely to be performed by situational wrongdoers with limited awareness.[29]

The basic intuition of the legal policy maker is to invest more in monitoring misconduct that is more severe (given its likely correlation with greater harm to society). Based on studies conducted with Lobel, it seems that when misconduct is likely to be viewed, at least by some people, as severe, there is less rather than more need to use rewards[30], which carry both monetary costs for the state and some social cost[31] for the whistle-blower him- or herself. The same argument seems to apply with greater strength to the good/bad people dichotomy, where there should be an increased focus on extrinsic measures when higher percentages of the population are unlikely to be interested in pursuing the behavior for internal reasons. In crime prevention, we focus most attention and levy the most severe punishments on the "worst" people, because the cost of even one person committing a crime such as murder is so high. We maintain this focus, even though the majority of the population will refrain from committing a crime based on their moral constraints.

However, when we incentivize whistle-blowers, we are not focusing on the worst members of society. Furthermore, in many cases incentivizing even one individual to behave in a cooperative way is sufficient. Similarly as discussed in Chapter 9, which focused on corruption, good people are more aware of the corrupting effect of money and the need to shield themselves from it, but they are less aware of the corrupting effects of prestige. Thus, the legal policy maker should invest more resources in the enforcement of monetary-based corruption and its prevention.

Therefore, the more we are interested in preventing genuinely bad behaviors, for which people intuitively recognize their wrongness, the more we are likely to focus

---

[29] But see Feldman, Y., & Halali, E. (2017) Regulating "good" people in subtle conflicts of interest situations. *Journal of Business Ethics*, 1–19, which demonstrates the greater efficacy of explicit measures, even in subtle contexts.

[30] Compare with the discussion in Chapter 6 on the interaction between the level of intrinsic motivation and the choice of legal instrument.

[31] As the individual is seen to be greedy rather than a hero.

on behaviors in which fewer people are actually likely to engage. This is true for three types of mind-sets individuals could have with regard to the law, which we discussed in this book in earlier chapters. The "bad people," those with a calculative mind-set are aware that wrongdoing is more likely to be enforced and punished. Situational wrongdoers find it harder to come up with justifications for clearly morally bad behaviors such as accepting money. Finally, in the case of the genuinely mindless individuals, it is more likely that such behavior will not be mistakenly engaged in without noticing.

8.3.2 *Uniform vs. Differentiated Regulation*

An even broader enforcement concern that lies at the heart of the law is how to ensure that regulatory initiatives facilitate compliance among as many people as possible while reducing law-abiding behavior among as few as possible. Is it even possible to regulate the behavior of both good and bad people using the same policy, or is differentiated regulation needed?

If we focus on the lowest common denominator and assume that all people have the same motivations, we decrease uncertainty and ensure some minimal compliance. Yet, much of the literature and research suggest that many types of motivations and levels of awareness affect compliance, proposing that a unified approach might be destructive to some people with more intrinsic motivations to comply. Such a one-size-fits-all policy might crowd out the motivation of those intrinsically motivated people. The key to developing effective enforcement, then, is to recognize its differential effect on different motivations, as well as on different segments of the population.

Taking this further, given the variations in people's motivation, should we take an across-the-board approach with regard to an average motivation, or should we invest the required energy needed to fine-tune approaches to be sensitive to the specific motivation of individuals? And who should be targeted – those who are internally committed to comply or those who are not?

In many accounts, the law's inability to determine whether it is dealing with good or bad people is one of the major factors that reduces its ability to use the knowledge presented so far in this book in a constructive way. Understanding the behavioral effects of law on different segments of the population and recognizing the pros and cons of each regulatory approach are likely to increase the ability to analyze more accurately the effect of law on a given population.

Many studies show the ill effects of a one-size-fits-all policy. For example, it may be possible that by creating ambiguous rules that make it difficult for bad people to evade the law, we might be responsible for moving some good people to the bad side.[32] Furthermore, in many contexts, good people are those who are more likely to

---

[32]   See Feldman, Y., & Smith, H. E. (2014). Behavioral equity. *Journal of Institutional and Theoretical Economics*, 170(1), 137–159, for a discussion of the advantage of ambiguity in deterring opportunistic individuals.

suffer from an approach to law that was originally designed to target bad people. As demonstrated in much research, when people have a strong intrinsic motivation, external interventions are not as important in influencing their behavior. In contrast, for those who are not capable of making choices themselves and have a weak internal locus of control, behavioral interventions that are rooted in paternalism may be the only effective means to facilitate their compliance.[33] A final argument against a uniform policy can be gleaned from the work of Costa and Kahn on energy conservation. They showed that informing people about their relative energy consumption had a different effect based on their political views: liberals were likely to decrease their usage, whereas conservatives were more likely to increase their usage.[34]

8.3.3 *Intrinsic vs. Extrinsic Motivation*

As suggested in the previous paragraph, with the growing recognition that strengthening intrinsic motivation is likely to lead to improved compliance, policy makers face the challenge of finding the right balance between targeting the internal motivation to obey and avoiding creating greater evasion of the law.[35]

An important field within the psychology literature investigates the interplay between extrinsic and intrinsic motivation.[36] Intrinsic motivation is the sense of morality inherent within the individual, whereas extrinsic motivation relies on incentives and rewards.[37] People often vary in their internal level of commitment to ethical behavior.[38]

Most generally, the crowding-out literature suggests that when people attribute their behavior to external rewards, they discount any moral incentives for their behavior, thereby lowering the perceived effect of intrinsic motivation. As applied

---

[33]   Fox, C. R., Bardolet, D., & Lieb, D. (2005). Partition dependence in decision analysis, resource allocation, and consumer choice. In R. Zwick & A. Rapoport (Eds.), *Experimental business research* Vol. III (pp. 229–251). Dordrecht: Springer.

[34]   Costa, D. L., & Kahn, M. E. (2010). Energy conservation nudges and environmentalist ideology: Evidence from a randomized residential electricity field experiment. National Bureau of Economic Research, Inc, Cambridge, MA. NBER Working Paper No. 15939

[35]   Compare also with the nudge vs. boost paradigm. Grüne-Yanoff, T., & Hertwig, R. (2016). Nudge versus boost: How coherent are policy and theory? *Minds and Machines*, 26(1–2), 149–183.

[36]   Harackiewicz, J. M., & Sansone, C. (2000). Rewarding competence: The importance of goals in the study of intrinsic motivation. In C. Sansone & J. M. Harakiewicz (Eds.), *Intrinsic and extrinsic motivation: The search for optimal motivation and performance* (pp. 79–103). San Diego, CA: Academic Press; Deci, E. L. & Ryan, R. M. (2000). The "what" and the "why" of goal pursuits: Human needs and the self-determination of behavior. *Psychology Inquiry*, 11(4), 227–268.

[37]   Deci, E. L., Koestner, R., and Ryan, R. M. (1999). A meta-analytic review of experiments examining the effects of extrinsic rewards on intrinsic motivation. *Psychological Bulletin*, 125(6), 627. See also Kasser, T., & Ryan, R. M. (1996). Further examining the American dream: Differential correlates of intrinsic and extrinsic goals. *Personality and Social Psychology Bulletin*, 22(3), 280–287.

[38]   Feldman, Y., & Lobel, O. (2009). The incentives matrix: The comparative effectiveness of rewards, liabilities, duties, and protections for reporting illegality. *Texas Law Review*, 88, 1151.

to regulatory incentives, crowding-out theory predicts that external incentives that use monetary rewards or punishments may undermine intrinsic motivations to comply.[39] For instance, paying people in return for donating their blood might lead donors to view the event as a transaction rather than a charitable act, thereby reducing the number of altruistic blood donations.[40]

Bowles has provided a summary of many of the studies on the crowding-out effect of incentives and on enforcement, but here are some notable examples.[41] Deci and Ryan found that tangible rewards undermine intrinsic motivation for a range of activities.[42] Following the "W effect" described by Frey and Jegen[43] with regard to the change in magnitude of the crowding-out effect, it is likely that with varying levels of intrinsic motivations among individuals, various sums of money will have correspondingly different effects on each subgroup. In a previous work with Lobel on how to incentivize whistle-blowers, we demonstrated that those who were intrinsically motivated were not significantly affected by the framing of monetary incentives, whereas those who were low on intrinsic motivation were affected by it.[44] Similarly, in my study with Perez, we found a direct relationship between the perception of incentives and intrinsic motivation levels: those who were low on intrinsic motivation were more likely to prefer deposits to fines, whereas the opposite was true for those who had high levels of intrinsic motivation.[45]

[39]   See, e.g., the work of Fher, in the following contexts: Fehr, E., & Gachter, S. *Do incentive contracts undermine voluntary cooperation?* University of Zurich, Institute for Empirical Research in Economics, Working Paper No. 34, Available at SSRN: http://papers.ssrn.com/sol3/papers.cfm%3Fabstract_id=313028; Fehr, E., & Falk, A. (2002). Psychological foundations of incentives. *European Economic Review*, 46(4), 687–724. See also Fehr, E., & Rockenbach, B. (2003). Detrimental effects of sanctions on human altruism. *Nature*, 422(6928), 137. For a general review, see Frey, B. S. (2007). *Not just for the money: An economic theory of personal motivation.* Cheltenham: Elgar; Akerlof, G. A. (1982). Labor contracts as partial gift exchange. *The Quarterly Journal of Economics*, 97(4), 543–569; Frey, B. S., & Jegen, R. (1999). *Motivation crowding theory: A survey of empirical evidence.* Center for Economic Studies & Information Institute for Econ. Research, Working Paper No. 245. Available at SSRN: http://ssrn.com/abstract=203330.

[40]   Titmuss, R. (1971). The gift of blood. *Trans-action*, 8(3), 18–26 argues that monetary payments to givers of blood could diminish the amount of blood given voluntarily.

[41]   Bowles, S. (2008). Policies designed for self-interested citizens may undermine the "moral sentiments": Evidence from economic experiments. *Science*, 320(5883), 1605–1609. See also Deci et al., *supra* note 36. Feldman, Y. (2011). The complexity of disentangling intrinsic and extrinsic compliance motivations: Theoretical and empirical insights from the behavioral analysis of law. *Washington University Journal of Law and Public Policy*, 35.

[42]   Ryan, R. M., & Deci, E. L. (2000). Intrinsic and extrinsic motivations: Classic definitions and new directions. *Contemporary Educational Psychology*, 25(1), 54–67. See also Gneezy, U., & Rustichini, A. (2000). Pay enough or don't pay at all. *Quarterly Journal of Economics*, 792, 799–800.

[43]   Frey, B. S., & Jegen, R. (2001). Motivation crowding theory. *Journal of economic Surveys*, 15(5), 589–611. See also Gneezy & Rustichini, Pay enough or don't pay at all.

[44]   See, Feldman & Lobel, *supra* note 38, at 1151.

[45]   Feldman, Y., & Perez, O. (2009). How law changes the environmental mind: An experimental study of the effect of legal norms on moral perceptions and civic enforcement. *Journal of Law and Society*, 36(4), 501–535.

Another issue addressed by the research on the intrinsic-extrinsic dimension that affects the ethicality of good people is the extent to which the behavior that the state is attempting to regulate is within the moral consensus of the population. In the study with Lobel described earlier, we highlighted the relationship between the severity of the misconduct and the regulatory mechanisms to prevent it: the greater the individual's perception of the severity of illegality, the less important was the choice of enforcement mechanism. In our analysis, we used severity of misconduct as a proxy for internal motivation.[46] In the group of participants who viewed the illegality as highly offensive, and hence had high levels of internal motivation to report it, the type of mechanism available to them to do so was largely irrelevant. Respondents expected the reporting levels of themselves and others to remain consistently high across all categories of legal mechanisms. However, when illegalities witnessed by potential enforcers were perceived as less severe, the use of high rewards and fines produced considerably higher levels of reporting than did low rewards. These findings suggest the importance of legal mechanism selection in instances where individuals do not have an ethical stake in compliance.

8.4 TAXONOMIES

Based on the behavioral trade-offs and enforcement dilemmas just reviewed, I discuss in Chapter 11 a long list of factors that could be used by policy makers to consider how to balance between the competing pros and cons of each type of legal intervention. In the current section, I will only discuss three examples to complete the argument raised in this chapter. Taxonomy is a solution to many of the concerned raised earlier, as it can facilitate the use of psychological and cognitive factors in the design, implementation, and enforcement of legal policy. Use of this taxonomy will make it easier to match legal policy to what we know about the behaviors, cognitions, and motivations of individuals to which it is addressed.[47]

A taxonomy for regulatory initiatives, as outlined in Chapter 11, should include the following relevant factors: type of regulated behavior, desired durability of the behavioral change, proportion of the target population whose cooperation is required for successful implementation of the mechanism, cost of enforcement, and cost of noncompliance. Let us examine some of those factors here.

---

[46] These included factors such as moral outrage, legitimacy, and perceived risk from the misconduct.
[47] Compare with Milkman et al., who propose the idea that there is a need to match the automaticity of the intervention and the automaticity of the underlying process that you attempt to modify. Milkman, K. L., Chugh, D., & Bazerman, M. H. (2009). How can decision making be improved? *Perspectives on Psychological Science*, 4(4), 379–383.

8.4.1 *Nature of the Regulated Behavior*

The first question that we need to address is what type of behavior we are looking to change. Is it the kind of behavior for which we need to rely on intrinsic motivation for people to perform well or is sustainability of key importance, given the high cost of enforcement? Do we want to increase the quantitative aspects of the regulated behavior – the extent to which one engages in it – as in recycling?[48] Or is the qualitative nature of the behavior more important, as in whistle-blowing or even blood donation (where we need people to be truthful about their health history) where the level of commitment to the action is critical. In the latter types of behaviors, we might give more weight to the decision process than the outcome. Furthermore, in legal contexts where "extra-role" activity, which is beyond what's needed in the law, is desired, the likelihood of reducing intrinsic motivation increases, and one should be more cautious in introducing extrinsic motives or nudges that may crowd out internal motivation.

8.4.2 *Sustainability of the Behavioral Change*

Whether the sought-after behavior requires a one-time decision or choices repeated over time will help determine the appropriate type of regulatory mechanism. In contexts such as enrolling in or choosing a pension plan, people are less likely to reverse their decision once they have made it. Sustainability is less important, and hence getting people to make the right choice (outcome, being the dominant focus) is more important than in areas such as health or nutrition, where choices need to be reaffirmed on a daily basis.

8.4.3 *What Proportion of the Target Population Needs to Cooperate*

In designing legal policy, one of the most important factors to take into account is whether the population is likely to have high levels of intrinsic motivation to comply with the regulated behavior. This is naturally more challenging when not much is known about the target population or when its levels of intrinsic motivation are heterogeneous. When a large proportion of the population has high levels of intrinsic motivation, policy makers can rely on non-coercive explicit measures or on softer types of implicit intervention such as nudges.

My earlier work has focused on divulging trade secrets, whistle-blowing, and recycling. This section illustrates the costs of compliance in these three behavioral contexts. In the area of trade secrets, everyone needs to be motivated to keep information confidential for the secret not to be disclosed, because if only a few people will be subject to legal consequences for disclosure, keeping company

---

[48] But this is not the case with regard to blood donations.

knowledge proprietary may be a futile endeavor.[49] Regulation should be designed to facilitate the cooperation of 100 percent of the target population, from those with the highest level of intrinsic motivation to those with the lowest level. In that context, policy should focus on the lowest common denominator, meaning those with the lowest level of intrinsic motivation to be loyal to the company. Since having a low level of motivations is likely to increase the chance of making "self-serving mistakes" and mistakes are costly, a greater emphasis should be placed on obtaining, at the very least, minimal compliance. Therefore, the price of harming the intrinsic motivation of committed employees might be secondary to making sure that even those without intrinsic motivation will be loyal to their employers.

The context of whistle-blowing is the exact opposite, where we only need the cooperation of some of the employees, who will go forward when some illegal activity occurs within the organization. Therefore, we mainly care about those who are high on intrinsic motivation. We might not even want to incentivize those without intrinsic motivation, for fear of generating false reports from bounty hunters, who are only interested in any rewards they might receive from exposing wrongdoing.

Finally, in the context of recycling, we are interested in long-term aggregate outcomes or a situation where as many people as possible will recycle as much as possible. In that context, there is no preference for either high or low intrinsically motivated individuals; therefore, the balancing consideration made by the policy maker is whether or not to use extrinsic motivation and through which types of incentives. In addition, though the ultimate goal may be to move as many people as possible toward environmentally responsible behaviors, the costs of noncompliance of one individual are not very high. In other words, in this context, the failure of a regulation to increase recycling is not costly since the goal is to increase the average level of recycling among the population. In the second half of this chapter, I use areas I have worked on in the past to demonstrate the previously mentioned regulatory trade-offs.

8.5 OPTIMIZING FREEDOM OF CONTRACTS FROM A BEHAVIORAL PERSPECTIVE: OUTCOME VS. PROCESS

In this section, we return to the trade-off between process and outcome through a psychological and behavioral analysis of contracting behavior.[50] As discussed also

---

[49] It should be noted that when speaking about trade secrets, the focus here is on the narrow definition of trade secrets, focusing on the core proprietary knowledge of a given company. Lobel, O. (2013). *Talent wants to be free: Why we should learn to love leaks, raids, and free riding*. New Haven: Yale University Press, who has argued for the importance of information spillover between firms. In that regard we wish to narrow our argument for the core knowledge of a firm, rather than the types of information that would be better off shared among companies. See also Feldman, The expressive function of trade secret law.

[50] Some of the text in the following section is based on earlier work on the therapeutic approach to contracts.

in the first chapter, the earliest research on the interaction between psychology and contracting focused on people's cognitive limitations. A whole array of studies in the 1990s addressed paternalism and the legitimacy and efficacy of limiting people's contractual choices. Twenty years later this same line of research advocates the use of nudges as a way to replace people's limited cognition, albeit still to a much lesser extent in the private law context.[51] As the argument goes, since people are not good at making decisions about themselves, greater state intervention might improve outcomes.

In an early work I took the opposite approach, focusing on the therapeutic effect of the process associated with freedom of contracts.[52] I examined the importance of people's voice and active participation in making contractual decisions and those elements' impact on shaping behavior in publicly desirable ways. My theory held that the more control that people had over the decision-making process, the better off they would be, even with a somewhat less optimal outcome.[53]

The direct relationship between control and well-being seems to be straightforward. Thompson summarizes it this way: when we have more control, "we feel better about ourselves, we are physically healthier, perform better under adversity, and are better able to make desired behavioral changes if we have a sense of behavioral control."[54] Thus, giving individuals more control of contractual terms increases their level of well-being.[55]

The social cognition literature highlights the important impact on well-being of daily activity aimed at achieving future goals. For example, Taylor and Pham[56] claimed that the ability to form a mental representation of one's goals has a positive influence on one's ability to cope with difficulties encountered while working toward those objectives.[57] Applying this concept to the value of personal involvement in the

---

[51]   See Eisenberg, M. A. (1995). The limits of cognition and the limits of contract. *Stanford Law Review*, 211–259, which attempts to draw an underlying theory of contract theory that takes into account human limits on the ability to calculate risk as a source for limiting freedom of bargaining and phrasing individualistic terms in several kinds of contracts. See also Larrick, R. P. (1993). Motivational factors in decision theories: The role of self-protection. *Psychological Bulletin*, 113(3), 440; Korobkin, R. (1998). Inertia and preference in contract negotiation: The psychological power of default rules and form terms. *Vanderbilt Law Review*, 51, 1583.

[52]   Feldman, Y. (2001). Control or security: A therapeutic approach to the freedom of contract. *Touro Law Review*, 18, 503.

[53]   Naturally the main limitation of that argument was that it was not clear how much people would be willing to give up in terms of the quality of their outcome.

[54]   Thompson, S. C. (1993). Naturally occurring perceptions of control: A model of bounded flexibility. In G. Weary, F. Gleicher, & K. L. March (Eds.), *Control motivation and social cognition* (pp. 74–93). New York: Springer.

[55]   Folkman, S. (1984). Personal control and stress and coping processes: A theoretical analysis. *Journal of Personality and Social Psychology*, 46(4), 839.

[56]   Taylor, S. E., & Pham, L. B. (1999). The effect of mental simulation on goal-directed performance. *Imagination, Cognition and Personality*, 18(4), 253–268.

[57]   For an application of the claim to more specific circumstances, see Rivkin, I. D., & Taylor, S. E. (1999). The effects of mental simulation on coping with controllable stressful events. *Personality and Social Psychology Bulletin*, 25(12), 1451–1462. See also Thompson, S. C. (1981). Will it hurt less if I can control it? A complex answer to a simple question. *Psychological Bulletin*, 90(1), 89.

bargaining process supports the advantages of using personally negotiated contracts and not prewritten form contracts, collective contracting, or state-mandated regulations.

It has been shown that civic participation enhances and empowers citizens' feelings of efficacy and belief in their ability to be part of the democratic process.[58] Public policy that undermines the focus on awareness and deliberation and supplants personal judgment and active involvement may undermine these positive processes.[59]

One cornerstone of the procedural justice literature is that the perception of a policy's fairness is crucial to the parties' willingness to accept the outcome of that policy. The work by Tyler and his colleagues has brought the implications of procedural justice into discussions in many areas of legal policy.[60] Two factors that may increase one's sense of procedural justice are having one's voice heard and having perceived control over the process. Naturally, being involved in negotiations over a specific contractual term is likely to increase both of those factors, especially in comparison to the default rule – especially so in the context of standard-form contracts in which one party holds complete control over the terms of the contract.[61] Consequently, it is quite plausible that negotiations will raise the sense of procedural justice and thus increase the tendency of people to respect the allocation of risks agreed to in the contract.

An additional psychological mechanism that is likely to support greater adherence to negotiated contract terms is cognitive dissonance. This theory suggests that when people actively choose to behave in a certain way, they are more likely to adapt their attitudes to their choice.[62] In other words, the mere fact that people choose to participate in an activity when no external justification is present causes them to

[58] Dalton, R. J. (2008). Citizenship norms and the expansion of political participation. *Political Studies*, 56(1), 76–98.

[59] Deci, E. L., & Ryan, R. M. (1980). Self-determination theory: When mind mediates behavior. *Journal of Mind and Behavior*, 1(1), 33–43. See also Friedman, M. I., & Lackey, G. H., Jr., (1991). *The psychology of human control: A general theory of purposeful behavior.* New York: Praeger.

[60] Tyler, T. R., & Blader, S. L. (2003). The group engagement model: Procedural justice, social identity, and cooperative behavior. *Personality and Social Psychology Review*, 7(4), 349–361.

[61] The case of default rules studied in the previous experiment also entails a situation in which rights are allocated without negotiations. Nevertheless, we assume that the lack of control in the standard-form setting is more extreme because in this case, control is shifted to the opposing party, whereas in a default-rule setting, control is shifted away from both parties to a third entity. Furthermore, unlike the case of default rules, there is no practical way to contract around a term in a standard-form contract. For a discussion and empirical demonstration of these differences, see Feldman, Y., & Teichman, D. (2011). Are all contractual obligations created equal? *Georgetown Law Journal*, 100, 5.

[62] The originator of this theory is Leon Festinger in his seminal book: Festinger, L. (1962). *A theory of cognitive dissonance*, Vol. 2. Stanford: Stanford University Press. For a broader account, see Bandura, A. (1986). *Social foundation of thought and action: A social-cognitive view.* Englewood Cliffs, NJ: Prentice Hall (pp. 469–470), in which he reviews his pioneering work on the intersection between self-autonomy and motivation. For a conceptual discussion of the contribution of choice to factors such as goal performance and persistence, see Ryan, R. M., & Deci, E. L. (2006). Self-regulation and the problem of human autonomy: Does psychology need choice, self-determination, and will? *Journal of Personality*, 74(6), 1557–1586.

feel more committed to that activity.[63] Presumably, the process of contracting, so long as it is the outcome of free choice, could lead to a deeper commitment to the contract's terms. Thus, the active choices that people make during negotiations are expected to decrease the likelihood that they will interpret the ambiguity in their own self-interest. In contrast, because in standard-form contracts people lack free choice with regard to the terms, no dissonance is created.[64] Indeed, in an article with Teichman – titled "Are All Contractual Obligations Created Equal?" – we showed the increased efficacy of negotiated contracts over standard-form contracts in strengthening people's intrinsic motivation to abide by the contractual terms.[65]

8.6 SHOULD LEGAL INSTRUMENTS BE SPECIFIC OR GENERAL?

Another example in a legal context, where a broader focus on the behavioral pros and cons could lead policy makers in a different direction, is the area of legal specificity, which was also discussed in Chapter 7 on the pluralistic effect of law. The question of how specific a law is a very relevant behavioral enforcement dilemma: it touches on theories related to explicit vs. implicit effects and differences between situations, between people, and between different mind-sets. To maximize the effect of legal intervention on behavior, the level of legal uncertainty should be determined based on the target population's different levels of intrinsic motivation and levels of awareness toward legal compliance.[66]

Regulations and contracts can be written along a spectrum of specificity, ranging from vague standards to more detailed and specific rules with particular examples. Behavioral and legal studies have reached conflicting conclusions about the optimal degree of specificity with which laws should be designed. From a behavioral standpoint, specificity is important to help people understand their goals and use their

---

[63] In the original study by Festinger, participants who received little compensation for engaging in a boring activity were more likely to think that the activity was interesting and rewarding in comparison to those who were highly compensated for the activity and hence did not need to justify to themselves their choice to engage in that activity. Festinger, L., & Carlsmith, J. M. (1959). Cognitive consequences of forced compliance. *The Journal of Abnormal and Social Psychology*, 58 (2), 203. For extensions of the theory to other domains of decision making, see, for example, Goetzmann, W. N., & Peles, N. (1997). Cognitive dissonance and mutual fund investors. *Journal of Financial Research*, 20(2), 145–158 (discusses investors' misperceptions of the past performance of their mutual funds as a personal justification for inaction).

[64] Cf., e.g., Coglianese, C. (2000). Assessing the advocacy of negotiated rulemaking: A response to Philip Harter. *New York University Environmental Law Journal* 9, 386, which discusses how cognitive dissonance may improve evaluation of a law when community members have set forth effort toward its framing.

[65] See Feldman & Teichman, *supra* note 61, at 5.

[66] Based on Boussalis, C., Feldman, Y., & Smith, H. E. (2017). Experimental analysis of the effect of standards on compliance and performance. *Regulation & Governance*. John M. Olin Center for Law, Economics, and Business, Discussion Paper No. 913.

cognitive resources in a focused manner. At the same time, ambiguity in the law can encourage good people to engage in creative interpretations of legal requirements, allowing them to justify unethical behavior, with limited awareness of the meaning of that behavior. By contrast, theories of crowding out, trust, and cooperation suggest that specificity can create resentment and lead to under-compliance and under-performance.

In legal scholarship, much of the debate on the optimal specificity of law has been influenced by the "rules versus standards" paradigm, in which standards are vaguer than rules; broadly speaking, rules are costlier to create, but cheaper to enforce. Kaplow's seminal paper on this topic [67] and many follow-up studies have translated the notion of "optimal specificity" as the "optimization of information costs."

Some economic analyses point to the benefits of vagueness from a rational choice perspective, but these benefits are often the flip side of the costs. Thus, vagueness can smooth out the liability function, which may reduce the cost of errors in selecting the point at which the sanction sets in.[68] Contracting parties often include vague terms in their contracts, which can serve as a "commitment device" to the contract, because they increase the cost of litigation on its content.[69]

An additional perspective comes from the multitasking paradigm that focuses on the problems that occur when some aspects of one's work are easier to monitor than others. According to the rational choice prediction, agents focus most of their work on the tasks for which they can be given an incentive.[70]

An additional line of research in law and economics focuses on the chilling effect of vagueness, which leads to a form of over-compliance. Ferguson and Peters argue, "The optimal amount of vagueness in a rule strikes a balance between the costs of loopholes, the chilling effect on economic activity, and the inefficiency created in the legal system."[71] Under a vague standard, uncertainty can cause damages to rise more quickly than social harms, leading people to reduce the expected liability by inefficiently over-complying. For example, Kyle Logue has noted how risk-adverse agents, when paying taxes, tend to over-comply with a vague law to avoid penalties for not complying.[72] Calfee and Craswell showed that even risk-neutral agents are subject to two contrasting behavioral effects of legal uncertainty: uncertainty reduces deterrence because of the prospect of escaping liability wrongfully (a false

---

[67] Kaplow, L. (1992). Rules versus standards: An economic analysis. *Duke Law Journal*, 42, 557.

[68] Craswell, R., & Calfee, J. E. (1986). Deterrence and uncertain legal standards. *Journal of Law, Economics, and Organization*, 2, 279.

[69] Choi, A., & Triantis, G. (2010). Strategic vagueness in contract design: The case of corporate acquisitions. *The Yale Law Journal*, 125, 848–924. See also Cooter, R. (1984). Prices and sanctions. *Columbia Law Review*, 84(6), 1523–1560.

[70] Holmstrom, B., & Milgrom, P. (1991). Multitask principal-agent analyses: Incentive contracts, asset ownership, and job design. *Journal of Law, Economics, & Organization*, 7, 24–52.

[71] Ferguson, M. F., & Peters, S. R. (2000). But I know it when i see it: An economic analysis of vague rules. *SSRN Electronic Journal*, 1.

[72] Logue, K. D. (2007). Optimal tax compliance and penalties when the law is uncertain. *Virginia Tax Review*, 27, 241.

negative), but in a variety of contexts, this effect is overshadowed by a tendency toward over-compliance, as in tax law.[73]

An additional way in which the behavioral literature contributes to the rational choice discussion is by emphasizing the distinction between compliance and performance.[74] Compliance is following the letter of the law, whereas performance measures whether people are making an extra effort to fulfill the spirit of the law.[75] There are also intermediate levels of behavior between compliance and performance that are sometimes called "beyond compliance" or "extra role behavior."[76]

8.6.1 Factors That Determine Optimal Levels of Specificity

Another way to determine the optimal level of specificity is to categorize the relevant factors into individual, situational, and doctrinal. Regarding individual factors, people who are risk lovers might be more likely to exploit ambiguity and misbehave more; in contrast, for risk-adverse people, ambiguity might create a chilling effect, inducing over-compliance. People who are high on the ethical scales measuring morality are less likely than people who are less ethical to look for loopholes and exploit ambiguity. Finally, regulations that target people who might be able to engage in deliberate reasoning may allow for more ambiguity.

Situational factors include the costs to society of individual misconduct: the higher the costs, the more that specificity is needed to prevent that misbehavior. In relatively simple, predictable situations, it might be appropriate to have more specific instructions. Another consideration is the degree of alignment between legal norms and morality or other forms of intrinsic motivation. If they are closely aligned, then we should choose less specificity because people are likely to interpret the law in a way consistent with the law. In addition, the higher the enforcement cost, the greater is the need to be specific.

In areas where expertise and moral or consensual power are very relevant, using invisible law such as nudges might outweigh the costs of informing people that the choice architecture presented to them is based on law.[77] With social issues for which preferences for publicly accessible process are strong and the solutions contested, more weight should be given to process in which more parts of the public are aware of its existence.

---

[73] See Craswell & Calfee, *supra* note 69, at 279.   [74] See Feldman & Smith, *supra* note 32.
[75] Garcia, S. M., Chen, P., & Gordon, M. T. (2014). The letter versus the spirit of the law: A lay perspective on culpability. *Judgment and Decision Making*, 9(5), 479.
[76] Kim, W. C., & Mauborgne, R. A. (1996). Procedural justice and managers' in-role and extra-role behavior: The case of the multinational. *Management Science*, 42(4), 499–515.
[77] See Steffel et al., *supra* note 27. See also Loewenstein et al., *supra* note 27.

8.6.2 *Behavioral Advantages of Specificity*

In this section and the following one, we present the beneficial and adverse effects of specificity in producing desirable behavior in a more analytical way. The main psychological construct in the behavioral literature that supports the importance of specificity is its effect on goal setting. The theory, which is highly influential in the management literature, claims (and data has shown) that specific, challenging goals result in higher performance than vague ones, such as "do your best." For example, Wood et al. reported 24 field experiments that found that individuals with specific, challenging goals either outperformed others or outperformed their own past performance when they had merely been instructed to simply "do their best."[78] A classic study conducted by Seijts and Latham compared the effect of giving people "do your best" instructions versus assigning distal and proximal goals and found that the combination of goals led to better performance than the former approach.[79] However, the "do your best" approach produced better performance than did the assignment of distal goals only. Therefore, this line of research seems to suggest that when specificity helps provide clear instructions and when it increases feelings of self-efficacy, it is superior to ambiguous standards or instructions. However, it should be noted that even the goal-setting paradigm recognizes contexts in which specific instructions can cause under-performance compared with ambiguous ones.

As suggested earlier, when considering the behavioral advantages of specificity, we must account not only for its cognitive but also its motivational effects. Indeed, behavioral research, particularly in behavioral ethics, has found a correlation between a preference for ambiguity and a desire to justify one's morally questionable behavior. Haisley and Weber, for example, found that people prefer ambiguous risks, when such ambiguity allows them to justify their unfair behaviors.[80] Dana et al. found that people are less generous in situations in which they can appeal to moral ambiguity to explain their selfish behaviors.[81] Similarly, Hsee found evidence that people make choices that satisfy their own preferences at the cost of not completing an assigned goal if they can exploit existing ambiguity about what decision could be considered to achieve the assigned goal.[82]

---

[78] Wood, R. E., Mento, A. J., & Locke, E. A. (1987). Task complexity as a moderator of goal effects: A meta-analysis. *Journal of Applied Psychology, 72*(3), 416.

[79] Seijts, G. H., & Latham, G. P. (2001). The effect of distal learning, outcome, and proximal goals on a moderately complex task. *Journal of Organizational Behavior, 22*(3), 291–307.

[80] Haisley, E. C., & Weber, R. A. (2010). Self-serving interpretations of ambiguity in other-regarding behavior. *Games and Economic Behavior, 68*(2), 614–625.

[81] Dana, J., Weber, R. A., & Kuang, J. X. (2007). Exploiting moral wiggle room: Experiments demonstrating an illusory preference for fairness. *Economic Theory, 33*(1), 67–80.

[82] Hsee, C. K. (1995). Elastic justification: How tempting but task-irrelevant factors influence decisions. *Organizational Behavior and Human Decision Processes, 62*(3), 330–337. See also Ayal, S., & Gino, F. (2011). Honest rationales for dishonest behavior. In M. Mikulincer & P. R. Shaver (Eds.), *The social psychology of morality: Exploring the causes of good and evil*. Washington, DC: American Psychological Association, 149–166.

8.6.3 *Behavioral Disadvantages of Specificity*

Much of the literature on the negative effects of specificity on compliance focuses on the attendant level of measurement and monitoring that such specificity enables. Even though the classic paper by Lazear, who based on his reading of the literature, argues that the piece-rate approach, in which people are evaluated based on how many units they produce, results in higher performance than a fixed-wage approach, aspects of the work that are not easily measured suffer from poor performance.[83] According to these theories, over time, people concentrate their effort strictly on the measured components of an activity, resulting in a decline in the overall quality of their work. Therefore, specificity combined with monitoring that focuses only on given measurable components (the letter of the law) seems to crowd out intrinsic motivation and decrease overall performance.[84] These inadvertent effects of measurement, such as the measurement paradox and the related multitasking effects problem, are exemplified in other leading theories of empirical economists.[85]

Similarly, Falk and Kosfeld demonstrated the effect of specificity on the principal-agent relationship in experiments in which the principal could either let an agent decide a production amount (ambiguous instruction) or the principal could set a lower limit for production (specific instruction).[86] When a specific lower limit was set, agents produced less than when the principal left the production levels to the agent's discretion. In *post hoc* questioning, agents stated that they saw the specified lower limit as a signal of distrust and therefore behaved less cooperatively. Specific instructions also give individuals less room for discretion, creating a situation in which they must be constantly looking for external instructions.

Along those lines Chou et al. showed how feelings of distrust, triggered by an overly specific contract, can lead people to low performance in a long-term contract and serve as an obstacle between the two sides in maintaining a cooperative long-term relationship.[87] These researchers cite a long list of negative psychological mechanisms, mostly related to motivation, which could be triggered when parties create a contract. Their conclusion is that when there is a less specific contract, employees will exert greater effect, strive for greater efficiency, and act in a more trustworthy way. The authors support these theoretical predictions with a series of experiments in which participants who were given a highly specific contract performed more poorly than those given a less specific contract. The authors

---

[83] Lazear, E. P. (2003). Teacher incentives. *Swedish Economic Policy Review*, 10(2), 179–214.

[84] Bowles, S., & Hwang, S. H. (2008). Social preferences and public economics: Mechanism design when social preferences depend on incentives. *Journal of Public Economics*, 92(8), 1811–1820.

[85] For example, See Holmstrom & Milgrom, *supra* note 70. See also Prendergast, C. (1999). The provision of incentives in firms. *Journal of Economic Literature*, 37(1), 7–63.

[86] Falk, A., & Kosfeld, M. (2006). The hidden costs of control. *American Economic Review*, 96(5), 1611–1630.

[87] Chou, E. Y., Halevy, N., & Murnighan, J. K. (2010). "The Hidden Cost of Contracts on Relationships and Performance," IACM 23rd Annual Conference Paper, available at SSRN: http://papers.ssrn.com /sol3/papers.cfm?abstract_id=1612376 (Posted: May 21, 2010).

compared the effect of a specific vs. a nonspecific contract requirement: "notify within one hour" vs. "notify as soon as possible." The specific term – "within an hour" – is not just clear and informative but is also framed in a way that completely limits choice; in comparison, the less specific condition – "as soon as possible" – is not only flexible but also gives the other party a strong signal of respect. It has been suggested that adding some detailed examples of work performance to a vague standard may be a way of achieving the best of both worlds.[88]

The interesting lesson to the dilemma we have just presented is that in contrast to much of the literature against specific instructions, when participants require information and guidance, as in the case of editing a document, we found that specificity increases performance even beyond what was required of them relative to the vague standard condition.

In summary, as will be suggested also in the chapter 11, in many cases, once we recognize the competing behavioral effects of a certain intervention, we should collect data prior to the implementation of that policy. The "Law of Good People" paradigm, suggests that we should care about multiple aspects of the interaction between law and human behavior because many may have a contradictory effect on human behavior. Once we recognize that the effect of law on behavior is multi-faceted and depends on various contextual factors, we can no longer make simple assumptions regarding the direction of the effect of legal intervention. The full perspective on the behavioral approach to law needs to be sensitive to the conflicting effects of any legal intervention and balanced with the specific goals of the legal doctrines based on empirical research and normative considerations such as those presented in Chapter 11.

---

[88]   Parchomovsky, G., & Stein, A. (2014). Catalogs. *Columbia Law Review*, 115, 165–209.

9

The Corruption of "Good People"

In previous chapters, we built the case that people's inability to recognize their own wrongdoings should be the primary behavioral consideration taken into account by policy makers as they attempt to modify and guide people's behavior. The abilities to present one's own behavior in noble terms and to modify a legal dilemma both ex ante and ex post are the main behavioral obstacles to influencing people to act in a socially desirable way. In earlier chapters – particularly Chapter 2 – we explained these mechanisms in great detail. In the current chapter, we examine some of the challenges that these mechanisms raise in a specific context – the fight against corruption. In no other area are these mechanisms so crucial for a number of reasons: first, corrupt behavior is – unlike other socially undesirable behaviors – usually legitimate (e.g., you decide, as a mayor, that a certain contractor should build a public building). Second, corruption is a matter of motivation: have you chosen a specific contractor because he or she is the most qualified or because you have a preexisting, personal relationship with that individual contractor? The literature we have reviewed suggests that people's ability to monitor themselves – whether recognizing a conflict of interest or noting how their own behavior may be influenced by ulterior motives – is impaired by the conflict of interest itself.

Shifting the focus of regulation from changing people's incentive structure to a much broader account of the cognitive and motivational mechanisms that explain the corruption of good people is the first step that regulators should take. As more data is collected on the factors responsible for misconduct, on the ways through which situational design changes people's ethical awareness, and on the efficacy of new types of interventions that should supplement rather than replace existing enforcement approaches, the toolbox that regulators use to deal with corruption will grow as well.

In previous chapters, we argued that wrongdoing could be committed not just by "bad" people or "calculative people" – self-centered parties who are willing to take advantage of another party's interests to promote their own interests. Decent

---

* This chapter includes revised texts from a paper "Using Behavioral Ethics to Reduce Organizational Misconduct" which will be published in 2018 in *Behavioral Science and Policy*.

individuals – "good people" – or "situational wrongdoers" under certain situational contexts might also promote their own interests at the expense of others, with limited awareness of the full ethical and legal ramifications of their behavior. Studies on the role of automaticity in human judgment and behavior[1] and on how good people come to do bad things[2] find that many individuals make unethical choices, not with the deliberate intention to act wrongly, but because they find themselves in situations that lower the barriers to misconduct. Bazerman et al., as well as Banaji and Greenwald,[3] discuss the concept of a blind spot to refer to people who fail to even recognize the unethical consequences of their own behavior. Thus, much of the harm that people cause stems from non-intentional and even non-deliberate misconduct.[4]

Clearly, as explained in Chapter 2, the degree to which good people act badly depends on the situation, their level of awareness of the wrongdoing, and their ability to overcome unconscious processes. The timing of the occurrence of the cognitive mechanism that allows good people to behave unethically is another determinant of subsequent behavior. For example, Shalvi et al. makes a distinction between ex ante mechanisms that allow people to engage in wrongdoing and focus mostly on the situation, and ex post mechanisms that are aimed at reducing the dissonance created by acting badly.[5] Gachter and Schulz distinguish between people's levels of dishonesty based on elaborated measurement of their scores in the dice-under-the-cup experiment, referring to a distinction between (1) unethical people who maximize their profits, (2) justified unethical people who are very sensitive to changes in the

---

[1] For the broader perspective, see Evans, J. S. B., & Frankish, K. E. (2009). *In two minds: Dual processes and beyond*. Oxford: Oxford University Press. For the role of automaticity in moral reasoning, see Haidt, J. (2001). The emotional dog and its rational tail: A social intuitionist approach to moral judgment. *Psychological Review*, 108(4), 814.

[2] For example, see Mazar, N., Amir, O., & Ariely, D. (2008). The dishonesty of honest people: A theory of self-concept maintenance. *Journal of Marketing Research*, 45(6), 633–644. See also Bersoff, D. M. (1999). Why good people sometimes do bad things: Motivated reasoning and unethical behaviour. *Personality and Social Psychology Bulletin*, 25(1), 28–39; Kidder, R. M. (2009). *How good people make tough choices: Resolving the dilemmas of ethical living*. New York: Harper; Cremer, D. D., Dick, R. V., & Murnighan, K. J. (2012). When good people do wrong: Morality, social identity, and ethical behaviour. In *Social psychology and organizations* (pp. 353–369). New York: Routledge; Hollis, J. (2008). *Why good people do bad things: Understanding our darker selves*. New York: Gotham Books; Banaji, M. R., & Greenwald, A. G. (2016). *Blindspot: Hidden biases of good people*. New York: Bantam Books. Note that the "good people" scholarship is usually different from the type of research conducted by Zimbardo on the Lucifer effect; see Zimbardo, P. G. (2008). *The Lucifer effect: Understanding how good people turn evil*. New York: Random House. These works generally try to explain how ordinary people end up doing evil or at least engage in gross criminal behaviors.

[3] See Hollis, *supra* note 2. See also Banaji & Greenwald, *supra* note 2.

[4] Mahzarian R. B., & Hardin, C. D. (1996). Automatic stereotyping. *Psychological Science*, 7(3), 136–141. See also Mazar et al., *supra* note 2. Bazerman, M. H., & Moore, D. A. (2008). *Judgment in managerial decision making* (7th ed.). New York: Wiley; Weber, J., Kurke, L. B., & Pentico, D. W. (2003). Why do employees steal? *Business & Society*, 42(3), 359–380; Shalvi, S., Gino, F., Barkan, R., & Ayal, S. (2015). Self-serving justifications: Doing wrong and feeling moral. *Current Directions in Psychological Science*, 24(2), 125–130. See further discussion of this point in Chapter 2.

[5] Shalvi, et al., Self-serving justifications doing wrong and feeling moral.

rules of the game, and (3) honest people who will not lie even in cases where the rules of the game make it more easily justifiable to do so.[6]

Therefore, many of those who are seen as "corrupt" in a given population are actually good people who are caught in situations that lead to corruption and who behave in a corrupt manner without wanting to and without being fully aware.[7] That is why we need to revisit the classic legal assumption that people's explicit self-interest explains their corruption. Based on this flawed assumption, sanctions are typically seen as the way to reduce corruption. As suggested by Chugh et al., however, incentives will be much less effective in changing the behavior of people who do not view themselves as doing anything wrong.[8] Expanding the toolbox to curb corruption is, thus, crucial.

9.1 BEHAVIORAL ETHICS AND THE REGULATION OF CORRUPTION

Studies of corruption and conflicts of interest describe numerous situations in which people who usually act in ways consistent with their professional and moral responsibilities allow their self-interest to prevail over fulfilling their professional duties. This could include a doctor who favors the interest of the pharmaceutical companies that invited him to conferences over that of his patients when writing prescriptions.[9] A mayor might favor the interest of those philanthropists who could help him in his future political career over those of the majority of the city's residents. In such situations, people can easily attribute their behavior to social motives as will be explained in the following sections.

Several psychological paradigms, such as bounded ethicality, blind spots, motivated reasoning, and self-deception, explain why this self-interested behavior takes precedence.[10] Behavioral ethics (BE) research has found that an effective way to

---

[6] In this experiment, participants were getting higher rewards when the number reported was higher. The design is usually such that participants enjoy anonymity. In more advanced version, participants were asked to throw the dice twice and then asked to report only on the first attempt.

[7] See Zamir, E., Teichman, D., & Feldman, Y. (2014). Behavioral ethics meets behavioral law and economics. In. E. Zamir & D. Teichman (Eds.), *The Oxford Handbook of Behavioral Economics and the Law*, 1. Oxford: Oxford University Press, pp. 213–241. See also Zamir, E., & Sulitzeanu-Kenan, R. (2018). Explaining self-interested behavior of public-spirited policymakers. *Public Administration Review*; http://onlinelibrary.wiley.com/doi/10.1111/puar.12825/full.

[8] Chugh, D., Bazerman, M. H., & Banaji, M. R. (2005). Bounded ethicality as a psychological barrier to recognizing conflicts of interest. *Conflicts of interest: Challenges and Solutions in Business, Law, Medicine, and Public Policy*, 74–95.

[9] Sah, S., & Fugh-Berman, A. (2013). Physicians under the Influence: Social psychology and industry marketing strategies. *Journal of Law, Medicine & Ethics*, 41(3), 665–672.

[10] Moore, D. A., & Loewenstein, G. (2004). Self-interest, automaticity, and the psychology of conflict of interest. *Social Justice Research*, 17(2), 189–202. For contrast, see also Rand et al.'s research paradigm on this topic, which suggests the opposite: Rand, D. G., Newman, G. E., & Wurzbacher, O. M. (2015). Social context and the dynamics of cooperative choice. *Journal of Behavioral Decision Making*, 28(2), 159–166. This argument was recently summarized in a meta-analysis that suggests that people's intuition is actually more likely to lead them to be cooperative.

minimize the corruption of good people is to determine which situations make it difficult for them to avoid unethical behavior and then design interventions that reduce the frequency of such situations. Yet this strategy may be difficult to implement when there is nothing inherently wrong with the behavior itself. For example, public officials are not necessarily misbehaving when they vote for a given regulation, promote a certain individual, or allow a certain commercial initiative to go forward. The only factor that would make such actions corrupt is an improper motive – for example, promoting an individual whose relative donated money to one's campaign. Determining motivation is difficult for outside observers and, given our proclivity to have ethical blind spots, difficult for each of us to do for ourselves.[11]

In addition, people often have mixed motives, acting for both legitimate and illegitimate reasons. When they operate according to various self-serving biases, particularly the objectivity bias, which causes people to downplay the effect of self-interest on their own behavior and hence view their motives as purely professional, they tend to mistakenly attribute their decisions to legitimate motivations.[12] Thus, a politician will convince himself that the only reason he is voting for a certain bill is the persuasive argument of a lobbyist, rather than the prospect of future financial support by the interest group represented by the lobbyist. We need to worry more rather than less that "softer" influence attempt (e.g., gifts, conference invitations), which might be seen as more legitimate based on current legal understanding, are the most dangerous ones according to the BE perspective. An invitation to give a keynote speech at a business conference, which gives politicians the ability to convince themselves that they are engaging in non-corrupt behaviors, may increase corruption more than a more blatantly criminal appeal, such as an envelope stuffed with cash, given as a donation.

The effect of softer incentives was found in my study with Halali, discussed in Chapter 3 that focuses on formal intervention,[13] in which participants were asked to fill out a survey reviewing a target institution that they hoped would hire them in the future to conduct and analyze those surveys; it thus presented a revolving door[14] scenario, where their current assignment and request to behave objectively are being corrupted by a subtle cue about what type of behavior would increase their future

[11] Hochman, G., Glöckner, A., Fiedler, S., & Ayal, S. (2015). "I can see it in your eyes": Biased processing and increased arousal in dishonest responses. Journal of Behavioral Decision Making, 29(2), 322–355.

[12] The concept is developed in Armor, D. A. (1998). The illusion of objectivity: Bias in the belief in freedom from bias. Unpublished doctoral dissertation, University of California, Los Angeles. It is reviewed among other approaches to the same bias in Pronin, E., Gilovich, T., & Ross, L. (2004). Objectivity in the eye of the beholder: Divergent perceptions of bias in self versus others. Psychological Review, 111(3), 781. For a more normative development in the context of ethical blind spot and conflict of interest, see Chugh et al., Bounded ethicality as a psychological barrier to recognizing conflicts of interest. They explain that people view themselves as more objective than other people and as such are unable to see themselves as being corrupt.

[13] See p.175 in Chapter 8.

[14] The "revolving door" usually refers to the movement of people between the public and private sectors. The fear is that people might think about the interests of their next employer, while still working for their current one.

employability. Participants were asked to answer two types of questions: those on the importance of the topics studied in the target institution and those evaluating the current researchers. We found that participants who were in the experimental condition where they were offered the option to work for the target institution were more likely to write favorable reviews of it. The promise of work did lead to an unethical bias. However, one would have expected the incentive-driven individuals to be more positive about the researchers than the topics studied in that context, as such reports are more likely to get them hired for additional experiments. Yet we found a corrupting effect with regard to their evaluation of the importance of the topics studied by the research center, but not for the evaluation of the researchers' benefits, although those researchers were in charge of rehiring them for their next job and would have been more likely to benefit the participants financially.[15] This analysis challenges current legal assumptions on the causes of corruption, which hold that greater financial incentives to be corrupt will increase corruption. In fact, BE suggests a more nuanced picture: the easier it is for good people to view themselves as good people, the more likely they are to be corrupt, irrespective of financial incentives. Thus, weaker, rather than stronger, financial connections between private sector interests and public sector employees might have a greater impact on fostering misconduct, at least for some of the good people and should be handled with caution, rather than being completely dismissed.

9.1.1 Challenging Situations

The ability of good people to engage in corrupted behavior can be strengthened by situational factors, as the concept of situational wrongdoers suggests. BE suggests that the situation effect on people's unethical behavior is much greater than is accounted for by the rational model of agents. For example, the fact that local governments across the world are more corrupt is less likely to be related to the types of people who choose to work in that branch. The hard-to-predict situational effects reduce the likelihood that focusing only on incentives will encourage ethical behavior, emphasizing the need for regulations that focus on the characteristics of the situation, as described in this section of the chapter.

9.1.2 Vagueness

Normative vagueness affects how people interpret their legal obligations. The rational-choice perspective holds that vagueness seems to deter people from attempting to find loopholes,[16] whereas BE research demonstrates that it sometimes

---

[15]   Feldman, Y., & Halali, E. (2017). Regulating "good" people in subtle conflicts of interest situations. *Journal of Business Ethics*, 1–19.

[16]   See Feldman, Y., & Smith, H. E. (2014). Behavioral equity. *Journal of Institutional and Theoretical Economics*, 170(1), 137–159.

does the exact opposite. For example, Schweitzer and Hsee show the effect of "elastic justification, where people take advantage of ambiguity in reality to choose an interpretation that supports their self-interest."[17] In a theoretical work with Smith[18] and a lab-based experimental study with Tcichman and Schur,[19] we confirmed that finding. The greater the ambiguity of the situation, the more people will feel confident in their own ethicality.[20] In a series of coauthored works on legal ambiguity, I demonstrated that unclear legal and organizational rules increase the likelihood that people's self-interest will take precedence over their professional duties.[21] Conversely, reducing people's ability to engage in elastic justification is likely to decrease the ability of good people to misrepresent the facts.[22] Thus, regulators who wish to curb corruption through legal means should craft relevant rules that are specific, rather than imposing general legal standards.[23] Since good people will most likely use ambiguity to their advantage, avoiding such language in the relevant legal and organizational codes is needed.

9.1.3 *The Danger of Non-monetary Influence*

Given the huge importance of incentives in public policy and the rational-choice perspective, policy makers usually assume that monetary rewards have the greatest influence on fostering corruption and hence should be subject to the greatest scrutiny. The BE perspective takes the opposite stance – that non-monetary rewards are harder to resist, especially by good people.

Classic studies on the corrupting power of money focus on politicians influenced by campaign donations[24] and on physicians whose health care decisions are affected by receiving drug industry money and perks.[25] In contrast, studies on European

---

[17] Schweitzer, M. E., & Hsee, C. K. (2002). Stretching the truth: Elastic justification and motivated communication of uncertain information. *Journal of Risk and Uncertainty*, 25(2), 185.

[18] See Feldman & Smith, *supra* note 16.

[19] Feldman, Y., Schurr A., & Teichman, D. (2013). Reference points and contractual choices: An experimental examination. *Journal of Empirical Legal Studies*, 103, 512–541. This paper is built on works of Moore et al., Bazerman et al., Feldman and Harel, and Feldman and Teichman, which all point to various factors that generate moral ambiguity and enable the individual to ignore the ethical dimension.

[20] Dana, J., Weber, R. A., & Kuang, J. X. (2007). Exploiting moral wiggle room: Experiments demonstrating an illusory preference for fairness. *Economic Theory*, 33(1), 67–80.

[21] Feldman, Y., & Harel, A. (2008). Social norms, self-interest and ambiguity of legal norms: An experimental analysis of the rule vs. standard dilemma. *Review of Law and Economics*, 4(1), 81–126. See also Feldman, Y., & Teichman, D. (2009). Are all legal probabilities created equal? *New York University Law Review*, 84(4), 980.

[22] See Feldman & Smith, *supra* note 16.

[23] However, see Boussalis, C., Feldman, Y., & Smith, H. E. (2017). Experimental analysis of the effect of standards on compliance and performance. *Regulation & Governance*, 97, for a discussion of the inadvertent effects of specificity on ethicality and performance.

[24] Lessig, L. (2011). *Republic, lost.* New York: Grand Central.

[25] Dana, J., & Loewenstein, G. (2003). A social science perspective on gifts to physicians from industry. *JAMA*, 290(2), 252–255.

financial markets have analyzed situations where there is no monetary connection
between an agent of a governing body and a private entity, but rather ties of shared
group identity, social class, or ideological perspective between regulators and those
being regulated.[26] A similar argument can be seen in the works of Kwak on cultural
capture, which focus on US financial markets, especially after the 2008 crisis and
how the cultural similarities between regulators and those being regulated, such as
graduating from the same schools and various common social ties prevented regulators from doing their job effectively.[27]

To recognize the effect of non-monetary influences on unethical behavior, there
is a need for additional controlled research studies on their impact. Despite the
growing recognition of the power of such influences – especially given the ability of
good people to rationalize their behavior – non-monetary influences, such as
receiving positive media coverage or invitations to prestigious conferences, are still
seen as less problematic legally. In addition, there seems to be greater tolerance of
those corrupted by such influences, compared to those corrupted by more direct
monetary incentives. Yet, regulators need to worry about non-monetary rewards at
least as much as they do about monetary ones.

9.1.4 *Partial Dependency and the Problem of Less Blatant Conflict of Interest*

A related issue to the impact of non-monetary influences is that of partial dependency, financial or otherwise. Again, the rational-choice perspective and the
BE research reach vastly different conclusions on this issue. According to the
rational-choice theory, partial financial dependency decreases the chances of corruption relative to full dependency. For example, a research center that is fully
funded by only one donor is more likely to produce research results in accord with
the interests of that particular donor. Hence, the traditional solution to that dependency problem is to diversify the pool of donors. However, BE research on topics
such as half-lies suggests that partial dependency may create more fertile ground for
corruption: good people will have more leeway to view themselves as not being fully
influenced by their dependency when it is only partial.[28] In that regard, when
regulators are able to partly solve a problem of conflict of interests, they might end
up creating a more problematic behavior from the perspective of the "Law of Good
People" paradigm developed in this book.

[26] Veltrop, D., & Haan, J. D. (2014). I just cannot get you out of my head: Regulatory capture of financial sector supervisors. *Academy of Management Proceedings*, 2014(1), 12898–12898. Shows based on data from the Dutch financial market that social identification between regulators and regulates might harm their ability to be impartial enforcers. See also Jones, D. (2000). Group nepotism and human kinship. *Current Anthropology*, 41(5), 779–809.

[27] Kwak, J. (2013). Cultural capture and the financial crisis. *Preventing Regulatory Capture: Special Interest Influence and How to Limit It*, 71–98.

[28] Fischbacher, U., & Föllmi-Heusi, F. (2013). Lies in disguise – an experimental study on cheating. *Journal of the European Economic Association*, 11(3), 525–547.

9.1.5 *Availability of Justifications*

As suggested earlier, the underlying assumption of most BE approaches is that individuals desire to view themselves as ethical agents. Therefore, people are more prone to unethical behavior in settings in which they can justify their behavior as ethical.[29] Conversely, when certain situations shine a spotlight on unethical elements of behavior, they may abstain from engaging in acts that promote their self-interest.[30] By using simple empirical measures of the features of particular situations, regulators can determine the common rationalizations that people use to justify corruption and then take a preemptive approach, perhaps by training people to recognize common justifications (e.g., everyone does it; no one would care; I am not responsible).[31]

9.1.6 *Corruption for the Sake of Others*

Another area in which rational-choice theory reaches conclusions opposite to those of BE research is in explaining why people engage in corruption for the sake of others. For example, unethical behavior can be engaged in by an agent, as by lawyers or accountants, by corporate directors or employees for the sake of the firm, or the shareholders, or for a cause, as when a politician acts on behalf of her constituents or a philanthropist directs funding to a specific group.

According to the rational-choice perspective, people are more likely to behave unethically when they expect to gain more from it, whereas BE research suggests that the opposite is often the case, at least for some of the people: people's misbehavior increases when they do it in their capacity to help others.[32] Some BE studies suggest that in some cases, people will act more unethically when they only enjoy part of the benefit rather than all of it,[33] or when they act in their professional capacity to benefit the corporation, or a client.[34] Furthermore, people are more

[29] Shalvi, S., Dana, J., Handgraaf, M. J., & De Dreu, C. K. (2011). Justified ethicality: Observing desired counterfactuals modifies ethical perceptions and behavior. *Organizational Behavior and Human Decision Processes*, 115(2), 181–190.

[30] For example, see Bazerman, M. H., Loewenstein, G., & Moore, D. A. (2002). Why good accountants do bad audits. *Harvard Business Review*, 80(11), 96–103. See also Feldman & Harel, *supra* note 21. They all point to various situational factors with a particular focus on legality, which could generate moral ambiguity that enables the individual to ignore the ethical dimension to the mechanisms such as wiggle room and elastic justification.

[31] By analogy, see a review of the rationales (e.g., "it's a new era") illegal downloaders of copyrighted files use to justify their behavior and the tactics used by both rights holders and regulators to fight these types of rationales. Feldman, Y., & Nadler, J. (2006). The law and norms of file sharing. *San Diego Law Review*, 43, 577.

[32] Gino, F., & Pierce, L. (2009). Dishonesty in the name of equity. *Psychological Science*, 20(9), 1153–1160.

[33] Wiltermuth, S. S. (2011). Cheating more when the spoils are split. *Organizational Behavior and Human Decision Processes*, 115(2), 157–168.

[34] Kouchaki, M. (2013). Professionalism and moral behavior: Does a professional self-conception make one more unethical?. *Edmond J. Safra Working Papers* (4). Available at https://papers.ssrn.com/sol3/papers.cfm?abstract_id=2243811.

likely to engage in more serious misconduct when they do it in a gradual rather than an abrupt way,[35] and when they harm many unidentified victims, rather than a specific individual known to them.[36]

Thus, corporate directors or executives may have a higher likelihood to make unethical choices when they are less likely to personally enjoy most of the fruits of their acts. Corruption is more likely in such contexts, which are probably more prevalent among corporate executives than are situations in which one individual stands to benefit directly from a corrupt act. Furthermore, in many corporate contexts, those agents and directors might not just engage in wrongdoing but also fail to intervene to halt corruption of others.[37]

9.1.7 Possible Nontraditional Interventions

Regulators thus need to be more aware of those cognitive mechanisms and situations that cause atypical suspects – good people – to be more likely not to follow their institutional responsibilities. Only after policy makers come to understand that a variety of states of mind and situations are conducive to corruption will they be able to develop policies that can address most corruption. Legal policy makers need to both revisit and expand the regulatory toolbox.

9.1.7.1 Ethical Nudges

The most well-known addition to the regulatory toolbox is the nudge, based on Thaler and Sunstein's book by that name.[38] They introduced the idea of interventions that could lead to behavioral change without limiting people's free choice. Different types of nudges have different effects and policy considerations. Well-established behavioral nudges, such as those related to practicing wellness and curbing energy consumption, have a long regulatory history. These classical nudges remind people to act to protect their true self-interest, such as by becoming healthier or saving money. In contrast, ethical nudges are far more complex, and their use requires further discussion. Ethical nudges generate different types of policy considerations because of the need to protect third parties (compared to traditional nudges that aim to protect the individuals themselves from their cognitive

---

[35] Shu, L. L., Mazar, N., Gino, F., Ariely, D., & Bazerman, M. H. (2012). Signing at the beginning makes ethics salient and decreases dishonest self-reports in comparison to signing at the end. *Proceedings of the National Academy of Sciences, 109*(38), 15197–15200.

[36] Amir, A., Kogut, T., & Bereby-Meyer, Y. (2016). Careful cheating: People cheat groups rather than individuals. *Frontiers in Psychology, 7*, 371.

[37] Pittarello, A., Rubaltelli, E., & Motro, D. (2016). Legitimate lies: The relationship between omission, commission, and cheating. *European Journal of Social Psychology, 46*(4), 481–491. For a work in progress in this context see Adi Libson, Directors' conflict-of-interest impact on passive behavior: Evidence from directors on the Tel-Aviv stock exchange (on file with author).

[38] Thaler, R. S., & Sunstein, C. (2008). *Nudge: Improving decisions about health, wealth, and happiness.* New Haven: Yale University Press.

limitations). They may be less effective than behavioral nudges because of people's greater temptation to stay biased in ethical contexts (i.e., to maintain their self-perception as ethical people). In addition, ethical nudges seek to suppress the actor's self-interest (e.g., making one less likely to give a job promotion to a friend) and therefore are likely to encounter greater motivational resistance.[39]

One of the most well-known examples of an ethical nudge is affixing one's signature to the beginning of a document, rather than at its end, which has been shown to reduce the incidence of unethicality.[40] This nudge is a practical and easy-to-implement measure that confirms that people change their behavior when reminded of their moral responsibility at the moment of decision making. However, such nudges should be implemented with caution, because making them into a law could make them too standard or routine, thus reducing their effect of reminding people of their moral and professional responsibility.[41]

9.1.8 *Rethinking the Use of Explicit Measures*

The main conceptual and practical change in regulating conflicts of interest in recent years is the emphasis on implicit interventions rather than explicit ones. The traditional approach focuses on explicit measures, such as financial incentives that reduce the motivation of individuals to engage in unethical misconduct; however, its effectiveness has been challenged by BE research on people's blindness to their own wrongdoing. In the paper with Halali described earlier on the relative effectiveness of explicit measures (texts describing the option of punishment for corruption and texts describing morality) versus implicit measures (word completion of words associated with morality and deterrence) in curbing corruption in a revolving door contexts, we found that explicit measures were better able to change behavior in subtle conflict of interest situations, with deterrence and morality messages having a similar effect; in line with some of the current criticism that questions priming techniques, implicit approaches were not effective in those situations.[42] Although we cannot fully explain the null effect of implicit measures, the fact that explicit measures were effective is in line with BE research on the importance of moral reminders and suggests that traditional enforcement mechanisms should continue to be used.[43] A possible, more legalistic approach to moral reminders is to use declarations more extensively. For example, before every

[39] See Feldman et al., *supra* note 7.
[40] Shu, L. L., Mazar, N., Gino, F., Ariely, D., & Bazerman, M. H. (2012). Signing at the beginning makes ethics salient and decreases dishonest self-reports in comparison to signing at the end. *Proceedings of the National Academy of Sciences, 109*(38), 15197–15200.
[41] This is an idea mentioned to me by Dan Ariely.   [42] See Feldman & Halali, *supra* note 15.
[43] Ayal, S., Gino, F., Barkan, R., & Ariely, D. (2015). Three principles to REVISE people's unethical behavior. *Perspectives on Psychological Science, 10*(6), 738–741.

meeting in which executives vote on decisions, they could be asked to sign a declaration stating that they understand the types of conflicts of interest that they need to reveal, that they do not have such conflicts, and that they know the relevant laws. Such repeated declarations can serve two purposes. From a behavioral perspective, actively writing a declaration prevents people from failing to announce a conflict of interest; such omissions can be downplayed in a person's mind more than can stating an outright lie.[44] From a legal perspective, writing a declaration in one's own handwriting reminds people that they can be prosecuted for perjury.

9.1.9 *Rethinking Deterrence in the Context of Corruption*

In Becker's well-known model, the effectiveness of enforcement as a deterrent to bad behavior is equal to the perception of expected (probability of detection x size of penalty) cost.[45] As expected, BE research challenges this equation.[46] If indeed good people are not fully aware of the unethical effect of their behaviors, then they are unlikely to accurately engage in cost-benefit analysis. As suggested in earlier chapters, the BE literature supports existing studies on deterrence, which argue the greater effectiveness detection likelihood relative to punishment size in reducing misconduct.[47] In many contexts, deterrence efforts could also convey moral norms of the impermissibility of certain behaviors, such as in areas of white-collar crimes, intellectual property violations, and tax evasion.[48] In those contexts, focusing on detection is much more likely to foster awareness of the ethical nature of behavior.[49] Frequent detection is effective in creating moral reminders and is better suited than enforcement to influence the behavior of good people, who are less likely to calculate the potential punishment they might receive, especially in cases where they do not even think that their behavior is corrupt. Thus, especially when dealing with gray behaviors that could be seen as corrupt, organizations and regulators should invest in detection rather than in penalty size, which assumes calculative mind-set.[50]

44 Spranca, M., Minsk, E., & Baron, J. (1991). Omission and commission in judgment and choice. *Journal of Experimental Social Psychology*, 27(1), 76–105.

45 Becker, G. S. (1968). Crime and punishment: An economic approach. In W. N. Landes (Ed.),. *The economic dimensions of crime* (pp. 13–68). London: Palgrave Macmillan.

46 See Feldman & Teichman, *supra* note 21. See further discussion of this point in Chapter 8.

47 Klepper, S., & Nagin, D. (1989). The deterrent effect of perceived certainty and severity of punishment revisited. *Criminology*, 27(4), 721–746.

48 Ariel, B. (2012). Deterrence and moral persuasion effects on corporate tax compliance: Findings from a randomized controlled trial. *Criminology*, 50(1), 27–69.

49 Mulder, L. B. (2016). When sanctions convey moral norms. *European Journal of Law and Economics*, 1–12. See also Feldman, Y. (2009). The expressive function of trade secret law: Legality, cost, intrinsic motivation, and consensus. *Journal of Empirical Legal Studies*, 6(1), 177–212 for the interaction between perception of costs and perception of the immorality of an act.

50 Fellner, G., Sausgruber, R., & Traxler, C. (2013). Testing enforcement strategies in the field: Threat, moral appeal and social information. *Journal of the European Economic Association*, 11(3), 634–660. For an approach that tries to separate them, see also Feldman, *supra* note 49. For the effect of small

9.1.10 Blinding

Another important tool in curbing corruption is to expand on the efforts to disguise personal information in job applications, as well as in various stages of criminal procedures to context related to conflict of interest. In employment discrimination, this practice has been shown to be highly effective in curbing implicit biases and the unconscious effects of self-interest. Based on that success, Robertson and Kesselheim edited a recent book on ways in which blocking information might prevent unconscious biases, which could be responsible for implicit corruption in many institutional contexts.[51] If people do not know what is in their best self interest in a given situation (e.g., who pays for their evaluation), their ability to be biased in that direction is undermined.

9.1.11 Targeted vs. Integrated Policy Perspective

In Chapter 11, we examine the approach policy makers need to take, given the variation between people. Clearly there are many types of people, and even good people have many different motives, some of which can impel them to do bad things. With regard to the concept of corruption, it seems that there are two main strategies for dealing with the heterogeneity of motivations and the frequent lack of awareness of corruption: (1) a targeted approach based on data collection and tailored toward a given situation and population and (2) an integrated approach encompassing a large number of regulatory tools attempting to deal with different mind-sets.

In a targeted approach, regulations address the specific situational factors that foster corruption for particular groups. For example, regulators might need to expand their focus from screening for illegal bank transfers to exploring the influence of non-monetary inducements, such as supportive media coverage and prestige. My work on pharmaceutical corruption suggests that scientists are mostly motivated by scientific prestige and self-fulfillment and therefore they sometimes cut corners in their research to achieve positive results for clinical trials. Focusing on financial fines is less relevant for this population but is more relevant when it comes to executives who engage in various evasive marketing practices to increase profits for the corporation and who define their success by financial success for the company rather than by scientific recognition.

The alternative integrated approach employs a set of regulatory tools, hoping to cover as many potential mind-sets of the regulated agents as possible. An example of an integrated approach is that proposed by Ayal et al. and discussed in more details

punishments, see Schurr, A., Rodensky, D., & Erev, I. (2014). The effect of unpleasant experiences on evaluation and behavior. *Journal of Economic Behavior & Organization, 106*, 1–9.

[51] Robertson, C. T., & Kesselheim, A. S. (2016). *Blinding as a solution to bias: Strengthening biomedical science, forensic science, and law.* Amsterdam: Elsevier, Academic Press.

in Chapter 4.[52] They call their approach REVISE, which is an acronym for REminding people not to use gray areas to justify dishonesty by setting subtle cues that increase the importance of ethical criteria; VIsibility, using procedures that increase people's awareness that they are being seen and recognized by other people who know them; and SElf-engagement, reducing the gap between people's abstract perceptions of their moral self-image and their actual behavior, which allows them to do wrong while still feeling that they are moral individuals.

9.1.12 *Inadvertent Interventions*

The behavioral approach to the regulation of corruption needs to focus not just on the tools used but also on recognizing that some existing tools might have the unintended consequence of increasing corruption, rather than curb it. In this section, we address those negative effects.

9.1.13 *Refining Disclosure*

Disclosure of conflicts of interest is one of the most commonly used approaches in legal contexts. Cain et al.'s research on disclosure's paradoxical effects (i.e., clients receive worse advice but do not discount their level of trust after the disclosure) is well known.[53] However, Sha's analysis of the impacts of those disclosures argues that the picture is more complex. Her research suggests that regulators can increase the effectiveness of disclosure regimes by adjusting the ways this disclosure is presented to the patients (e.g., it's best to present the disclosure as mandatory rather than voluntary and best presented by a third person rather than by the doctor herself).[54]

9.1.14 *The Four Eyes Principle*

The idea that a transaction that needs to be approved by two people, rather than just one, is less likely to be corrupt is a well-established concept within both the corporate and political worlds. Intuitively, involvement of more people seems likely to reduce corruption. However, this concept might backfire, according to Weisel and Shalvi, who show that when people work together in dyads, in certain conditions, they are more likely to engage in wrongdoing than they would have individually.[55] Clearly further research is needed to understand the mechanisms that underlie this surprising effect. Their work challenges the current regulatory perspective that the four eyes

---

[52] See Ayal et al., *supra* note 43.

[53] Cain, D. M., Loewenstein, G., & Moore, D. A. (2005). The dirt on coming clean: Perverse effects of disclosing conflicts of interest. *Journal of Legal Studies*, 34(1), 1–25.

[54] Sah, S., Loewenstein, G., & Cain, D. M. (2013). The burden of disclosure: increased compliance with distrusted advice. *Journal of personality and social psychology*, 104(2), 289.

[55] Weisel, O., & Shalvi, S. (2015). The collaborative roots of corruption. *Proceedings of the National Academy of Sciences of the USA*, 112(34), 10651–10656.

principle is an effective tool in curbing corruption.[56] Here, too, policy makers might decrease the inadvertent effects of work done by dyads by changing the responsibilities assigned to each member of the pair as well as their relevant responsibilities. When each individual has different responsibilities, there is room to speculate that the collaborative effects will be curbed.

9.1.15 *Language Considerations in the Framing of Ethical Codes*

The final approach I discuss here is probably the most traditional one: ethical codes. There are conflicting views regarding their efficacy,[57] but there is some evidence that ethical codes can be made more potent by drawing on newer BE approaches that focus on a combination of explicit and implicit ethical interventions. For example, in work I did with Francesca Gino and Maryam Kouchaki on the language of ethical codes, we showed that using the word "employees" instead of "we" was more effective in curbing employees' unethical behavior[58]. We explained this effect as related to the more forgiving nature of "communal" codes (that use the phrase "we" often throughout the code), which causes people to be more committed to the organization while signaling to employees that they might be forgiven for their misconduct. Thus, the focus on good people requires the need to pay attention to very subtle changes in the language of ethical codes being used by companies.

9.2 SUMMARY

In this chapter, I contrasted the behavioral ethics and the rational-choice perspectives on how to reduce corruption. Notably, I suggested that when considering the corruption of good people, whose motivation and awareness of the ethicality of their own behavior are limited, the BE approach can provide valuable insight into regulating corruption. I conclude with the following three reasons to add behavioral ethics to the regulatory toolbox. First, it helps identify situations when misconduct is more likely to occur, thus alerting policy makers to either consider methods to alter those situations or to increase scrutiny over them. Second, BE research suggests that some of the tools based on the rational-choice theories have some unintended consequences, especially when applied to good people. Finally, BE research suggests some additional tools that could be used by policy makers to more effectively curb corruption. By expanding the toolbox, as well as the type of people whose behavior we should worry about, collecting data on the particulars of a given

---

[56] Irlenbusch, B, Mussweiler, T., Saxler, D., Shalvi S., Weiss, A. (2016). Similarity increases collaborative cheating.

[57] O'Fallon, M. J., & Butterfield, K. D. (2005). A review of the empirical ethical decision-making literature: 1996–2003. *Journal of Business Ethics*, 59(4), 375–413.

[58] Kouchaki, M., Feldman, Y., & Gino, F. (2017). Expressive effects of ethical codes: An experimental survey of US employees' interpretation, understanding and implementation of institutional ethical policies. Unpublished on file with the author.

situations, and using a differentiated approach (when data exists) or an integrated approach (when there is not enough data), policy makers will be able to offer a more comprehensive and effective approach to address corruption. The overuse of the criminal law perspective in the fight against corruption and the need to look for a smoking gun and for a blatant conflict of interest should be completely abandoned, given the findings of behavior ethics as incorporated in the law of good people approach. The next chapter will focus on employment discrimination, which is an area of law in which the principles of the law of good people have already been recognized, partly because the behavioral literature on social cognition is highly developed.

10

Discrimination by "Good" Employers

The field of employment discrimination, to a greater extent than other areas of the law, already accounts for non-deliberative explanations of people's motivation and awareness, both jurisprudentially and doctrinally. Hence, the decision to focus on this area was derived to a large extent from its incorporation of the behavioral ethics approach, which looks to implicit processes and not smoking guns as sources of misconduct. Employment discrimination is far more pervasive than people are willing to admit, and the law should be moving from an *ex post* treatment to an *ex ante* design of the hiring and firing situation, given the newer understanding of how individuals make decisions.

Legal scholars, notably Krieger, have suggested that a large proportion of biased employment decisions results not from discriminatory motivations but from a variety of unintentional judgment errors of categorization.[1] Similarly, from a behavioral perspective Agerström and Rooth demonstrate the importance of System 1 reasoning in hiring decisions.[2] Specifically, their study found that participants' likelihood of

---

[1] Krieger, L. H. (1995). The content of our categories: A cognitive bias approach to discrimination and equal employment opportunity. *Stanford Law Review*, 47(6), 1161. See also Krieger, L. H. (1998). Civil rights perestroika: Intergroup relations after affirmative action. *California Law Review*, 86(6), 1251. Krieger, L. H., & Fiske, S. T. (2006). Behavioral realism in employment discrimination law: Implicit bias and disparate treatment. *California Law Review*, 94(4), 997; Hart, M. (2005). Subjective decision-making and unconscious discrimination. *Alabama Law Review*, 56(3), 741; Jolls, C., & Sunstein, C. R. (2006). The law of implicit bias. *California Law Review*, 94, 969–996; Rich, S. M. (2011). Against prejudice. *George Washington Law Review*, 80(1), 1–101; Reeder, G., & Pryor, J. (2008). Dual psychological processes underlying public stigma and the implications for reducing stigma. *Mens Sana Monographs*, 6(1), 175; Fiske, S. T., Cuddy, A. J., & Glick, P. (2007). Universal dimensions of social cognition: Warmth and competence. *Trends in Cognitive Sciences*, 11(2), 77–83; Uhlmann, E. L., Brescoll, V. L., & Machery, E. (2010). The motives underlying stereotype-based discrimination against members of stigmatized groups. *Social Justice Research*, 23(1), 1–16; Anderson, L., Fryer, R., & Holt, C. (2006). Discrimination: Experimental evidence from psychology and economics. In W. M. Rodgers (Ed.), *Handbook on the economics of discrimination* (pp. 97–118). Cheltenham: Edward Elgar.

[2] Agerström, J., & Rooth, D. (2011). The role of automatic obesity stereotypes in real hiring discrimination. *Journal of Applied Psychology*, 96(4), 790–805.

hiring people who are overweight was affected by their implicit attitude toward obesity. In addition, in this area of law, there is the consideration of various types of discrimination, intentional and non-intentional, as well as recognition of regulators' limited ability to know what is on people's minds when they make hiring decisions.

Thus, this book's discussion of employment discrimination is relatively short because expounding on the impact of dual-reasoning systems on employment discrimination would be like preaching to the choir. Rather than describing new ways to understand employment discrimination, this chapter examines why the behavioral ethics approach is so highly developed in this area, which can help us understand how it can be effectively applied to other fields. After all, a main aim of this book is to raise awareness of implicit and unconscious processes in accounting for people's behavior in other legal areas, such as how people interpret contracts or approve transactions in the context of corporate law.[3]

This chapter also addresses why the research on the power of implicit biases in employment discrimination has had a minimal impact on legislation in this area – even though the traditional legal scholarship is aware of the importance of accounting for implicit discrimination. Given the richness of the behavioral findings on implicit employment discrimination, the lack of full responsiveness of the law is particularly frustrating. By and large, current employment discrimination laws are still much better suited to deal with calculated wrongdoers than with situational wrongdoers, and most of the progress in reducing employment discrimination is occurring outside traditional legal contexts. We argue that adopting the *ex ante* treatment by legal policy makers, rather than waiting for harm to occur before regulating it, would enable the law to address situational wrongdoers. While law and economics scholars recognize the advantages of an ex ante design, there is relatively little attention to incorporating situational design into the law.

10.1 IMPLICIT DISCRIMINATION

One of the reasons for the recognition of the influence of System 1 reasoning in employment discrimination is the greatly developed research on social cognition on intuitive and non-deliberative mechanisms.[4] The processes leading people to discriminate are often unconscious – especially those involved in the first stage where people's genuine primary prejudice is generated. Cognitive psychological research has been supplemented by social psychology research on intergroup psychology focusing on stereotyping processes as one of the central processes guiding implicit

---

[3] See Krieger & Fiske, *supra* note 1, at 997. See also Dasgupta, N. (2004). Implicit ingroup favoritism, outgroup favoritism, and their behavioral manifestations. *Social Justice Research*, 17(2), 143–169.

[4] Greenwald, A. G., & Banaji, M. R. (1995). Implicit social cognition: Attitudes, self-esteem, and stereotypes. *Psychological Review*, 102(1), 4.

discrimination.[5] Within this literature, Fiske's work is especially promising because it offers a more nuanced and multidimensional approach to discrimination.[6]

As discussed in earlier chapters, there are two systems of reasoning: automatic, intuitive, and mostly unconscious processes (labeled System 1) and controlled and deliberative process (labeled System 2).[7] In the context of employment discrimination, An ample body of research has shown that both conscious and unconscious processes interact without the individual's full awareness that discrimination even occurs.[8]

Crandall and Eshleman provide insights into the processes through which discrimination is generated.[9] They propose that a "suppression-justification model" results in either the expression or the suppression of discrimination. In this model, discrimination is or is not generated as a result of a two-stage cognitive process. In the first stage, an automatic, genuine, primary prejudice is generated in which individuals are automatically evaluated based on their membership in a certain social group. In the second stage, the expression of the genuine prejudice in the form of discriminatory behavior is either suppressed or justified by beliefs, values, and social norms.

In the next section, I differentiate between "good employers" who engage in intuitive discrimination and "bad employers" who engage in deliberative discrimination, as well as the likelihood of certain types of discrimination to occur. Although these distinctions are important from the liability perspective, they are even more significant in developing extralegal approaches that prevent discrimination from being generated or suppressed once it occurs. Only by accounting for the processes that underlie people's discrimination can we predict differences in how discrimination occurs and to whom it is targeted.

10.2 IMPLICIT DISCRIMINATION AND DIFFERENTIATED DISCRIMINATION

With Kricheli-Katz and Porat, I have conducted theoretical and empirical studies of differentiated discrimination focusing on both implicit and explicit

[5] Tajfel, H. (2010). *Social identity and intergroup relations.* Cambridge: Cambridge University Press. See also Taifel, H., & Turner, J. C. (1979). Realistic group conflict theory. *Social Psychology of Intergroup Relations,* 33–47. For reviews, see Fiske, S. T. (1998). Stereotyping, prejudice, and discrimination. In D. T. Gilbert, S. T. Fiske, & G. Lindzey (Eds.), *The handbook of social psychology* (Vol. 2, 4th ed., pp. 357–411). New York: McGraw-Hill.

[6] Fiske, S. T. (2000), Stereotyping, prejudice, and discrimination at the seam between the centuries: Evolution, culture, mind, and brain. *European Journal of Social Psychology,* 30, 299–322.

[7] Stanovich, K. E., & West, R. F. (2000). Individual differences in reasoning: Implications for the rationality debate? *Behavioral and Brain Sciences,* 23(5), 645–665. See also Evans, J. S. (2003). In two minds: Dual-process accounts of reasoning. *Trends in Cognitive Sciences,* 7(10), 454–459.

[8] See Krieger & Fiske, *supra* note 1, at 997. See also Mitchell, G., & Tetlock, P. E. (2006). Antidiscrimination law and the perils of mindreading. *Ohio State Law Journal,* 67, 1023.

[9] Crandall, C. S., & Eshleman, A. (2003). A justification-suppression model of the expression and experience of prejudice. *Psychological Bulletin,* 129(3), 414–446.

processes.[10] We noted that although employment anti-discrimination laws prohibit specific forms of employment discrimination based on race, sex, religion, and age, these laws do not take into account the different mechanisms generating each of those forms.[11] Rather, the laws take a blanket approach, applying similar remedies and prohibitions to each form. To identify the specific mechanisms motivating each form of discrimination, we reviewed four types of discrimination identified in the theoretical and empirical literature. The first form is taste-based discrimination, which occurs when disparities are the result of discriminators' likes and dislikes of certain social groups. With this form of discrimination, the discriminator is willing to forgo material gain to cater to his or her preferences.[12] Two other forms of discrimination are statistical discrimination[13] and mistaken-stereotypes discrimination, and both arise due to cultural beliefs about social groups.[14] These beliefs tend to center on ability and performance, with members of certain social groups perceived as performing better than members of other groups in particular contexts. Generally speaking, when cultural beliefs are statistically supported, people who take these statistics into account (without testing them in the individual case) engage in statistical discrimination. When cultural beliefs are statistically erroneous, people practice mistaken-stereotypes discrimination. The fourth form of discrimination is normative discrimination, which occurs when people act in accordance with their normative evaluations and moral judgments. With this form of discrimination, people are discriminated against not because it is perceived to be costly to interact with them, but because their actions are viewed by others as normatively wrong. For the most part, the literature on the different forms of discrimination does not pay much attention to the reasoning mechanisms underlying each. Nonetheless, it is possible to speculate on those mechanisms and the connection between the type of discrimination and the likelihood that implicit discrimination will occur.[15]

[10]   Feldman, Y., & Kricheli-Katz, T. (2015). The human mind and human rights: A call for an integrative study of the mechanisms generating employment discrimination across different social categories. *Law & Ethics of Human Rights*, 9(1), 43–67; in a follow up working paper with Haggi Poart and Tami Kricheli-Katz, we have conducted a series of game based experiments that attempt to compare empirically between these types of discrimination.

[11]   Title VII of the Civil Rights Act of 1964 prohibits employment discrimination on the basis of religion, race, and sex. The Age Discrimination in Employment Act of 1967 (ADEA) protects certain applicants and employees who are 40 years old and older from discrimination. Both laws are enforced by the US Equal Employment Opportunity Commission (EEOC).

[12]   Becker, G. S. (1957). The theory of discrimination. See also Arrow, K. (1973). The theory of discrimination. *Discrimination in Labor Markets*, 3(10), 3–33; Arrow, K. J. (1998). What has economics to say about racial discrimination? *Journal of Economic Perspectives*, 12(2), 91–100.

[13]   Phelps, E. S. (1972). The statistical theory of racism and sexism. *American Economic Review*, 62(4), 659–661.

[14]   In using the term "cultural beliefs," we refer to learned, sometimes unconscious, shared beliefs about the respect, social esteem, and honor associated with types or categories of people compared to other types or categories of people. In the United States, for example, beliefs about social esteem are also associated with beliefs about differences in ability and competence in the tasks that are valued by society. Ridgeway, C. L., & Correll, S. J. (2006). Consensus and the creation of status beliefs. *Social Forces*, 85(1), 431–453.

[15]   For some discussion in economics on the connection between taste-based discrimination and implicit discrimination, see Bertrand, M., Chugh, D., & Mullainathan, S. (2005). Implicit discrimination. *American Economic Review*, 95(2), 94–98.

Parallel to the research on automatic and implicit discrimination, social psychology research suggests that people in social interactions categorize each other immediately and intuitively and place others into membership in social groups accordingly. Thus, for example, people tend to immediately categorize each other by sex and skin color. These categories tend to have associated cultural beliefs about the characteristics of group members; for example, cultural beliefs about women may be that they are more communal, emotional, and expressive than men.[16]

Based on research about how the human mind works and about how people interact, we have argued that the ways in which social interactions and the human mind work in relation to each of these categories of employment discrimination – race, sex, religion, and age – differ from one another; therefore, to better address each form of discrimination, those differences across categories need to be taken into account.

To better understand how the differences across categories may play out differently and result in differing discriminatory outcomes, we analyzed gender, race, and age discrimination in the United States.[17] Because these categories are based on salient physical features that are easily and quickly recognized, people immediately categorize others by them and automatically and intuitively rely on these categories in their perception and evaluation of others.[18] The cultural beliefs that are associated with these categories – for example, women are "less assertive" and "more communal" than men – are therefore immediately evoked whenever people interact.

10.3 DIFFERENCES ACROSS FORMS OF DISCRIMINATION

When employers make discriminatory decisions on the basis of these salient features, discrimination may function differently depending on the type of decision the employer is expected to reach (e.g., hiring, firing, or promotion), the level of information available to the employer on the candidate (e.g., personal background information), the way alternatives are framed (e.g., comparatively, in absolute terms), and the situational constraints on the possibility to deliberate (e.g., time to decide, accountability).

[16] Deaux, K., & Kite, M. E. (1987). Gender stereotypes. *Gender Belief Systems: Homosexuality and the Implicit Inversion Theory*, 11(1), 83–96; Eagly, A. H. (1987). *Sex differences in social behavior: A social-role interpretation*. Hillsdale, NJ: Erlbaum; Wagner, D. G., & Berger, J. (1997). Gender and interpersonal task behaviors: Status expectation accounts. *Sociological Perspectives*, 40(1), 1–32.

[17] See Feldman & Kricheli-Katz, *supra* note 10. Our analysis relied on works of scholars such as Brewer, M. B., & Lui, L. N. (1989). The primacy of age and sex in the structure of person categories. Social Cognition, 7(3), 262–274.

[18] Ridgeway, C. L. (1997). Interaction and the conservation of gender inequality: Considering employment. *American Sociological Review*, 62(2), 218. See also Ridgeway, C. L. (2011). *Framed by gender: How gender inequality persists in the modern world*. Oxford: Oxford University Press.

10.3.1 *Familiarity*

Kricheli-Katz and I predicted that in hiring decisions, job candidates' visible traits (gender, race, age) would play a larger part in giving rise to implicit discrimination than less visible traits such as religion and sexual orientation.[19] However, visible traits play less of a role in promotion and firing decisions, when employers know much more about their employees' abilities and performance than what they see on the surface. In other words, employers are likely to have more information on which they can make deliberate decisions, compared to the earlier hiring stages where, for certain social groups, the level of information on each candidate is minimal and the reliance on stereotypical information is greater. Thus, familiarity increases use of System 2 reasoning, while lack of it increases the reliance on System 1 processes.[20]

10.3.2 *Frequency of Social Interactions*

The frequency of the social interactions that take place between members of different groups affects the occurrence of discrimination. Whereas we tend to have family or household members of both genders and of different ages, we are less likely to share a household or to have relatives of other races and religions. Daily interactions between men and women and between people of different ages reinforce many of the cultural beliefs and stereotypes about gender and age in social relations. When interactions between members of different groups – such as those of different races and religions – are less frequent, other, more institutional mechanisms, such as the media, the law, or differential organizational positions of power, may be more important in generating and reinforcing such cultural beliefs. We can therefore predict that new information, especially information regarding a job candidate's performance and personal qualities, such as his or her warmth and good nature, will reduce employers' race- and religion-based biases to a smaller extent than their biases against people of a different gender and those of different ages. For example, information regarding the applicant's volunteer work will reduce race- and religion-based biases of employers to a greater extent than biases resulting from their cultural beliefs regarding gender and age.

10.3.3 *Statistical Enforcement*

Statistical unethicality recognizes the difficulty in determining the state of mind of the individual wrongdoer. This concept is based primarily on ideas developed in the

[19] See Feldman & Kricheli-Katz, *supra* note 10. in a follow up working paper with Haggi Poart and Tami Kricheli-Katz, we have conducted a series of game based experiments that attempt to compare empirically between these types of discrimination.

[20] Greenwald, A. G., & Krieger, L. H. (2006). Implicit bias: Scientific foundations. *California Law Review*, 94(4), 945–967.

area of employment discrimination, in which one can only evaluate whether an employer's hiring or promotion decisions reflect discriminatory practices by looking at them in the aggregate.[21] Work done by Porat and Posner on aggregation and the law has laid the theoretical groundwork for learning about people's behavior based on aggregated data.[22] In regulating the bounded ethicality of people in making hiring and firing decisions, aggregation may enable a better understanding of their various ethical biases, which might not even be clear to those making such decisions. Such an approach is especially important for dealing with situations in which people believe their choices are solely determined by relevant and permissible considerations: only aggregated data of their decisions over time can allow for a closer look at their full set of motives. The relative success of this concept in the area of employment discrimination law,[23] where the idea is that it is only possible to identify employment discrimination in the aggregate, should be expanded to more areas of law related to ordinary unethicality, where it is hard to understand the state of mind of the wrongdoers.

10.4 WAYS TO REDUCE IMPLICIT DISCRIMINATION BY "GOOD" EMPLOYERS

Efforts to reduce implicit discrimination need to consider the many legal contexts in which non-deliberate reasoning is likely to play a role in hiring and firing decisions. Such efforts also need to address discriminatory processes that operate on different levels of intentionality and awareness. The approach advocated in the book is an evidence-based combination of education, regulation, and differentiated enforcement.

10.4.1 *Masked Applications*

The masked applications approach is a relatively new method that assumes that hiring managers might, at least partially, discriminate unconsciously and are prone to automatic biases generated by stereotyped information, even though they may deny or be unaware of those biases. It calls for the removal of stereotypical information (i.e., gender, age, immigration status, and marital status) from application files and as well as the occasional use of "blind" interviews, in which the employer cannot see the candidate. In one of the classic studies on masking personal information, Goldin and Rouse showed that musicians who performed auditions behind a screen, thereby concealing their gender and age, were more likely to pass the audition and be hired than those candidates who performed in

---

[21] Compare with Sturm, S. (2001). Second generation employment discrimination: A structural approach. *Columbia Law Review, 101*, 458–668.
[22] Porat, A., & Posner, E. (2014). Offsetting benefits. *Virginia Law Review, 100*, 1165.
[23] See Sturm, *supra* note 21.

full view.[24] However, Lumb and Vail found that an attempt to help non-European candidates get accepted to medical school by masked application was unsuccessful, possibly due to the ability of application evaluators to recognize the applicants' country of origin through other details in the application.[25] In a study conducted in Sweden by Åslund and Skans, it was found that anonymous applications were effective in eliminating the effects of both race and gender discrimination in the first stage (i.e., being invited for the interview).[26] However, chances of subsequently being hired were improved only for applicants of a different gender but not for those of different races. In a study conducted in the Netherlands by Bøg and Kranendonk, which focused mostly on ethnicity, a small effect of masking identity was found in invitation-for-interview decisions, but it completely disappeared in the hiring process.[27] In a European study of the academic marketplace for those with doctorates in economics, masking personal information was shown to have a reverse effect in that fewer female applicants received invitations for interviews, relative to the traditional approach.[28]

10.4.2 *Two-tier Expressive Approach*

Another approach that accounts for the fact that there are both good and bad people and that both implicit and explicit discrimination are likely to occur stems from an idea first advocated by Krieger.[29] Given the focus on good people and bad people and the need to differentiate between them based not just on the results of their behavior but also on their motivations, it might be helpful to come up with different names for each type of discrimination based on the distinction between implicit and explicit discrimination. Such an approach prevents a situation where people who engage in situational wrongdoing and those engaged in intentional wrongdoing will be treated in a similar way. Such similar treatment undermines the social condemnation that intentional wrongdoers could receive for engaging in discriminatory practices.

Scholars have suggested various ways the law and employment practices can be redesigned to be better able to reduce implicit employment discrimination. Hiring

---

[24] Goldin, C., & Rouse, C. (1997). Orchestrating impartiality: The impact of "blind" auditions on female musicians. *National Bureau of Economic Research.* doi:w5903.

[25] Lumb, A. B., & Vail, A. (2000). Difficulties with anonymous shortlisting of medical school applications and its effects on candidates with non-European names: Prospective cohort study. *British Medical Journal,* 320(7227), 82–85.

[26] Åslund, O., & Skans, O. N. (2012). Do anonymous job application procedures level the playing field? *Industrial and Labor Relations Review,* 65(1), 82–107.

[27] Bøg, M., & Kranendonk, E. (2011). Labor market discrimination of minorities? Yes, but not in job offers. *Munich Personal RePEc Archive.* https://mpra.ub.uni-muenchen.de/33332/.

[28] Krause, A., Rinne, U., & Zimmermann, K. F. (2012). Anonymous job applications of fresh Ph.D. economists. *Economics Letters,* 117(2), 441–444.

[29] See Krieger, *supra* note 1.

and promotion procedures can be redesigned based on the social and cognitive research into how people make these decisions, for example, use of a diversified hiring team, made up of individuals likely to be more sensitive to candidates from minority groups; this should help reduce the impact of implicit discrimination. This idea is based on Jolls and Sunstein's concept of prohibiting consciously biased decision making, which suggests that the presence of population diversity in an environment tends to reduce the level of implicit bias[30]; they further argue that anti-discrimination laws reduce implicit biases because people have more opportunities to see people from various backgrounds in the workplace: "The law does not simply protect an immediate victim or set of victims from behavior deemed to be unlawful; instead, the law tends to shape and affect the level of implicit bias of all those present simply by exposing people to more positive exemplars of availability and affect heuristics."[31] In addition, "government affirmative action plans may operate as a form of direct debiasing"[32] due to the mere exposure to more employees from underrepresented minorities. The most efficient way to ensure diversity is to be committed to it, as reflected by organizational models and priorities.[33] Finally, after the fact, the litigation process in the courtroom could be redesigned to be better able to uncover implicit bias.[34]

10.4.3 *Education and Debiasing*

Training against implicit racial biases has been shown to be an effective tool in the ex ante approach to the regulation of implicit discrimination because of its ability to change people's intrinsic motivation.[35] It is important to recognize the role of internal motivation in reducing discrimination versus that of external motivation, which is promoted by the law.[36]

Levinson and Smith, in their 2012 book, *Implicit Racial Bias Across the Law*, argue that implicit racial bias is not only invisible but is also largely unintended; hence, coercion is likely to be unproductive in changing behaviors that are based on such

---

[30]   See Jolls, & Sunstein, *supra* note 1. See also Lowery, B. S., Hardin, C. D., & Sinclair, S. (2001). Social influence effects on automatic racial prejudice. *Journal of Personality and Social Psychology*, 81(5), 842–855; quote on p. 851. they found that a "simple fact of administration of an in-person IAT by an African American rather than a white experimenter significantly reduced the measured level of implicit bias".

[31]   See Jolls & Sunstein, *supra* note 1.   [32]   Ibid., p. 984. See also Krieger, *supra* note 1.

[33]   Rhode, D. L. (2012). Women and the path to leadership. *Michigan State Law Review*, 1439, 1439–1471.

[34]   Pederson, N. B. (2010). A legal framework for uncovering implicit bias. *University of Cincinnati Law Review*, 79(1), 97–153.

[35]   This follows the line of research of Lebrecht, S., Pierce, L. J., Tarr, M. J., & Tanaka, J. W. (2009). Perceptual other-race training reduces implicit racial bias. *PLoS ONE*, 4(1). See also Rudman, L. A., Ashmore, R. D., & Gary, M. L. (2001). "Unlearning" automatic biases: The malleability of implicit prejudice and stereotypes. *Journal of Personality and Social Psychology*, 81(5), 856–868.

[36]   Bartlett, K. T. (2009). Making good on good intentions: The critical role of motivation in reducing implicit workplace discrimination. *Virginia Law Review*, 1893–1972.

biases.[37] They suggest, instead, the importance of employees' internalization of values of diversity in the workplace. However, this line of work cannot address those people who *want* to act on the basis of their intentional biases.

10.4.4 *Ex ante Design of the Job Interview: Joint vs. Separate*

In her recent book, *What Works: Gender Equality by Design*, Bohnet outlines a situational design approach to reducing employment discrimination against women that incorporates elements of both the BLE and BE models.[38] In an earlier paper, Bohnet et al. showed that negative stereotypes regarding race are weaker when people evaluate others in a between-subject comparison, rather than in a within-subject comparison.[39] They explained this finding by arguing that comparing multiple candidates requires more deliberative System 2 reasoning than does making a simple yes-or-no evaluation of a single candidate, which more strongly activates System 1 thinking. Thus, when people need to decide between two or more candidates at the same time, their System 2 reasoning is activated, and so they are more likely to monitor and reduce the potentially disruptive effect of stereotypes on their decision making.

10.5 CONCLUSION

In this short chapter, we have shown how employment discrimination law has embraced the concept of dual reasoning and the related notion of implicit discrimination. Understanding why this area of law has been open to the importance of implicit process and of the distinction between "good" and "bad" employers may be helpful in our efforts to advance these concepts in other legal areas. At the same time, it is important to note that even within this area of law, there is still a gap between the legal literature and the legal doctrine, and this gap in itself can teach us important lessons on the barriers to full integration of the good people rationale within more areas of the law.

[37] Levinson, J. D., & Smith, R. J. (Eds.). (2012). *Implicit racial bias across the law*. Cambridge: Cambridge University Press.
[38] Bohnet, I. (2016). *What works: Gender equality by design*. Cambridge, MA: Belknap Press of Harvard University Press.
[39] Bazerman, M. H., Bohnet, I., & Van Geen, A. V. (2012). When performance trumps gender bias: Joint versus separate evaluation. Report No. 8506867, Harvard Kennedy School Faculty Research Working Paper Series.

11

Summary and Conclusion

In this book, I created the infrastructure for the neglected area of research on human behavior in legal theory and practice – behavioral ethics. People's inability to fully capture the social, legal, and moral meaning of their behavior and the variation in people's cognition and motivation toward the law challenge the main ideas behind both legal liability and legal enforcement. In a world that assumes there are only calculative individuals, the set of tools and the predictions about human behavior are relatively clear-cut. Yet the good people typology introduces complications and complexity. It does not replace the traditional model, but it increases the number of models that legal policy makers need to deal with simultaneously.

This book's basic premise is that, for policy making purposes, we can treat a given population as if there are types of people: the traditional "calculated" wrongdoers; the genuinely moral individuals whose wrongdoing is based only a blind spot with limited awareness to their wrong doing; and the most challenging group of "situational" wrong-doers, those who use various social and situational cues to justify (to themselves) their unethicality. The bad/calculated people the law always focused on are not about to disappear, but they are just one of at least three types of people whose wrongdoing should be regulated both *ex ante* and *ex post*.[1] We also know that there are individual differences and variation within each group, as discussed in Chapter 6. Complicating the situation further is that many in the largest group of "good people" might still be somewhat aware of their wrongdoing. As shown in Chapters 2 and 5, many of the cognitive mechanisms that people use make them somewhat unaware of the processes through which they justify unethicality. The variation both in the level of awareness of wrongdoing and mechanisms used to allow people to break the law while still feeling that they are normative individuals makes it even more difficult to regulate "good people."[2]

---

[1] Although the ex post part is far more discussed in law, mainly through the concept of negligence; for a classic discussion, see Terry, H. T. (1915). Negligence. *Harvard Law Review*, 29(1), 40–54.

[2] For example, Tenbrunsel, A. E., Diekmann, K. A., Wade-Benzoni, K. A., & Bazerman, M. H. (2010). The ethical mirage: A temporal explanation as to why we are not as ethical as we think we are. *Research in Organizational Behavior*, 30, 153–173.

In this final chapter, I present concluding thoughts on the interaction between behavioral ethics and law. I examine the important role of intrinsic motivation in a "good people world," given the overwhelming evidence of its ability to change both their perception and behaviors.[3] I then present a taxonomy that would help the state organize its regulatory and enforcement efforts. I conclude with a discussion of limitations in BE research, unanswered questions, and research efforts needed to answer them, so that states will be able to more effectively regulate the behavior of both good and bad people.

There are three main approaches to designing interventions: an integrated approach, where all means are used simultaneously; a consecutive approach, where the different interventions are used one after the other toward a smaller and smaller portion of the population; and the differentiated approach, in which a different approach is adopted for each situation. The most relevant conceptual framework for the differentiated approach is a taxonomy that includes the most relevant factors when attempting to implement and enforce a policy initiative: the type of regulated behavior, the target population, the cost of enforcement and of noncompliance, and the proportion of the population whose cooperation is required for successful implementation of the mechanism.

11.1 THE INTEGRATED APPROACH

Given the difficulty of determining individuals' awareness of the unethical nature of their decisions, BE suggests focusing on aggregating people's decisions as proof of wrongdoing. As noted in the previous chapter that focused on employment discrimination, that area of the law incorporates most fully the behavioral ethics approach. The focus on aggregated enforcement can be understood by analogy from work in the area of employment discrimination, as discussed in the previous chapter,[4] where the inability to penetrate people's minds has led, in some cases, to an aggregated approach to evaluating decision making. Beginning with *Griggs* v. *Duke Power Co.* (1971), the US Supreme Court has recognized that although it is not mandated that the workforce of a company should replicate the composition of the general population, statistical disparity between the two can be used as compelling evidence of employment discrimination under a disparate impact theory[5]. According to this theory, even if it is impossible to prove that the employer intended to treat candidates differently, the fact that the employer used criteria that resulted in discrimination against a class of individuals is sufficient to establish illegitimate discrimination.

[3] See Chapter 6, which deals with individual variance.
[4] Fienberg, S. E. (Ed.). (2012). *The evolving role of statistical assessments as evidence in the courts.* New York: Springer Science & Business Media. Krieger, L. H. (1995). The content of our categories: A cognitive bias approach to discrimination and equal employment opportunity. *Stanford Law Review,* 47(6), 1161.
[5] Shoben, E. W. (1983). The use of statistics to prove intentional employment discrimination. *Law and Contemporary Problems,* 46(4), 221–245.

Similarly, in the realm of bounded ethicality, rather than assuming bad intentions when we cannot prove them, it may be possible to collect data on ethical decisions over time and create criteria to be applied if the aggregation of behaviors indicates that one should have been aware of the negative effect of one's actions. For example, misuse of office supplies or the improper acceptance of gifts may be considered misbehavior even if any one instance of such conduct is merely questionable. A sufficient number of marginal instances can warrant sanctioning, regardless of the actor's intent. Important jurisprudential work needs to be done to justify increasing one's responsibility for one event based merely on the fact that it has been repeated. However, given the difficulty of determining responsibility for isolated events and the ability of System 2 to predict the likelihood that such unethicality will recur, a solution of this type may be necessary and appropriate.

Research into the dual-reasoning systems, the crowding-out effect, and intrinsic versus extrinsic motivation makes clear that people react to the law in more ways than previously assumed. This book therefore advocates an integrated approach that incorporates both nontraditional and traditional methods of regulation and enforcement. This approach reflects a change not only in the mix of interventions used but also in their design and sensitivity.

Yet, even an integrated approach finds it difficult to determine ex ante the people who are likely not to comply with the law. We have suggested various methods to account for this variation in the population: acoustic separation, use of a taxonomy, and accounting for the level of intrinsic motivation toward a specific legal doctrine. For example, legal instruments, such as regulations and contracts, can be designed in ways that differentiate between the motivations of good and bad people to meet their obligations[6]; differences in cultures can be addressed when attempting to change tax compliance norms. Designing rules in a legitimate way and creating effective deterrence methods can also help reinforce traditional mechanisms of enforcement, which will affect both good and bad people. *Ex post*, the research paradigm can help courts and other enforcement agencies understand the severity and intentionality of various misconducts.

11.1.1 *The Sequential Approach to Behaviorally Based Regulation*

Probably the most coherent approach to regulation that takes into account the different functions of law, the differences between people, and the differences between situations is the paradigm of responsive regulation.

---

[6] For an illustration of this point, see Feldman, Y., & Smith, H. E. (2014). Behavioral equity. *Journal of Institutional and Theoretical Economics*, 170(1), 137–159. See also Feldman, Y., & Teichman, D. (2011). Are all contractual obligations created equal? *Georgetown Law Journal*, 100, 5; Feldman, Y., & Lifshitz, S. (2011). Behind the veil of legal uncertainty. *Law & Contemporary Problems*, 74, 133.

According to Ayres and Braithwaite's responsive regulation pyramid of regulation approach, most people in a population react to less strict interventions.[7] The stricter interventions will be used in a sequential way toward the portion of the population that does not react to previous more lenient messages.[8]

According to Tyler and Trinker,[9] it is possible to design interventions based on people's intrinsic motivation, beginning with those that target considerations of morality, fairness, and social values and then moving to a harsher approach to the minority of people who are more calculated wrongdoers. Similar arguments were made in the context of using trust-based approaches to virtuous people in society.[10] This sequential move from soft to hard regulation may align with a move from nontraditional and situational enforcement, which focuses on good people, to traditional enforcement, which is always in the background but will come into play when nontraditional enforcement fails. However, while the approach of Tyler and that of Ayres and Braithwaite holds that soft regulation is mostly preferable to hard regulation, we recognize that nontraditional means such as nudges suffer from many limitations that make them inferior to traditional enforcement methods that involve deliberation.

The rest of the chapter focuses on two main strategies that legal policy makers can adopt to address variation among people: reducing the impact of ethical biases by changing people's motivation and using taxonomies that offer a set of considerations to take into account when fitting the right type of intervention to a specific behavior.

11.2 TAXONOMY AS A TOOL TO MODIFY THE ONE-SIZE-FITS-ALL POLICY

The taxonomy presented here highlights the areas in which greater scrutiny of the ethical behavior of individuals should be exercised. It takes into account both traditional factors, such as the level of monitoring, intrinsic loyalty toward the organization, and compliance with prevailing norms, as well as nontraditional factors: the type of individual we are attempting to regulate, the moral "wiggle room" of the situation, the relative availability of excuses for justifying behavior, and whether the task can be accomplished without cognitive focus. As suggested in earlier chapters, various policy trade-offs will emerge because each intervention has its own pros and cons. Trade-offs

---

[7] Ayres, I., & Braithwaite, J. (1995). *Responsive regulation: Transcending the deregulation debate.* Oxford University Press on Demand.

[8] For some of the recent work in this tradition, see Leviner, S. (2008). A new era of tax enforcement: From big stick to responsive regulation. *University of Michigan Journal of Law Reform, 42,* 381. See also Baldwin, R. (2014). From regulation to behaviour change: Giving nudge the third degree. *Modern Law Review, 77*(6), 831–857; Alemanno, A., & Spina, A. (2014). Nudging legally: On the checks and balances of behavioral regulation. *International Journal of Constitutional Law, 12*(2), 429–456.

[9] Tyler, T. R., & Trinker, R. (2018). *Why children follow rules: Legal socialization and the development of legitimacy.* Oxford: Oxford University Press.

[10] Pettit, P. (1995). The cunning of trust. *Philosophy & Public Affairs, 24*(3), 202–225; Cherney, A. (1997). Trust as regulatory strategy: A theoretical review. *Current Issues in Criminal Justice, 9,* 71.

and dilemmas include the following: should there be public discourse on nudges, should we worry more when people make decisions in a group context, should we revise deterrence to deal with non-deliberative effects, and how can we affect good people without harming the credibility of state treatment of the bad ones.

11.2.1 *What Is the Nature of the Behavior?*

The key component is the behavior the policy maker wishes to promote, and its nature will determine the relative importance of intrinsic motivation. Why one engages in recycling or organ donation is not important[11]; for the most part, policy makers only care only about the activity level and willingness to pay for compliance. In other contexts, however, such as whistle-blowing or even blood donation, intrinsic motivation seems to play a larger role. Furthermore, in legal contexts, where "extra-role" activity is desired, the cost of harming intrinsic motivation increases and one should be more cautious in introducing extrinsic motives. Where there is a high cost of enforcement or a great need for sustainability of behavior, there may need to be a stronger reliance on deliberation and preventing illegality.

11.2.2 *What Proportion of the Target Population Needs to Cooperate for the Policy to Work?*

Another important dimension is what proportion of the target population should be targeted when the level of intrinsic motivation is heterogeneous. In earlier research, I focused empirically on the ability to change the behavior of people in three types of activities: recycling and file sharing, which I put in a category of "the more the merrier"; whistle-blowing, which I put in the category of "it only takes one to help"; and divulgence of trade secrets, which can be put in the category of "it only takes one to harm." These three examples help us think about the importance of being aware of legal contexts when determining how to change the behavior of a given population with regard to a given doctrine.

In the area of trade secrets,[12] everyone needs to be motivated for the secret not to be disclosed, because even if only a very few people are not affected by the legal instrument, it may be futile to keep company knowledge proprietary. Clearly the value of the trade secret diminishes when more than a handful of unauthorized

[11]   But this is not the case with regard to blood donation.
[12]   It should be noted that when speaking about trade secrets, the focus here is on their narrow definition, which focuses on the core proprietary knowledge of a given company. Lobel, O. (2013). *Talent wants to be free: Why we should learn to love leaks, raids, and free riding*, Vol. 1. New Haven: Yale University Press, has argued for the importance of information spillover between firms. In that regard, we wish to narrow our argument for the core knowledge of the firm, rather than the types of information that would be better off shared among companies. See also Feldman, Y. (2009). The expressive function of the trade secret law: Legality, cost, intrinsic motivation and consensus. *Journal of Empirical Legal Studies*, 6(1), 177.

people know about it. In this context, we have to focus on the lowest common denominator, meaning that those with the lowest level of intrinsic motivation to be loyal to the company should be the focus of the regulation. Since variation in motivations is likely to increase the chance of making mistakes and mistakes are costly in such contexts, a greater emphasis should be given to making sure that at the least we get minimal compliance by all employees. The price of harming the intrinsic motivation of committed employees might be secondary to making sure that even those without intrinsic motivation will be loyal to their employers.

The whistle-blowing context is the exact opposite, where we only need the cooperation of some of the employees who will go forward when some illegal activity occurs within the organization. Therefore, we mainly care about those who are high on intrinsic motivation and may not even want to incentivize those without intrinsic motivation due to a fear of generating false reports from bounty hunters.

Finally, in the context of recycling[13] and file sharing,[14] we are interested in averaging or in a situation where as many people as possible will recycle as much as possible or buy media content legally. Outcomes are important, but they are long term and aggregate. Although the ultimate goal is to move as many people as possible to environmentally responsible behaviors, private noncompliance is not very costly. In such a situation, we have no preference for either high or low intrinsically motivated individuals; therefore, the policy maker must balance whether or not to use extrinsic motivation and through which types of incentives. In this context, making a few mistakes in targeting people's motivations is not costly since the effort is to increase the average level of recycling.

11.2.3 Is There a Moral Consensus with Regard to the Behavior in Question?

Another important dimension derived from the research on intrinsic versus extrinsic motivation is the extent to which the behavior that the state is attempting to regulate is within the moral consensus of the population.[15] When there is a moral consensus and a population is likely to have a high level of intrinsic motivation to comply, the policy maker could rely on non-coercive explicit measures or an increase in the proportion of softer types of implicit intervention.

In my work with Lobel,[16] we found that the level of moral consensus had an interesting effect on regulation: the greater the perception of severity of the

13 Feldman, Y., & Perez, O. (2012). Motivating environmental action in a pluralistic regulatory environment: An experimental study of framing, crowding out, and institutional effects in the context of recycling policies. *Law & Society Review*, 46(2), 405–442.
14 Feldman, Y., & Nadler, J. (2006). The law and norms of file sharing. *San Diego Law Review*, 43, 577.
15 See in this context the discussion in Chapters 4 and 6 of Aquino's work on the accessibility of morality. Aquino, K., & Reed II, A. (2002). The self-importance of moral identity. *Journal of Personality and Social Psychology*, 83(6), 1423.
16 Feldman, Y., & Lobel, O. (2009). The incentives matrix: The comparative effectiveness of rewards, liabilities, duties, and protections for reporting illegality. *Texas Law Review*, 88, 1151.

misconduct, the less important was the choice of regulatory mechanism. In our analysis, we used severity of the misconduct as a proxy for internal motivation.[17] In the group of participants who viewed the illegality as highly offensive, and hence had high levels of internal motivation for reporting, the type of mechanism available to them to do so was largely irrelevant. Respondents expected their own reporting levels and those of others to remain consistently high across all categories of legal mechanisms. Thus, in areas where the misconduct is expected to trigger high internal motivation, there is less need to invest in incentive mechanisms.

However, when illegalities witnessed by potential enforcers were perceived as less severe, the use of high rewards and fines produced considerably higher levels of reporting than the use of low rewards. These findings suggest the importance of legal mechanism selection in instances where individuals do not have an ethical stake in compliance. In such cases, triggering external motivation through regulatory policy takes on a far greater role in promoting reporting activity. Therefore, regulatory agencies may consider providing high monetary rewards when the goal is to incentivize reports in contexts that evoke less moral outrage, such as tax evasion.

The same argument seems to apply to the good/bad people dichotomy: a greater focus on extrinsic measures should be used in areas where higher percentages of the population are unlikely to explicitly be interested in pursuing the behavior. That is why crime prevention focuses on the bad person, even though the vast majority of the population will be restrained from committing a crime by their moral constraints. However, the harm caused by even one person committing a crime is so high that we focus on harsh, extrinsic methods.

11.2.4 *How Long Does the Behavior Change Need to Last?*

Whether the behavior only occurs once or is repeated is another important consideration. For example, in encouraging enrollment in a pension plan, the focus is on the initial decision; getting people to participate (outcome being the dominant focus) is important. Once they have made their choice, people are less likely to reverse it; sustainability is less important than in areas such as health or nutrition, where choices need to be reaffirmed on a daily basis. Similarly, the focus on expressive versus invisible law is also dependent on context. In areas where the expertise of the state as well as the moral or consensual bases are high, highlighting the expressive law might outweigh the costs associated with informing people that the choice architecture presented to them is based on law. In social issues in which preferences for a deliberative process are strong and existing legal solutions are contested, more weight should be given to process. Focusing on trust may be more important in areas that are difficult to monitor, whereas focusing on directed regulation is desirable when enforcement costs are relatively low.

---

[17] This factor included items such as moral outrage, legitimacy, and perceived risk from the misconduct.

11.2.5 *What Is the Cost of Noncompliance?*

In some situations, the costs of noncompliance are disproportionately large relative to the benefits of targeting intrinsic motivation. Since variation in motivations is likely to increase the chance of regulation being ineffective and mistakes are costly, in-depth analysis of the level of desirable compliance and its counter-costs becomes crucial. In the context of trade secrets, one egregious leak may be detrimental to a company,[18] while with many environmental protections, a failure of one individual to recycle is not consequential because what are important are long-term and aggregate behaviors. Some private noncompliance is thus not very costly.

11.3 NEW DIRECTIONS IN BEHAVIORAL ETHICS AND THE LAW

In addition to the three approaches suggested earlier, more general ideas could be used to change the unethical and illegal behavior of good people.

11.3.1 *Situational Design*

Given the fact that many individuals make choices without full awareness, it might make sense to place more of the responsibility for wrongdoing that occurs in organizational contexts on the organization itself. Doing so will incentivize the organization to design the situation in a way that will facilitate compliance and discourage wrongdoing. This shift in responsibility should be reinforced by state regulation and legal policy, which would focus on making it hard for people to find rationales for noncompliance.

11.3.2 *Smarter Use of Uncertainty*

Legal ambiguity has varying effects both on the ability to understand the meaning of various concepts in laws, contracts, and organizational codes and on subsequent decision making. Haisley and Weber, for example, found that people prefer ambiguous risks when such ambiguity allows them to justify their unfair behavior.[19] Dana et al. found that people are less generous in situations in which they can use moral ambiguity to explain their selfish behavior.[20] Similarly, Hsee found evidence that people make choices that satisfy their preferences at the cost of not completing an

---

[18] At the same time, here too an overly broad definition of trade secrets and misappropriation can have detrimental consequences to innovation. See Lobel, *supra* note 12. See also Feldman, *supra* note 1.

[19] Haisley, E. C., & R. A. Weber. (2010). Self-serving interpretations of ambiguity in other-regarding behavior. *Games and Economic Behavior*, 68(2), 614–625.

[20] Dana, J., Weber, R. A., & Kuang J. Xi. (2007). Exploiting moral wiggle room: Experiments demonstrating an illusory preference for fairness. *Economic Theory*, 33(1), 67–80.

assigned goal, if they can exploit existing ambiguity about what decision can be considered as having achieved the assigned goal.[21]

11.3.2.1 Intrinsic Motivation and Implicit Unethicality

Finally, the most obvious but not less important approach could be not to assume good people's implicit or somewhat explicit unethicality and work with it, but rather to attempt to at least change some of the motivation that underlies it.

11.3.2.2 The Dynamics of the Unethicality of Situational Wrongdoers

As mentioned earlier, the role of intrinsic motivation is related to the broader discussion that lies at the heart of behavioral ethics: the interaction between motivation and cognition, particularly how people's motivation toward the law affects the likelihood of transgressions happening with limited awareness. The literature reviewed in Chapter 2 suggests the important role of enhanced self-control, which is mostly associated with System 2 reasoning, in curbing unethicality. Thus, heightening the awareness of people that they need to behave ethically might force System 2 to kick in. However, to the extent that we view this awareness as the product not only of the situation but also of the motivation to avoid doing harm, policy makers should do more than target people's cognitive awareness: they need to also make people want to avoid engaging in that wrongdoing. Thus, whether people are "good" or "bad" seems to be related both to motivation and cognition. Furthermore, the distinction between the two types of good people makes the interaction between motivation and cognition even more complex. The genuinely moral individual will only do bad things under conditions of limited cognition (blind spot). However, situational wrongdoers are somewhat aware that what they are doing is bad, but their motivation is too weak to prohibit them from using justifications to allow themselves to do it. Seeing that everyone is parking illegally mostly reduces their motivation to follow the rules and increases their ability to view themselves as good people while parking illegally, despite knowing perfectly well that it is illegal. Clearly, when such behavior becomes a habit, there will be more and more reliance on automatic reasoning; hence, with limited motivation to comply with the law, we might see an increase in people engaging in misconduct that does not cause any active moral dilemma for them. Such processes are hard to measure in classical short-term psychological experiments but are widely recognized in the sociological research on internalization.[22]

---

[21] Hsee, C. K. (1995). Elastic justification: How tempting but task-irrelevant factors influence decisions. *Organizational Behavior and Human Decision Processes*, 62(3), 330–337.

[22] For a review on internalization and socialization processes with regard to wrongdoing, see Feldman, Y. (2003). Experimental approach to the study of normative failures: Divulging of trade secrets by Silicon Valley employees. *University of Illinois Journal of Law, Technology, and Policy*, 105, which uses this literature to understand Silicon Valley engineers' practices of trade secrets' divulgence.

11.3.2.3 Can We Create Good People?

The previous description, combined with earlier chapters that examined the role of morality in legal compliance (Chapters 3 and 5) raised the question of the feasibility of increasing levels of intrinsic motivation to obey the law. This section draws attention to another aspect of intrinsic motivation: its ability to reduce non-deliberative biases and thus make the automatic system more ethical. The goal of legal policy can thus be reformulated to create a situation in which people are intrinsically motivated not to be cognitively biased to their own unethicality.

A growing number of studies demonstrate that by changing people's motivation, we are able to change their non-deliberate wrongdoing.[23] The best-known research is by Devine, who has studied automatic and controlled components of stereotypes and prejudice and the ability to change those automatic components.[24] In different works on the topic Inzlicht and his collaborators[25] found that people can be motivated to overcome their unethical biases. While such a line of research might undermine the justification for this whole book, it is important to note that it is unclear to what extent this change is durable over time. I am not yet aware of a study that has compared, for example, the efficacy of nudges vs. intrinsic motivation in changing people's ethical behavior in the long run. However, from the literature it seems that motivation can sometimes change implicit biases without any cognitive tricks, mostly through changing people's intentions.

This accords with another of our basic premises – that there has been too much attention to the role of cognitive mechanisms in influencing behavior and too little focus on the important role of intrinsic motivation. What we learn from scholars such as Bazerman, Tenbrunsel, Devine and Inzlicht is that intrinsic motivation matters for behaviors with limited cognition. Even under legal policy that is sensitive to non-deliberative choice and even with various nudges that communicate directly

---

[23] It make sense to remember at this stage the earlier works on learning conducted by Skinner, whose approach to learning focused directly (albeit not explicitly) on changing people's automatic reasoning (think of Pavlov's famous findings regarding the effect on dogs' reaction to noise associated with food). In that regard much of the research on learning has tended to focus on changing people's automatic behavior. The possibility of repeating such trials to make people's System 1 more ethical seems to be unrealistic for any liberal mind. Nonetheless, it is possible to think of some religious rituals as attempting to make people's automatic behavior more moral. This concept is discussed from a different perspective in the research on embodiment and religion; see, for example, Zhong, C. B., & Liljenquist, K. (2006). Washing away your sins: Threatened morality and physical cleansing. *Science*, 313(5792), 1451–1452.

[24] Devine, P. G. (1989). Stereotypes and prejudice: Their automatic and controlled components. *Journal of Personality and Social Psychology*, 56(1), 5.

[25] See, for example, Teper, R., Segal, Z. V., & Inzlicht, M. (2013). Inside the mindful mind: How mindfulness enhances emotion regulation through improvements in executive control. *Current Directions in Psychological Science*, 22(6), 449–454; Milyavskaya, M., Inzlicht, M., Hope, N., & Koestner, R. (2015). Saying "no" to temptation: Want-to motivation improves self-regulation by reducing temptation rather than by increasing self-control. *Journal of Personality and Social Psychology*, 109(4), 677; Inzlicht, M., Schmeichel, B. J., & Macrae, C. N. (2014). Why self-control seems (but may not be) limited. *Trends in Cognitive Sciences*, 18(3), 127–133.

with people's automatic systems, motivation plays an important part in regulating good people and facilitating their compliance, rather than just punishing them for their unethicality. In the next section, we focus on the implementation of these arguments in the area of motivational training.

11.3.3 *Motivational and Cognitive Training in Reducing Ethical Biases*

Bazerman and Tenbrunsel have suggested various techniques for people to become aware of their limited ability to recognize their ethical failings and so reduce their prejudices and in general behave more ethically.[26] For example, focusing on the "should" rather than the "want" self, Bazerman and Gino[27] suggested that people should consider beforehand what "want" desires might come into play at moments of decision making. They can then be better prepared to resist these desires and instead implement a decision based on their ethically sound "should" preferences. Bazerman and Gino use the example of a common interview question asked of job applicants: What pay has a competing employer offered you? The "want" self is likely to wish to inflate the number, encouraging the applicant to lie to the potential employer. By anticipating this, one can come up with a more acceptable answer, such as "I'm not comfortable sharing that information," which serves the applicant's self-interest but also does not violate moral rules. This "should" vs. "want" approach recognizes areas in which people might cut corners and tries to anticipate those situations in advance.

In a series of experiments, Devine et al. showed that it is possible to train people to be less affected by their implicit racial biases and that this change is long lasting.[28] At a minimum, these experiments support the claim that even if we are unaware of the automatic components of our behaviors, we may be able to control them after participating in training. In the field of social cognition, which is mostly related to employment discrimination, there seems to be consensus that stereotypes can be altered with various training techniques.[29]

11.3.3.1 Behavioral Ethics and the Rise of Behavioral Insight Teams

It is impossible today to analyze the relationship between law and the behavioral sciences without accounting for the enormous success of the behavioral insight

---

[26] Bazerman, M. H., & Tenbrunsel, A. E. (2011). *Blind spots: Why we fail to do what's right and what to do about it.* Princeton: Princeton University Press.

[27] Bazerman, M. H., & Gino, F. (2012). Behavioral ethics: Toward a deeper understanding of moral judgment and dishonesty. *Annual Review of Law and Social Science, 8,* 85–104.

[28] For example, Devine, P. G., Forscher, P. S., Austin, A. J., & Cox, W. T. (2012). Long-term reduction in implicit race bias: A prejudice habit-breaking intervention. *Journal of Experimental Social Psychology, 48*(6), 1267–1278.

[29] Blair, I. V. (2002). The malleability of automatic stereotypes and prejudice, *Personality & Social Psychology Review, 6,* 242; Monteith, M. J. et al. (2002). Putting the brakes on prejudice: On the development and operation of cues for control. *Journal of Personality & Social Psychology, 83,* 1029.

teams (BITs) that have sprung up worldwide.[30] In fact, the most important change in behavioral-legal scholarship in recent years has been the BIT revolution, based on the influential nudge approach.[31] BITs advise governments on how to use knowledge derived from psychology and behavioral economics to shape people's behavior in socially desirable ways.[32] In 2010, the United Kingdom set up the Behavioural Insights Team, popularly called the "Nudge Unit," to apply behavioral research findings to public policy.[33] In July 2013, news sources reported that the White House was planning to assemble a similar team in the United States. According to a government document, the team would aim to "scale behavioral interventions that have been rigorously evaluated, using, where possible, randomized controlled trials." The document also described several policy initiatives that had already benefited from implementation of these behavioral insight teams: getting people back to work; improving academic performance; and increasing college enrollment and retention, retirement savings, adoption of energy-efficient measures, and tax compliance.

Despite criticism of the BITs from those concerned about "big brother" and "nanny state" policies, the great interest in applying behavioral insights indicates a growing consensus among regulators about the validity and effectiveness of bringing behavioral economics into law. A leading behavioral economist and advisor to the UK's Behavioural Insights Team, Richard Thaler, distills his advice for policy makers into two succinct points: first, if you want to encourage some activity, you need to make it easy, and second, you cannot create evidence-based policies without evidence.

The policies adopted based on the work of the BITs vary considerably. Most of the initiatives focus on setting consumer defaults and understanding choice

---

[30]   For more elaboration on this point, See Feldman, Y., & Lobel, O. (2015). Behavioral trade-offs: Beyond the land of nudges spans the world of law and psychology. In A. Alemanno & A. L. Sibony (Eds.), *Nudge and the law: A European perspective.* Oxford: Hart.

[31]   Sunstein, C. R., Pratt, S., & Thaler, R. H. (2014). *Nudge: Improving decisions about health, wealth, and happiness.* New Haven: Yale University Press. For a recent collection of papers on nudge see Alemanno & Sibony, Nudge and the law.

[32]   The EU, a latecomer to this game, has recently established a task force that published a guideline report, describing how policy makers should use psychology when implementing behaviorally based legal policy in areas related to health and consumer choices. In recent years, many organizations such as the World Bank and the OECD have prepared reports identifying behavioral sciences as one of the main focuses of governments. Both the UK and US governments rely increasingly on insights from behavioral sciences, especially with regard to non-deliberative choice by individuals. See Behavioural Insights Team, The Behavioural Insights Team Update report 2013–2015 (2015), www.behaviouralinsights.co.uk/wp-content/uploads/2015/07/BIT_Update-Report-Final-2013–2015.pdf; For the report of 2016–7 see http://www.behaviouralinsights.co.uk/publications/the-behavioural-insights-team-update-report-2016-17. See also Executive Order – Using Behavioral Science Insights to Better Serve the American People whitehouse.gov (2015), www.whitehouse.gov/the-press-office/2015/09/15/executive-order-using-behavioral-science-insights-better-serve-american; for their latest report see https://sbst.gov/download/2016%20SBST%20Annual%20Report.pdf and René van Bavel et al., Applying behavioural sciences to EU policy-making: Policy brief (2013), http://ec.europa.eu/dgs/health_food-safety/information_sources/docs/30092013_jrc_scientific_policy_report_en.pdf. See also Alemanno & Sibony, *supra* note 30.

[33]   For a review of the history and achievements of this unit, see Halpern, D. (2016). *Inside the nudge unit: How small changes can make a big difference.* New York: Random House.

architecture. Such initiatives consider ways in which decision making can be improved by packaging information and choices differently, for example, by changing the set default to opt-out rather than opt-in. Success stories have included improvements in school nutrition, increased use of paperless printing, and increased enrollment in pension plans and health insurance.[34] As with the behavioral analysis of law, the focus of the BIT movement is on improving choices in contexts related to finance, health, the environment, and energy.[35]

BITs, however, have been far less effective in regulating ethical behaviors that are clearly the domain of legal doctrines and are largely subject to traditional regulatory and enforcement practices.[36] The literature on the BIT approach to mainstream legal enforcement is weak, mostly because it lacks the conceptual ability to influence areas that are being regulated by substantial legal doctrines such as administrative law, contract law, and tort law. Because of these limitations, hardly any legal scholars[37] are currently active in leading BIT initiatives or within academic frameworks aimed at generating knowledge for these initiatives.[38] I hope that the suggested shift to BE also leads to a conceptual change and increased legal scholarship on the BIT initiative.

11.3.3.2 The Challenges of Ethical Nudges

In Chapter 4, we discussed the overlooked difference between the effectiveness of "cognitive" nudges and that of "ethical" nudges: nudge-like measures are more effective in a heuristics-and-biases context than in the context of unethical behavior. In the former context, nudges are often used to align people's decisions with their true self-interest (e.g., saving more money), whereas in the context of unethical behavior, they seek to suppress the actor's self-interest (e.g., making one less likely to give a job promotion to a friend) and are therefore likely to encounter greater motivational resistance from people to overcome these ethical biases[39]). Indeed, as described in Chapter 1 in the discussion of the differences between behavioral ethics and behavioral economics, BITs around the world address bounded rationality, helping people achieve more desirable solutions by removing decision-making constraints; however, it is much more difficult to remedy biases associated with

[34] Sunstein, C. R. (2014). *Simpler: The future of government*. New York: Simon & Schuster.

[35] Shu, L. L., Mazar, N., Gino, F., Ariely, D., & Bazerman, M. H. (2012). Signing at the beginning makes ethics salient and decreases dishonest self-reports in comparison to signing at the end. *Proceedings of the National Academy of Sciences*, 109(38), 15197–15200.

[36] Most of its focus has been on pension savings, health issues, energy savings, and being smarter consumers.

[37] With the exception of Cass Sunstein, who is a legal scholar.

[38] For example, BX2015 | Behavioural Exchange Insights Conference 2015, BX2015 | Behavioural Exchange Insights Conference 2015 (2016), www.bx2015.org.

[39] Zamir, E., Teichman, D., & Feldman, Y. (2014). Behavioral ethics meets behavioral law and economics. In. E. Zamir & D. Teichman (Eds.), The Oxford Handbook of Behavioral Economics and the Law, 1. *Oxford: Oxford University Press*, pp. 213–241.

behavioral ethics, because doing so deals with people's motivation to obey the law and with their sense of morality. In addition, people often do their best to ignore the ethical challenges of a given situation. Attempting to cause people to behave more ethically is complex because the various BE mechanisms do not provide indications of whether the good people are indeed "good." In the classical BIT approach, the behaviors to be modified are those that most people would try to avoid if they spent enough time thinking about them (e.g., saving for retirement), whereas in BE, when talking about doctrines such as implicit corruption, it is not clear whether there is any objective factor toward which individuals should work in the sense that they would regret it if they failed to accomplish it. This is not the case when it comes to ethicality, where people's main self-interest is to preserve their self-conception as ethical people and not necessarily to actually behave ethically. Thus, in the ethical world, with the exception of the enforcement authorities, there is no external threshold to their level of ethicality. However, in the financial world, the energy world, and the health world (which are the bread and butter of the cognitive biases), the external threshold will be the price of gasoline, their health, and their weight.[40]

Therefore, the effect of ethical nudges is more limited than that of more typical nudges attempting to improve levels of saving or health. In financial and health matters, people's true self-interest is always present, and reminding them of it helps. In contrast, in ethical nudges, most people's true self-interest is to maintain their self-image of ethicality, not to behave ethically. Therefore, nudges help only to the extent that they succeed in challenging individuals' self-image as moral people. However, they may be more effective for the genuinely good people whose unethicality is mostly the product of automatic and largely unconscious biases. For such individuals, nudge-like measures might help them overcome these biases.

The limited attention paid to the improvement of ethical decision making is evident in other domains. At present, behavior-based legal policy does not deal with the much larger issues of how to create a just society, how to generate respect for the rule of law, or how to use the law to decrease various automatic processes that are involved in corruption, intolerance, and discrimination. The psychological discussion of non-deliberative choice remains on the margins of legal theory; it assists states in mobilizing citizens to save energy or save for their pensions, but it does not help people become more ethical or states more just.[41]

To summarize: first, the "Law of Good People" paradigm paradigm and the new intervention methods advocated by nudge and BIT, rather than modifying the traditional mechanisms of the state, have unjustifiably abandoned them, without

[40] For a very smart analysis of the usage of ethical nudges in enforcement of unethicality in corporations see Haugh, T., The ethics of intracorporate behavioral ethics. *California Law Review Online*, 8(1). SSRN: https://ssrn.com/abstract=2982434.
[41] This is not to undermine the importance of these initiatives; however, those types of interventions do not really deal with areas of legal substance such as conflict of interest, employment discrimination, and rule of law.

conducting the required empirical and normative evaluation of the advantages and disadvantages of new soft intervention techniques relative to the traditional ones.[42] Second, exploring the behavioral, social, legal, and institutional aspects of a wide spectrum of situations in which BITs can prove effective and legitimate makes it easier to integrate these types of interventions within the legal arsenal.

11.3.4 The Perils of Changing People's Non-deliberative Ethical Choices through External Regulatory Interventions

Scholars such as Bartlett suggest that for people to be able to change their implicit associations, they need to believe that they have autonomy and free choice or else any external intervention might backfire.[43] The argument goes that using some form of legal intervention or deterrence, which by definition calls for some restriction on people's autonomy, might negatively affect the ability of people to reduce implicit bias. It is possible to argue that changing people's level of intrinsic motivation may seem to be futile, as external motivation techniques such as incentives may crowd out and inhibit altruistic motivations. However, some studies do support the idea that extrinsic motivation can increase intrinsic motivation. The relationship between regulation and intrinsic motivation is a complicated one and is affected by several variables. For example, my work with Smith and Boussalis explored the interrelations between specificity, fairness, and monitoring. As described in Chapter 7, specificity in itself can interact with both morality and deterrence in any given context. This line of research is supported by work on the expressive function of the law, described in Chapter 3, with a focus on the ability of law in the areas of trade secrets, environmental law, and file sharing to change people's perception of what is moral.[44]

As described in more detail in Chapter 7 on the pluralistic account of law, the crowding-out literature generally finds that extrinsic motivation undermines intrinsic motivation. Fehr[45] argued that when people attribute their behavior to external rewards, they discount their moral incentives for their behavior, thereby lowering the apparent effect of intrinsic motivation. For example, paying people to donate blood causes donors to view the donation as a transaction, rather than a charitable act, eroding altruistic blood donations. Similarly, in a series of lab-based experiments, Deci and colleagues argued that "tangible rewards tend to have

---

[42] Compare with the work of Milkman, K. L., Chugh, D., & Bazerman, M. H. (2009). How can decision making be improved? *Perspectives on Psychological Science*, 4(4), 379–383.

[43] Bartlett, K. T. (2009). Making good on good intentions: The critical role of motivation in reducing implicit workplace discrimination. *Virginia Law Review*, 1893–1972. Her argument is mostly based on the research conducted by Plant, E. A. & Devine, P. G. (2001). Responses to other-imposed pro-black pressure: acceptance or backlash? *Journal of Experimental Social Psychology*, 37, 486.

[44] See discussion on pp. 60, 62, 108.

[45] Fehr, E., & Falk, A. (2002). Psychological foundations of incentives. *European Economic Review*, 46 (4), 687–724.

a substantially negative effect on intrinsic motivation."[46] In a similar vein, Marshall and Harrison suggested that the use of incentives can damage self-esteem, resulting in the perception that professionalism is no longer valued.[47]

Thus, external interventions can sometimes have reverse effects.[48] Inzlicht and colleagues examined the effect of motivation (internal-autonomous vs. external-controlled) on people with explicit prejudice. They showed that intrinsic motivation techniques focusing on increasing autonomy were more successful than using control to motivate prejudice reduction. In a second study that replicated the same type of motivations, but by using priming, a similar pattern emerged, where controlled motivation had what they called an "ironic" effect on prejudice.

Yet a more nuanced view holds that the effect of incentives is not linear, but rather that "intermediate" payouts have a disproportionately high crowding-out effect compared with low or high payout levels. Tenbrunsel and Messick argued that a weak system of sanctions produces worse results than having no sanctions at all.[49] By introducing a sanctioning system, the principal changes the evaluation of the problem from an ethical dilemma to a business decision, consequently shifting individual considerations away from ethics and toward self-interest.[50] Research done by Devine et al. has shown that explicit racial bias was moderated by internal motivation to respond without prejudice, whereas implicit racial bias was moderated by the interaction of internal and external motivation to respond without prejudice.[51] Specifically, they found that high internal, low external participants exhibited lower levels of implicit race bias relative to other participants. They developed concept scales related to the existence of individual difference in the

---

[46]   Deci, E. L. (1971). Effects of externally mediated rewards on intrinsic motivation. *Journal of person-ality and Social Psychology*, 18(1), 105. See also Deci, E. L., Koestner, R., & Ryan, R. M. (1999). A meta-analytic review of experiments examining the effects of extrinsic rewards on intrinsic motivation. *Psychological Bulletin*, 125(6), 627–668.

[47]   Marshall, M. (2005). It's about more than money: Financial incentives and internal motivation. *Quality and Safety in Health Care*, 14(1), 4–5.

[48]   Legault, L., Gutsell, J. N., & Inzlicht, M. (2011). Ironic effects of antiprejudice messages. *Psychological Science*, 22(12), 1472–1477.

[49]   Tenbrunsel, A. E., & Messick, D. M. (1999). Sanctioning systems, decision frames, and cooperation. *Administrative Science Quarterly*, 44(4), 684–707.

[50]   One caveat is that in many cases external rewards can enhance intrinsic motivation. The interpersonal context in which the extrinsic motivation is introduced, or even the verbal cues attached to the sanctions, can determine how much we intrinsically value the extrinsic reward. For example, a child being reprimanded by a parent, whose opinion the child greatly values, may experience a greater increase in motivation to behave well than if the same reprimand were issued by a teacher with whom the child has little rapport. Nevertheless, the consensus in the literature suggests that in most instances attempts to externally control people's behavior can have considerable counterproductive results in the long term. For a review of some of these conflicting effects, see Deci et al., *supra* note 46.

[51]   Devine, P. G., Plant, E. A., Amodio, D. M., Harmon-Jones, E., & Vance, S. L. (2002). The regulation of explicit and implicit race bias: The role of motivations to respond without prejudice. *Journal of Personality and Social Psychology*, 82, 835–848.

internal level of motivation to avoid prejudice.[52] Similarly as discussed earlier, Bartlett found that when people who do not have the internal motivation to avoid racial bias are being threatened or coerced, they are unable to change their evaluation in the same way as people who have a stronger commitment to avoid racial bias. Her work highlights the challenge of motivating people to change without feeling coerced.

The variation in the efforts of people with high and low motivation to avoid prejudice suggests the legitimacy of dealing with people as having different moral responsibilities. This is particularly salient, given the research showing that stereotypes can be altered and changed with training. Our conclusion in earlier chapters that "good people" do not choose to do wrong, but rather interpret the situation in a way that will allow themselves to feel moral, suggests that we need to revisit their moral judgment analysis. People do not make moral decisions in a vacuum. Hence, the focus in behavioral choice is not just making morality salient through nudges on situational design, but on making it clearer to people that they have a position that might affect their moral judgment.

Furthermore, from a policy-making perspective, the relevant question might not be whether intrinsic motivation can increase compliance or performance, but whether and when intrinsic motivation outperforms extrinsic motivation in securing desirable behavior. In contexts in which intrinsic motivation is more successful in securing compliance, policy makers must make sure that the standard extrinsic motivators provided by law (e.g., sanctions and incentives) do not undercut intrinsic motivations.

Is it also the case that we can make people become more ethical? When an individual tries to reduce racial bias, he or she has to address only one dimension of character and behavior. Reducing racial bias thus seems to be simpler than situations regarding ethical behavior, where people have to choose from a number of options and have less clarity of what is the right thing to do. Acting ethically is related to many dimensions: honesty, rule compliance, cooperation, and many more attributes that make changing intrinsic motivation so challenging.

Even though increasing intrinsic motivation is likely to positively affect behavior, extrinsic motivation can be effective in discouraging wrongdoing. In addition, we still need to address the behavior of those with low intrinsic motivation to act ethically. We fully support education and training as important tools in making people more likely to obey laws, but to present them as the only tools will be neither effective nor practical.

In concluding this part, it seems that despite the limitations of focusing on motivation's effect on ethical behavior, states should recognize that education and training can be effective tools to enable people to deal with many ethical problems.

[52] Plant, E. A., & Devine, P. G. (1998). Internal and external motivation to respond without prejudice. *Journal of Personality and Social Psychology, 75*, 811–832.

Yet people will only make a lasting change in their behavior when they change what they think is the right thing to do. In a sense, nudges are like rules that ensure that people do not engage in self-deception, but in and of themselves they can never be a permanent solution that will lead to changing people's intrinsic motivation. Finding ways to change people's intrinsic motivation in a non-coercive way is likely to help reduce people's ethical biases.

11.4 LIMITATIONS OF BEHAVIORAL ETHICS AND THE FUTURE OF LAW AND BEHAVIORAL ETHICS

Behavioral ethics makes an important contribution to the BLE literature, supporting the view that the self-serving effects of motivation on cognition allow people to do harm when it serves their self-interest without feeling guilty about their actions. The BE literature highlights the mechanisms and biases that prevent people from fully understanding that their behaviors are sometimes self-interested and unethical. Uncovering these biases is especially important because as demonstrated society is harmed by the bad deeds created by good people, which are not yet targeted by state interventions.

Yet, admittedly, the ability of the current BE literature to recommend how to translate its findings into law is limited. Many important aspects are still being debated in the literature, both theoretically and methodologically. Within the concept of bounded ethicality, the interrelations between automaticity, awareness, and controllability are still the subject of controversy, and potential solutions are elusive. Furthermore, we know more about the effect of System 1 on System 2 – which is of descriptive interest – than about the effect of System 2 on System 1 – which is of greater normative interest. Even one of the most momentous questions for the law – are we intuitively good or bad – seems to be affected by context more than was previously assumed. In addition, the degree to which the good/bad aligns with individual differences is more limited than anticipated and seems to vary across different behaviors and contexts.

The lack of consensus among researchers on basic concepts limits the ability to base policies on BE findings. For example, would giving people more or less time to make behavioral choices increase or decrease the likelihood that they would engage in wrongdoing?[53] How can we answer that question, if we do not yet know the meaning of methods such as time pressure (how much time) and ego depletion (how hard)? Finally, BE's call for a differentiated treatment of good and bad people rests on the assumption that good people are genuinely unable to recognize the wrongness of their behavior. However, there is very little research on that topic, especially

---

[53] for conflicting perspective on the topic see on one hand the dissenting views of Rand, D. G., Greene, J. D., & Nowak, M. A. (2012). Spontaneous giving and calculated greed. *Nature*, 489(7416) 427–430. On the other hand, see Shalvi, S., Eldar, O., & Bereby-Meyer, Y. (2012). Honesty requires time (and lack of justifications). *Psychological Science*, 23(10), 1264–1270.

from a legal enforcement perspective, which limits the ability to remove responsibility from those good people, because it is very hard to rule out the option of their playing it dumb to avoid punishment.

Methodological issues also limit the ability of policy makers to translate the knowledge accumulated in behavioral ethics into public policy. Very abstract experimental paradigms make it hard to draw direct practical conclusions from lab experiments (e.g., there is a difference between the conflict of interest situations studied in labs and the ones people face at work where they believe that their career is on the line). The unethical behavior studied in the lab often involves people reporting a number from dice that they throw or the number of questions they answer or what number they see on a computer screen. In the real world, unethical behaviors are much more complex and are done without any deliberation, which raises doubts on the external validity of some of the lab studies involving unethical behavior. In addition, data is collected from laboratory experiments that show only the short-term effects of various ethical manipulations, such as priming and ethical nudges. Numerous problems could account for why some of these effects may get diluted in the field; for the most part, the law is more interested in the long-term effects of these practices. Unfortunately, most of the research in BE has been in a few areas of micromanagement of workplace behavior, which is not entirely suitable for incorporation into legal theory and policy-making. Finally, debate continues on the validity of methods such as IAT and fMRI regarding the consistency of measures and predictability of behavior across situations.

Indeed, the book leaves us with many unanswered questions that future research should discuss and refine: How blind is a blind spot from a legal perspective of responsibility? Can we combine traditional methods with the new BIT-type methods? What knowledge is needed to offer legal policy makers a formula for optimally balancing traditional intervention methods with nontraditional ones? Can we combine traditional and nudge-like interventions without harming either approach? What values are more important when attempting to increase the efficacy and legitimacy of nudges (e.g., making people aware of the nudges)? Can we know *ex ante* in what mode of reasoning people will be when making a decision about the law? Can we know in advance the effect that similar interventions would have on the two types of good people as well as on the bad people in every policy context?

More specifically, from a jurisprudential perspective, who is the real person from an ethical perspective: the 2-second individual or the 20-second individual? The one who acts without deliberation or the one who is calculative?[54] Given research that shows people can internalize changes in automatic mechanism such as stereotypes and become less biased through training, should we impose a legal duty on people to engage in such ethical courses and impose liabilities on those who do not pass them?

---

[54]   Frankish, K. (2010). Dual-process and dual-system theories of reasoning. *Philosophy Compass*, 5(10), 914–926.

Should states impose costs on organizations that do not design their environments to facilitate ethical behavior?

More research into these types of questions could dramatically change the legal enforcement literature in at least two ways: first, it will enable legal policy makers who seek to modify behavior through regulation to account for its effect on both deliberative and non-deliberative choice processes. Second, any behavioral attempt to regulate the behavior of people will have to account for the various behavioral trade-offs imposed by normative considerations, for the relative advantages of traditional enforcement mechanisms, and for institutional constraints imposed by the legal culture of different states. This will enable the core ideas of ethical decision-making and automatic behavior to be applied to broader societal problems. In the long term, it is my hope that the combination of behavioral ethics with the behavioral analysis of law will create a new branch of legal scholarship, in which scholars with detailed knowledge of legal doctrines become involved in the theory and subsequently the practice of mechanism design and behavioral engineering. Behaviorally trained legal scholars will play a prominent role in creating a theory that will ensure greater integrity in the regulation and enforcement of contractual, corporate, and administrative duties. Their involvement could change our understanding of how to design contracts to reduce justifications for breaching them. Corporate law could be designed in a way that agents will be less likely to believe that what's good for them is good for the company. Tax law could be formulated such that it will be harder for honest taxpayers to avoid paying taxes due to ambiguity or a lack of clear instructions of what is the right thing to do. Tort law could be designed with a better understanding of how people really make mistakes, and procedural law could account for self-serving biases in how people understand their contribution to the dispute. Hopefully, this book could help generate more research by legal scholars into the implications of behavioral ethics for their fields of expertise and consequently a richer and adaptive legal approach will emerge.

Index